PENGUIN BOOKS

THE MANCHESTER CC

Ed Glinert's passion for p
gift for digging out obscure stories, have made him one of the most
acclaimed writers about urban life and city histories. He is the author
of *The London Compendium, Literary London, East End Chronicles* and
West End Chronicles, and leads a variety of walking tours. Ed has lived
in Manchester for many years, and now he has turned his attention to
this great centre of industry, revealing the city in a new light.

The MANCHESTER Compendium

A Street-by-Street History of England's Greatest Industrial City

Ed Glinert

PENGUIN BOOKS

PENGUIN BOOKS

Published by the Penguin Group
Penguin Books Ltd, 80 Strand, London WC2R ORL, England
Penguin Group (USA) Inc., 375 Hudson Street, New York, New York 10014, USA
Penguin Group (Canada), 90 Eglinton Avenue East, Suite 700, Toronto, Ontario, Canada M4P 2Y3
(a division of Pearson Penguin Canada Inc.)
Penguin Ireland, 25 St Stephen's Green, Dublin 2, Ireland
(a division of Penguin Books Ltd)
Penguin Group (Australia), 250 Camberwell Road, Camberwell, Victoria 3124, Australia
(a division of Pearson Australia Group Pty Ltd)
Penguin Books India Pvt Ltd, 11 Community Centre, Panchsheel Park, New Delhi – 110 017, India
Penguin Group (NZ), 67 Apollo Drive, Rosedale, North Shore 0632, New Zealand
(a division of Pearson New Zealand Ltd)
Penguin Books (South Africa) (Pty) Ltd, 24 Sturdee Avenue, Rosebank, Johannesburg 2196, South Africa

Penguin Books Ltd, Registered Offices: 80 Strand, London WC2R ORL, England

www.penguin.com

First published by Allen Lane 2008
Published in Penguin Books 2009
1

Copyright © Ed Glinert, 2008
All rights reserved

The moral right of the author has been asserted

Typeset by Rowland Phototypesetting Ltd, Bury St Edmunds, Suffolk
Printed in England by Clays Ltd, St Ives plc

978–0–141–02930–6

www.greenpenguin.co.uk

Penguin Books is committed to a sustainable future
for our business, our readers and our planet.
The book in your hands is made from paper
certified by the Forest Stewardship Council.

To the memory of Marian Walsh

Contents

Acknowledgements

I am indebted to my editor, Margaret
Bluman, for suggesting Manchester as the
subject of a follow-up to *The London Compendium*, and to my agent, Faith Evans, for
her continued support and encouragement.
Many other people at Penguin, such as
Rosie Glaisher and Marcella Edwards, were
supportive of the project from the
beginning.

Help and advice came from a number of
quarters, particularly Mark Gorman and
Gill King. Many thanks also to Mike Ash-
Edwards, Jeremy Beadle, Celia Boggis, Bela
Cunha, Dhun Daji, Maureen Gaskell, Dave
Hammonds, Victor Hyman, Andrew Lukas,
Terry McCaughey, Graeme McIver, John
Nicholson, Adele, Juliet, Martin and Simon

Rose, Elena and Marcello Rosenbaum,
Jonathan Schofield, Val Stevens, David
Stone and Howard Stubbings.

The staff at Manchester Central Library,
particularly Paula Moorhouse, were always
on hand to provide me with cuttings,
books and advice. Chetham's Library was
an invaluable source of material, and so
many thanks to Michael Powell and his
colleagues.

As always many thanks to Katy Walsh
Glinert for accompanying me on jaunts to
the furthest corners of the metropolis – even
to Angel Meadow, the 'new' Hulme and
Strangeways – and patiently listening to
me reciting large chunks of the text in
preparation.

Introduction

Manchester is Britain's most important city after London; a dynamic centre of energy, one-time hub of the country's cotton industry, the cradle of liberalism, birthplace of a world-renowned orchestra in the Hallé, long-time setting for one of the world's greatest independent newspapers in the *Manchester Guardian*, home of one of the world's most popular football teams in Manchester United, and famed for its innovative groups such as the Fall, Joy Division and the Smiths.

It has been home to the unreconstructed capitalist and the devout radical, the flamboyant architect and the sober scientist, the raving cleric and the inspired music-maker, the rabble-rousing demagogue and the selfless philanthropist – embracing the full range of human activity as befits Britain's second city.

As a major city Manchester is a relatively new phenomenon. Two hundred and fifty years ago it barely registered on the national consciousness. Manchester had no elected local government and its population numbered little more than 10,000. When Daniel Defoe conducted his *Tour Thro' the Whole Island of Great Britain* in the 1720s he could still justly describe Manchester as 'one of the greatest, if not really the greatest meer village in England'. At that time there was little to distinguish the town from hundreds of other similar places dotted around the English landscape. It had made no significant contribution to the country's history or culture, and there was no reason to suppose

this would change. But thanks to the accident of its geography and the ingenuity of its citizens Manchester became one of the most powerful cities in the British Empire. By the middle of the nineteenth century Benjamin Disraeli could justifiably write in his 1844 novel *Coningsby*, 'Manchester is as great a human exploit as Athens.'

Manchester lies in a bowl between the Pennines and the Cheshire Plain. In AD 79 the Romans built a fort at Castlefield which lasted several centuries before being abandoned. The town developed at a different site near the modern-day cathedral. It was conveniently near the sea, bringing the world's goods to local ports, close to the hills with their fast-flowing rivers, whose power would be harnessed in the Industrial Revolution, and close to the markets created by the proximity of so many towns and villages. Important long-distance roads crossed through it.

Manchester had long enjoyed trade in textiles such as fustians, woollens and 'Manchester velvet', an early form of corduroy. The climate – damp and temperate – is ideal for treating cloth. In the fourteenth century Flemish weavers settled here and vastly improved the local textile industry. But it was the decision of the Duke of Bridgewater in 1761 to cut a canal from his Worsley mines to Manchester that revolutionized the local economy. The price of coal dropped, and new industries opened near the waterside. Entrepreneurs, merchants and machine-makers were soon attracted to

Manchester. At the end of the eighteenth century the local invention of new machines such as the spinning jenny and water frame revolutionized textile work. Goods could now be mass produced and a new type of building – the mill or factory – was created thus enabling as many workers as possible to produce as many goods as was feasible. These mills no longer needed to be situated by fast-flowing rivers in the countryside; they could be erected in the city centre. Consequently Manchester changed from a small, insignificant town surrounded by fields, into an economic powerhouse and a hub of energy, the major manufacturing centre in Britain for cotton goods and heavy machinery, what the historian Asa Briggs has described as 'the shock city of the industrial age'.

The great romantic writer Thomas de Quincey, who was born in the city centre in 1785, provided the most vivid description of that period: 'In this place trade is the elysium and money is the god. I cannot sit out of doors but I am nosed by a factory, a cotton-boy, a cotton-dealer, or something else allied to that most detestable commerce.'

With the growth in industry came a huge increase in population. The number of inhabitants in Manchester rose from 15,000 to 70,000 in the second half of the eighteenth century. By 1800 there were around 90,000 people living locally, and their number continued to grow at an unprecedented rate.

Nearly seventy years after the opening of the first English canal in Manchester another major transport revolution started here: passenger railways. The world's first station, Liverpool Road, opened in Manchester's Castlefield in 1830. Manchester was soon at the centre of a huge network of commuter lines, and by the mid-nineteenth century was home to some of the greatest engineering companies of the railway age.

Throughout the nineteenth century Manchester remained a major textile centre, not just for cotton-spinning but also for clothes

manufacture, which took place in a quarter that arced round from Ancoats to Shudehill and Piccadilly to Chorlton-on-Medlock. Local firms such as Ryland's specialized in shirts and underwear, while around a third of the world's waterproof garments were made at the Mackintosh plant in Chorlton-on-Medlock. It was not just textile manufacturing that took place in Manchester, though. There were coal pits, power stations and heavy engineering in east Manchester, where locomotives, engines and even cars were produced. The city became a great distribution centre for the region's goods. Even then Manchester was not satisfied. In the 1890s it devised an ingenious solution to reduce the cost of imports: the building of a ship canal to bypass Liverpool's high charges, which made the city one of the world's great ports.

As the commercial and industrial centre of the early modern age Manchester was at the forefront of political developments of the time. Its nineteenth-century merchants, the archetypal *laissez-faire* capitalists, included Richard Cobden, who became the single most influential figure on Victorian liberal politics, a fierce exponent of representative democracy at home and peace through free trade abroad. But there was an obvious downside to the capitalists' wealth. Though the people had jobs, they were paid barely above subsistence level and had little in the way of free time, independence or freedom. Living and working conditions were so desperate that in 1842 the average age of death among Manchester's working class was seventeen. To improve their lot they often rebelled. They demonstrated, rallied, raged and went on strike, and their demands were often met by force, especially on 16 August 1819 in what became known as the Peterloo Massacre when fifteen people died and more than 400 were injured during a rally demanding parliamentary reform. The widespread poverty turned Manchester into a centre for reform and radicalism. Here Marx and Engels researched much of the *Communist Manifesto* (at Chetham's

Library), the trade union movement was born (at 103 Princess Street in 1868), and the suffragettes staged some of their most dramatic coups.

The city had no democratic representation until the Manchester Corporation was formed in 1838. This late start didn't stop its elected council from becoming one of the most powerful in the land, operating from the grandest town hall in the country. And it was municipal politics that dominated the next century. However, as the twentieth century wore on, the Corporation began to demonstrate a growing unwillingness to allow any sort of independent life to flourish in the city. At the end of the Second World War it produced a megalomanic blueprint for the future – the 1945 Manchester Plan – fuelled by the idea that social engineering devised at Town Hall level could provide solutions to the age-old problems of poverty, overcrowding and unhappiness. Adding to the devastation caused by enemy wartime bombing, vast chunks of the city were to be wiped away to satisfy the demands of the plan's instigator, city surveyor Rowland Nicholas. The Town Hall and much of the Victorian centre would be demolished and rebuilt from scratch. There would be skyscrapers resting on podiums connected by elevated walkways surrounded by dual carriageways – a dehumanized nightmarish concrete world born out of the utopian desires which the Corporation brazenly promoted until they came crashing down in the horrors of the Hulme Crescents and Fort Ardwick.

By the 1970s much of central Manchester had been needlessly destroyed, including the warren of courts and basement dives north of Market Street, the gorgeous galleried Lancaster Arcade near Victoria station and Harry S. Fairhurst's masterpiece – York House – the city centre's most remarkable twentieth-century building. In their place came block after ungainly block of glass and granite towers – Piccadilly Plaza, UMIST,

Crown Square and worst of all the Arndale Centre – which went up without any thought of their effect on the well-being of the city, without any attempt to integrate them into the landscape, dwarfing all human scale and warmth and plaguing Manchester.

The tragedy of the 1996 IRA bombing of Manchester city centre gave the authorities the opportunity to repair past mistakes. Sadly, opportunity has been lost again. There have been too many misguided projects clouded by PR hype. The Arndale Centre was cosmetically reworked instead of being razed. New eyesores have gone up in the shape of the Piccadilly Gardens pavilion, the fake 'heritage' pubs by the cathedral, and the awkward street furniture of Exchange Square, arrivals as ungainly as the failed experiments of the 1960s.

Yet despite the city's much vaunted obsession with elected politics its most interesting and successful new developments have been those wrought by individuals acting independently of the Town Hall and central government: Humphrey Chetham, late-medieval merchant who founded Chetham's, one of the world's great libraries; the machine-makers of the late eighteenth century, such as Richard Arkwright; the scientist John Dalton, originator of atomic theory in his George Street laboratory; the *Manchester Guardian*'s guiding spirit, C. P. Scott; the theatre impresario Annie Horniman; the warehouse king Harry S. Fairhurst.

To this list can be added entrepreneurs of recent decades who have made the city buzz: Bob Scott, founder of the Royal Exchange theatre; Tony Wilson with Factory Records; the small-scale designers of New Mount Street and Castlefield; the property developer Tom Bloxham and his Urban Splash team; and the architects Ben Kelly, Stephenson-Bell and Ian Simpson. They have made Manchester invigorating and enticing, a city of endless fascination, whose intricate history pours out of every location.

How to Use *The Manchester Compendium*

The Manchester Compendium is a guidebook with a difference. It contains no lists of hotels, restaurants, nightclubs and tourist attractions. It is not a companion to the city's many glossy PR tracts. It has no connection with the Town Hall, tourist board or locally based newspaper groups.

It is a history of Manchester presented not as a chronological narrative but area by area, street by street, building by building where incidents and stories have occurred. Unlike in other guidebooks these topics are not presented as thumbnail sketches but fleshed out in great detail, so that the reader gets a full history of a particular landmark presented in a usable format that lends itself both to reading at leisure and checking out on foot.

Every important story in Manchester's history has been considered: from the Roman settlement at Castlefield, built only a few decades after the crucifixion of Jesus Christ, to the Peterloo Massacre; from the early days of the Industrial Revolution to the birth of the computer at Manchester University; from Manchester United's days by a chemical works in Clayton to George Best's playboy period, with a full supporting cast en route – Thomas de Quincey, John Dalton, Richard Cobden, Elizabeth Gaskell, Charles Hallé, the Pankhursts, L. S. Lowry, Anthony Burgess, Mark E. Smith, Morrissey

– against an exciting array of backdrops: the Victorian warehouses of Princess Street; the Gothic palaces of the Victorian merchants; the Free Trade Hall, as well as the less splendid but no less interesting architectural eyesores of the late twentieth century: the Hulme Crescents, the Arndale Centre, Fort Ardwick . . .

Entries have been arranged first by area under chapters such as City Centre (Main Streets) or South Manchester, then by smaller areas within, where appropriate, followed by streets listed in alphabetical order. Entries on each street have been laid out with the walker in mind: they start at one end and proceed in order of location to the other end. The same is then done for the other side of the street. Buildings that have been demolished are listed in a different font.

The need for this book is obvious. Manchester has been poorly served by literature. Detailed histories of the city that can be placed alongside Peter Ackroyd's *Biography of London* or Stephen Inwood's *History of London* are hard to find. Those histories that do exist are heavy with accounts of the Peterloo Massacre, Manchester's Victorian architecture and post-war economic decline but do not contain serious consideration of recent phenomena such as the rise of the city's twentieth-century music scene – as if

one would contemplate a history of
say St Petersburg and make no mention of
Shostakovich. The Manchester resident or
visitor eager to snap up information is
poorly served as the idea of uniting all
aspects of city life into one book has never
previously been attempted. *The Manchester
Compendium* addresses this need.

City Centre: Main Streets

Manchester city centre is surprisingly small, barely a mile east–west and north–south, fitting into what was the medieval town. From the mid-eighteenth century the demands of industry meant that the surrounding land was needed for the mills, factories and wharves that powered the growing industries, and the population was forced to live away from the old town, which then became the commercial sector. The modern-day city centre can be divided into small neighbourhoods – Castlefield, Knott Mill and Smithfield – with main streets such as Albert Square, Deansgate and Princess Street forming a frame around them.

Albert Square

Manchester's main meeting place, the civic and political heart of the city, was created between 1868 and 1877 around the monumental Town Hall, one of Britain's greatest municipal buildings. The Town Hall's size and stature make Albert Square a formidable rival to the town squares of similar European cities, even if there is no visual spectacle to match Munich's Marienplatz striking clock or the figures of Prague's astronomical clock to draw in visitors.

Before the nineteenth century Albert Square was Hall Field, open land sloping down to the River Tib. By the time the Town Hall was being planned in the early 1860s there were houses all around, pubs such as the Engravers' Arms, a smithy and a coffee-roasting works. The site now occupied by the Town Hall was Town's Yard, location of the fire brigade and the Corporation workshops.

After the Town Hall was erected Albert Square became the setting for demonstrations and major civic events. In September 1885 the socialist thinker William Morris spoke here at an open-air meeting on the subject of free speech. A biographer, J. Bruce Glasier, described him as being that day 'lion like, not only because of his shaggy mane, but because of the impress of strength of his whole front'. On VE Day,

8 March 1945, thousands gathered in the early afternoon to hear a broadcast by prime minister Winston Churchill officially announcing the news of the Allies' victory. While waiting they were entertained by the Manchester Police Band who performed popular songs of the time. There was considerable applause after Churchill's speech, but the loudest cheers came after the sounding of the last 'all clear'. On 12 July 1961 the Russian cosmonaut Yuri Gagarin, the first man in space, appeared on the Town Hall balcony to rapturous applause. More recently the kind of events that used to take place here have shifted to new civic areas such as the Castlefield arena and Exchange Square.

Modern refurbishment has not been kind to the centre of Albert Square. The paving is over-elaborate and the pedestrianization the latest in a long line of unsatisfactory schemes which have included a bus terminus, cab stands and an awkward network of small roads and traffic islands.

● **Adolphe Valette**'s 1910 Impressionist painting *Albert Square, Manchester*, which can be seen in the main Manchester Art Gallery, shows a shadowy figure that looks like L. S. Lowry, who had been one of his pupils, wheeling a barrow in the fog in front of the Albert Memorial.

centre

The centre of the square is dominated by Thomas Worthington's Albert Memorial which preceded the better-known London version.

Albert Memorial

The first monument built to commemorate Prince Albert, Queen Victoria's consort, is an elaborate open-arched Gothic canopy designed 1862–7 by Thomas Worthington to house Matthew Noble's marble statue of the prince. It is profusely decorated with statuary allegorically representing Albert's interest in art, commerce, science and agriculture. The memorial was cleaned at great expense in the 1970s after some councillors had asked for it to be destroyed.

▶ Thomas Worthington's architecture, p. 100.

north side

The north side of Albert Square contains two large Victorian office blocks: Nos. 1–7 Princess Street of 1877 and the Northern Assurance Buildings (9–11 Princess Street) of 1902.

east side

Manchester Town Hall

Fittingly for a city that prides itself as a municipal power on a scale rivalling the great city-states of European history, Manchester Town Hall is the grandest, greatest and most imposing building in the region. It was built from 1868–77 to the Gothic designs of Alfred Waterhouse, whose winning plan, one of 136 entries, while not the most handsome, was the one the judges felt would make best use of the light, the ventilation and the awkward triangular site.

The Corporation had specified no preference for the building's architectural style, but to emphasize Manchester's newly found wealth from textiles Waterhouse chose as his model the thirteenth-century Gothic cloth halls of Flanders. He built in brick faced with stone from the West Yorkshire Spinkwell quarries for the exterior, ashlar for the interior, and placed above the main entrance a 286-foot-high clock tower. Waterhouse also included much statuary on the façade. General Agricola, the Roman who founded Manchester in AD 79, is honoured with a statue over the main doorway. Above him are Henry III and Elizabeth I, and there are also statues of Thomas de la Warre, founder of what is now the cathedral. On the ground floor is a Sculpture Hall displaying busts of great figures from Manchester history, such as the scientists John Dalton, with glassware at his feet, and William Joule, cross-legged, leaning on an elbow.

Inside the building Waterhouse's skill becomes apparent. Seven staircases lead up from the ground floor, some grand and imposing, others spiralling mysteriously at the corners of the building. On the first floor are the Lord Mayor's rooms, the Conference Hall, which contains the original council chamber with its huge Gothic

Militants v. *moderates*

Town Hall politics had never captured the interest of the Manchester public until the early 1980s when, after more than a century of mostly predictable bouncing between Liberal, Conservative and Labour administrations, a more interesting development emerged: internecine warfare within the ruling Labour Group.

On the one side were the young, secular, iconoclastic new councillors: graduates, teachers and social workers, armed with a heavy dose of Tory-bashing polemical bluster. On the other side was old-school Labour – the manual workers – who held the positions of power. The challengers insisted that Labour councillors carry out their manifesto commitments, but the ruling old guard had little interest in Labour policy or democracy. They took their cue not from the party statements but from an elite of mostly Catholic party power brokers who drank in the smoky workingmen's clubs of east Manchester.

The raging political battle for control was described in the *Manchester Evening News* of 1983 and 1984 as a tussle between militants (revolutionary and dangerous) and moderates (responsible and experienced). In reality it was a contest between those who had a vision for a new Manchester and those who had presided over a city that had lost confidence and the wherewithal to make competent decisions.

The new challengers wanted to rebuild the city; the old guard wanted to knock it down.

The struggle for control, which mirrored the machinations taking place within the party nationally, was ironic given that over the years successive governments had consistently eroded the power of councils and handed control over the police, gas, electricity and water to quangos. Nevertheless in 1984 the challengers took control, and the dour but capable Graham Stringer became council leader. He began running Manchester with a degree of imagination that hadn't been seen locally since the days of Richard Cobden, working with business and government agencies to repair the crumbling city, investing in new buildings and ideas. Some schemes were hopelessly ambitious (two failed and embarrassing Olympics bids), some inspired (the regeneration of Castlefield, the canals and east Manchester; the exposure of corruption within Greater Manchester Police; the repopulation of the city centre) and some simply wrong (the part destruction of the Free Trade Hall, the revamping of Piccadilly Gardens, the creation of Exchange Square). Yet most have succeeded in bringing people, prestige and prosperity to Manchester, achievements lacking in the record of the previous rulers.

chimney-piece, oak screen and wrought-iron galleries where the press and public sat, and the Great Hall, the building's *tour de force*, which John Ruskin called 'the most truly magnificent Gothic apartment in Europe'. In the panels of the Great Hall's hammerbeam roof are the gilded coats of arms of the nations with which Manchester traded, and on the walls are Ford Madox Brown's twelve murals illustrating episodes from Manchester's history.

Around the Great Hall is the centre of the building, lit by the surrounding courtyards (often used as a Victorian setting in TV dramas), while throughout the profusion of cloister-like corridors, spiral staircases, bridges and stairwells creates a wonderful sense of drama.

The Town Hall was officially opened on 13 September 1877 with a grand ceremony marred only by the refusal of Queen Victoria to attend. So desperate was the Corporation to secure the monarch's presence that councillors even insisted that the artist Ford Madox Brown should not choose the story of Peterloo for one of his frescoes of Manchester's history for fear of offending the Queen. It was all in vain. Victoria disregarded all entreaties, and Benjamin Disraeli, the prime minister, was left to notify the city cryptically that it was 'out of the power of Her Majesty to be present on this interesting occasion'. One reason, undisclosed at the time, was that the Queen was unhappy that Manchester Corporation had commissioned a statue of the regicide Oliver Cromwell. She was also wary of being seen on the same platform as the one-time fiercely radical Manchester mayor, Abel Heywood, who had once been imprisoned for distributing publications which argued for the abolition of the monarchy.

Such was Manchester's penchant for empire building that by the 1920s it considered the Town Hall too small. E. Vincent Harris was commissioned to build an extension on an adjacent site to the south, and it is there that the council now meets. Yet, ironically, when the Corporation commissioned chief surveyor Rowland Nicholas to draw up the Manchester Plan of 1945 for rebuilding the city after the Second World War, he decided the main Town Hall was now too big, and suggested a streamlined – and hugely expensive – modernist replacement. Fortunately for Manchester his proposals were shelved.

● Regular tours of the building take place.

south side: Mount Street to Southmill Street
The only side of Albert Square to complement the magnificence of the Town Hall site is the south with its profusion of romantic-looking Gothic Victorian office blocks and the Thomas Worthington-designed Memorial Hall, created not in the rigid Flemish Gothic of the Town Hall but in the colourful Venetian-style Gothic promoted by John Ruskin.

St Andrew's Chambers, No. 21
At the corner with Mount Street is St Andrew's Chambers, built in 1872 by George Redmayne, a pupil of Waterhouse, for the Scottish Widows Assurance Society. It is clad in Darley Dale stone and features in the roundel above the door a relief of a woman with a box labelled 'fund', a kneeling monk and a standing boy.

Carlton House, No. 20
To the west of St Andrew's Chambers is Carlton House, originally Bridgewater Buildings, also made of Darley Dale stone and built in 1872, though considerably less interesting visually than St Andrew's Chambers. It originally housed the headquarters of the Bridgewater Canal company and the offices of architects Clegg and Knowles.

Albert Chambers
Clegg and Knowles designed Albert Chambers, adjacent to Carlton House, in 1873 for the Manchester Corporation Gasworks.

Memorial Hall, corner with Southmill Street
Thomas Worthington, one of the great mid-Victorian Gothic architects, designed the hall with funds left over from the construction of the Albert Memorial in 1866 to commemorate the bicentenary of the creation of the Unitarian Church by 2,000 ministers who had left the Church of England. The polychromatic brickwork, contrasting voussoirs, stone tracery and windows, either single or grouped in threes, constituted a glorious example of the Italianate Gothic according to the art critic John Ruskin. The ground floor has been spoiled by being converted into the Square Albert pub.

Lloyds House, between Southmill Street and Lloyd Street
A Gothic warehouse, the city's first purpose-built packing warehouse for a shipping company, dates back to 1868 and was designed by Speakman and Charlesworth.

▶ Harry S. Fairhurst's warehouses, p. 43.

west side
The west side of Albert Square is a travesty, ruined by the 1970s demolition of the nineteenth-century buildings, which were replaced with bland corporate blocks of a deliberately low-key design so as not to detract from the Town Hall. Long demolished is the office at Nos. 12–13 which until 1945 was the headquarters of the famous *Bradshaw's Railway Guide*, named after George Bradshaw who first devised a timetable for services in the 1830s.

Cross Street

In many ways Cross Street is Manchester's most attractive main thoroughfare, home to stylish Baroque-style Edwardian office blocks, eccentric oddities such as Mills & Murgatroyd's former Ottoman Bank of 1889, with its corkscrew chimneys, at Nos. 56–60, and the immense Royal Exchange. The most impressive part is the junction with King Street, dominated by Charles Heathcote's monumental late nineteenth-century baroque-revival office blocks: fanciful, flamboyant *fin-de-siècle* architecture at its finest.

In the nineteenth century there were more small workshops than epic buildings on Cross Street. In one of these, at No. 13, Benjamin Dancer, the Victorian photography pioneer who invented the microphotograph, opened a shop in 1845. Dancer was soon supplying thermometers and microscopes to James Prescott Joule, the foremost physicist of his day, who described Dancer's wares as 'the first made in England with any pretensions to accuracy'. In 1842 Dancer took the earliest known photograph of Manchester – the cutler's shop at 1 Market Street.

No longer standing at the corner with John Dalton Street is the Prince's Tavern where the writer Thomas de Quincey was born in 1785.

west side: John Dalton Street to Market Street

Mr Thomas's Chop House, No. 55

A rarity in Manchester given the recent destruction of so many ancient city-centre pubs is Mr Thomas's Chop House, a slender, exquisitely designed Edwardian tavern.

Royal Exchange

Once the trading floor for Manchester's powerful cotton industry, when it was supposedly 'the biggest room in the world' and controlled around 80 per cent of the global trade in finished cotton, the Royal Exchange now houses a spectacular futurist theatre-in-the-round whose plays are among the most eagerly awaited in the city.

The current Exchange is the fourth such building on or near the site. The first Exchange stood in the Market Place, fifty yards north of the present one. It was replaced in 1809 with a hall that occupied only a small part of today's complex and was nearly destroyed three years later by a mob protesting at the borough reeve's decision to allow supporters of the hated government ministers Castlereagh and Addington to host a lunch there. In 1815 the building was engulfed in flames after a riot over the price of potatoes. John Edward Taylor, who went on to found the *Manchester Guardian*, was accused of inciting the rioters by brandishing a placard urging 'Now or Never'. He sued the Tory MP who alleged his involvement and won the case.

In January 1819 the radical demagogue Henry 'Orator' Hunt, en route to a demonstration in Manchester seven months before his appearance at the Peterloo Massacre, stopped his carriage outside the Exchange and began taunting members with a banner proclaiming 'Hunt and Liberty' and 'Universal Suffrage'. He continued his protest until, according to one eyewitness, he was 'saluted with every mark of indignant contempt and was obliged to give up his intentions'.

The Exchange was closed on 17 August 1819, the day after Peterloo, when reports swept through Manchester that 50,000 men were marching on the town from the north ready to attack the bastions of the state. A lesser drama in 1834 saw the free-trade pioneer John Bright make a public stand against the unpopular Corn Laws. Standing on a chair, he addressed the members until they threatened to call the police. An atypical member of the Exchange a decade later was the pioneering Communist Friedrich Engels, a capitalist of sorts by day, who once described himself as a 'queer sort of businessman who cheered when there was a panic on the Exchange'.

The building was extended a number of times over the decades and by the 1920s the Exchange hall had become the largest trading room in the world. By this time the Royal Exchange had 11,000 members. There were 500 brokers, nearly 2,000 yarn agents, 300 waste dealers, 200 bleachers, 150 finishers and 1,000 shippers from the scores of cotton towns located within twelve miles of the building. On a typical trading day the Exchange would be packed with thousands of soberly dressed, top-hatted merchants bartering, bantering, haggling and haranguing each other for the best prices. Trading continued until the 1960s when the Lancashire cotton industry, having failed to manage labour relations and embrace new technology successfully, found itself stifled by overseas competition. Amalgamations, mergers and closures followed, and the Exchange closed down on 31 December 1968 – by which time there were only fifteen cotton mills left in the area.

Fears that the building would become a white elephant, or be demolished, were eased when the 1969 Theatre Company moved in and commissioned Levitt, Bernstein Associates to build a theatre. The architects devised an ingenious seven-sided steel-and-glass module suspended from four massive columns which seats 740, making it the largest theatre-in-the-round in the world. Since its opening in 1976, the Royal Exchange has staged mostly classic theatre and revivals. The complex also contains a café, exhibition space, theatre bookshop, craft shop and in a different section some stylish boutiques. The great trading hall remains with the closing prices still on the wall. The Exchange was damaged by the 1996 IRA bomb, resulting in the theatre company temporarily playing in Castlefield while the building was repaired.
▸ Corn Exchange, p. 92; Manchester School of Theatre, p. 26.
east side: Market Street to Princess Street
𝔐𝔞𝔫𝔠𝔥𝔢𝔰𝔱𝔢𝔯 𝔊𝔲𝔞𝔯𝔡𝔦𝔞𝔫 (1879–1968)
The *Manchester Guardian*, the city's greatest ever newspaper, founded in the wake of the 1819 Peterloo Massacre, moved from its Market Street base (p. 12) to new premises here in 1879.

At that time its editor, Charles Prestwich (C. P.) Scott, had been in the chair seven years. He stayed at the helm of the paper for fifty more years and became the greatest newspaperman of the era. Scott would arrive by bike from his Fallowfield home, the Firs, at 6 p.m. every day with a packed meal of eggs, salt and milk, occasionally splashing out to include an apple. He would then begin planning the long leader which, according to W. P. Crozier, one of his leading journalists, was '*the* prime instrument of policy, *the* voice, persuasive or protestant, for whose utterance, more than for any other single purpose, he believed the paper to exist'.

Not all the long leaders were spiked with wisdom. On 11 September 1908 Scott wrote: 'We cannot understand to what practical use a flying machine that is heavier than air can be put.' Nevertheless, under him the *Manchester Guardian* was transformed from a paper which simply had a high local standing into one with major international status – *the* voice of English liberalism. To ensure its success the *Guardian* kept in touch with national affairs through the wire, and copies of the paper were sent by night train to Euston and St Pancras stations, from where they could be taken by bicycle to the grand houses of Belgravia and Westminster where the opinion-formers lived.

C. P. Scott led public opinion on a number of issues and championed unfashionable causes: Irish Home Rule, Zionism, opposition to the Boer War. He excelled at spotting talent and in his time hired Neville Cardus, Howard Spring, Arthur Ransome and Malcolm Muggeridge, who remembered on his first day Scott 'sitting at his desk, his eyes bright blue, his flesh rosy, his beard white and truculent; a high-minded Sir John Falstaff, looking a little mad'. Scott required from his writers one thing more than anything else: what he once called 'moral earnestness'. No doubt with this in mind he devised the maxim 'comment is free, but facts are sacred', although he conveniently ignored the entreaty when, after telling Malcolm Muggeridge to write a disparaging leader

Neville Cardus joins the Manchester Guardian

Rusholme-born, working class and self-educated, Neville Cardus was the *Manchester Guardian*'s most celebrated twentieth-century writer, an expert on music and cricket. Yet his rise wasn't smooth. At the age of eighteen in 1908 he used to stand outside the building and gaze longingly at the windows imagining that inside 'Samuel Langford, greatest of all writers on music, was meditating on Brahms over his desk'.

Cardus's break came eight years later when he wrote to editor-proprietor C. P. Scott asking to be taken on as a clerk – anything, as long as he could work in the building. With his application Cardus included two samples of his writing, an essay on the composer Granville Bantock and another on metaphysics. He was granted an interview with Scott at the editor's grand Fallowfield home, the Firs (p. 170), arrived at the appointed hour, and was shown by a maid into a room decorated in the fashionable William Morris style, but unheated, despite the cold weather. When Cardus took a book down at random from the shelf he found the pages uncut.

An hour passed before Scott appeared. The two men spoke about a variety of topics and at length about George Bernard Shaw. 'He's beginning to look old at last – don't you think so?' asked the editor as if, Cardus later mused, 'we all lived on the same intellectual and social plane'. Scott bade the would-be journalist goodbye and a few days later sent him a note stating that Cardus might be able to assist him in a 'semi-secretarial way'. The work meant that Cardus, to his chagrin, had to go to the Firs, rather than Cross Street, every day, and he did so for a month – without pay – before being dismissed. An opening into an exciting world had been tantalizingly revealed then slammed shut in his face. A few months later came a letter explaining that there was a vacancy for a reporter. 'Would Mr Cardus like to come for an interview next week?'

Cardus handwrote many of his reviews late at night and sent a driver to Cross Street with them. Occasionally he would dictate pieces over the phone, which could lead to problems of comprehension. He once described the diva Elizabeth Schwarzkopf as a 'quite eloquent singer', which the copy-taker on the other end of the line typed out as a 'white elephant singer'. No editor checking the copy thought this odd and the phrase went in uncorrected, to Cardus's and Schwarzkopf's deep embarrassment. He once used the phrase 'from thence' in a piece and received a courteous rebuke from C. P. Scott. Cardus dared to argue that Fielding had used it in *Tom Jones*, and so had Smollett. 'Did they?' replied Scott. 'Neither Mr Fielding nor Mr Smollett would have used it twice in my newspaper.'

Offered an attractive sum to move to London and write for the *Evening Standard*, Cardus chose to stay in Manchester. Many were surprised by his decision, but as he later explained: 'You only had to tell any musician in Europe, anybody who was anybody in fact, that you belonged to the *Manchester Guardian* and at once they met you not as a pressman, not as a journalist, but as a writer, free and civilized.'

---

about a gas holder that had been erected in the city, he remembered that the paper was carrying an advert from the very gas company. He ordered Muggeridge to drop the leader with the advice, 'There are occasions on which truth should be economized.'

Scott became owner of the paper as well as editor in 1907. Following his death in 1932 ownership was wrapped up in the Scott Trust, which still ensures that no one powerful magnate can emerge as sole proprietor à la Rupert Murdoch. As the twentieth century proceeded the paper's power brokers became increasingly preoccupied with thoughts about how London perceived their paper. Was it taken seriously? Why was it excluded from the Newspaper Proprietors' Association which negotiated with the trade unions? Should the *Manchester Guardian* be a provincial paper dealing with local news and a smattering of national affairs or a national newspaper that just happened to be based in Manchester?

On 24 August 1959 the paper dropped 'Manchester' from its masthead. Ironically, sales immediately increased in Manchester, possibly because locals had previously felt the paper to be too provincial. But it was an admission of northern inferiority that encapsulated problems that Manchester is still wrestling with. Confusingly, and with typical *Guardian* fudge, the editor, Alastair Hetherington, stayed on in Manchester until 1964. In leaving the city that year the *Guardian* lost its original *raison d'être* – to provide an alternative, independent provincial view of society – and soon became part of the metropolitan liberal establishment.

▶ The *Guardian* on Market Street, p. 12.

Cross Street Chapel

Manchester's main Nonconformist place of worship, now in its fourth building on the site, was originally the Dissenters' Meeting House, built for the Revd Henry Newcome in 1694, five years after the Toleration Act allowed non-Anglican Protestant places of worship.

During the eighteenth century Cross Street Chapel became a centre of support for the Hanoverian line to the throne, while its opponents, the Jacobites, who wanted the Crown to go to the Catholic Stuarts, worshipped at the Collegiate Church. Simmering tension between the two groups boiled over in June 1715 when a Jacobite mob led by blacksmith Thomas Syddall smashed through the doors of the chapel and overturned the pews. Syddall was hanged a year later for a different crime. Thirty years afterwards his son, also Thomas, was hanged for his part in the 1745 Jacobite uprising, and his head displayed at Manchester's Market Cross.

Later in the eighteenth century the chapel became a home from home for those with maverick social and religious views, and members of its congregation were responsible for a number of major local developments including the nearby Manchester Academy, where John Dalton taught, the Manchester Infirmary on Piccadilly Gardens, and the founding of the *Manchester Guardian*.

The original chapel was destroyed in the Second World War. Its 1950s replacement stood as a welcome and restrained antidote to the ebullient baroque commercial office blocks nearby but was demolished in the 1990s. In its place Holford Associates built the blandest of sandstone, glass and granite office blocks, with a room for worship on the ground floor.

▶ St Mary (The Hidden Gem), p. 78.

Deansgate

Manchester city centre's longest street runs rigidly straight north–south along the edge of the city centre less than 100 yards east of the River Irwell. Its name may refer to the long-lost River Dene or perhaps bears homage to the Danes who invaded Manchester in the ninth century, the 'gate' suffix being similar to '*gatten*', the Scandinavian word for street.

Deansgate takes the course of the Roman road that ran from Chester to Carlisle, and connects Manchester's two oldest local settlements, the Roman fort at Castlefield and the medieval community that grew up around the cathedral. It also boasts a number of elegant buildings: the former court at No. 184; Elliot House opposite; and at Nos. 62–66 the Barton Building (Hayward's), a palazzo of 1875 which still contains some of its original mahogany fittings. There are also quaint old pubs such as the Sawyers Arms, the Northwest's tallest building in the Beetham Tower and the extraordinary Gothic bulk of the John Rylands Library.

west side: Bridgewater Viaduct to Victoria Bridge Street

John Rylands Library, south junction with Wood Street

One of the world's great libraries is housed in a cathedral-like Gothic creation built in red sandstone to the designs of Basil Champneys. It is named after the multi-millionaire cotton magnate John Rylands, whose fortune financed its building from 1890–99 under the guidance of his widow, Enriqueta Augustina Rylands. What began as Rylands's own small library of theological works has since expanded to become a barely rivalled collection, containing such rarities as the second-century St John Fragment (the oldest existing edition of the New Testament), the second largest collection of works by the pioneering printer William Caxton, a first edition of Shakespeare's Sonnets, and more than 12,000 books produced between 1475 and 1640. There is also material dating back to the third millennium BC, artefacts written on papyrus, linen, parchment, wood, bone, bark and bamboo, and manuscripts and archives in all the major languages and subjects, encompassing literary, historical, genealogical, biblical, medical, legal and scientific texts. Since 1972 the library has been owned by Manchester University and is open to the public. It was restored at great cost from 2004–07.
▸ Chetham's Library, p. 95.

House of Fraser/Kendal's, between King Street West and St Mary's Street

What was Kendal's for seventy years, Manchester's most fashionable department store, became House of Fraser in 2005, losing its unique identity and exclusive cachet. The store was first opened by James Watts on the corner of Deansgate and Parsonage Lane in 1796, and later moved to 99 Deansgate, opposite the current site (now Waterstone's). In 1835 Messrs Kendal, Milner and Faulkner bought the premises and at the end of the nineteenth century expanded over the road, the two Deansgate sites being linked by an underground passage. A new owner in 1919 was Harrod's which renamed the store accordingly but changed it back after protests from staff and customers,

following which it became Kendal's. The current building, with its façade of frosted glass in the Art Deco style, was devised by J. W. Beaumont in 1939. Twenty years later the House of Fraser bought out Harrod's, but it was not until the £25 million refit in 2005, by which time the store had declined more than expected, rather like Lewis's on Mosley Street, that the name of House of Fraser replaced Kendal's.
▸ Lewis's, p. 13.

Mancunian Film Corporation (1930s), No. 54

The Manchester film company, responsible for a succession of joyous, low-grade romps in the middle years of the twentieth century, was set up by John E. Blakeley at 54 Deansgate in 1934. The first production, *Love, Mirth and Melody*, showcased a collection of music-hall acts, the scenes connected by a threadbare storyline, and was shot in London, not Manchester. The film sank without trace so quickly that the British Board of Film Classification has no record of it at all. The company's next production, *Off the Dole*, starring George Formby, was more successful, and Mancunian moved to new offices, first to nearby 3 Parsonage, and then to a larger site in Rusholme, where it opened its well-known studio.
▸ Mancunian Film Studio, Rusholme, p. 170.

east side: Cateaton Street to Chester Road
No. 1 Deansgate

The 2003 construction of No. 1 Deansgate, a block of luxury flats faced with glass which sits on a podium of shopping units, was greeted ecstatically in the press as proof of Manchester's arrival as a progressive European city. The building was designed by the firm of Ian Simpson who himself owns one of its apartments, as do the footballers Gary Neville and Ryan Giggs. There are views of the Fylde coast from the top floor.

Beetham Tower, No. 301, between Great Bridgewater Street and Trafford Street

Astonishment greeted the rise of the forty-seven-storey glass Beetham Tower in 2005, its height amid the relative dwarfs that comprise the rest of the Manchester skyline ensuring it is visible from the countryside beyond the city.

The lower levels are occupied by a Hilton Hotel; the upper storeys contain offices, the Sky Bar – offering its patrons the best views over the city – and 219 luxury apartments, all but four of which were quickly sold when put on the market. The forty-seventh-floor split-level penthouse was bought not by the footballer Wayne Rooney, as reported in the press, but by Ian Simpson, the architect himself. Simpson, who was also responsible for No. 1 Deansgate and the Urbis museum, then announced his intention to build a winter garden inside by planting twenty-four olive trees and oaks.

Despite its immensity Beetham Tower has little to offer architecturally. Its one trick – the slightly cantilevering upper half of the building – fails to detract from the monotony of the striped glass façade that recedes into opaqueness towards the top, as if the building were disappearing into the clouds, an unoriginal device taken from Jean Nouvel's unbuilt Parisian *Tour Sans Fin*.

Market Street

One of Britain's busiest shopping streets, home to the usual chainstores as well as the infamous Arndale Centre, was originally Market Stede Lane, a link between the medieval Market Place and the daub holes where Piccadilly Gardens now stand. By the eighteenth century its most imposing property was Palace House on the south side, which acquired its name after the owner, a Mr Dickenson, hosted Bonnie Prince Charlie, the Young Pretender, when his Jacobite forces invaded Manchester in 1745.

By that time Market Street was the growing town's main terminus for stagecoaches. The vehicles used to gather outside the Royal Hotel on the corner with Mosley Street but could go no further as the road began to narrow to only five yards, with just two feet of pavement on either side. One of the most popular coaches was Mathew Pickford's 'Flying Wagon' which took four and a

half days to reach London. By 1830 journey times had improved and Sherman's 'Telegraph' took just eighteen hours. It left three times a week at 5 a.m., with stops for breakfast at Macclesfield, lunch at Derby and supper at Leicester, the horses being changed eighteen times in all. The best-known London coach was the 'Peveril of the Peak', so-called after the 1823 Walter Scott novel, now the name of one of Manchester's most popular pubs.

The arrival of some coaches was particularly anticipated. For instance, in December 1816 crowds waited excitedly on Market Street for news of the Spa Fields political demonstration in London, which many believed might give rise to an insurrection. As the coach bearing the news pulled into Market Street the crowd rushed towards it but the guard, thinking the vehicle was about to be attacked, aimed his pistol at the ringleader, Josiah Booth, and threatened to shoot him if he didn't back away. In the mêlée word spread that the Spa Fields rioters in London *had* taken the capital and revolution was imminent. Mancunians celebrated by going on the rampage, but later discovered that the events had petered out.

One coach which failed to arrive in Manchester with its full complement of passengers was the vehicle that left Liverpool on 30 November 1819 with the leading political journalist William Cobbett on board. Cobbett had just returned to Britain from America, but the authorities refused to allow him into Manchester as he had brought with him the bones of Thomas Paine, author of the radical *Rights of Man*, whose posthumous presence, so they feared, might induce revolutionary fervour in the local population only a few months after the Peterloo Massacre.

The last stagecoach to London, the 'Defiance', ran in 1841. Soon the great coaching inns were redundant. Even the Bridgewater Arms, which the poet laureate Robert Southey called 'a spacious inn' in *Letters from England* (1808) and from where

Thomas de Quincey sets out in his short story 'The English Mail Coach', was demolished.

In 1832 Benjamin Hyam, an Ipswich-born Jew, capitalized on Manchester's longstanding success in textiles by opening what is believed to be the world's first tailor's shop at №. 26. A ready-to-wear suit cost 10s 6d. In the 1840s the remaining houses on Market Street were demolished so that more shops could be built. On Sundays when the shops were closed thousands would head to Market Street just to gaze in awe at the goods on offer in the windows.

Market Street was also a great publishing centre. *The Times* described it as 'sedition corner' for the radical *Manchester Observer*, founded in 1818, was based here. The *Manchester Observer* was one of the first newspapers to pioneer popular journalism aimed at the literate working class. Its editor James Wroe was present at Peterloo in 1819, and was the first person to describe what took place there as the 'Peterloo Massacre'. Ironically Peterloo was the paper's undoing, for a new paper that arose out of the events – the *Manchester Guardian* – soon took many of the *Observer*'s readers and Wroe ceased publication in 1821. In its last edition he wrote: 'I would respectfully suggest that the *Manchester Guardian*, combining principles of complete independence, and zealous attachment to the cause of reform, with active and spirited management, is a journal in every way worthy of your confidence and support.'

Market Street in the twentieth century remained at the centre of Manchester life. During the 1926 General Strike a lorry containing empty milk churns and bedding, driven by student blacklegs, was overturned here and set on fire by the crowd. The street was the setting for a couple of strange incidents in the Second World War. At the start of the war the celebrated Manchester City goalkeeper Frank Swift was put on traffic duties on Market Street. His presence, rather than solving congestion, only added to it as curious motorists kept stopping to

gawp at him. At 3 p.m. on Christmas Eve 1940 three aircraft appeared over Market Street with their bomb-doors open. Thousands fled in a panic from what they thought was a Luftwaffe raid that had escaped the warning sirens. But their fears proved groundless as the planes were British, dropping road-safety leaflets, not bombs.

In the late 1960s the warren of small alleys on the north side of the street was bulldozed to make way for the Arndale Centre. Also destroyed were scores of basement beat clubs which had been closed down in a wave of overzealous policing targeted at what the force called the 'long-haired, drug-taking menace'. So determined were the Manchester police to get rid of the clubs that they pressed successfully for parliamentary legislation to help them, resulting in the Manchester Corporation Act of 1965, the only piece of legislation ever passed specifically to stop people enjoying themselves.

Despite being part of the main St Albans to Carlisle road (the A6) Market Street was blocked off to vehicles in 1983. By day the street is thronged with shoppers, but at night it becomes a no-go zone to all but the most foolish or anti-social. Millions of pounds have been spent on cluttering the road with ungainly street furniture, bollards and even escalators leading to fast food outlets, all of which will make the cost of converting the road back to vehicular use in the near future even more costly.

north side: Corporation Street to Piccadilly
Arndale Centre, between Corporation Street and High Street
All cities have covered shopping centres but none has one quite as unloved as Manchester's Arndale Centre, a thirty-acre mall lying between Market Street and Withy Grove. The Arndale takes its name from one-time owners the Arndale Property Trust which began buying the land on the north side of Market Street in 1955. A decade later demolition of the dark alleyways, nightclubs and antiquated shops that filled the area began. The new mall planned for the

site would be designed by Hugh Wilson and Lewis Womersley who were also responsible for the incorrigible Hulme Crescents (p. 129). Here they erected monolithic concrete blocks containing retail outlets, multi-storey car parks and flats, coating the entire complex in hideous buff tiles that led to it soon being nicknamed the biggest toilet in Britain. In the basement a covered market consisted of little more than stalls of a dubious quality dumped in a dank and dismal crypt, and by Cannon Street was a bus station whose roof was too low to accommodate the buses and had to be rebuilt. The construction of the Arndale also meant that a huge section of the city centre was now under cover, away from natural light and cordoned off from the public at night, a restriction of the city's use from which Manchester has never recovered.

The 1996 IRA bomb which exploded on Corporation Street only yards from the Arndale's western wall damaged some of the structure but the Cromford Court residential section was particularly resilient. On the morning of 15 June, the day of the bomb, 77-year-old Cromford Court resident Danny O'Neill, who was nursing a bout of flu, ignored the knock of the caretaker who had been sent round to clear all the residents out of the block before the suspected bomb detonated. When the blast shook the ducks off his wall, he merely turned over in his bed. Three days later he emerged to the amazement of local housing officials and asked: 'I'm feeling much better, what should I do?'

The bomb caused considerable damage to the mall, and much discussion about the Arndale Centre's future filled the newspaper pages. But the opportunity to scrap the entire complex and start again was not taken. Instead cosmetic tinkering has seen some – only some – of the yellow tiles removed and the covered market cleaned up. The Arndale of the twenty-first century remains a testimony to the worst of 1960s corporate planning: ugly architecture, uninspiring chainstores, dismal eateries,

pubs serving beer in plastic skiffs and an overwhelming sense of despondency.

Brooke Bond, No. 29 (site now covered by Arndale Centre)

The well-known tea merchant's was founded at 29 Market Street in 1869 by Arthur Brooke. He added the name 'Bond' not in deference to a joint owner but simply because he liked the sound of the word.

Manchester Guardian (1819–79), No. 29

The *Manchester Guardian*, now simply the *Guardian* and based in London, was founded in 1819 on Market Street by textile merchant and would-be journalist John Edward Taylor, who may have been responsible for the account of Peterloo that appeared unsigned in *The Times* on Wednesday 18 August, two days after the massacre.

Deciding that the local papers were not accurately reflecting the horror people felt after the violence, Taylor and some political friends raised money to set up their own newspaper. The prospectus for what they called the *Manchester Guardian* explained that it would 'zealously enforce the principles of civil and religious Liberty, warmly advocate the cause of Reform [and] endeavour to assist in the diffusion of just principles of Political Economy'. The first *Manchester Guardian* was published as a four-page edition on Saturday 5 May 1821. It cost 7*d* and appeared weekly.

At that time Manchester was growing rapidly as an industrial and commercial centre, and the increase in population boosted the paper's circulation. By 1825 the *Manchester Guardian* was selling over 3,000 copies, and was soon leading the campaign for Manchester to have its own representation in Parliament. However, Taylor was regularly being criticized by former associates for relinquishing his earlier radical stance. For instance, ten years after Peterloo he was no longer supporting universal suffrage. A former colleague, Archibald Prentice, was horrified. He bought the *Manchester Gazette* and moved it to the left of the *Manchester Guardian*. But it was the *Guardian*, not the *Gazette*, that survived.

Taylor remained editor until his death on 6 January 1844. His successor, Jeremiah Garnett, supported the Liberal Party and took up unpopular causes such as equal rights for Roman Catholics. He was in charge when the *Manchester Guardian* became a daily after the tax on newspapers was removed in 1855. The paper moved in 1879 to Cross Street, where under the formidable C. P. Scott it regained its earlier role as a major organ of radicalism.
▶ The *Manchester Guardian* on Cross Street, p. 6.

Debenham's, between High Street and Tib Street
One of Manchester's most impressive Art Deco blocks was designed in 1932 by the Fairhurst firm, the city's greatest architects of twentieth-century warehouses, for the Rylands textile company on an irregular site where no two roads meet at a right angle. The building is steel-framed and clad in Portland stone, features towers at either end of the long Market Street elevation, and zigzag patterns and exuberant ornamental metalwork on the façade. Though it had been intended as a warehouse, parts of the building were soon let to different shops, including Marks & Spencer, and to the Midland Bank. A beacon with a revolving searchlight was placed on the roof in the 1950s to aid aeroplanes flying into Ringway. That decade it became a department store – Paulden's – and since the 1970s has been Debenham's.
▶ House of Fraser/Kendal's, p. 9.

south side: Mosley Street to Exchange Street
Lewis's (1879–2001), corner with Mosley Street
One of Manchester's best-known department stores until its shock 2001 closure was founded in Liverpool in 1877 by David Lewis, who three years later opened a Manchester branch here. Shoppers were soon marvelling at the then unusual notion of being allowed to walk round without being pressured into buying. Early attractions included Manchester's first escalator, a 2s 9d watch and the biggest soda-fountain in the

Empire. The fountain was situated in a basement that was also an entertainments palace, housing stereoscopic machines, distorting mirrors and penny-in-the-slot Edison phonographs, and which was once flooded with two feet of water to reproduce Venice in miniature.

Lewis's adopted American-style advertising by taking space in newspapers in which it openly quoted the store's prices. It dealt in cash only and frowned on credit, which other shops allowed, alongside the slogan: 'Save for it, and save money.' Unlike the London department stores Lewis's success was based not just on retailing but on manufacturing. For instance, in the 1880s it employed 300 tailors and 300 cobblers.

In 1908, and again in 1929, the shop was extended on the same site, swallowing up a number of small courts to become the biggest department store in Britain outside London. Decline set in over the last decades of the twentieth century, and even though its closure was a surprise Lewis's was by then a sorry sight, the staff having long given up trying to impress. The site has since been taken up by Primark.
▶ Marks & Spencer's early days, p. 161.

Clarion Café (1903–36), No. 50a
Manchester's main early twentieth-century left-wing meeting-place-cum-café opened in 1903 and was soon visited by the leading writers H. G. Wells and George Bernard Shaw, who came to see the William Morris-designed room, the walls of which were adorned with quotations from his writings.

The Clarion was more than just a radical headquarters; it was part of a nationwide movement based around Robert Blatchford's widely read radical *Clarion* newspaper. Blatchford, who was second only to William Cobbett as a writer of popular political journalism in the nineteenth century, saw his Clarion movement as 'Cavalier socialism', as opposed to what he claimed was the Roundhead faction personified by the dour, self-righteous Keir Hardie. When in 1900 Hardie became the Labour movement's first MP Blatchford labelled him a 'sanctimonious prig who makes my flesh creep'. Hardie in turn derided Blatchford for 'introducing frivolity into the movement. Socialism is a serious task.'

There were also Clarion rambling and cycling clubs (Christabel and Sylvia Pankhurst were devotees of the movement), and Clarion vans, which ferried the self-styled Clarionets round the region and into the remote Derbyshire countryside, upon which they would descend en masse. Their trademark song was 'England arise, the long night is over' and they conducted open-air meetings outside the village chapel to drum up support for Socialism. The Clarion shut in 1936.

Anti-Corn Law League headquarters
(1838–42), **Newall Buildings** (site covered by Royal Exchange)
Manchester led the campaign to scrap the Corn Laws, one of the most unpopular pieces of legislation of the early nineteenth century, from **Newall Buildings** on Market Street. The Corn Laws had been passed at the end of the Napoleonic Wars to protect British wheat from foreign competition. They allowed merchants to hold grain in bond until prices reached what the owners thought was the highest they were likely to go. This kept the price of bread artificially high, to the detriment of the poor.

Intense opposition to the law came from a variety of groups, not just the working class and radicals, who saw the legislation as a symbol of the ruling aristocracy's feudal authority, but also from merchants, who were unable to make profits from the monopoly. The league itself was a middle-class movement, many of whose members also belonged to the Manchester Chamber of Commerce. They made it the best organized political pressure group of the era. They adopted what are now considered modern methods of campaigning – printing handbills, hosting fund-raising balls, aiming different publicity material at the various target groups – and directly leafleted every voter in the country (some 100,000 people) via the new penny post.

To support its cause, in 1840 the League built a hall in Manchester which became the Free Trade Hall, the most important building in the city's history. Two years later the League moved to London to be nearer Parliament. Robert Peel, the Conservative prime minister, repealed the Corn Laws in 1846, despite intense opposition from within his party, and Manchester politics briefly became the most influential in the country.
► Free Trade Hall, p. 29.

Mosley Street

Mosley Street, once the most important and most handsome street in Manchester but now little more than a tram route, links the two main centres of St Peter's Square and Piccadilly Gardens. It was built over fields at the end of the eighteenth century and named after the Mosley family who owned the manor of Manchester from 1596 to 1838 and whose descendant was the 1930s British Union of Fascists leader, Oswald Mosley.

In the early nineteenth century Mosley Street was lined with elegant residences bought by wealthy merchants such as Nathan Meyer Rothschild, paterfamilias of the famous banking family, but it was too central a location to remain residential for long. With the economic growth of Manchester Mosley Street soon became a prime location for offices and warehouses, which led the rich to decamp to the suburbs. Mosley Street's remaining houses were torn down in the mid-nineteenth century and it then became solely commercial.

On a street that is home to two of the city's most important cultural institutions – the Manchester Art Gallery and the Portico Library – the most imposing structure for more than a century was a warehouse, the garish **Milne Buildings** (situated between Spring Gardens and Booth Street), described by Nikolaus Pevsner as 'the most startling in Manchester' on account of its superimposed giant columns. **Milne Buildings** was demolished in the early 1970s to widespread dismay. Yet its replacement, **Eagle Star House**,

with its long bands of smooth concrete, was
a classic of its kind, the best Manchester
building of the period, though admittedly
a dark one for English architecture. Early
in the twenty-first century it too was
demolished.

west side: St Peter's Square to Market Street
Royal Bank of Scotland, south corner with
York Street
Edward Walters, architect of the Free Trade
Hall, designed Manchester's last glorious
palazzo for the Manchester and Salford
Bank in the 1860s. Beautifully proportioned,
it sits on a huge rusticated base and was
extended by Barker & Ellis in the 1880s, with
further developments by Fairhurst's in 1975.
Nathan Meyer Rothschild's address
(1806–11), north corner with York Street
Nathan Meyer Rothschild bought the property at the corner of Mosley and York streets
after his marriage in 1806. By then the man
who went on to found the famous banking
dynasty, the man whom Lord Byron
described as a 'true Lord of Europe' in *Don
Juan* (1819), had been in Manchester seven
years. Rothschild had moved here from
London because the town was the centre of
the new cotton industry and he wanted to
oversee the exporting of locally made cotton
goods to Frankfurt.

Despite speaking little English, Rothschild
soon developed a reputation for aggressive
selling. Rothschild's fellow businessmen
regarded him with suspicion, maybe even
jealousy, and demanded cash down when he
wanted to buy anything. Perhaps their sus-
picions were justified. When a rival once
asked Rothschild for the secret of his success,
he replied: 'Minding my own business.' And
Rothschild could be rather vulgar. At one of
his concert parties, presented by Louis Spohr,
the violin virtuoso, he congratulated the
musician, jingled some coins in his pocket
and explained: '*That's* my music.'

In 1808 Rothschild bought huge quantities of gold from the East India Company,
then the most powerful firm in the world,
and used it to finance the British government's battles in the peninsular campaign.

Rothschild wound up his Manchester affairs
in 1811 but continued to prosper.

J. Gibbons Sankey's Mercantile Bank in
Portland stone now stands on the site.
Harvest House/Richard Cobden's office
(1830s), Nos. 14–16
Manchester's first commercial building
created in the Italian *palazzo* style was
Harvest House, built for the calico printer
Richard Cobden in 1839. Cobden was one of
the most formidable politicians of the nineteenth century. He rose to prominence in
1830s Manchester as a vociferous opponent
of the hated Corn Laws, and was a leading
figure in the so-called 'Manchester School'
of politicians and merchants pushing for
free trade, minimum state interference in
business and international cooperation.
Cobden was also one of the staunchest pro-
ponents of the idea of electing a council to
run the town's affairs. When the Manchester
Corporation was established in 1838 he
became one of its first aldermen.

Harvest House came about through a
meeting at the Ottoman Club, Constanti-
nople, between Cobden and the architect
Edward Walters. Cobden asked Walters to
create a warehouse for him in central Manchester, and after securing the property
wrote to his brother, Frederick, 'The architect assures me that if I were to put up my
house tomorrow I might have 6,000 guineas
for it . . . I gave 3,000. There being but one
opinion or criterion of a man's ability – the
making of money – I am already thought a
clever fellow.'

By 1840, when he moved into No. 16,
Cobden was said to be one of the best-
travelled men in Britain: he had visited
much of Europe and even made it to the
United States. In 1841 he was elected MP for
Stockport. Five years later the Corn Laws he
had fought against for so long were
repealed. But Cobden was not just a money-
maker. He was also an advocate of the arts
and bemoaned his fellow merchants who
'might be seen in the evenings smoking clay
pipes and calling for brandy and water in
the bar parlours of homely taverns. If they

possessed a little of the mind of the merchants and manufacturers of Frankfurt and Chemnitz they would become the de Medicis of England instead of glorifying in being the toadies of a clodpole aristocracy.'

One reason why Cobden's name doesn't resound down the ages with the gravitas of Victorians such as Gladstone or Disraeli is his lack of relentless political ambition. When Lord John Russell invited him to join his Liberal cabinet in the late 1840s he declined so that he could visit various European countries to spread the word about free trade. It was a typically selfless and philanthropic move, and led in 1851 to his proposing in Parliament a motion for the reduction of armaments, a move that fitted in with his opposition to intervening in the affairs of other countries on the grounds that such actions hit trade. 'England has no interest apart from the preservation of peace,' he explained in opposing the Crimean War.

Though derided now in some circles as a right-wing figure, Cobden was simply an iconoclast and a progressive. He believed that powerful nations should work to promote business and culture, not war, and that greater international accord in trade would lead to less conflict: peace through free trade.

► Anti-Corn Law League headquarters, p. 14.

Manchester and Salford Bank, No. 10, north of Marble Street

Richard Tattershall's four giant-order Corinthian columns frame what looks like a temple – a temple to banking. It was built in 1836 for the Manchester and Salford Bank, and is now occupied by a building society.

Birthplace of the Football League/Royal Hotel (1827–1908), corner of Mosley Street and Market Street

A plaque on the wall of the Abbey Bank notes how in April 1888 the Football League was created at a meeting that took place in the Royal Hotel, which then stood on this site. The League was the North's answer to the Football Association, the body formed

by southern clubs in 1863 to codify the mostly random rules that then barely regulated the game. Those clubs, formed from the public schools and military, were gentlemen amateurs; however, in the North there was a desire to have a professional game in which players were paid. In July 1885, after four years of debate, the Football Association had legalized professionalism, but the northern clubs felt that an *ad hoc* fixture list of friendlies and FA Cup matches was not enough to sustain interest, and pushed for a new type of competition.

Two men were the main force behind the new Football League – J. J. Bentley and William McGregor. Bentley, secretary of Bolton Wanderers, was also a top-class referee who wrote up reports of matches he reffed in the local newspapers. It was Bentley who was behind the staging of the FA Cup Final in Fallowfield in 1893, the only time the final has been played in the city. McGregor was a Scottish draper and a director of Aston Villa, and it was he who devised the simple but revolutionary idea of getting clubs to play each other every year, home and away, with points awarded for results – a format that was eventually accepted across the world as the best method for judging teams.

On 2 March 1888 McGregor wrote to the leading northern and Midlands clubs setting out his ideas. He chose not to involve southern teams as at that time they were either deemed not good enough or considered too set in their ways to adapt to the new style of competition. The first meeting of the clubs was held at Anderson's Hotel in London on 23 March 1888, but it was at the second meeting, at Manchester's Royal Hotel on 17 April, that the name 'Football League' was coined. It was not McGregor's choice. He wanted 'Football Union', but that was considered too similar to Rugby Union and was voted out.

The teams that formed the original Football League were Accrington, Aston Villa, Blackburn Rovers, Bolton Wanderers, Burnley, Derby County, Everton, Notts County, Preston North End, Stoke City,

West Bromwich Albion and Wolverhampton Wanderers. The first season of the Football League began in 1888 and the first champions were Preston North End.
▶ Manchester United, p. 189.

east side: Piccadilly to St Peter's Square
Portico Library, north junction with Charlotte Street

The Portico, a subscription library dating back to the early nineteenth century, was the brainchild of two businessmen, Michael Ward and Robert Robinson, who visited Liverpool's Lyceum Library in 1796 and thought of opening in Manchester something that would 'unite the advantages of a news room and library on an extensive and liberal plan'.

Ward and Robinson won support from 400 leading Manchester figures and devised a system whereby subscribers were also the owners, paying thirteen guineas at the outset and two guineas a year to belong. The Mosley Street site was chosen as it was in an elegant part of the city, close to where many would-be members lived. Thomas Harrison was appointed architect, and between 1802 and 1806 he created one of the first classical revival buildings in England, the façade based on the north elevation of the Temple of Athena Palias at Priene, even though he had failed to make it as far as Greece on his Grand Tour.

The Portico's first secretary was Peter Mark Roget, a doctor at the Infirmary on Piccadilly, who in 1805 produced a 'classed catalogue of words on a small scale' – the *Thesaurus of English Words and Phrases* – which has posthumously made him universally known. The library chairman from 1849–84 was the Revd William Gaskell, husband of the novelist Elizabeth. Early users included the opium-eating writer Thomas de Quincey and the pioneering scientist John Dalton, who was given free admission in return for 'superintending the going of the clock'. The library also had non-bibliographic uses. It provided the venue for the dinner given in honour of the Duke of Wellington's opening of the Manchester–Liverpool Railway in 1830, which went ahead without the Iron Duke after his carriage was stoned by a mob still angered over Peterloo and the accidental death on the railway line of the politician William Huskisson.

One early attraction of the Portico was its stock of London papers, then not widely available in the town. But the fears of initial detractors, that Manchester couldn't support so bold a venture, were proved half right in 1920 when the library sold the ground floor to the Bank of Athens, a space now occupied, predictably, by a pub. The library is today confined to the upper floor and members are obliged to use the old tradesmen's side entrance on Charlotte Street to gain access.
▶ Chetham's Library, p. 95.

Manchester Art Gallery
Few cities outside London can match the breadth and quality of Manchester's main art gallery, which contains the country's best collection of Pre-Raphaelites. The gallery is housed in Charles Barry's classical revival building of 1827–35, originally home of the Manchester Institution for the Promotion of Science, Literature and the Arts, which provided exhibition space and lecture rooms for scientific bodies.

In 1882 the owners offered the building and its contents to the Corporation for free, provided that councillors spent £2,000 a year for twenty years on new works of art. The Corporation's Art Gallery Committee bought enthusiastically and accumulated an impressive collection by the end of the nineteenth century. An inspired choice was Ford Madox Brown's monumental Pre-Raphaelite painting *Work*, bought for £400 on the recommendation of *Manchester Guardian* editor C. P. Scott. Other major acquisitions, including a set of Turners, came through bequests from wealthy Mancunians. The creation of the Art Fund in the 1960s allowed galleries to save for buying major works. Manchester duly obtained Baccicio's *St John the Baptist* and Stubbs's *Cheetah and Stag*. In 1979 the

Assheton Bennetts donated a collection of seventeenth-century Dutch and Flemish paintings, and in 1993 Sidney Bernstein, founder of Granada TV, bequeathed a collection that included works by Chagall and Modigliani.

The relationship between the gallery and Manchester politicians has not always been fruitful. One mayor, pointing to the paintings at a function in the early twentieth century, was heard saying to a VIP: 'None of your manufactured stuff, lad. Real masterpieces there, and all 'and-painted.' But that was nothing compared to the alderman sitting next to the Pre-Raphaelite artist William Holman Hunt at the opening of the gallery who scribbled a note to a colleague that read: 'Who or what is a Holman hunt [*sic*]?' Even as recently as the 1980s there was a strong feeling within the left-wing Labour Group that any spending on the art gallery was a criminal waste of money that should have gone into the bottomless well of housing repairs.

► Former Manchester Academy of Fine Arts, John Dalton Street, p. 77.

Oxford Street

Work began in the 1790s on a new route to link St Peter's Fields with the Wilmslow turnpike. In the nineteenth century many of the buildings on the east side of Oxford Street backed on to wharves of the Rochdale Canal, but these have long been filled in. By the early twentieth century the street was a centre for entertainment with theatres such as the long gone Hippodrome and the Prince's. Later in the century its cinemas made it the centre of Manchester nightlife, but these were closed piecemeal from the 1970s and now no cinemas survive here.

west side: River Medlock to Lower Mosley Street

Medlock Bridge

The young Thomas de Quincey, the fêted local-born writer, was mercilessly taunted by the boys working at the factory that stood here by the river Medlock, as he made his way from the family home, Greenhay, to

school early in the nineteenth century. The factory lads were particularly irked about the boots de Quincey and his brother, William, wore, and teased them with a series of mocking chants. When William, the braver de Quincey, challenged the ringleader to a fight, the taunting stopped, and he sent the enemy packing with a shower of stones. Thomas, the more cerebral de Quincey, was sufficiently haunted by the experience to incorporate it into his autobiographical masterpiece *Confessions of an English Opium Eater* (1821).

► Greenhay, p. 135.

Cornerhouse

Manchester's major arts centre occupies a split site by Oxford Road station. The main building, on Oxford Street, was converted from a furniture warehouse in the early 1980s. It contains an exhibition space, a café, a bar, a well-stocked arts bookshop and, rare for the Northwest, an arthouse and repertory cinema. The building by Whitworth Street West, with its stylish frosted-glass 1930s frontage, was designed by Charles Swain, who was also responsible for Manchester City's former Maine Road stadium.

Tootal, Broadhurst and Lee Building, north of Rochdale Canal

A gorgeous terracotta-clad late-Victorian office block, typical of so many *fin-de-siècle* Manchester textile headquarters, was built by J. Gibbons Sankey for the Tootal textile company in 1898. The building sports a variety of epic features: loading bays, giant-order Corinthian columns, angular towers, flagpoles and, on the corner with Great Bridgewater Street, two beefy stone figures which strain to hold up the weight of the upper storeys.

► YMCA building/St George's House, Peter Street, p. 28.

Hippodrome Theatre/Gaumont Cinema, between Great Bridgwater Street and Chepstow Street

The Hippodrome variety theatre that opened on this site on Boxing Day 1904 was designed by Frank Matcham, the leading theatre builder of the day. It had a sliding roof, space for 100 horses and a large area that could be filled with water for aquatic events, a feat proudly promoted in the programme as 'A foot to a Fathom of Water at a touch of a lever.'

The theatre closed in 1935, when the sign was moved to a new theatre with that name in Ardwick, and it was rebuilt as a cinema, the Gaumont, with an interior designed by the renowned Russian Theodore Komisarjevsky, former director of Moscow's Bolshoi, who emigrated to Britain after Lenin's directive about putting 'theatre into coffins'. The Gaumont was popular with GIs in the Second World War and renowned for its singalongs during which the words of popular hits were run on the screen and the audience encouraged to join in what was an early form of karaoke.

It was here on New Year's Eve 1961 that Ian Brady and Myra Hindley, the Moors Murderers, enjoyed their first date, watching *El Cid*. After the cinema closed in 1974 the venue became a nightclub, Romanoff's (later Rotters), which itself closed in 1991. The building was then demolished and replaced with a car park. To the immediate north is the Picture House, a former cinema which has been preserved but has suffered the ignominy of being turned into a McDonald's.

Prince's Buildings, north of Chepstow Street
The buff terracotta façade and tall stark chimney line are all that remains of Birkett's original Art Nouveau 1903 office block.
east side: St Peter's Square to River Medlock
Plaza, immediately south of the Odeon
Business was bad at the Plaza nightclub in the late 1950s until Mecca made Jimmy Savile manager. Savile, with his shock of multi-coloured hair, began hosting lunchtime discos in 1959, and was soon attracting as many as 2,000 punters, although anyone who smelt of drink, had a dirty shirt or was wearing unpressed trousers would be turned away by the tough ex-miners from Savile's former Yorkshire colliery days who patrolled the door and were even known to

shave the sideburns off particularly hairy revellers. The Plaza sessions also attracted a large number of truanting schoolchildren, and when local headteachers complained Savile, with trademark cheek, responded: 'You've had it too easy for too long. If you make your school more attractive than my dancehall you can keep them.' The venue later became the Tropicana but has since been demolished.
▸ Hacienda, p. 61.

The Music Box/Jilly's, No. 65
Long a popular city centre club/rock venue, in the 1970s it was Fagin's, with a small bar beneath known as Rafters. It was there that the Joy Division played their second ever gig (as Warsaw) on 31 May 1977, their manager, Rob Gretton, being the DJ. The group went on stage at one in the morning, but only a handful of punters were left in the building and singer Ian Curtis began picking fights with them. At a later Rafters gig Curtis ripped the stage apart, throwing the wooden pieces at the audience, and deliberately dropped a pint pot on the floor so that he could roll around in the broken glass like his hero, Iggy Pop.

On 14 April 1978, at the Stiff/Chiswick Challenge, the group impressed a watching Tony Wilson, then in his early days as an impresario, and when Curtis berated Wilson later that night with a string of cusses for not promoting the group on his Granada TV programme Wilson booked them a slot. He later signed the band to his fledgling Factory Records label, reaping considerable critical success following the release of their first album, *Unknown Pleasures*, in 1979. The venue is now the Music Box-cum-Jilly's.
▸ Factory Records, p. 176.

St James's Building, Nos. 65–95
The grandest and most imposing of Manchester's Edwardian office blocks is an immense baroque construction clad in Portland stone, built by Clegg, Fryer and Penman for the Calico Printers' Association in 1912. No expense was spared on the external design; the frontage with its seven storeys and twenty-seven bays even features

aedicules that act as the façades of miniature 'buildings'. Inside there are more than 1,000 rooms, reached via a grand entrance hall that looks more like that of a Monte Carlo casino than of a Manchester office block. However, the back, overlooking the Rochdale Canal, is plain and unadorned – why waste money on something that few would see, no doubt mused the owners. Unfortunately, there is no opportunity to catch an appropriate glimpse of this immense Beaux Arts creation owing to its claustrophobic location, crammed into the textile warehouse area around Oxford Street.

Palace Theatre, north junction with Whitworth Street

An ornate late-Victorian grand theatre, one of the main venues in Manchester for long-running shows, it opened as the Palace of Varieties, a music hall, in 1891. There was considerable opposition from local Methodists, concerned about the effect lewd entertainment might have on public morals, and though the Palace's first programme was one of grand ballet it was soon staging music hall – exactly what the Methodists feared – with performers such as Little Tich, Dan Leno and Marie Lloyd.

When music hall declined after the Great War the Palace took to conventional drama and Christmas pantomime, with occasional shows by major stars. When Danny Kaye played there in June 1949 the queues stretched along Oxford Street as far as the Central Library. There were fears that the Palace would close in the 1970s but instead it was refurbished, and it reopened in 1981 with Bob Scott, who oversaw the creation of the Royal Exchange Theatre, as managing director. The booking of star names and major touring companies has filled the auditorium since.

Palace Hotel/Refuge Assurance building, south junction with Whitworth Street

The Palace Hotel, built as the Refuge Assurance company's headquarters, is an exuberant, lavishly designed, *fin-de-siècle* construction with a tower that is one of Manchester's best-known landmarks. Three buildings in all, the first went up from 1891–5 and was designed by Alfred Waterhouse, the architect responsible for Manchester Town Hall, who chose the finest materials: ceramic tiles, Carrara marble, terracotta, parquet flooring and stained glass. Waterhouse also incorporated a number of clever technical devices: the heating was supplied by steam piped in from the nearby Bloom Street power station, and it had a communications system of pneumatic tubes in which messages in leather capsules were sent around the building.

To recruit staff in the early days a Refuge official would stand on the corner of the street stopping every third person with the question: 'Would you like a job here?' The company was soon enjoying considerable success, and Paul Waterhouse, son of Alfred, was commissioned early in the twentieth century to build an extension. It was he who devised the striking clock tower, described by Professor C. H. Reilly as 'like a tall young man in flannel trousers escorting two charming, but somewhat delicate, old ladies dressed in lace'.

The third building on the site, the one along Whitworth Street, was constructed in 1935, resulting in a formidable complex backing on to the River Medlock. With its sheer elevations faced in glazed white brick, the rear of the building is as spectacular as the garish frontage, and it featured strikingly in the climax of Val Guest's 1960 Manchester-based thriller *Hell Is a City* in which the detective played by Stanley Baker chases a criminal across the roof.

The Refuge company moved to Cheshire in 1987, and two years later the building was converted into a hotel.

● The Refuge is still under construction in Adolphe Valette's 1910 Impressionist oil painting *Oxford Road, Manchester*, which can be seen at Manchester Art Gallery.

Italy in Manchester

The Italianate styles of building were brought to Manchester early in the nineteenth century by a succession of architects who provided the city centre with its most conspicuous look. For much of the Victorian period almost every new major public building was given the Italianate treatment, often with the inclusion of a feature commemorating an existing Italian structure.

● **Albert Hall**, Peter Street. Architect W. J. Morley used the church of Santa Maria della Spina in Pisa as his inspiration.

● **Albert Memorial**, Albert Square. Thomas Worthington's design was also based on the church of Santa Maria della Spina in Pisa.

● **Athenaeum**, Princess Street. The entrance is reminiscent of Domenico Fontana's porch to the Palazzo della Cancelleria in Rome.

● **Britannia Hotel**, Portland Street. Its outline echoes the Fondaco dei Turchi in Venice.

● **Free Trade Hall**, Peter Street. The front is based on the Gran Guardia Vecchia at Verona.

● **Memorial Hall**, Albert Square. The top floor exhibits the window tracery of the Ca' d'Oro on the Grand Canal in Venice.

● **Police Courts**, Minshull Street. The bell tower shows similarities with that of San Marco, Venice.

● **Royal Bank of Scotland**, 25 St Ann's Square. The linking of the main block with the manager's house recalls the Palazzo Pandolfini in Florence.

Peter Street

Manchester's most famous building (the Free Trade Hall), its most glamorous hotel (the Midland), and the location of the best-known event in its history (the Peterloo Massacre of 1819) can all be found on Peter Street, which runs between Deansgate and St Peter's Square.

Peter Street was built through St Peter's Fields in 1793 to replace a cart track and named in honour of the now demolished St Peter's church. There was a flower garden on the south side where the Free Trade Hall now stands, leading to a windmill, remembered in nearby Windmill Street. As there were few buildings the surrounding land was regularly used as a rallying place for protesters in the early nineteenth century, a time of considerable political unrest.

On 4 November 1816 a demonstration called to discuss the 'present distressed state of the country' took place on St Peter's Fields. The following March around 12,000 people gathered here to support the Blanketeers, unemployed Lancashire spinners and weavers marching to London to protest to the Prince Regent, each of whom took with them a blanket to keep warm. During the rally the protesters were violently moved on by the King's Dragoon Guards, who arrested their leaders and cleared the crowd, chasing around 300 marchers to Stockport, where they attacked them again.

Around 8,000 people assembled in St Peter's Fields on 8 January 1819 to hear the Reform leader, Henry Hunt, who was seeking support for a declaration to be sent to the Prince Regent stating that 'the only source of all legitimate power is in the People' and that 'all Governments, not immediately derived from and strictly accountable to the People, are usurpations and ought to be resisted and destroyed'. Seven months later, on 16 August 1819, St Peter's Fields held its last and most notorious demonstration when a charge by the military at a huge crowd gathered to support parliamentary reform resulted in the Peterloo Massacre (see below).

Peter Street and St Peter's Fields were fully built up in the 1840s, around the time that the Anti-Corn Law League erected a

continued on p. 25

The Peterloo Massacre

I met murder on the way/He had a mask like Castlereagh – from 'The Mask of Anarchy', Shelley, 1819

Eleven people died and more than 400 were injured at St Peter's Fields on 16 August 1819 when soldiers charged through a crowd of 60,000 demonstrating peacefully for parliamentary reform. The event, one of the most violent episodes in English political history, became known as the Peterloo Massacre, the most infamous event in Manchester history.

Peterloo was one of several demonstrations to take place around Peter Street in the early nineteenth century, a period marked by low wages, high prices and social distress. By 1819 there was much indignation against what was seen as a corrupt parliamentary system, and in the summer the radical Patriotic Union Society called a demonstration for 16 August, a public holiday. Speakers booked included Mary Fildes, whose involvement in campaigns for birth control led to her being accused of promoting pornography, and Henry 'Orator' Hunt, a supporter of annual parliaments, universal suffrage and the secret ballot, who was due to speak on 'real Reform and rational Liberty'.

In the weeks leading up to the demonstration the authorities condemned the holding of what they called seditious assemblies, and set up a network of spies and informers to monitor the activities of the many radical groups in Manchester and south Lancashire. They were worried that there might be a riot as a number of local political activists had been training on the moors with pikes and firearms. Those involved in local radical organizations, united by the desire to attain the vote by force of argument, not violence, had sent out instructions that demonstrators were to carry no weapons.

Nevertheless on the day itself the authorities assembled a formidable security force: around 400 Special Constables, 1,500 soldiers from the 15th Hussars, the Royal Horse Artillery, and the Manchester and Salford Yeomanry, a body of local shopkeepers, publicans and merchants.

On the morning of 16 August hundreds of people began arriving early at St Peter's Fields holding banners proclaiming 'Annual Parliaments', 'Vote by Ballot', 'Universal Suffrage' and 'No Corn Laws'. As the size of the crowd increased, local magistrates, meeting in a Mr Buxton's house in Mount Street overlooking St Peter's Fields, decided they would arrest Henry Hunt once he began speaking, before he could rouse the crowd, and disperse the marchers – as they had done during the earlier 'Blanketeers' rally.

At 1.30 p.m., with events proceeding peacefully and Hunt by the hustings (corner of Windmill Street and South Street), the magistrates convinced themselves that the town was in 'great danger' and panicked. They instructed Joseph Nadin, the deputy chief constable, to arrest Hunt. When officers tried to reach the hustings they found their way through the crowd blocked and called for help from the part-time Yeomanry, stationed on Cooper Street. The Yeomanry surged towards the demonstrators, killing an infant in the process – the first casualty of the day.

In St Peter's Fields they became separated and panicked, drawing their weapons at the protesters, each 'waving a bloody sword/ For the service of their Lord', as Shelley described it in 'The Mask of Anarchy'. To William Hulton, chairman of the Lancashire and Cheshire magistrates, watching from the Mount Street house, the people were at fault. He shouted to Lieutenant Colonel L'Estrange, the commander of the military forces, 'Good God, Sir, don't you see they are attacking the Yeomanry? Disperse them.' The Revd Charles Ethelston read the Riot Act and Colonel L'Estrange ordered the 15th Hussars to rescue the Yeomanry, who violently and bloodily cleared the crowd from St Peter's Fields, killing eleven people and injuring more than 400. Of those killed, five were sabred, three trampled, one hit with a stone, one was crushed and one fell down a cellar.

By 2 p.m. the field was 'strewed [with] caps, bonnets, hats, shawls and shoes', according to Sam Bamford, the Middleton radical. 'Several mounds of human beings still remained where they had fallen, crushed down and smothered. Some of these still groaning – others with staring eyes, were gasping for breath and others would never breathe more.'

The politics of Peterloo

The first few decades of the nineteenth century, enshrined in public imagination as the elegant age of the Regency, were a time of severe political repression in England. The corrupt electoral system meant that membership of the House of Commons was decided by a small franchise of wealthy men. Parliamentary seats could be bought and sold, or handed down like family heirlooms. A thriving, growing town such as Manchester had no parliamentary representation (nor even its own elected council) yet the deserted village of Old Sarum, Wiltshire, had its own MP.

The Conservative government of Lord Liverpool, fearful of the kind of revolutionary activity recently witnessed in France, was intent on stamping out all dissent and free speech. But when the victory over Napoleon's forces at Waterloo in 1815 gave way to economic recession, there were riots, demonstrations and an increase in radical activity. After a missile was thrown through the glass window of the Prince Regent's coach before the opening of Parliament in January 1817, the government suspended habeas corpus, which meant that anyone considered a danger to the state could be imprisoned without trial. Its restoration in March 1818 led not to complacency but to renewed demands for parliamentary reform at a series of well-attended public meetings, culminating in the Manchester gathering at St Peter's Fields on 16 August 1819.

The aftermath of Peterloo

On the day after the violence in St Peter's Fields placards appeared in London proclaiming: 'Horrid Massacres at Manchester'. They had been brought there by Richard Carlile, one of the speakers the authorities wanted to arrest along with Henry Hunt, but who had escaped arrest after being spirited away from the scene by local radicals and hidden at a secret location. But it was James Wroe, editor of the radical newspaper the *Manchester Observer*, who was present at St Peter's Fields, who coined the phrase 'Peterloo Massacre'.

Another local journalist, John Edward Taylor, had discovered that *The Times*'s John Tyas, the only reporter from a national newspaper to attend the rally, had been arrested and imprisoned, and was therefore unable to file his report. Taylor sent an account to the paper himself, even though he had left the scene early. Radicalized by the events, he began to plan a new local paper closer to his own views, which he published for the first time on Saturday 5 May 1821 as the *Manchester Guardian* (p. 12).

The authorities were unrepentant about the carnage in Manchester. Lord Liverpool's government supported the action of the magistrates and the Yeomanry, while the Home Secretary, Viscount Sidmouth, sent a letter of congratulations to the Manchester forces, praising their actions. In December 1819 Parliament passed further repressive measures in the shape of the Six Acts, which banned public meetings of more than fifty people and gave magistrates powers to search any property or person for arms.

At the inquest into the death of one of the victims, the coroner John Lees refused to accept any evidence critical of the authorities, and the hearing was adjourned, later being declared null and void on a technicality. In 1822 members of the Manchester Yeomanry were acquitted of any wrongdoing at their trial at Lancaster Assizes. However Henry Hunt, who had been arrested at Peterloo, was found guilty at his trial in York the following March of 'assembling with unlawful banners at an unlawful meeting for the purpose of exciting discontent' and was gaoled for two years. Samuel Bamford, the Middleton radical, was one of three people given a year's sentence.

'The Mask of Anarchy' – Shelley and Peterloo

On hearing in Italy news of the events in Manchester the poet Percy Bysshe Shelley, a sympathizer of the radical cause, responded immediately with the vitriolic 'The Mask of Anarchy'. Written in the form of a popular ballad, the poem is a venomous indictment of the politicians he blamed for the social conditions – 'the triumph of Anarchy' – that had resulted in the Peterloo Massacre.

In the poem Shelley imagines a dream in which Lord Castlereagh, the Leader of the House of Commons; Lord Eldon, the Lord Chancellor; and Lord Sidmouth, the Home Secretary, are disguised in masks. Castlereagh is Murder ('I met murder on the way/He had a mask like Castlereagh'), Eldon is Fraud ('Next came Fraud, and he had on/Like Eldon, an ermined gown'), and Sidmouth, Hypocrisy ('Like Sidmouth next, Hypocrisy/On a crocodile rode by'). The poem ends with the memorable lines: 'Rise like Lions after slumber/In unvanquishable number/Shake your chains to earth like dew/Which in sleep had fallen on you/Ye are many – they are few.' Although 'The Mask of Anarchy' was written soon after Peterloo it was not published until 1832, thirteen years after the events, as Leigh Hunt, Shelley's publisher, believed it to be too controversial and libellous to be released while the accused were alive.

Peterloo also earns mentions in various Manchester-based novels. In Mrs Linnaeus Banks's *The Manchester Man* (1874), Mr Chadwick is attacked by the Yeomanry and defended by Jabez Clegg, a scene which echoes a real-life incident in which Mrs Banks's grandfather John Daniels was similarly assailed until rescued by one of his own weavers. In Howard Spring's epic novel *Fame Is the Spur* (1940), the hero, J. Hamer Shawcross, a venal Labour politician modelled on Ramsay MacDonald, inherits as a child a sword that had been used to strike down a demonstrator at the massacre and uses it metaphorically to scythe his way through British politics.

wooden pavilion on the site eventually occupied by the Free Trade Hall (now a hotel). By the end of the century Peter Street had become, along with Oxford Street to the south-east, Manchester's main thoroughfare for theatres and music halls. Only the Theatre Royal (now a disco) remains from that era.

north side: Deansgate to St Peter's Square
Albert Hall
An exuberant buff and yellow terracotta church and hall, similar only in name to London's Albert Hall, it was built as a Wesleyan Mission Hall in 1910 by Samuel Collier, a Methodist minister, who wanted it as a riposte to the many local night-time venues. 'Within a distance of 500 yards along Peter Street and Oxford Street,' Collier explained, 'there are ten places of amusement, nine of which are theatres and music halls seating 25,000 people and bringing great crowds – perhaps the largest in the city on one thoroughfare at night – and 22 licensed houses. In no area in Manchester is there to be found more men, women and young people to whom an appeal ought to be made in the name of Christ.'

In wartime the hall hosted midweek Hallé concerts after the Free Trade Hall was bombed. On the night of the Munich air disaster, 6 February 1958, many were turned away, so full of worshippers was the hall. The Methodist centre closed in 1971 due to the declining numbers of local residents, and after lying empty for over a decade was renovated as a bar.

Gaiety Theatre (1878–1959), opposite the Theatre Royal
Under the ownership and management of Annie Horniman, in the early twentieth century the Gaiety became one of the most celebrated theatres in the country, home to Britain's first repertory company, staging early runs of local plays such as Stanley Houghton's *Hindle Wakes* (1912) and Harold Brighouse's *Hobson's Choice* (1915).

The first theatre on the site, Edward Garcia's Gaiety Theatre of Varieties, opened in 1878. It burned down five years later and

was rebuilt as the Comedy Theatre in 1884, and was where *La Bohème* was first premièred in Britain in 1897. By 1903 the venue had become the Gaiety Theatre, but this was soon closed down by the city's watch committee on the grounds of obscenity.

Four years later Annie Horniman, granddaughter of the tea merchant John Horniman, arrived in Manchester to continue the crusading theatre productions she had overseen since inheriting the family fortune in 1893. Horniman had financed a season of plays at the Avenue Theatre, London, featuring the first public performances of works by W. B. Yeats and George Bernard Shaw, and in Dublin she had funded the opening of the Abbey Theatre. Her first productions in Manchester were staged at the Midland Hotel, but she also hired Frank Matcham, the leading theatre architect of the day, to redesign the Gaiety. Here she put on works by Euripides and Shaw, but more importantly she also introduced Britain's first repertory system – a quick turn-over of programme with a regular team of players and producers.

Intent on discovering a major new English dramatist, Horniman encouraged local writers. 'If Lancashire playwrights send their plays to me,' she announced, 'I shall pledge myself to read them through. Let them write about their friends and enemies – about real life.' Through this initiative she found Allan Monkhouse, Stanley Houghton and Harold Brighouse – the Manchester School of Theatre. The movement was shortlived however, and disbanded during the Great War. Nor was it universally praised, even within the city. James Agate, one of the leading theatre critics of the day, claimed that the Manchester School was overrated and that Houghton's *Hindle Wakes* was a 'bright flash in what turned out to be a very small pan'.

Around this time Neville Cardus, who went on to become one of the *Manchester Guardian*'s most fêted writers, took a job at the Gaiety bar, having fled the printer's where he was apprenticed after fighting with

The Manchester School of Theatre

● *Hindle Wakes*, Stanley Houghton, 1912

Set in the mill town of Hindle, near Wigan, during Wakes Week, the play centres around Alan Jeffcote, the mill owner's son, and Fanny Hawthorne, who decide to sneak off to Llandudno for some fun. While they're away, Fanny's best friend Mary drowns. When she returns to Hindle and her parents discover where she's been, they insist she and Alan marry. Alan, however, is already engaged and Fanny, a proto feminist with her own agenda, announces: 'I'm a Lancashire lass, and as long as there's weaving sheds in Lancashire I shall earn enough to keep me going.'

Hindle Wakes was first performed not in Manchester but at the Aldwych Theatre, London, and enabled Houghton to take up writing full time. He moved from Manchester to the capital, and then to Paris, but was taken ill and on returning to Manchester in 1913 died of meningitis. A 1931 film version of the play starred Sibyl Thorndike, who had appeared in the Gaiety run.

● *Hobson's Choice*, Harold Brighouse, 1915

The best-known and most revived work of the Manchester School of Theatre is named after an antiquated saying which originated in the Bull Inn, Spitalfields, east London. There, Thomas Hobson used to hire horses to Cambridge coach operators on the proviso that they always chose the horse closest to the stable door, i.e. they had no choice at all – Hobson's choice. It was Stanley Houghton, not Brighouse, who intended using the phrase as the title for a play, but having jotted down the idea he died before he could use it. His note was found by Brighouse, who was compiling a memorial edition of Houghton's plays.

Set in 1880 in a cobbler's in Eccles, the play centres around Hobson, the tyrannical owner, who has consigned his eldest daughter, Maggie, to tend to him eternally, only for her to plan a way of breaking free of her travails. The play was turned into a film in 1953 by David Lean and starred Charles Laughton as the formidable Hobson.

a colleague. Cardus was so ashamed at having lost his chance of learning a trade at the printer's that he never told his family of his dismissal but left the house each morning at six o'clock, walked the three miles into the city centre, waited until nine for the library to open, and then spent hour after hour there before it was time to go to the theatre to sell chocolates.

The Gaiety was sold to a cinema group in 1921. Some shows were staged in the 1950s, but it closed in 1959 and was replaced by an office block, Television House.

south side: Lower Mosley Street to Deansgate

Midland Hotel, between Lower Mosley Street and Mount Street

Manchester's greatest hotel, an immense Renaissance-style block clad in red brick, polished granite, and pink and brown terracotta, was built by the Midland Railway Company between 1898 and 1903 to the designs of Charles Trubshaw. The site had previously been occupied at various times by Cooper's Cottage, the Casino music hall, and the Gentlemen's Concert Hall (p. 63). The hotel should have been built a few yards west to front Central station, the Midland Railway company's Manchester terminus, in the same way that the Midland Hotel fronts St Pancras at the London end of the line. However, funds ran out and construction was delayed for twenty years.

The hotel opened on 5 September 1903. It was considerably better equipped than any other in Manchester. There was a Palm Court, Turkish baths, hairdressers, tailors, a chemist, a post office, continental restaurants, 400 bedrooms, 100 baths and air-conditioning to protect guests from the smoky Manchester air. There was also a concert-hall-cum-theatre, included as compensation to the owners of the Gentlemen's Concert Hall, which had been demolished to make way for the Midland, and to bridge the gap between the building and the station a covered passageway was erected to connect the two. The hotel theatre staged the first plays produced by Annie Horniman when she arrived in Manchester from Dublin in 1907, although she was forced out when the manager discovered her smoking. Ironically, the hotel also put on 'smoking' concerts, which women could attend only if accompanied by a man, and young men only if permission had been granted by their employer. These were abandoned after the First World War. Another feature removed at that time was the Winter Garden, where Israel Sieff had married Rebecca Marks, daughter of one of the founders of Marks & Spencer, Michael Marks, in 1910.

Famous users and guests of the Midland have included the car manufacturers Charles Rolls and Henry Royce, the thriller writer Edgar Wallace and Winston Churchill. Rolls and Royce first met in the hotel's Grill Room in 1904 and decided to go into business together (see below). Edgar Wallace locked himself in his room for two days to finish a film script. Winston Churchill ate eighteen oysters, washed down with a bottle of Pommery and Greno champagne, before speaking at the nearby Free Trade Hall in 1929, returning to the hotel afterwards for a five-course dinner that lasted until the early hours.

When the great actor Laurence Olivier stayed at the Midland in the 1970s while filming *Brideshead Revisited* at Granada TV, the fire alarm went off in the early hours of the morning. Derek Grainger, *Brideshead*'s producer, raced through the corridors waking the cast but despite knocking repeatedly on Olivier's door had to wait some time before he got a response. 'What is it?' asked the great actor. 'Larry, Larry, there appears to be a fire.' 'Really? Oh, bad luck. Do let me know if there's anything I can do,'

came the reply, followed by a shutting door. Perhaps Olivier was sympathizing with the hotel's best-known long-term resident at that time, *Coronation Street*'s Albert Tatlock (the actor Jack Howarth), whose tenure was spoiled, so he claimed, by having to attend the fire drill which he tried to avoid by hiding in his room until found by the manager.

The Midland was spared by German bombers during the Second World War supposedly because Hitler had chosen it for the local Reich headquarters after his planned invasion. But more of a threat to its future was British Rail, who took over the running when the railways were nationalized after the war. They had let the Midland's St Pancras hotel deteriorate and had failed to maintain the fabric of this building, damaged by the hundreds of trains using the nearby Central station every day. British Rail sold the Midland to the Holiday Inn group in the 1980s and they restored it, retaining many of the original features such as the marble corridors, the double-arched coach entrance, the rococo lettering and the reliefs of the Wyvern, the mythical beast that was the Midland Railway's logo.

Until recently the Midland was still an ideal location for Mancunians looking to enjoy a post-Hallé concert coffee or afternoon tea, as Rachel Rosing does in Howard Spring's 1935 novel of that name, but twentieth-century changes have brought the introduction of an antisocial door policy and the quality of the refreshments has similarly declined.

► Grand Hotel, p. 98.

St George's House, between Mount Street and Museum Street
A monumental block, its size in keeping with the other buildings on the south side of the street, St George's House neatly complements the adjacent Midland Hotel in its use of terracotta but has a façade that is oddly asymmetrical. It was constructed in 1911 as the YMCA building which the promotional brochure described as a 'City of Refuge from the Temptations of the City' on its

Rolls meets Royce

Lunching in the Grill Room of the Midland Hotel on 4 May 1904, Henry Royce,
motor mechanic and engineer, was introduced to Charles Stewart Rolls, a wealthy
motoring enthusiast. Royce had already
developed his own 10 hp motor car, which
he believed to be superior to the one he
had been using to travel around Knuts-
ford. Rolls, who owned a car sales business
in London, had set the world land speed
record of 93 mph in 1903. At their Midland
meeting Rolls hailed Royce as 'the man I
have been looking for for years', and
agreed to become sole distributor of
Royce's cars. The new Rolls-Royce company was formed in 1906, the year in
which Rolls won the Isle of Man TT race,
reaching a speed of 70 mph. Their first
works were at Cooke Street, Hulme
(p. 131), which they soon outgrew, moving
to Derby in 1908. Two years later Rolls
became the first British air accident victim
when his plane crashed during a display in
Bournemouth.

opening. Architect John Henry Woodhouse
gave it a reinforced concrete frame, one of
the city's first, and created one of the most
elaborately designed buildings in Manchester, with no two rooms of the same
dimensions. There was a billiard room,
smoking room, dining room and photo-
graphic dark room, and on the top floor a
1,200-sq.-ft swimming pool and running
track. As with New York's YMCA, the
main bulk of the building could be turned
into a hall large enough to hold 1,000
people.

In February 1936, during his only trip to
Manchester, George Orwell, then a struggling writer researching what became *The
Road to Wigan Pier*, his renowned polemic
on middle-class attitudes to the labour
movement, stopped off at St George's
House, the local headquarters of the Youth
Hostel Association. Orwell wanted to cash a
cheque, as he had only 3d in his pocket, but
was turned down. He then went to Bootle

Street police station and asked the officer in
charge to find him a solicitor who would
vouch for him. The policeman refused and
so Orwell found himself penniless in a
strange city. 'Frightfully cold. Streets
encrusted with mounds of dreadful black
stuff which was really snow frozen hard and
blackened by smoke,' he recalled in his
diary. At a pawnbroker's on Chester Street
near the modern-day Macintosh Village the
owner refused to take his raincoat but gave
him 1s 11d for his scarf, which at least
allowed the great writer to spend the night
in a doss house.

Royale's/Theatre Royale, between Museum
Street and Southmill Street
A nightclub now occupies what was the
third home of Manchester's oldest theatre,
the Theatre Royale, designed by Irwin and
Chester in an emphatic classical style, with a
huge pediment and two immense fluted
Corinthian pillars framing a Carrara marble
statue of Shakespeare leaning on one elbow.

In 1847, two years after the theatre
opened, Charles Dickens appeared here as
Captain Bobadil in Ben Jonson's *Everyman
in His Humour*. Twelve years later the
theatre's owner, John Knowles, who had
driven the 'Peveril of the Peak' coach
between Manchester and London, invited
Henry Irving, then in his twenties, to join
his company as leading actor and stage manager. Irving found to his amazement that
the Manchester audience and critics were
'more discriminating and consequently
more severe' than those he had previously
encountered. Over the next five years he
received great acclaim in many of Shakespeare's leading male roles including Lear,
Brutus, Shylock and Iago. When Irving
made his farewell appearance the audience
rose as one and sang 'God Be With You Till
We Meet Again'.

The theatre was converted into a cinema
in 1927 and later became a bingo hall. Plans
to demolish it in 1960 and build an office
block, as had befallen the Gaiety opposite,
were thwarted, and after closing in the 1970s
it soon reopened as a nightclub, Royale's.

Free Trade

> Other great halls in England are called after a royal patron, or some figure of traditional religion. Only the Free Trade Hall is dedicated to a proposition –
> A. J. P. Taylor, 1957

Free trade, the economic doctrine that dominated the first half of the nineteenth century and eventually split the Tory Party, orginated in London in 1820 but was taken up vehemently in Manchester in the 1830s. Led by Richard Cobden, a calico manufacturer, and John Bright, a Rochdale-born cotton merchant, the newly enriched Manchester merchants began to challenge the political power of the ruling landed aristocracy who opposed free trade.

Cobden and Bright, who embodied the so-called 'Manchester School', believed that free trade between nations would not only increase domestic wealth but generate international understanding. But they felt that their financial dealings were being hampered by Parliament's protection of farmers and landowners through the Corn Laws which set an artificially high price for imported corn. They also objected to paying high import duty on raw cotton, the ingredient most vital to their wealth.

During the 1840s the pro-free trade/anti-Corn Laws movements gathered momentum as Cobden and Bright, by now MPs, kept the pressure on Robert Peel, the Conservative prime minister, whose wealth was inherited – it came from the family textile mills – whereas theirs was a result of their own endeavours. Although Peel was sympathetic to free trade, he had been elected on a platform of maintaining the Corn Laws. However, when the 1845 Irish Potato Famine forced 3 million Irish to rely on cheap imported corn, which was illegal under the Corn Laws, Peel repealed the Act.

On 15 May 1846 an alliance of Conservatives, Whigs and independent free trade-supporting MPs voted to change the Corn Laws, a decision which split the Conservative Party and forced Peel to resign. The occasion was marked with a banquet in the Free Trade Hall attended by some 3,000 guests who at midnight were treated to a rousing rendition of the song 'There's A Good Time Coming, Boys'. Manchester had led the way, as John Bright, the leading free trader, explained to the audience when speaking here in 1851: 'We are called the Manchester Party and our policy is the Manchester policy, and this building I suppose is the school room of the Manchester School.'

► Richard Cobden's Mosley Street office, p. 15.

Free Trade Hall (Radisson Edwardian Hotel), west of Southmill Street

> A gesture grand our city made/By putting up a Hall to Trade/But saddest fate to think upon/The hall remains though trade has gone – *Manchester City News*, 1930

Manchester's greatest building – concert hall, public-speaking place, home to the Hallé Orchestra, and now a hotel – was built by the city's merchants to honour their campaign for free trade and stands on the site where eleven people were killed and hundreds injured during the 1819 Peterloo Massacre.

The Free Trade Hall's origins were humble. The first hall, a simple building with no architectural pretensions known as the Pavilion, was erected in eleven days in January 1840. The city's wealthy merchants, such as Richard Cobden, now had a venue to host meetings and run their campaign for the abolition of the Corn Laws and the introduction of commerce unconstrained by government policy – free trade. The hall was underused, however, and was demolished two years later when the Free Trade movement, then based in Manchester, decided that a more suitable permanent building was needed.

Its 1843 replacement, the first building to be known as the Free Trade Hall, was

Architecture of the Free Trade Hall

The Free Trade Hall is Manchester's grandest *palazzo* building. Its façade is based on the Gran Guardia Vecchia at Verona, even though it is unlikely that the architect, Edward Walters, ever visited that part of Italy. An impressive ground-floor arcade is supported by sturdy piers whose spandrels contain the shields of the Lancastrian towns associated with the Anti-Corn Law movement. The dominant first floor, the *piano nobile* of Renaissance architecture, contains pedimented windows framed by coupled Ionic columns, above which carved figures represent Arts, Commerce, Manufacture, Agriculture and Free Trade, with out-stretched arms inviting the nations of the world to embrace British commerce. Those of the four continents then known (Europe, Asia, Africa and America) can be found in the tympana of the arches.

The interior of Walters's building featured a continuous gallery that stood only nine feet above the ceiling of the stalls, thereby creating an intimate atmosphere. It was destroyed when a bomb which fell on the building in December 1940 left only the Peter Street façade and South Street side intact. The hall was restored to the designs of Leonard Howitt from the City Architect's Department (there being insufficient funds to hire a prestigious 'name' architect), and he chose an austere, stripped-down Art Deco look, hurriedly executed so that the building's opening would coincide with the 1951 Festival of Britain. Howitt's work was removed at the end of the twentieth century for the conversion of the building into a hotel, but the façade remains.

hastily built and uninspiring. 'Dirty cold and comfortless', the *Manchester Guardian* described it, while Tory opponents of free trade decried it as 'Cobden's Cemetery'. Nevertheless it was regularly used. Charles Dickens chaired an evening for the local Athenaeum cultural society here on 5 October 1843, after being elected president of the Athenaeum Grand Soirées.

To celebrate the abolition of the Corn Laws in 1846 the free traders decided to build a new, grander hall. An architectural competition was set up and won by Edward Walters, responsible for the lavishly decorated cotton warehouses on Charlotte Street in what is now Chinatown. His hall, designed as a Lombardian *palazzo*, opened in 1856, and soon became a truly public hall. The one-time headquarters of free trade was now not just the home of free speech but the setting for political debates, society AGMs, public meetings, literary readings and dramatic performances. Dickens appeared again, this time in the Wilkie Collins play *The Frozen Deep*, in August 1857, and entertainment on other nights

was provided by ventriloquists, comedians and circus acts such as Charles Blondin, the tightrope walker. But above all the hall was home to the Hallé Orchestra, which first played here on 16 December 1856 and continued to use the building until the 1990s (see box on pp. 31–3).

Of the many political rallies held at the Free Trade Hall the most celebrated took place on New Year's Eve 1862, when local cotton workers and manufacturers assembled to show support for the northern states of the USA during the American Civil War, even though Manchester was suffering economic hardship because no raw cotton was being exported from the South. It was an action that Abraham Lincoln described as 'an instance of sublime Christian heroism which has not been surpassed in any age or in any country'.

On 13 October 1905 the hall was the setting for a Liberal Party pre-general election rally that became one of the most significant events of the suffragette movement. The campaign's leaders Christabel Pankhurst and Annie Kenney were incensed that the

The Hallé Orchestra at the Free Trade Hall

The Hallé takes its name not from its city of origin, like most orchestras, but from its founder. It was the brainchild of the German-born musician Charles Hallé, a friend of Chopin, who fled Paris during the 1848 revolution and came to Manchester to take charge at the Gentlemen's Concert Hall on Lower Mosley Street (p. 63). In 1857 Hallé was invited to form an orchestra to play a series of concerts during Manchester's Great Art Treasures Exhibition. When the exhibition closed, it looked as if the orchestra would disband too. But Hallé decided to maintain it at his own expense as the Hallé Orchestra – the first professional symphony orchestra in Britain.

The Hallé's first concert took place at the Free Trade Hall in January 1858. Attendance was poor but Hallé was determined to make the orchestra a success. He wanted to show the world that Manchester Man was more than just a vulgar, self-made capitalist, as depicted by Charles Dickens in *Hard Times*'s Josiah Bounderby, but had an appreciation of beauty and aesthetics as well.

The orchestra and its leader prospered. So formidable was Hallé's reputation by the time of his death in 1895 that the Hallé Orchestra Concerts Society managed to secure the services of the formidable Hans Richter, then the most fêted conductor in the world, to take over the orchestra. Richter, however, could not disentangle himself from his contractual obligations in Vienna for four years and, when he first arrived, he was greeted with discontent about an English orchestra being conducted by a non-Englishman, and complaints that Germans were dominating music.

Although Richter showed little interest in the new music of Stravinsky or Debussy, he did approve of Elgar, and one of the highlights of his regime was the première of Elgar's first symphony here on 3 December 1908, conducted by the composer himself. In the audience was the nineteen-year-old Neville Cardus, who later became Manchester's foremost music critic. Looking back on the première, Cardus explained how 'those of us who were students were excited to hear at last an English composer addressing us in a spacious way, speaking a language which was European and not provincial'. It was around this time that it became *de rigueur* to wear evening dress at the Hallé (it remains so for the musicians), a state of affairs that gave rise to feelings of superiority in some concertgoers over those unable or unwilling to attend. Cardus later recalled how Hallé concerts were the 'prerogative and privilege of the few . . . the upper-middle classes of Bowdon, Eccles

Liberal government had recently 'talked out' a parliamentary debate on women's suffrage and decided that the rally would be ideal for launching their new, more militant tactics. As Winston Churchill (then a Liberal) rose to speak, Annie Kenney shouted: 'Will a Liberal government give women the vote?' She was ignored. A few minutes later Christabel Pankhurst jumped up on her chair and repeated the question. The Chief Constable of Manchester asked the women to put the request in writing. Annie Kenney did so, but a few moments later she and Pankhurst saw Sir Edward Grey read the note in an amused manner. This annoyed the women so much they began to unfurl the suffragettes' banner, whereupon stewards and plain-clothes police ejected them from the hall as they shouted: 'Answer the question!' Intent on getting herself arrested to win more publicity for her campaign, Pankhurst spat in the face of two policemen in the lobby and struck an inspector in the mouth. The two women were charged with disorderly behaviour, which led to Pankhurst admitting: 'We got what we wanted.

and Victoria Park. "Carriages at 9.30," was an announcement in the programme.'

After Richter was forced out in 1911, the Hallé ambitiously approached Richard Strauss to take over. When he turned them down, the management settled for Michael Balling, but he returned to Germany for good when the Great War broke out and anti-German feeling in Manchester was running high. Balling's departure, however, proved a blessing in disguise, for Thomas Beecham, who later founded the London Philharmonic Orchestra and the Royal Philharmonic Orchestra, became the Hallé's musical adviser. He ushered in a new golden era for the orchestra under the dynamic Hamilton Harty, conductor from 1920–33, who gave the first English performances of such major symphonies as Mahler's ninth and Shostakovich's first. Harty also broadened the concerts' appeal by encouraging working people to attend, even if they could only afford to stand at the back on the heating grid, as the folk singer Ewan MacColl recalled in his autobiography.

During Harty's tenure the expected duration of each piece was printed in the programme, except that no one was sure if the stated time was Richter's or Hallé's. Harty slowed many of the pieces down until Neville Cardus threatened to bring in an alarm clock and set it for what he perceived to be the acceptable length of time. Meanwhile, the philosopher Samuel Alexander

would sit in the front row and read the *Manchester Guardian* if he didn't understand the music.

After Harty's departure the orchestra's fortunes waned and the baton was taken by a number of guest conductors. At the outbreak of the Second World War the government requisitioned the Free Trade Hall, which was almost destroyed by a bomb, and the orchestra lost many of its personnel. Yet it was when the Hallé was at its lowest ebb that it received its greatest boost: the appointment of John Barbirolli, chief conductor of the New York Philharmonic, as musical director.

When Barbirolli joined the orchestra in 1943 it had only twenty-six musicians and no home. Yet the strictures of war also produced more demand for simple pleasures such as concerts. Barbirolli's enthusiasm fired the musicians and the Hallé performed admirably in a variety of settings, including Belle Vue's King's Hall and the Paramount cinema on Oxford Road (now the Odeon). Barbirolli radically altered the repertoire, removing what he called 'the "piano racket" [which] decreed that no orchestral concert was possible without a piano soloist playing one of three concertos – Grieg's, Rachmaninov's second or Tchaikovsky's first'. He also introduced new themed nights and arranged for the Hallé to tour abroad as ambassadors for Manchester.

Yes, I wanted to assault a policeman.' They were jailed at Strangeways.

The hall continued to be the setting for political rallies throughout the first half of the twentieth century. On 9 May 1931 the Communist Party called a 'People's Congress' to campaign against attempts 'to impoverish and degrade the working class'. Three years later, on 25 November 1934, a public meeting arranged by the British Union of Fascists under the banner 'Fascism Explained! Hear how fascism will save your

Country and your job' ended in chaos when a member of the audience interrupted the fascist leader, Oswald Mosley, and was attacked by a steward. Fighting broke out and stewards used rubber truncheons to restore order.

A German bomb destroyed the interior on 22 December 1940, and it wasn't until 1951 that the rebuilt hall, the work of the city architect Leonard Howitt, opened. That the new building had been completed in a rush, and with insufficient thought given to

The Free Trade Hall reopened in 1951 after the bomb damage was repaired. Over the next two decades, under Barbirolli's stewardship, the Hallé enjoyed its most successful run; the recordings from that period, particularly those of the Sibelius symphony cycle, were greeted enthusiastically. Though Barbirolli gradually relinquished his contacts with the orchestra as the 60s drew to a close, when he died of a heart attack in 1970 it was obvious that his replacement would face an uphill struggle for recognition. James Loughran, who arrived from the Scottish Symphony Orchestra, performed creditably throughout the 1970s, as did his replacement, Stanislaw Skrowaczewski in the 1980s, but they lacked the dynamism of their illustrious predecessor. No such accusation could be made, however, of the flamboyant Japanese-American Kent Nagano, who arrived amid much publicity as the Hallé's saviour in 1991 and raised the orchestra's profile at a time when its finances were in disarray and its repertoire had become safe and predictable. It was he that smoothed the way for the orchestra's move to the Bridgewater Hall, where it now continues to prosper under Mark Elder.

▸ The Bridgewater Hall, p. 64.

its reconstruction, was evident in the unimpressive backstage area, the substandard bar and catering facilities, the poor acoustics and the absence of a box office to sell tickets, which wasn't incorporated until 1973.

After the 1960s fewer political meetings were held here. Instead there was a growing number of rock concerts, the most notable being those by Bob Dylan in 1966 and the Sex Pistols ten years later (p. 34). Long-running complaints about the sound quality, and rumours that a new purpose-built concert venue was being created for the Hallé Orchestra, continued into the 1980s when plans for the Bridgewater Hall were unveiled. Despite the absence of a large public hall in Manchester, the Free Trade Hall's owners, Manchester city council, decided to close the venue and sell it to developers for conversion into a hotel. To the council's embarrassment, objectors were dismissed by the councillor in charge of the city centre as 'middle-class tossers'. Consequently Manchester has ruined its greatest building to the dismay of the local population keen to preserve the integrity of something so central to the city's history.

Great Northern Square

Not so much a square in the traditional sense of the word as an open space at the junction of Peter Street and Deansgate, Great Northern Square is one more scheme – along with the revamping of Piccadilly Gardens, the relocation of the Shambles Square pubs and the cosmetic reworking of the Arndale Centre – that future generations of Mancunians will come to rue. To create Great Northern Square a number of popular buildings were destroyed, including part of the Great Northern Goods Warehouse (since refurbished into a Cineplex), the Gallery nightclub and the Toptapi Turkish eaterie that was take-away, casual café and smart restaurant in one. The open space, as predicted, has become a wind tunnel, surrounded by the predictable run of 'designer' bars and cafés which does little to enhance one of Manchester's major junctions.

Rock music at the Free Trade Hall

As the twentieth century proceeded non-classical music began to appear in the programme. In March 1956 a concert featuring the radical American black singer Paul Robeson was booked for the small Lesser Free Trade Hall at the top of the building. As the American government had refused to let Robeson out of the country, seizing his passport because of his Communist activities, the event took place without the presence of its star. The night was billed as 'Let Paul Robeson Sing' and featured only his recorded voice.

Two years later Muddy Waters, the leading Chicago blues performer of the time, brought with him to England a raucous electric band that played the Free Trade Hall to boos from members of the audience, who knew only his acoustic music and thought electrically amplified music vulgar. Most of them were unaware that Waters hadn't played folk blues since the 1940s.

The first of many rock gigs to take place at the Free Trade Hall was an appearance by Bob Dylan on 17 May 1966. Similar controversy greeted Dylan's decision to play an electric set. Although this time the audience *were* aware of Dylan's similar conversion from an acoustic to an electric sound, many fans felt that he had betrayed the purity of the folk idiom and his own political integrity by lining up with a rock band. Boos and slow handclaps rang out during the electric parts of the set, and the tension increased when an irritated fan shouted: 'Judas.' Dylan quickly retorted, 'I don't believe you. You're a liar,' and turning to his band urged them to play 'fucking loud', before launching into 'Like A Rolling Stone'. The events were captured on a bootleg album that was released under the erroneous title *Live At The Albert Hall*. The night's mythical status increased following the 2001 publication of C. P. Lee's book *Like The Night*. But more prosaic claims suggest that most of the boos were directed at the poor sound quality, which meant half the audience could hear only the keyboards and the other half only the singing, rather than at Dylan's conversion, and that most of the audience was broadly supportive of the singer's new direction.

When the Who played here in 1970 the hall's management wrote in the engagements book: 'Dirtiest group to have used the hall. NOT AGAIN.' Three years later Genesis, with Peter Gabriel fronting, part-recorded their 1973 *Genesis Live* album, one of rock's few aesthetically successful live LPs, here.

The most significant gigs to take place at the Free Trade Hall occurred in the summer of 1976. On 4 June that year two Bolton students, Howard Trafford and Pete McNeish, promoted the Sex Pistols' first northern appearance in the Lesser Free Trade Hall. The gig, billed in the local listings magazine with the warning: 'Eat your heart out on a plastic tray if you miss them,' failed to draw much of a crowd,

Piccadilly Gardens

Where London has Piccadilly Circus, Paris the Arc de Triomphe and Berlin the Brandenburg Gate, Manchester has at its centre the new Piccadilly Gardens – a shabby square of muddy grass and play fountains flanked by an awkward concrete wall, bus station, tram lines and ugly office block.

In pre-industrial times the land was covered by the daub holes from which people took their clay to build houses. The ponds became ornamental lakes in the late eighteenth century when Oswald Mosley, Lord of the Manor of Manchester, donated the land to the authorities for building an infirmary. After the Infirmary moved to south Manchester in 1908 it seemed the building might become either a reference library, a new Royal Exchange or an art gallery. Instead it was demolished in 1910 and the site landscaped.

and when Malcolm McLaren, the Sex Pistols' manager, went out into Peter Street looking to entice inside any likely looking punters he found the street swarming with police. Thoughts that the officers had turned up to preempt any violence that might accompany the Pistols were soon quashed by news that there had been an armed robbery nearby.

A month later, on Tuesday 20 July, Trafford and McNeish, by then renamed Howard Devoto and Pete Shelley, again put on the Pistols, supporting them as Buzzcocks, Manchester's first punk group. That night the Pistols premièred what became their first single, 'Anarchy In The UK', in front of an audience of about 100 people. Few gigs, especially ones so badly attended, have inspired the birth of so many new bands. Among those watching the Pistols on those two nights were Ian Curtis, Bernard Summer and Peter Hook, who formed what became Joy Division and, after Curtis's suicide, New Order; Mark E. Smith of the Fall, Manchester's longest-running band; Mick Hucknall, who set up a punk group with a rockabilly bent, Crispy Ambulance, before launching his career as a supper-club singer *par excellence* with Simply Red; and Morrissey, never one to rush things, who belatedly formed the Smiths, Manchester's most fêted rock group.

► Manchester music, p. 67.

The authorities now turned their attentions to the Infirmary's replacement. One idea was for a vast cathedral to be designed by R. H. Carpenter. The plan came to nothing. Then in 1917 the conductor Thomas Beecham announced, 'I will build in Manchester an opera house that shall be of size and importance not less than those of any other opera house in London or any continental towns with the exception of Paris and Petrograd.' Unfortunately

Beecham went bankrupt before he could see the project through. In the 1930s formal flower beds – Piccadilly Gardens – were laid out as a temporary measure. A bland and predictable choice, they were at least popular and provided Mancunians with a rare patch of attractive open space in the heart of the city. A glimpse of how they looked can be gained from L. S. Lowry's 1954 painting *Piccadilly Gardens*.

The gardens could have remained in this pleasant state for ever, but in the 1990s councillors began itching for change. However they were unable to come up with a scheme that might have added to Manchester's reputation. They uprooted the flower beds, filled in the sunken levels, and replaced them with a flat lawn, which squelches into mud during the long rainy season, and is dotted with fountains, an unfortunate choice in a city already overendowed with natural water. The opportunity to rid the area of the unnecessary bus station was not taken, its presence ensuring that the nearby shopping units have continued to attract mostly bottom-of-the-market outlets.

Although the Mosleys had donated the land on condition that it would always be kept for public use, the council sold the space on the Portland Street side of the gardens to a developer, the Argent Group, in the 1990s. Argent hired the architects Allies and Morrison's to build an office block, but the ungainly result has infuriated locals. Its unsuitability is only slightly tempered by the pointless concrete wall near the tram lines that looks like a chunk of masonry left behind by accident after the redevelopment was completed in 2002 but, surprisingly, turns out to be a piece of architecture designed by Tadao Ando in a style similar to that he had previously used in Beverly Hills and Tokyo.

Lowry and Lowry

L. S. Lowry, Manchester's best-known artist, sat in Piccadilly Gardens one cold day in 1957 musing over a letter he had received from a young girl in Heywood asking his advice about studying art. Enticed by her name – Carol Ann *Lowry* – he was contemplating replying when, looking up, he saw through the winter gloom a bus going to Heywood. This convinced him to pay the youngster a personal visit, rather than simply sending a letter, and he took the bus on the long journey to her house. Despite the age difference (he was seventy, she was thirteen), they struck up a friendship, social and professional, which was so strong that she became an art teacher and the sole beneficiary of his will.

north side (Piccadilly)
Manchester Infirmary

The eighteenth-century Infirmary was aimed at those who couldn't afford doctors' fees, but after the Peterloo Massacre of 1819 the scores of wounded demonstrators who came here for treatment were mostly dealt with unsympathetically. For instance, when Dr Ransome asked James Lees, a 25-year-old weaver from Delph whose head had been cut by a sabre, whether he had now had enough of meetings and Lees replied 'No,' the doctor ordered the wounded man to leave the hospital immediately. In 1908 the Infirmary moved to a greenfield site in Chorlton-on-Medlock, and the building was demolished soon after.

east side (Portland Street)
No. 1 Piccadilly Gardens

Given its most central and important of locations, the decision to build a new office block here at the beginning of the twenty-first century gave Manchester the chance to show the world its determination to introduce the best in design and architecture to the city centre. Unfortunately, Allies and Morrison's No. 1 Piccadilly Gardens looks more like a multi-storey car park than a prestigious landmark building on a major

strategic site. To add to the absurdity the bright red brick is merely a decoration, rather than a structural feature, for the 2003 block has a steel frame.

south side (Parker Street: Portland Street to Mosley Street)

Parker Street, which also acts as the south side of Piccadilly Gardens, was lined with warehouses until these were destroyed in the Manchester Blitz of 22–23 December 1940. The day after the destruction a van from the Ministry of Information toured the streets with the BBC's Godfrey Baseley, originator of *The Archers*, shouting out instructions to locals on what they should do next. A week after the bombing the huge basements of the burnt-out buildings were converted into water-storage tanks so that Manchester firemen would have a ready source of water should more bombs fall.

The Piccadilly side of the road is now occupied by a bus station, which exists solely as a result of the inability of Manchester and its surrounding towns to devise a county-wide bus network as in London, whereby buses connect suburbs, passing through rather than finishing at the city centre. Indeed such is the long-standing hostility between the cities of Manchester and Salford that none of the score of buses that ply the Wilmslow Road/University corridor take the logical route across the Irwell into Salford and all terminate at Piccadilly instead, clogging the streets here while those of Salford city centre remain eerily quiet.

The Chinatown side of Parker Street consists of Piccadilly Plaza, an archetypal 1960s shopping mall and office block complex. The three buildings that comprised the original plaza – Piccadilly Hotel, Sunley Tower and Bernard House – were designed as an esoteric architectural joke, a modernist take on the Albert Square/St Peter Square trio of Town Hall, Town Hall Extension and Central Library. It was unveiled in 1959 as one of Manchester's first property speculation schemes, built in the hope of attracting takers rather than for a specific client. The complex would be big, bold and brash, *the* symbol of a new post-war, post-industrial Manchester. In the fashion of the time the new buildings would be connected by a podium, with obscured entrances to the offices and a spiral entry ramp for cars into the hotel. All-weather pedestrian bridges, similar to those in Minneapolis, would link the site to similar buildings around what is now Chinatown.

Piccadilly Plaza opened in 1965. The Manchester establishment was ecstatic. 'This is a most exciting development,' claimed Manchester Corporation. 'A wonder of the new age,' waxed the *Evening Chronicle*. 'Glistening in glass and concrete, modern as a sputnik,' raved the *Daily Mail*. Of the three sections, the least appetizing was evidently the Piccadilly Hotel, with its cantilevered block overhanging Portland Street. The most attractive was Bernard House, topped with a playful jagged roof. In between was Sunley Tower, named after its developer, Bernard Sunley.

Once Mancunians had recovered from the shock of having architecture from the set of *Thunderbirds* dominating its centre, they realized that Piccadilly Plaza was not the trail-blazer of a new era but an aberration. Users soon found themselves frustrated by the obscured entrances, the complex's inaccessibility and the prospect of having to enter a building to use shops within rather than walking into them from the street as is usual. By 1967 only eleven of the forty units had been let. The quality of the companies who rented space was typified by a cheap-and-nasty fish and chips outlet and amusement arcades. One exception was Piccadilly Radio, one of the early independent stations, which was housed here in the 1970s and early 80s.

Renovation was carried out in the late 1990s, but this too was botched. Sunley Tower was rebranded City Tower, while Bernard House, the best of the three blocks, was demolished, thereby ruining the homogeneity of the complex and rendering the retention of the other two constructions farcical. Promises that the shopping units would be revamped to attract up-market clients have also proved to be overoptimistic, the only exception being Marks & Spencer.

▸ The Arndale Centre, p. 11.

Piccadilly Hotel

Readers of the *Evening Chronicle* in 1961 were assured that the proposed Piccadilly Hotel was to be 'the finest in Europe'. The project's architects assumed that by the late 1960s all guests would arrive by car, so one of the hotel's novelties was that people would be able to drive straight into the foyer, enclosed on one side by glass and on the other by 'invisible walls of warm air'. There was no street entrance for pedestrians. This led to the absurd sight of guests walking up the spiral concrete driveway that was the hotel's only entrance, clutching their luggage and moaning about the architects' rejection of Newton's laws of gravity.

Once it was completed, it was clear that the Piccadilly Hotel, with its shockingly bleak brutalist concrete, would not even be the best in Manchester. At lunch during the official opening on 16 March 1965 a twenty-foot length of ceiling broke loose during the fish course. The mess was cleared and the meal was resumed. Alas at the end of the next course the same thing happened again. A few years later several bar staff were dismissed for serving watered-down gin.

Infamous early guests, according to local legend, included the Kray twins, who journeyed to Manchester in the mid-1960s, were met at the train station by the police, and escorted to a top-level parley with local villains at the hotel. There they were told to leave town immediately and were duly escorted away by the same officers.

City Tower (Sunley Tower)

Piccadilly Plaza's promoters claimed that its new skyscraper, Sunley Tower, would look like Le Corbusier's United Nations building. In one respect it did, in that it was also a lofty slab, but as it was executed by Covell Matthews and Partners, rather than the renowned Swiss, it displayed none of the latter's ingenious finesse. The tower's twenty-four storeys show a blank concrete face to Piccadilly Gardens, but on the less seen Chinatown side the concrete façade is decorated with printed-circuitry motifs standing out in relief. During its construction in 1961 Sunley Tower was captured in cinematic glory, providing the backdrop to Julie Christie's stroll through the city in John Schlesinger's *Billy Liar*.

Portland Street

Portland Street's transformation from a dirt track on the edge of town in the early nineteenth century into the setting for some of Manchester's most flamboyant cotton showrooms mirrored the town's development. For instance, in 1820 Manchester had 126 warehouses, but by 1830 there were more than 1,000. As Howard Spring later noted in his 1934 novel *Shabby Tiger*, Portland Street had become the setting for Manchester's greatest trading houses and hotels, 'grim and strong as prisons'.

The grandest of these was the remarkable Cook and Watts building (now the Britannia Hotel), but there were also less ostentatious workplaces such as the Portland Street mill run by Henry Houldsworth, who in the 1840s bought the British patent rights for machine-embroidered fabrics. Portland Street retained its impressive appearance until wartime bombing, which left sizeable gaps, later filled in with a collection of high-rise monstrosities which ignored the old building line that so enhanced the street. Remarkably, two tiny Georgian pubs – the Circus Tavern and Grey Horse, among the smallest in Britain – remain, near the junction with Princess Street.

south side: Piccadilly to Oxford Street
Queen's Hotel, No. 1
The Queen's Hotel, which stood at the corner of Piccadilly and Portland Street, was converted from an older property in 1845 and was the first hotel opened specifically for railway travellers. It became renowned for its turtle soup. It was here that a number of major Manchester events of the early

twentieth century took place. In November 1905 Manchester City held an auction of their entire playing staff, the backbone of the team that had won the 1904 FA Cup, after being forced into selling as punishment for making illegal payments. Manchester United pre-empted the sale by directly approaching the players they wanted. Defender Herbert Burgess, Alec 'Sandy' Turnbull and Jimmy Bannister moved across the city, and three years later United won their first League Championship.

A meeting crucial to the development of the Middle East took place in the Queen's on 9 January 1906. The Zionist leader Chaim Weizmann, then a research chemist at Manchester University, met the Tory party leader Arthur Balfour, who had just resigned as prime minister, to discuss the possibility of a Jewish homeland. Balfour could not understand why Weizmann and his fellow Zionists were so hostile to the idea of Jews being persuaded to settle in Uganda, east Africa. Weizmann convinced the politician otherwise. 'Mr Balfour, if you were offered Paris instead of London, would you take it?' he asked. When Balfour expressed amazement at the idea and responded, 'But London is our own!', Weizmann retorted, 'Jerusalem was our own when London was a marsh.' Balfour was taken aback and asked, 'Are there many Jews who think like you?', to which Weizmann replied, 'I believe I speak the mind of millions of Jews.' The meeting led to the Balfour Declaration which stated that 'His Majesty's Government looks with much favour on the establishment of a Jewish state in Palestine,' an announcement that eventually resulted in the founding of modern Israel in 1948, with Weizmann as the country's first president.

The Queen's was demolished in the early 1960s to make way for a flyover that was never built, and was replaced with Charles, White & Hood's unsightly steel-and-glass commercial block, itself recently demolished.

▶ Weizmann in Cheetham Hill, p. 160.

Portland Hotel

Three Edward Walters warehouses form the Portland Hotel, one of Manchester's oldest. The wing nearest Piccadilly is Brown's Warehouse, built 1851–2 in York stone. Strangely the *piano nobile* is on the second floor. Walters built the taller Kershaw, Leese and Sidebottom warehouse alongside Brown's in 1852. Completing the trio is the E. & J. Jackson warehouse of 1858.

Britannia Hotel

Manchester's greatest nineteenth-century textile warehouse was the 1858 Cook and Watts building, now the Britannia Hotel, inside which some 600 staff displayed a variety of finished goods that included linens, carpets, dresses, umbrellas, bags, satchels and corsets. As Cook and Watts wanted somewhere suitably flamboyant to show off their wares, they hired the architects Travis and Mangnall to create a Florentine palace, using a variety of different styles – Italian Renaissance, Elizabethan and French Renaissance – on each floor, and crowning each corner with a large tower and Gothic rose windows. Travis and Mangnall continued their lofty ambitions on to the roof, which features four stocky pavilions with wheel windows. Only at the rear, which the impressionable businessman, arriving at the Portland Street entrance by cab, wouldn't see, was adornment skipped, leaving just plain brick.

Owner James Watts was the archetypal Manchester man of yore: a self-made, free-trade supporting dissenter. His country seat, Abney Hall in Cheadle, was where Prince Albert stayed when he came north to open the 1857 Art Treasures Exhibition at Old Trafford. Three employees – Messrs Kendal, Milne and Faulkner – bought out the original Watts shop on Deansgate and turned it into what became Kendal's, for decades Manchester's most glamorous store (p. 9). The Watts Warehouse closed in 1972 and its future looked bleak. However, the authorities rejected consent to demolish it in 1977 and the building was sold to the Britannia

group two years later. Little of the original interior remains.

► Midland Hotel, p. 26.

Princess Street

A breathtaking sweep of Victorian export warehouses complete with exotic location-based names – Brazil House, Asia House et al – sweep down Princess Street from its junction with Portland Street towards the River Medlock. In the cotton industry's heyday these warehouses were owned mostly by Germans or Greeks and used for displaying goods in sumptuous surroundings. Astonishingly the Corporation contemplated demolishing most of them in the early 1970s to build a roundabout and new ring road, but desisted before it was too late. Many of the blocks have recently been converted into apartments.

west side: Mancunian Way to Albert Square

Factory Records HQ (1990s)/Paradise Factory, Nos. 112–116

Tony Wilson's Factory label, central to Manchester's status as a major late twentieth-century music city, bought the building for their new headquarters in the early 1990s. In-house designer Ben Kelly, who was responsible for creating the look of Factory's Haçienda nightclub, remodelled the block, inserting a zinc roof and installing a board-room table that hung from the ceiling until the Happy Mondays sat on it. As stylish as the design was the cost hastened the demise of Factory, and when the label went bankrupt in 1992 the directors 'celebrated' with an anarchic party that spoiled much of Kelly's work. At least Factory could take solace in the value of its back catalogue – New Order, James, A Certain Ratio et al – or so Wilson thought, only to be handed a letter signed by him in blood in 1979 stating that 'we don't own the music, the musicians own the music . . .' The Paradise Factory, a mostly gay nightclub, has used the building for much of the time since.

► Factory's Withington HQ, p. 176.

Asia House, No. 82

Built 1906–9 by the Refuge Assurance Company as an example of early property speculation, this impressive Edwardian warehouse, with its odd trapezoid shape, was first occupied by the Oxford Packing Company, and by 1910 was home to thirty-six shipping companies. While some of the public areas are elaborately designed and the ornate façade of sandstone, brick and marble is dotted with baroque features, the offices themselves are utilitarian. To the sides of the building there are gated private lanes. At the back flows the River Medlock.

Central House

By the Rochdale Canal stands Central House, designed by two Scottish architects, Corson and Aitken, in the Scottish baronial style, as evident from its large corner tourelles and steeply pitched slate roof.

east side: Cross Street to Mancunian Way

Athenaeum

A landmark in Manchester's architectural history is the Athenaeum, now part of the Manchester Art Gallery. It was the first major local nineteenth-century building that was neither classical nor Gothic. Instead Charles Barry chose the Italian Renaissance palace or *palazzo* style, using his own Travellers' Club in London's Pall Mall as the model. The design meant that the ground floor was to be used for storage while the main business – the cultivation of the arts – could be carried out on a low-lying first floor: the *piano nobile*. The format provided local architects with a ready-made model for the new warehouses springing up throughout Manchester, even if each successive *palazzo* was less stylish, less assured than the original.

The Athenaeum opened in 1839 for 'literary, political and scientific uses', established by 'a number of gentlemen who felt a desire to bring together in such a club the class of superior mercantile servants and young men'. Karl Marx later called it 'virtually the only home of the muses in Manchester', and its first members included some of the most important figures in Manchester society,

among them the progressive merchants Richard Cobden and Robert Owen. The Athenaeum soon came to be famous for its literary soirées, at the first of which Charles Dickens spoke on the conditions for juveniles in London prisons, stressing the need for educating the poor. The interior was destroyed in a fire in 1874, after which an incongruous mansard roof was added.

The City Art Gallery (p. 17) took over the building after the Second World War and for fifty years it was used for exhibitions and lectures. Despite the gallery's recent costly renovation project, linking the Athenaeum with the main wing, the front entrance on Princess Street is still unnecessarily closed, suggesting to passers-by that the building is redundant.

Mechanics' Institute, No. 103

The first meeting of the Trades Union Congress took place here from 2–6 June 1868, delegates presenting papers on political economy, the role of apprentices and picketing. The building, designed by J. E. Gregan in 1854, had opened as the new home of the Mechanics' Institute, a body founded in 1825 to foster understanding between the different classes, or what the co-founder, the banker Benjamin Heywood, called 'mutual confidence and regard between the working man and his employer'. The Mechanics' Institute would teach men the 'application of science to mechanical and manufacturing art'. Unfortunately, few mechanics turned up and those who did came mostly from the lower-middle class. No. 103 became a technical school in 1883, and was later a training college and school of commerce. In the 1990s it was briefly home to the National Museum of Labour History, whose exhibits are now based at the Pump House on Bridge Street (p. 89).

▶ Working Class Library, p. 188.

New Union, No. 111

Believed to be the second oldest gay pub in the country, the New Union opened as Dusty Miller's in 1823, catering for the navvies who dug the Rochdale Canal that runs alongside, and soon after became the

Union. Sometime around 1960 the pub began to welcome homosexuals openly, but in 1965 the licensee was imprisoned for 'outraging public decency'. When he was released, it became the New Union.
▸ The Village, p. 98.

St Peter's Square

St Peter's church, which gave the square its name, was demolished as long ago as 1907, following a huge drop in local population numbers. The territory the church covered has been preserved as a green space and is the setting for Manchester's cenotaph, designed by Edwin Lutyens in Portland stone in a style similar to his London model.

Since 1934 St Peter's Square has been dominated by the vast bulk of the Central Library. After it was finished the council made plans to open up St Peter's Square into Albert Square and create a new civic centre, only to find that the Friends Provident company had already bought the site at the corner of Mosley and Dickinson streets. A vote on placing a compulsory purchase order failed by one. Instead a Town Hall extension was built on the corner of Lloyd and West Mosley streets. The square has been spoiled by the haphazard nature of its architecture and the ugly shapes of the Metrolink station.

Central Library

At first sight Manchester's main municipal library, with its Pantheon-like dome and neoclassical features, is an impressive sight, a suitably grand setting for so important an institution. But as a working library it disappoints, for the architect, E. Vincent Harris, was more concerned with obtaining the correct classical proportions than with providing a practical building.

On the ground floor, which should be the main floor, there is little space for books – its main staple – and just two rooms: the commercial library and the strangely named General Readers section, little more than a second-rate suburban branch incongruously located within the city's main library.

The bulk of the open collection is in the first-floor reading room, reached by two impressive staircases and a tortuously slow and cramped lift, thereby making it practically inaccessible to children, anyone hampered by infirmity or those carrying a stack of volumes. The reading room also suffers from a notorious echo, which transforms the merest sound into a hurricane. It is, however, beautifully designed, encircled by twenty-eight Tuscan columns and centred with an Italianate well-head. Elsewhere in the building are the excellent Local History section (first floor), the Arts and Music Library (second floor) and the Literature and Language section (fourth floor); in the basement is the Library Theatre.

Since the 1980s the council has run down the service, closing the Jewish Library, removing vast numbers of esoteric books from the main reading room and allowing students to treat the place as a social club.
▸ Chetham's Library, p. 95.

Whitworth Street

Joseph Whitworth was a pioneering mechanical engineer whose nineteenth-century machines were among the first to be capable of measuring to within one ten-thousandth of an inch. He also invented the mechanical street sweeper, vital in cleaning Manchester's grimy thoroughfares. The south side of Whitworth Street rivals Princess Street as the setting for an impressive succession of Edwardian textile warehouses. Those east of Princess Street – Whitworth House, Bombay House – are mostly functional but of period interest; those further west, such as India House, magnificent and unforgettable in their ambition.

north side: Oxford Street to Aytoun Street
Bridgewater House/News on Sunday
(1987), Nos. 58–60
Built in granite and faience in 1912–14 for Lloyd's Packing Warehouse Ltd, its architect was Harry S. Fairhurst, whose ingenious designs revolutionized commercial architecture in Manchester in the boom period that followed the opening of the Ship Canal.

In 1987 Bridgewater House was home to
the disastrous left-wing paper *News on
Sunday*. A brave attempt to capitalize on the
gap in the market for a nationwide socialist
newspaper, it was hampered by intent that
was greater than initiative. Basing a
national, rather than a regional, newspaper
outside London meant it was too distant
from Whitehall, from well-informed rival
journalists who could share stories, from
advertising agencies and from a ready pool
of experienced potential employees. More
worryingly, most senior staff had never
previously written for a national title, the
head of personnel had never worked in that
department, and the head of finance had
never drawn up accounts for a company
before.

In the week leading to the launch, staff
engaged in an odd way of preparing for
publication by going on a 'deafness aware-
ness course' that consisted of walking
around Manchester wearing earplugs. By
then the original editor, John Pilger, the
campaigning investigative reporter, had
quit, angered at the incompetence around
him, and was contributing pieces to rival
titles criticizing a paper that no one had yet
seen.

Just before the newspaper's first appearance the potential readership was stunned
into disbelief by the crassness of the launch
slogan: 'No Tits But Lots of Balls'. Unsurprisingly the first editions were damp
squibs. Readers were unfazed by stories of
strikes in Mexico and Brazilians selling
kidneys for cash, and were soon shunning
a paper written in a sloppy, contrived,
non-intellectual style devoid of all the
usual national newspaper production
qualities.

The paper was soon lurching from one
financial crisis to another. Huge sums of
money were lost, including the pension
contributions of several Labour-run councils. When millionaire businessman Owen
Oyston offered to take over the paper and
provide a cash injection, the shareholders
couldn't agree on his proposals and he quit,

leaving no alternative benefactor, and the
newspaper folded.

▶ *Manchester Evening News*, p. 89.

Twisted Wheel (1965–71)

Manchester's best-known mod era nightclub moved to Whitworth Street from
Brazenose Street in 1965. The music, provided by in-house DJ Roger Eagle, who later
founded Eric's punk club in Liverpool, was
strictly R&B, but when this sound went
mainstream in the British charts club-goers
demanded ever more obscure numbers.
They began championing little-known US
records under the catch-all title 'Northern
Soul', the term invented by music journalist
Dave Godin. Having visited the club Godin
concluded that Northern soul fans preferred
the fast sounds from northern US cities
such as Chicago and Detroit, while their
London counterparts preferred their black
music from the Deep South studios of
Memphis and Muscle Shoals.

The club promoted some of Britain's first
all-nighters, attracting hundreds of revellers
from as far away as Scotland and the Midlands. It also put on acts such as Ike and
Tina Turner, who were amazed at the
ecstatic reception they got from the white
crowd when in America their set was
already considered outdated by the black
community.

As the Twisted Wheel was alcohol-free,
members compensated by bringing in with
them copious amounts of drugs, even
though possession of even a handful of
amphetamines could result in a six-month
sentence. The police, meanwhile, were only
too keen on launching raids at which
officers would line up clubbers in the street
outside, plant a bag of proscribed pills at the
feet of a random punter, and then watch as
the bag was kicked along till it landed by an
unsuspecting dupe, who would then be
arrested for possession. The Twisted Wheel
closed in 1971 and the building became
Placemate 7. It is now Legends.

▶ The Hacienda, p. 61.

south side: Fairfield Street to Oxford Street
Lancaster House

One of Harry S. Fairhurst's most flamboyant creations, Lancaster House is an immense terracotta block, impressive and exuberant, its lofty corner 'wedding-cake' tower and cupola dominating the corner of Princess and Whitworth streets. It was built as a packing warehouse for Lloyd's in 1907–10 but no longer serves the textile trade. Sadly the base has been spoiled by conversion into a so-called 'Irish' pub.

Cambrian Buildings

Surprisingly not a Fairhurst creation, but the work of the much lesser known J. D. Harker, and completed in 1908. Cambrian Buildings was later joined on to Lancaster House and connected with adjacent India House by means of a huge Art Nouveau iron gate with pendant lamp.

India House, Nos. 73–75

Built by Harry S. Fairhurst from 1905–9 for Lloyd's Packing Warehouse company, to a design brief urging him to provide as much light as possible for clients who would be carefully examining cotton goods. There also had to be room for loading and unloading, and suitable storage area. Fairhurst clad the building in Aberdeen Correnie granite at the base, with red Accrington brick and glazed sienna tiles at higher levels. In the basement was machinery that allowed as many as 2,500 pieces of cloth to be folded, stamped and packed, ready for the dockside, in three hours. A magnificent Impressionist view of the building can be seen in Adolphe Valette's 1912 painting *India House*, owned by the Manchester Art Gallery.

City Centre: Districts

Away from main roads such as Deansgate and Market Street the character of the city centre changes, shaped by the smaller areas which retain their traditional names, or in some cases have earned popular new ones, such as Spinningfields and The Village.

CAMPFIELD

A thin sliver of land between Quay Street and Liverpool Road, adjacent to Castlefield, Campfield is named after the Roman camp that was situated here early in the first millennium. During medieval times the area was covered with open fields beside the small village of Manchester where local inhabitants gathered to voice their grievances.

In 1831 around 100,000 people came to Campfield to show their support for parliamentary reform. The main speaker was the Manchester banker Benjamin Heywood, who, according to an anonymous bystander, spoke 'in a low tone of voice, with some hesitation and was badly heard', which may explain why, despite being elected that May as MP for Lancaster, he soon quit Parliament, his voice too weak for politics. The meeting elapsed peacefully unlike the demonstration in 1819 that had resulted in the infamous Peterloo Massacre.

Campfield was covered with streets in the mid-nineteenth century and has remained mostly intact since – a rare example, for Manchester, of a late-Georgian estate. At the west end of Campfield lies Granada TV and with it the *Coronation Street* studio set, its cobbles and scruffy demeanour contrasting sharply with the Georgian elegance of nearby Byrom Street and St John Street.

Lower Byrom Street
west side
Museum of Science and Industry (main building)
Just off Liverpool Road in an 1880-built warehouse lies the main building of the sprawling Museum of Science and Industry

housed in five buildings on a seven-acre site. Inside this block is a permanent exhibition on Manchester's once powerful cotton industry, the hands-on Xperiment! Gallery, and an informative section on the city's vital role in scientific discovery, with rooms devoted to John Dalton, originator of atomic theory, and Ernest Rutherford, who first split the atom, among others.

► Museum of Science and Industry, Liverpool Road, p. 52.

east side

ℌall of Science

Crowds of more than 3,000 people used to attend the lectures on politics and social issues at the ℌall of Science in the middle decades of the nineteenth century. Among the many Chartists, socialists and radicals, a regular visitor was the German business-man and pioneer of Communism Friedrich Engels, who worked with Karl Marx. Engels couldn't praise the programme of events organized at the hall highly enough. 'At first one cannot get over one's surprise on hearing in the Hall of Science the most ordinary workers speaking with a clear understanding on political, religious and social affairs,' he once wrote. The Museum of Science and Industry's Air and Space Gallery now occupies much of the site.

► Mechanics Institute (birthplace of the TUC), p. 40.

Quay Street

The quay was created in 1734 by Edward Byrom at the point where the road meets the River Irwell. The river had been made navigable in the 1720s to allow access to the sea at Liverpool via the River Mersey.

north side: Water Street to Deansgate

Opera House

An impressive building capable of holding 3,000 and a rare survivor among city-centre theatres, the Opera House now stages more mainstream musicals than high culture. It opened on Boxing Day 1912 as the New Theatre, but closed when its owners went bust in March 1914. It reopened eighteen months later in

October 1915 as the New Queen's Theatre, where Thomas Beecham staged operas on a lavish scale never before seen in Manchester. Finally, in 1920, the venue became the Opera House. Here Noël Coward's *Operette* was premièred, and Emlyn Williams and Sybil Thorndike starred in *The Corn Is Green*.

The Opera House thrived in the 1950s, showing the latest American musicals such as *Oklahoma* and *South Pacific* (with a then unknown Sean Connery), but audience figures declined in the 1960s, and, when the building closed in 1979, its future looked

---

A Taste of Honey

Watching the Terence Rattigan play *Variations on a Theme* at the Opera House in the 1950s, the teenage Shelagh Delaney thought it so bland and trivial that she was convinced she could do better. Delaney took a fortnight off work to adapt for the stage her novel *A Taste of Honey*, which tells the story of a Salford girl made pregnant, shockingly for the time, by her black lover, and which the film director Lindsay Anderson later described as a 'work of complete, exhilarating original-ity'. In 1958 Joan Littlewood took *A Taste of Honey* to London where it had a long West End run and won several awards. Delaney also wrote the screenplay for the film, partly shot in Salford, which stands as one of the great works of British cinema.

The play and film have lived on musi-cally in the lyrics of a host of Smiths and Morrissey songs. Episodes and dialogue from the film appear in songs such as 'What Difference Does It Make?' ('I'll prob-ably never see you again'), 'Asleep' ('Sing me to sleep') and 'Reel Around The Fountain' ('You're the bee's knees, but so am I', and 'I dreamt about you last night, and I fell out of bed twice'). The Smiths' plaintive 'This Night Has Opened My Eyes' is an even more deliberate tribute.

► Morrissey meets Marr, p. 186.

bleak. After a brief stint as a bingo hall an Arts Council campaign saw the theatre reopen in 1984 for stage shows. Like the Palace Theatre it now puts on mostly musicals.

Sunlight House

With touches of Art Deco and between-the-wars modernism, Sunlight House, an office block of 1932, is one of Manchester's most striking buildings. It was named after its creator, the developer, entrepreneur and architect Joe Sunlight who was born in Russia as Josif Schimschlavitch and took his new 'illuminative' title from the model village of Port Sunlight in Cheshire. After visiting Chicago in search of architectural inspiration, Sunlight conceived the Manchester building as a full-scale skyscraper – forty storeys in all – but was foiled by the Ministry of Town and Country Planning which refused to let him have more than fourteen floors. Nevertheless Sunlight House was the first skyscraper to be built in the north of England, and the tallest building in the city until the CIS Tower went up in 1962.

south side: Deansgate to Water Street

Cobden House Chambers, No. 19

One of the largest surviving Georgian houses in Manchester, 19 Quay Street was the birthplace of the college that became Manchester University. The squat brick property was built in 1775 for the Byroms, one of eighteenth-century Manchester's most important families, and was home from 1836–43 to the leading political campaigner Richard Cobden. It was here that Cobden staged a number of meetings of his successful pressure group, the Anti-Corn Law League (p. 14).

In the early 1850s Cobden leased the building to the trustees of the calico-buyer John Owens, who wanted to set up a college that would provide a classical education similar to that of the two ancient universities: Oxford and Cambridge. Owen's College opened in 1851, but was not an immediate success and by 1856 the number of students

attending was alarmingly low. One day the professor of chemistry, standing in the doorway, was asked, 'Maister, is this th' neet asylum?' and replied, 'Not yet, my man, but if you come in six months' time I fear it will be.' The college did prosper, however. Its lecturers included some of the most gifted scientists of the time, such as Edward Frankland, who pioneered the idea of the valency system of chemical bonding, and Henry Roscoe, who made advances in photochemistry and devised a way of preparing vanadium in a pure metallic state. Another remarkable figure was the tutor and lecturer William Stanley Jevons, whose 1865 tract *Coal Question* drew attention to the possible exhaustion of energy supplies. The following year Jevons was appointed professor of logic and philosophy at Owens, and in 1870 he unveiled before the Royal Society his 'logical piano' – a primitive computer which performed calculations using pulleys, switches and piano-like keys.

Once the college began setting exams (run by the University of London), student numbers soared, and it became apparent that the Quay Street building was too small. A new site in Chorlton-on-Medlock was found and Alfred Waterhouse, architect of Manchester Town Hall, was hired to build more ambitious premises for what in 1880 became Manchester University. No. 19 Quay Street then became the Manchester County Court and remained so until 1990. The building is now home to solicitors who have maintained the eighteenth-century features, including the elegant staircase and its metal banister, without which the staircase would collapse.

► Manchester University, p. 120.

Granada Television, Quay Street at Atherton Street

Coronation Street, Brideshead Revisited and *World In Action* made Granada Television Britain's most enterprising independent television company in the early years of independent broadcasting. It was founded in 1956 by cinema-chain owner and producer Sidney Bernstein who chose the name

'Granada' out of love for the Spanish city of that name. Ironically, he was initially opposed to the idea of commercial television, fearing that it carried 'such a great propaganda power that it could not be entrusted to any bodies other than a public corporation'.

Bernstein located the company in Manchester after studying weather charts, believing that in the rainy city people were more likely to stay in, and his choice was crucial to the post-war regeneration of the area, even if at first it horrified many of the new staff. To silence sceptics he commissioned Ralph Tubbs, who had worked on the Festival of Britain, to design a stylish HQ. The channel began broadcasting on 3 May 1956 with the announcement: 'From the North, this is Granada.' Early programmes included *A Visit to the Walker Art Gallery*, the documentary *Youth Is Asking* and the unusual sight of Manchester City winning the FA Cup, captured in a detailed documentary about the team's return from Wembley.

Within four years Granada had premièred what would become its most successful show, *Coronation Street*, which its creator, Tony Warren, initially wanted to call *Florizel Street* until he was dissuaded by criticism that the name sounded like that of a detergent. *Coronation Street* was first screened on 9 December 1960. It began as an entertaining reflection of working-class, inner-city Manchester life, set in a small community inspired by Ordsall's Archie Street, named Weatherfield – a pun on Manchester's eternally bad weather and Campfield, the area in which the studio is located. At first the programme was too stagey, too obvious a homage to Northern melodrama, and viewers were shocked to hear characters speaking with northern accents rather than in RADA-trained neutral enunciation. But by the 1970s the storylines had improved considerably and *Coronation Street* had become a nationally networked social institution. Although it was wrapped in sentimentality, nostalgia and moral con-

servatism, it was also trenchant, witty and engaging, played by a powerful cast of actors such as Pat Phoenix (Elsie Tanner) and Bernard Youens (Stan Ogden), who had mostly been raised in local rep theatres and the now defunct Mancunian Film Studio.

Competition from the BBC in the form of *EastEnders* led Granada to open the set to the public in 1988. People could walk along the cobbled street itself (never a real street, but part of the studio) and drink in the Rovers' Return pub, as well as tour the recreations of Downing Street (used in *First Among Equals*) and Baker Street (from the Jeremy Brett version of Sherlock Holmes). The Granada Studio Tour was however spoiled by the owners' decision to incorporate the attractions into an American-style theme park, and it was no surprise when the venture closed in 1999.

Since Bernstein's death in 1993 the company has declined, no longer able to produce shows of the calibre of *World In Action*, its fêted investigative programme (1963–98), the early 1980s adaptation of Evelyn Waugh's *Brideshead Revisited* or *University Challenge*.

► Mancunian Film Studio, p. 170.

CASTLEFIELD

The Roman birthplace of Manchester and setting for its first modern-style industry is now a major tourist site, thanks to the sprawling Museum of Science and Industry, which incorporates the world's first railway station. It is also a popular night-time spot with its bars set near the canal basin.

The Romans built four successive forts in Castlefield, south of modern-day Liverpool Road, after Agricola, general and governor, arrived in Britain in AD 77. On vanquishing the hill tribes in the West, Agricola subdued the 'blue-shielded Brigantes' of the North. He set up camp in York and set the Brigantes to work building small forts such as the one at Manchester, where his troops camped by a sharp sandstone crag alongside a loop of the river Medlock, near its confluence with the Irwell. The contours of the terrain led the Romans to give it the name 'Mamucium' – place of the breast-shaped hill – from which the word Manchester later derived.

The first fort, built *c.* AD 80, was simply a ditch and mound with timber defences on top, but over the next three centuries it was developed into a major fortification. Around the fort a village or *vicus* grew, to supply the needs of the soldiers. There were drinking dens and brothels, and an active smithing industry, as the discovery of more than thirty small furnaces during archaeologist Barri Jones's 1972 dig showed.

After the Romans left the area around the year AD 410 the fort was abandoned, and Manchester grew on a separate site, further north by the cathedral. When the historian Camden visited the town in the sixteenth century he noted how much of the last fort remained, and that it was known popularly as the Castle-in-the-field, hence the name for the area – Castlefield. As the population of Manchester grew locals began plundering the site for building material. By the twentieth century almost no trace of the last fort remained.

Ironically, given the antiquity of this area, it was here that some of Manchester's first modern-style industry began in 1764 after the Duke of Bridgewater's Canal opened to bring coal to Manchester. The Rochdale Canal followed in 1805, and twenty-five years later it was in Castlefield that the world's first railway station – Liverpool Road – was opened.

By the mid-nineteenth century Castlefield was a canal and rail centre, and a hub of industry, with dyers and vitriol manufacturers working near those employed in the water-side warehouses. The area's industrial importance continued until the 1960s, but after the goods traffic left Liverpool Road station, and the warehouses by the canals closed, Castlefield lost its purpose and turned into a dead land of disused railway viaducts, rotting canals and derelict

sites. Revival in the 1980s came courtesy of entrepreneurs such as the bookmaker Jim Ramsbottom, who spotted the potential at what he called 'the wrong end of Deansgate'. There was also much input from Manchester city council and the now-defunct Greater Manchester Council, which developed one of the most successful urban-regeneration schemes Britain has ever seen, reworking Castlefield as a centre of tourism and leisure. Modern service sector industries and media companies moved into what remains one of the most fascinating areas in Manchester, the canals reopened, the rivers were cleaned up, the old warehouses refurbished and the decaying buildings revamped as smart apartment blocks – the estate a living example of how to unite industrial archaeology with modern living and leisure.

Beaufort Street

A reconstructed gateway, ditches and wall of the Roman fort, built of red sandstone to resemble the original as closely as possible, can be found off Beaufort Street. Explanatory boards relate the history of the site.

Castle Street

This small winding cobbled street leading from Deansgate to the Castlefield Canal Basin is practically an island as it is entirely surrounded by the Bridgewater and Rochdale canals. It has recently become something of a Victorian period piece thanks to the faithful restoration of the original industrial buildings such as the Merchant's Warehouse (see Bridgewater Canal, p. 102).

Collier Street

Roman Fort

The sole remaining piece of Manchester's Roman fort, a stone block dating from *c.* AD 200 – once described by the renowned historian A. J. P. Taylor as the 'least interesting Roman remains in Britain' – stands under railway arch No. 95 in a disused timber merchants' yard off Collier Street. When in the 1840s it was announced that a railway would be cut through the site, there were a few Roman blocks still standing, and the Duke of Ellesmere held up construction so that they could be preserved.

Liverpool Road

The world's first railway station, Liverpool Road, opened in 1830 on what was then the quickest route out of Manchester leading to the turnpike road for Liverpool. Originally the street was Priestnor Road, its first houses built at the end of the eighteenth century; within a few decades they had been divided into flats for those working on the nearby canals and rivers. Despite the intensity of industrialization in Castlefield, the sub-sequent decline of the area in the 1970s, and its recent revival as a tourism and leisure centre, Liverpool Road retains on its south side much of the original mix of rickety houses, corner pubs and small shops.

north side: Water Street to Deansgate
World's first railway station (Liverpool Road)

Liverpool Road, the world's first station, now part of the Museum of Science and Industry, was built by George Stephenson for the Liverpool and Manchester Railway Company in 1830. Although there were earlier railways, the Liverpool and Manchester line was the first with two tracks, timetables and stations.

Constructing a railway line to connect the two cities as a way of overcoming problems caused by the freezing of the canals in winter had first been discussed in 1822. A public company was formed in 1824, but attempts to push a bill through Parliament were thwarted. A Miss Byrom and a Mrs Atherton, who owned the land around Liverpool Road, objected to the siting of the station, while the Old Quay Canal Company, which feared for the commercial future of the River Irwell they ran once the railway opened, claimed the surveyors had made a number of inaccurate calculations such as placing the river Irwell thirty feet above Vauxhall Road even though it lay five feet below. The bill was withdrawn and resubmitted more successfully in 1826.

Once work started the railway builders discovered major physical problems along the 31-mile route that needed to be over-come, particularly in Chat Moss, the huge tract of swampy land near Warrington. More than 70,000 square yards of spoil were tipped into one part of the moss without success. Eventually young larch trees from Botany Bay Woods were laid together herring-bone style to solidify the land. A different kind of problem came with the construction of the Sankey Viaduct over a canal: nine arches, each fifty feet wide, were needed to take the line across.

Originally the railway company contemplated using horse-drawn carriages but as these would have been able to reach a maximum speed of only 15 mph the idea was dropped in favour of steam locomotives. Trials were held at Rainhill to choose an engine, and George Stephenson's 'Rocket' was considered the best. There were also livestock considerations. Summoned before a Parliamentary committee in 1825, George Stephenson was asked: 'Suppose now, one of these engines to be going along the railroad at the rate of nine or ten miles an hour, and that a cow were to stray upon the line and get in the way of the engine, would that not, think you, be a very awkward circumstance?', to which the engineer memorably replied: 'Aye, very awkward indeed for the coo.'

At first only one station between the cities was planned, halfway, at Newton le Willows. This was later changed so that there would be a Manchester terminus – at Liverpool Road. With no prototype for how a station should look, Liverpool Road took the form of a typical late-Georgian terrace. There were two entrances – for First and Second Class – and a brick property on the corner was adapted as the station agent's house. As for travellers starting from other towns, it was announced that those standing alongside the line could signal to the driver by waving a handkerchief or umbrella if they wanted the train to stop, an option no longer available.

Everything was ready for the first run on 15 September 1830. Both cities were agog. Passengers marvelled at the idea of travelling between the two metropolises in just over an hour, rather than over much of the day, even though medical men had warned potential passengers of the dangers travelling at high speeds might present for their health. Some 700 people crammed into eight special trains for the opening journey, while a crowd of around 50,000 stood at various points alongside the line to watch. Henry Booth, the railway company's treasurer, was particularly excited: 'From west to east and from north to south, the mechanical principle, the philosophy of the nineteenth century, will spread and extend itself. The world has received a new impulse. The genius of the age, like a mighty river of the new world, flows onwards, full, rapid and irresistible.' At Liverpool Road stood the poet Alfred Lord Tennyson. He peered down at the tracks but handicapped by short-sightedness assumed the vehicles ran in grooves embedded into the metal. The mistaken impression inspired him to write the line: 'Let the great world spin forever down the ringing grooves of change' in the poem 'Locksley Hall' (1842). The actress Fanny Kemble, who was also in the crowd watching the celebrations, noticed something more redolent of strained industrial relations in Manchester. 'High above the grim and grimy crowd of scowling faces, a loom had been erected, at which sat a tattered, starved-looking weaver, evidently set there as a representative man, to protest against the triumph of machinery and the gain and glory which the wealthy Liverpool and Manchester men were likely to derive from it.'

And it was this sense of political and social injustice that impinged on the day. As the first train drew into Liverpool Road weavers threw stones at the carriage of the prime minister, the Duke of Wellington, to show their distaste for his military association with Peterloo and his opposition to the Reform Bill. At the station a greater crowd prevented him reaching the official opening luncheon. He left hungry amid boos and jeers.

But a greater drama had occurred already. When the procession stopped at Parkside, halfway along the route, the VIPs ignored warnings not to wander on the track and William Huskisson, President of the Board of Trade, slipped and fell into the path of a locomotive, which rolled over his leg. Seriously injured, he was taken to Eccles where he deteriorated. Surgeons tried in vain to save him but he died later that evening, the first railway casualty.

When Liverpool Road station opened, the surrounding land was semi-rural. Hulme Hall, a grand house, stood barely a mile in the distance. The railway company soon realized the location was not central enough, and in 1844 rerouted the line so that the Manchester terminus was at Hunt's Bank (now Victoria). It seems perverse that Liverpool Road lasted as a station only fourteen years, although it did stay open for goods until 1975. After it closed completely there were fears that the site would be sold for redevelopment. Railway enthusiasts, local historians and conservationists lobbied to save the station. Greater Manchester Council carried out a survey, and after deciding to use the site as part of a new museum bought the buildings for £1. In the early 1980s the station was converted into part of the new Museum of Science and Industry. Steam trains run on the original tracks for a short distance during the summer. In the basement is the museum's Underground Manchester section, with its reconstruction of an 1868 sewer and 'The Making of Manchester' exhibition on the city's history.

Power Hall

The Museum of Science and Industry's engines and locomotives are stored in the Power Hall, built in 1855 as a freight shed. The hall is home to the largest collection of working steam engines in the world and also contains examples of the many vehicles that

Railways in Castlefield

Castlefield offers the visitor not just a bewildering assortment of waterways but an equally baffling labyrinth of railway lines. These are best seen at the canal basin, where tall viaducts decorated with castellated effects in mock honour of the vanished 'castle' (the Roman fort) fill the sky.

The main line, heading west from Deansgate, was originally known as the Manchester, South Junction and Altrincham Railway. The intention was not to build it high above the ground on a viaduct but to drain a section of the Bridgewater Canal, which the authorities deemed to be redundant with the growth of the railways, and lay the tracks at ground level. This ambitious plan was soon dropped and instead a viaduct was constructed of more than 50 million bricks. It is this line that branches at Collier Street in Castlefield, the northern section to Eccles, the southern towards Trafford Park.

Only parts of the Castlefield viaducts that took trains into the Great Northern Goods Warehouse on Watson Street (preserved, but now part of a leisure complex) remain, as attempts to trace the route on street level will show. To the immediate south of the goods warehouse viaduct is the line that took trains into Central station. This was one of Manchester's main termini, built by the Midland Railway to link Manchester to St Pancras via the East Midlands until it closed in the late 1960s. Some of the lines which went into Central station are now part of the Metrolink system, whose trams can be seen heading across the area on yet another viaduct.

used to be made in Manchester, including those built at Ford's first European plant in Trafford Park (p. 190).

Lower Campfield Market/Air and Space Gallery

The 1876 glazed market hall was built on the site of Acres Fair which was held here after

it moved from St Ann's Square. Originally food was sold in the market, and it later became an exhibition hall. It is now the Museum of Science and Industry's Air and Space Gallery, with exhibits that include a Shackleton bomber, a Spitfire and an (unused) Japanese kamikaze plane.

► Manchester's aviation history, p. 178.

St Matthew, east of Barton Street
Charles Barry's 1825 church, a monumental Gothic construction, was demolished in 1951, one of many casualties of the diminishing population of city-centre Manchester during the twentieth century. The picturesque Sunday school building opposite is now offices.

Upper Campfield Market

One of two neighbouring cast-iron market halls built by Travis and Mangnall in the 1870s, it became the temporary home of the Royal Exchange Theatre after the 1996 IRA bomb.

Spanish Cultural Delegation

On the corner of Liverpool Road and Deansgate stands the former Free Library, designed by Meek and Allison in 1882. Its façade features sculptures and the city's coat of arms, but it is the open internal layout that shows the architects' ingenuity. A covered brick inner arcade provides a dramatic setting for a restaurant, hairdresser and the Spanish Cultural Delegation.

south side: Deansgate to Water Street

The Ox (Oxnoble Inn)

Although it was the only pub in Britain named after a potato, its uniqueness was destroyed at the beginning of the twenty-first century when it was changed to the Ox. The unusual name came from the Oxnoble potatoes of Norfolk which used to be unloaded at the nearby Potato Wharf.

Outdoor Events Arena, south of Potato Wharf
The open space off Liverpool Road situated by an arm of the Bridgewater Canal is used for outdoor events. It was here that thousands of Mancunians gathered in 1994 to hear the announcement of which city would

be chosen to host the 2000 Olympics. When International Olympic chief Jose Samaranch appeared on TV to reveal the choice there was a momentary hush in the crowd, even though no one believed it would be Manchester. After Samaranch announced the winner as Sydney, the crowd launched into a spirited version of the Monty Python song 'Always Look On The Bright Side Of Life'.

Potato Wharf

There was much excitement in Manchester in 1841 when a ship from Dublin sailed up the Irwell bearing a cargo of potatoes, which were unloaded near where Potato Wharf now stands, and then returned to Ireland with coal from Fitzgerald's pit in Salford. 'Such are probably the small beginnings of Manchester's future greatness as one of the ports of the United Kingdom,' wrote the *Manchester Guardian* prophetically. Potato Wharf is now the name of a winding street off Liverpool Road heading towards the canals, which has been revitalized in recent years with apartment blocks and offices taking the place of the closed-down industrial sites. It also allows access to the spectacular Giant's Basin, a circular weir built by James Brindley to carry surplus water between the River Medlock and the Bridgewater Canal, which is one of the great engineering wonders of Manchester.

CHINATOWN

Manchester's Chinatown, symbolized by a huge ornate arch on Faulkner Street, is filled with restaurants and ethnic grocery stores occupying the Victorian cotton warehouses, following one of the most successful regeneration stories in the city's history.

The area was first built over in the eighteenth century around the 1786 church of St James. Neighbouring streets were given names that honoured royals – George III and Queen Charlotte – and several important eighteenth-century institutions located their headquarters here, including

the Scientific and Medical Society on Faulkner Street, which later became Owens College Medical School, and the Literary and Philosophical Society on George Street. On the main roads surrounding the St James's estate this trend continued into the nineteenth century with the Portico Library (established in 1806); the Manchester Institution, now the City Art Gallery (1835); and the Athenaeum on Princess Street (1837). Within a few decades commercial pressure resulted in residents moving away and warehouses being built.

Following the publication of the council's 1945 Manchester Plan the roads between Mosley Street and Portland Street were identified for demolition. The nineteenth-century buildings were to be replaced by lofty towers of granite and glass as the city chose to remodel itself in the American fashion. However, in the late 1960s, in the wake of the disastrous Piccadilly Plaza scheme to the north and the rise in building costs, the scheme was quietly abandoned.

When the textile businesses in the area began to close in the following decade the lower floors of the buildings were gradually taken up by Chinese restaurateurs, each attracted in turn by the previous buyers, as well as the cheap rents. Mostly the restaurants were run by settlers who had arrived in the 1950s from rural parts of Hong Kong, where their land had been bought up by the government looking to expand the urban area. The Chinese arrivals chose to go into catering, as there was little competition, and a quick return on capital meant that funds could be sent back home.

By the 1970s it was evident that a new Chinatown had emerged. Alongside the restaurants there are now shops selling Chinese medicines, supermarkets stocking a vast range of Oriental goods and food, gift shops, casinos and bookmakers where Chinese is spoken. In 1987 a striking and lofty arch, the first true Imperial Chinese arch in Europe, was erected on Faulkner Street. It is painted red and gold, and adorned with dragons and phoenixes, colours and symbols of luck and prosperity. Chinatown has continued to prosper, its popularity enhanced by the retention of the Georgian grid pattern of streets and the resistance to the unimaginative rebuilding that has tainted other parts of the city.

Charlotte Street

Barely changed by the development mania that has gripped Manchester since the Second World War, the street is still lined with Edward Walters's 1850s stone-faced palazzo-style textile warehouses: Charlotte House, Austin House, No. 34, and Fraser House, from west to east. Each features a short flight of steps leading from street level to the principal showroom, and there are iron-framed lifting devices at the rear. Since the demise of the cotton industry these have mostly become offices for the Chinese community.

Faulkner Street

The Imperial Chinese Archway, built by a team of engineers from Peking, and decorated with ceramics, lacquer, paint and gold leaf, dominates Faulkner Street, an attractive street of Chinese restaurants, Oriental grocery stores and offices. The cotton warehouses here are not as flamboyant as those of Charlotte Street, for the merchants who paid for these buildings in the late nineteenth century chose not to spend their money on external decorations on what was a side street.

George Street

Along with Faulkner Street, George Street contains Chinatown's main stretch of Chinese restaurants and supermarkets. Before the Second World War the street was home to the Manchester Literary and Philosophical Society, an organization whose members and speakers made some of the most significant advances in the history of British science.

north side
Manchester Literary and Philosophical Society (1799–1940), No. 36

John Dalton, James Prescott Joule and Ernest Rutherford are among the eminent scientists who revealed their findings in papers read first at 36 George Street, one-time home of the Manchester Literary and Philosophical Society.

Dalton came to Manchester in 1793 to take up a post as professor of mathematics and natural philosophy – what would now be called 'science' – at the New College on Mosley Street. He had been a schoolteacher in Kendal, where, thanks to the sadistic regime of the time, he was obliged to pin down the boys while his brother flogged them. In Manchester Dalton lived at a number of addresses in what is now Chinatown, including 18, 27 and 35 Faulkner Street, and 10 George Street. A devout Quaker, he led a more philanthropic life here, devoting himself to chemistry and meteorology.

In 1793 Dalton demonstrated that evaporation and condensation were not chemical but physical changes in water. A year later he identified colour-blindness, which is known as Daltonism in some countries. But he is best known for his findings on atomic theory deriving from the experiments conducted at 36 George Street, which he revealed at lectures given here early in the nineteenth century.

Dalton was the first chemist to propose formally that elements consisted of small indivisible particles, which are chemically indestructible; that atoms of different elements differ by their weight which is relative to the weight of the simplest element, hydrogen. Dalton assigned atomic weights to the atoms of the twenty elements he was familiar with and invented a system of classification in which oxygen was assigned a ring, hydrogen a ring with a dot in the middle, and nitrogen an upright line. Although Dalton's atomic weight theory was untouchable, his classifications were not successful, and it was left to the Swede Jöns

Jacob Berzelius to devise the modern-day, simple letter notation such as 'O' for oxygen and 'He' for helium.

Because many of Dalton's documents were destroyed when the Lit and Phil building was bombed in the Second World War, no one is certain how he arrived at the details of his theory. Ironically, the first figure to suggest that atoms might themselves be made of smaller particles was Dalton's obituarist, R. A. Smith, in a Lit and Phil Society paper in 1856, twelve years after Dalton died.

In 1818 Dalton turned down a chance to run the scientific side of a polar expedition. He explained that he would not be able to stand life at sea and that he did not wish to disrupt his chemistry work. A more likely explanation was that continued absence from Manchester would have prevented him from maintaining his daily weather records, which he kept for fifty-seven years.

At a lecture held here on 2 November 1841 James Prescott Joule, the leading physicist of the era, gave his ground-breaking talk on the 'electric origin of the heat of combustion'. News of these findings first appeared before the public in the pages of the *Manchester Courier* in 1847. No science journal would publish them, for at that time scientists believed that heat was a material called caloric – a weightless fluid which existed in all substances and was released when they were warmed up. Joule later carried out a number of breakthrough experiments in heat and energy in the laboratory at his father's house in Salford.

A later scientific giant involved in the society was the New Zealander Ernest Rutherford who in a Lit and Phil paper posited that the atom itself contained a fascinating, sub-microscopic world, a nucleus around which smaller particles orbited, one of the fundamental scientific concepts of the twentieth century.

The society now organizes events at a number of Manchester venues.

▶ Ernest Rutherford at Manchester University (p. 122).

south side
Cold War nuclear shelter, between Princess Street and Dickinson Street
A high wall and windowless brick building are the only clues to Manchester's 1950s nuclear bunker that lies below Chinatown. Officially the Guardian Underground Telephone Exchange, it was built in 1954 by Polish immigrants, chosen because they couldn't speak English and would not be able to divulge its secrets. It was covered until 1967 by D Notice restrictions, which meant that publications were not able even to mention its existence.

The bunker cost £4 million, provided by the United States, and its purpose was to house civil servants and local dignitaries deemed worthy of saving in the event of a nuclear war. Inside was stocked six weeks' supply of dried and tinned food, and there was a kitchen, bar, dining room, dormitories, artesian well, fuel tanks and two generators known as Jayne and Marilyn. To enhance the quality of life for those who might have been lucky enough to be incarcerated within, artificial windows and scenery were painted on to some of the walls.

If the Guardian Exchange had been needed, a 35-ton concrete slab would have slammed into place over the entrance, which could only have been opened from the inside using hydraulic jacks. However the bunker had a short life as a viable means of protection from a potential nuclear bomb. By 1960 technology had moved on and it was apparent that if a thermonuclear device fell on the city it would wipe out everything, even the bunker. Nevertheless the shelter was maintained until the late 1970s, the six switchboards manned twenty-four hours a day, 365 days a year, so that they could be used by British Telecom, even if employees were infuriated by the constant hum of the air conditioning and dazzled by the glare of the fluorescent lights.

From the Guardian Exchange a 1,000-foot tunnel runs west to Salford and a slightly shorter one east to Ardwick, emerging at the surface at Lockton Close. The entrance to the Salford shaft can be found on Islington Street in the city centre.

• Other local sites which would have assumed vital strategic use during a nuclear war include the Manchester Regional War Room, built in 1952 below the Alexandra Hospital, Cheadle, where military operations for the area would have been coordinated, and the Manchester Corporation Control Centre under Greystoke Hall, Palatine Road, West Didsbury.

FINANCIAL DISTRICT

The land between Cross Street and Mosley Street has traditionally been Manchester's financial centre. The first bank to open here was Albert Heywood's of 1772, which meant that merchants no longer had to transport cash to London by coach under heavily armed guard. The Bank of Manchester was established in 1829 on the corner of Brown and Market streets. Others soon followed nearby. Although much business has now moved away from the centre, this is still the most elegant section of the city, with a concentration of fabulously ornate *fin-de-siècle* buildings.

Back Pool Fold
The winding, twisting alley is built on the site of a medieval ducking pool and a Tudor mansion, Radcliffe Hall, which was used in Elizabethan times as a prison for Roman Catholics caught illegally attending Mass. On the morning of 15 June 1996, shortly before the Manchester IRA bomb exploded, the Army Bomb Squad set up base on Back Pool Fold outside the long-standing Sam's Chop House pub. Anxious to prevent an explosion, they engaged their 'pigstick disrupter', a device fired by robot at a vehicle suspected of containing a bomb to ascertain its contents before any attempt is made to disable it. In this case the plan was unsuccessful for the bomb exploded exactly one second before the army timer was able to begin its task.

Brown Street
The *Manchester Evening News* was launched from an office on Brown Street on 10 October 1868 by Mitchell Henry, a local businessman hoping to win election to Parliament as a Liberal. When Henry lost he swiftly dropped his interest in the newspaper, but the title was saved by two Manchester businessmen, Peter Allen and his brother-in-law John Edward Taylor, son of the John Edward Taylor who founded the *Manchester Guardian*. Thus was born the fruitful association between the two long-running Manchester papers which still exists today. In 1879 the *Evening News* moved to Cross Street to share offices with the daily (p. 6).

L. S. Lowry, Manchester's most fêted artist, worked as a rent collector for the Pall Mall company offices based at 6 Brown Street from 1910–52. He was obliged to visit houses in Longsight, Old Trafford and Hulme, but as long as he brought in the money his bosses never queried what he did throughout the day, much of which was spent not rent-collecting but researching subjects for his paintings or going home to Pendlebury to work on them. Lowry strove to keep separate his two lives. He feared that professional artists would dub him a 'Sunday painter' if they discovered what he did during the week. When he retired after forty-two years with the firm, there was no send-off. 'I shan't be in tomorrow,' he simply told colleagues – and he wasn't.

With its position in the heart of Manchester's financial district, Brown Street features a number of lavishly designed banks and company buildings. Nos. 46–48 were once Brooks' Bank, founded by Sir William Cunliffe Brooks of Barlow Hall, the mansion near Southern Cemetery that partly survives as a golf clubhouse. The 1868 building has been altered but the unusual prickly ironwork on the veranda remains in place.

Cooper Street
On the day of the Peterloo Massacre – 16 August 1819 – the Manchester Yeomanry

set up base on Cooper Street, and after
Deputy Chief Constable Joseph Nadin
ordered officers to arrest Orator Hunt,
the main speaker at St Peter's Fields, the
Yeomanry swarmed along Cooper Street,
where they accidentally killed an infant, the
first casualty of the day, as they raced
towards the demonstration.

In 1824 Cooper Street became the first
home of the Mechanics Institute, one of
several similar bodies throughout England
set up to educate the working classes, particularly in science, at a time when there
were no free schools. Yet many considered
the Manchester body pompous and preten-
tious, and a breakaway version opened in a
timber yard on Brazenose Street in the
1840s.

By that time Cooper Street had become
commercialized. Johann Georg Kohl, a
German visitor to Manchester in 1844 wrote:
'Here stand the great warehouses, five or six
storeys high, all large and imposing, some of
them stately and elegant, at night . . . brilli-
antly lighted from top to bottom.' In the
early twenty-first century Cooper Street has
been home on Saturday nights to the kitsch
nightclub Tiger Lounge in the former Freemasons' Hall at No. 5, the same building
that in the 1970s housed George Best's
Oscar's nightclub.

► Mechanics Institute, Princess Street, p. 40.

Kennedy Street

A once charming, barely noticeable back
street, close to busy Princess Street, it presented an unbroken line of quaint Victorian
buildings until early in the twenty-first century when two of the delicate properties in
the middle of the street, which had been left
to deteriorate, collapsed and had to be
demolished. Conservationists were furious,
for the buildings were owned by Trafford
Park Estates, whose managing director, Neil
Westbrook, is a former Lord Mayor of
Manchester.

Still standing at the northern end of the
street is the Law Library, an admirable
example of fanciful, mid-nineteenth-century

Venetian Gothic revival architecture. At
the southern end is the Vine Inn with its
gorgeous Art Nouveau lettering and green
tiling, and the adjacent City Arms pub,
where many a political deal has been struck
by the ruling Labour Group of the council,
to whom it is a home from home.

King Street
*between Cross Street and Spring Gardens only;
for the section west of Cross Street, see p. 78*

The king of central Manchester streets,
named in 1735 in support of the exiled Stuart
kings, is lined with some of Manchester's
most exclusive shops west of Cross Street
and some of its most handsome office
blocks here in the Financial District. At first
King Street was residential, but by the 1830s
most houses had been taken over by
businesses. In 1845 the Bank of England
opened a branch at No. 82, and this was
followed by a number of other banks, which
made this area the financial heart of Manchester.

north side: Cross Street to Spring Gardens
𝕸𝖆𝖓𝖈𝖍𝖊𝖘𝖙𝖊𝖗 𝕿𝖔𝖜𝖓 𝕳𝖆𝖑𝖑 (1825–1911)
Manchester's first 𝕿𝖔𝖜𝖓 𝕳𝖆𝖑𝖑, at the corner
of Cross Street and King Street, opened in
1825, not for the council, which then didn't
exist, but for the Police Commissioners.
Architect Francis Goodwin modelled it on
the Erechtheion of Athens, the dome based
on the Athenian Tower of the Winds –
Greek architecture conferring integrity on
Manchester's growing democracy.

When the city's first elected council was
formed in 1838, those in charge of the building refused to let councillors hold meetings
in the 𝕿𝖔𝖜𝖓 𝕳𝖆𝖑𝖑 and so the politicians had
to make do with 𝖄𝖔𝖗𝖐 𝕳𝖔𝖙𝖊𝖑 next door
instead. In 1844 the body of the late scientist
John Dalton, resting in a mahogany casket,
lay in state at the 𝕿𝖔𝖜𝖓 𝕳𝖆𝖑𝖑 in a room
covered with black drapery. Forty thousand
people paid their respects before the coffin
was taken to Ardwick Cemetery in a mile-
long cortège.

By the 1860s the Manchester Corporation
was at last allowed access, but the politicians

deemed the building too small to hold the city's growing ambitions and Alfred Waterhouse was commissioned to design a monumental new Town Hall on Albert Square. The old one became a reference library and survived until 1911, when it was demolished apart from the façade, which was re-erected in Heaton Park. On the site Charles Heathcote's sturdy baroque-style branch of Lloyd's Bank of 1915 now stands. Its banking hall features marble pillars, carvings and decorations in the grandest styles.

● Other impressive Charles Heathcote buildings in Manchester include two at this junction: the Eagle Insurance building (at the south-west corner) and the Northern Rock Building Society (south-east corner). Nearby at 1–3 York Street is Heathcote's flamboyantly designed Parr's Bank (now the Athenaeum).

▶ Manchester Town Hall, Albert Square, p. 2.

York Hotel

Manchester's first elected council – thirty-four merchants and ten shopkeepers – met in the York Hotel, which stood near the junction with Cross Street, in 1838. They had been refused use of the adjacent Town Hall by the various public bodies that ran the building and feared, correctly, that their powers were on the wane. It was in the York Hotel that year that local mill owners and politicians formed the Anti-Corn Law League, hoping to force a change in the law over the fixed price of bread, a campaign crucial in securing Manchester's status as a city of influence and prestige.

▶ Anti-Corn Law League headquarters, Market Street, p. 14.

55 King Street/Former National Westminster Bank

One of the few successful examples of 1960s modernism in Manchester stands on the site of the York Hotel. The fortress-like building was designed by Hugh Casson, who had overseen the architecture of the 1951 Festival of Britain. It has a double hammerhead shape and is clad in rough, hand-tooled, ribbed Swedish granite. Unprotected by

legislation, the building was redesigned in 1998 by Stephenson Bell, who kept the white marble office entrance but opened up the ground floor to shops and restaurants.

▶ The 1960s architecture of Piccadilly Plaza, p. 36.

Reform Club

The last Manchester building to be created in the Venetian Gothic style that was all the rage in the mid-nineteenth century was the Reform Club, designed by Edward Salomons, who was also responsible for what is now the Jewish Museum in Cheetham Hill. The York sandstone façade, with its huge double-light windows, features a veranda where speakers, mostly supporting the Liberal Party, used to address crowds waiting on the street below. William Ewart Gladstone, then prime minister, was guest of honour at the opening ceremony on 17 October 1871. It was here that Winston Churchill gave his election victory speech in 1906, having just won the seat of Manchester North West. In recent years the building has housed an up-market nightclub and an expensive restaurant.

south side: Spring Gardens to Cross Street
HSBC/Midland Bank

Edwin Lutyens's Portland stone block of 1933–5, built for the Midland Bank, is one of Manchester's most impressive twentieth-century buildings. The shape cleverly plays with the notion of 'sacred geometry', mathematics with supposed divine properties, in that the proportion of the base to the middle section and the middle to the top section is equal to that of the Golden Ratio (about 2/3), the supposed ideal measurement of antiquity. The walls slope slightly inwards – 1 inch in every 11 feet – so that the building appears taller than it is. Although Lutyens wanted a marble border in the banking hall the bank persuaded him otherwise on the grounds that 'a considerable number of people in Manchester wear nails in their boots and the risk of slipping is even greater than it is in London'. The interior rather incongruously and bravely resembles a typical Wren church.

Ship Canal House

A steel-framed Harry S. Fairhurst construction of 1924–6, based on Charles Holden's unrealized Board of Trade building in Whitehall, Ship Canal House was the tallest building in Manchester when erected and it required an Act of Parliament to allow it to be built this high. Michael Waterhouse, grandson of the Town Hall architect, Alfred, spoilt Fairhurst's work by slapping the Atlas Assurance Company headquarters as close as possible to Ship Canal House in 1929: there is no gap between the two buildings.

Former Bank of England

A rare Manchester building by Charles Cockerell, best known for his work on the monumental classical St George's Hall in Liverpool, was the first provincial branch of the Bank of England, and opened in 1826. In 1971 Century House, a nine-storey brown glass office block, typical of the anti-social corporate architecture style of the period, was added at the back. Despite being the first building in Manchester with air-conditioning, it was gone within twenty years, replaced by a worse eyesore, Holford Associates' unlovely fifteen-storey office block, which has reduced Cockerell's original building to the status of an entrance foyer.

Prudential Assurance Building

An 1880s block typical of Alfred Waterhouse in its use of red brick and terracotta, a style popularly dubbed 'Waterhouse slaughterhouse'.

Spring Gardens

Spring Gardens contains the most lavishly designed stretch of ornate, turn-of-the-century, baroque-style banks in Manchester. George Nicholson, who lived at No. 9 early in the nineteenth century, produced the first vegetarian cookery book in 1803. It contained recipes of 'one hundred perfectly palatable and highly nutritious substances which may be easily secured at an expense much below the price of the limbs of our fellow animals'.

east side: Market Street to Mosley Street
Parr's Bank/The Athenaeum, north junction with York Street

A baroque red sandstone building of extraordinary flamboyance, it was designed by Charles Heathcote for Parr's Bank in 1902. Heathcote provided Art Nouveau motifs in the ironwork, and arched windows with paired Doric columns supporting huge scrolled brackets that are purely decorative. Inside are columns of Pyrenean marble which arrived on the Manchester Ship Canal, were transferred to a barge, taken along the Rochdale Canal to a wharf near Spring Gardens, and from there sent on an even more demanding journey by horse and cart to reach the bank. After the council sanctioned demolition in 1972 the Victorian Society successfully pushed for its survival. The mahogany banking hall is now a bar. Some of the original stained glass survives.
▶ Refuge Assurance building, p. 20.

National Provincial Bank, No. 41

One of Alfred Waterhouse's lesser known buildings, an early home to the Manchester Ship Canal Company, is an exuberant and powerful baroque creation which features giant Doric pilasters topped with similarly epic Ionic pilasters and a flamboyant roofline studded with Renaissance effects. To the south at Nos. 43–45 is Charles Heathcote's former Lancashire and Yorkshire Bank of 1890, which looks so much like an Italian baroque church it is worth contemplating how absurd such a sight appears in this highly commercialized, godless district.

GAYTHORN

Gaythorn, shabby and despoiled, stands by a bend in the River Medlock south of Whitworth Street West. For over 100 years until the 1980s the area was home to huge gas cylinders that towered over the grimy low-rise factories. By then most of the local industry had shut down. The opening of the Haçienda nightclub in a former yacht warehouse here in 1982 revitalized what was a depressed area, and other venues were soon clamouring for an address close to the dramatic backdrops of railway viaducts, canals and decaying Victorian brickwork. Although the Hacienda is long gone there are still many night-time venues in the area, and the decline of Gaythorn has halted.

In the early nineteenth century Gaythorn was home to a savage community living in densely packed housing by the Medlock prone to intense humidity and even flooding. The poor ventilation and drainage riddled these subterranean lairs with damp and germs. During the cholera epidemics of the 1840s the town authorities sealed them up to stop the spread of the disease.

Typical was a room nine by ten feet accommodating ten people in a building abutting two outside toilets meant for 250 people. In the 1840s waves of poor Irish immigrants fleeing the potato famine began to settle here, as it was the only place they could afford in Manchester. Soon the area was nicknamed 'Little Ireland', its inhabitants treated derisively by the rest of the town. Even the *Manchester Guardian*, when commenting on the police attempts to close down illegal whiskey stills, described how the officers were subject to the 'almost murderous spirit of violence that exists in the breasts of some of the lower orders of Irish'.

The nightmarish conditions of Little Ireland were first exposed in 1842 by the campaigning doctor James Phillips Kay. He found the area to be 'the haunt of hordes of thieves and desperadoes who defy the law, and is always inhabited by a class resembling savages in their appetites and habits'. Writing more than a decade later, German social historian Jakob Venedey claimed with some black humour that 'Little Ireland was discovered during the period of the cholera epidemic. Until then, all the inhabitants of Manchester hurried past the place and turned their gaze away.' Venedey went on to describe how 'hundreds were evicted from their cellars. Hundreds rotted alive next to the unburied dead. And the endless

pestilence that was raging there had taken such a grip that all fumigation and cleaning were useless and the decision had to be made to brick up many of these pits.'

The most infamous descriptions of Little Ireland came from the German Communist Friedrich Engels, whose *Conditions of the Working Class in England*, written in 1844, first appeared only in German. By the time the book was translated into English in the 1870s Little Ireland had been cleaned up to build the Manchester South Junction & Altrincham Railway and the new Oxford Road station. Nevertheless Engels's description remains the most potent historical account of a desperate area:

> In a rather deep hole, in a curve of the Medlock and surrounded on all four sides by tall factories and high embankments, covered with buildings, stand two groups of about 200 cottages, built chiefly back to back, in which live about 4,000 human beings, most of them Irish. The cottages are old, dirty, and of the smallest sort, the streets uneven, fallen into ruts and in part without drains or pavement; masses of refuse, offal, and sickening filth lie among standing pools in all directions . . . The race that lives in these ruinous cottages, behind broken windows, mended with oilskin, sprung doors, and rotten doorposts, or in dark, wet cellars, in measureless filth and stench must surely have reached the lowest stage of humanity.

Later that century most of the dwellings began to be replaced by factories and workshops, and Gaythorn became entirely commercialized.

▶ Engels in Red Bank, p. 163.

New Wakefield Street
The Green Building, No. 19
The most unusual of the many new developments that have appeared in Manchester since the early 1990s is the Green Building. A drum-like, green-coloured block of flats, faced with much wood panelling on the façade, it was designed by the renowned architect Terry Farrell, who was also

responsible for London's Charing Cross station and the new MI6 building. Environmental concerns were uppermost in mind; carbon emissions are 60 per cent of those in similar blocks, and there are a wind turbine and underfloor heating. There is even a nod to Le Corbusier's pioneering work in Marseilles, for the building incorporates a 120-place nursery and doctors' surgery.

Oxford Road Station Approach
Oxford Road station
The station's late-1950s wooden frontage, the work of R. L. Moorcroft, British Rail's regional architect, is one of the most unusual sites in Manchester. The façade features a wooden conoid, a basic shell design later made famous in the Sydney Opera House.

Whitworth Street West
north side: Deansgate to Oxford Street
The Hacienda (1982–97), Nos. 11–13 Britain's most celebrated 1980s nightclub was opened by Tony Wilson's Factory Records and New Order in the former International Marine Centre, a yachting warehouse, on 21 May 1982. Inspiration for the venture came from the anarchic and eccentric French agitprop group the Situationists, from whom Wilson borrowed the phrase 'The Hacienda must be built' and incorporated symbolism used in the club's motifs.

On the opening night the main attraction, surprisingly, was the comedian Bernard Manning, who moaned to the bemused crowd: 'I've played some shit-holes in my time, but this is really something.' Cabaret Voltaire brought their unique blend of samples and electro pulses on the second night, and in 1984 a barely known Madonna performed there. Less successful were the East European avant-garde noise specialists Einstürzende Neubauten, who were banned after attacking the cast-iron columns with pneumatic drills.

Despite the Hacienda being the follow-up to Wilson's revered Factory nights at the Russell Club in Hulme, there were few

patrons in the early days. But gradually the Hacienda's appeal grew. Punters were lured by Ben Kelly's austere industrial décor – not a potted plant or plush carpet in sight – the whiff of bohemian glamour associated with the Factory label, and the uncompromising dance music supplied by high-quality DJs such as Mike Pickering (later of M People) and Dave Haslam.

By the mid-1980s the Hacienda had attained the kind of legendary status not associated with a nightclub since the days of London's Who/Maximum R&B period Marquee and Liverpool's Cavern. The clientèle was nattily dressed, the owners as fashionable as it was possible to find, and the music ingeniously mixed – snatches of Syd Barrett-era Pink Floyd, Troublefunk, Yello and George Clinton – often aided by A Guy Called Gerald and Graham Massey of 808 State, who would bang on the DJ booth door and hand over tapes of deranged twenty-minute bleeps and bloops that were played in full. Only Morrissey, it seems, was unimpressed, recalling in the Smiths' song 'How Soon Is Now?' a depressing night he spent in the Hacienda.

By the late 1980s the soundtrack was mostly acid house, and the club at its most popular. But the growth in numbers came with a price, for there was a similar increase in the number of patrons intent simply on causing trouble, and a rise in the number of ecstasy-peddling drug dealers. The owners were mortified. The drugs laws meant they were legally able to provide one type of drug – alcohol – at agreed prices that made them barely solvent, but were not allowed to peddle the more popular ecstasy pills that made the dealers rich.

The combination of drugs, drug dealers and associated criminals, rather than a demise in the quality of the music, ruined the club. A police clampdown following the 1989 death of sixteen-year-old Claire Leighton after taking an ecstasy pill here was opposed by Manchester city council, previously a keen advocate of destroying the club scene, whose leader, Graham Stringer, wrote to the magistrates court explaining that the Ħacienđa made a 'significant contribution to active use of the city centre core' in line with the government's own policy of regenerating urban areas.

But it was Wilson who voluntarily closed the club, temporarily, after gunmen threatened door staff – which simply moved the problem elsewhere. The Ħacienđa soon reopened with airport-style security measures, but in 1992 Factory Records went bankrupt, compounding the club's problems, and the violence continued. When Mike Pickering had a knife pulled on him he quit, and revellers began to turn to new venues such as Paradise Factory and Sankey's Soap. The Ħacienđa closed for good in June 1997 and was demolished soon after to be replaced by an unsightly block of flats which uses the Hacienda name.

Twenty Four Hour Party People
Scenes from Michael Winterbottom's *Twenty Four Hour Party People*, a 2002 film about Factory Records and the Ħacienđa scene, take place in what looks like the inside of the club but was in fact a film set expertly re-created in an Ancoats warehouse. A thousand clubbers were invited to act as extras, making up a crowd of revellers dancing to records played by the regular Ħacienđa DJs. A couple of days after filming finished the replica version was demolished.

► Twisted Wheel, p. 77.
Ritz

I could hear them playing all the hits/at that mecca of modern dance, The Ritz – John Cooper Clarke, 'Salome Maloney', 1978

The longest-running nightclub in Manchester opened in the early years of the twentieth century as an up-market ballroom, where the glamour easily toppled over into kitsch thanks to the chandeliers, tasteless wallpaper, and notorious bouncing dancefloor, as sent up by John Cooper Clarke in his cutting rap poem 'Salome

Maloney', which perfectly captured the stiletto and sleeked-back sideburns scene. The Ritz featured in the 1961 film *A Taste of Honey*, which was why Morrissey, a great fan of the film, arranged for the Smiths to have their first gig at the Ritz, on 4 October 1982. As well as the Smiths supporting pop funk band Blue Rondo A La Turk, the show, promoted by Andrew Berry, 1980s hairdresser to the stars, and later subject of Morrissey's solo single 'Hairdresser on Fire', featured a drag act and a dance troupe.
south side
The Green Room, Nos. 54–56
The renowned experimental theatre is based in the railway arches near Oxford Road station and dates back to the Green Room Society of the 1920s, set up to encourage new drama writers. The original venue on Liverpool Road in Castlefield was destroyed in the Second World War, and a variety of different addresses was used until a place was found for it underneath the arches in 1987.

GREAT BRIDGEWATER

The awkwardly shaped section of land bounded by Peter Street, Oxford Street, the Rochdale Canal and Deansgate is home to some of Manchester's biggest public buildings, including the Bridgewater Hall, G-Mex, the adjacent convention centre and the Great Northern leisure complex. But the area is lucky to survive at all in its present state. The *Guardian* in April 1961 presented proposals to flatten the land to make way for new flats and a bus station. Pedestrians would have to negotiate the area several feet up on 'sky walkways'. Of course nothing came of the scheme.

After the closure of Central station in the late 1960s the area fell into decline. Revival followed the Greater Manchester County Council's ambitious restoration of the old station into the G-Mex Exhibition Centre in the mid-1980s. In the early 1990s came the opening of the Metrolink tram line that runs through the locale and the building of the Bridgewater Hall, which in turn has led to further multi-million-pound projects.

A significant coup for Manchester was being chosen as the venue for the 2006 Labour Party conference, held at G-Mex.

Great Bridgewater Street
north side: Deansgate to Oxford Street
Chepstow House
Built by Speakman and Charlesworth in 1874 for Samuel Mendel, the vastly wealthy cotton magnate, Chepstow House was one of the most technologically advanced Manchester textile buildings of the period. The ground floor was used for storage, and the basement, with its fourteen hydraulic presses, for packing goods. Below it runs the River Tib, which was diverted to accommodate the building's foundations. Chepstow House was converted into flats in the 1990s.
► Mendel at Whalley Range, p. 175.
Peveril of the Peak, east junction with Chepstow Street
The strangely named Peveril of the Peak, covered in lime green glazed tiles and occupying a triangular site, is one of the last surviving pre-twentieth-century pubs in central Manchester. *Peveril of the Peak* was the title of a Walter Scott novel of 1822, and was the name used by one of the best-known stagecoaches that plied the route between Manchester and London. Inside the pub none of the insensitive modernization that has ruined so many similar establishments has been allowed, and drinkers come from afar to play the table football machine with its legendary Yeovil-like slope.
► Wellington Inn, p. 96.
south side: Oxford Street to Deansgate
Lee House, No. 90
An architectural oddity in that the building is designed like a Chicago skyscraper with long sleek bands that would benefit from being spread over twenty-plus floors even though only seven were built. The architect, Harry S. Fairhurst, who was responsible for a series of powerful Manchester textile

warehouses early in the twentieth century, most of which survive, visited the United States for inspiration and returned to Manchester determined to build Europe's tallest block, only to see his plans thwarted in the slump of the late 1920s.
► Bridgewater House, p. 41.
Briton's Protection
At the corner with Albion Street stands the ornately designed and unspoilt Briton's Protection pub. Built in 1795 and for a time an army recruiting office, it is furnished with rich wood and decorated with cut glass, and has become a haven for real ale drinkers and those who want to relax in sumptuously ornate surroundings. Until a change occurred in the Manchester male psyche in the 1980s, the pub wouldn't serve women. The landlord once ejected Deborah Curtis, wife of Joy Division's ill-fated leader Ian, purely on gender grounds. Plans announced in 2006 to the dismay of Mancunians revealed that the pub might be moved to a different site to accommodate yet more new flats, thereby negating one of the reasons why people would want to move back to the city centre in the first place.
► Wellington Inn, p. 96.

Lower Mosley Street
Cooper's Cottage, home of the avid eighteenth century horse-racing enthusiast William Cooper, who used to walk from Manchester to Doncaster for the St Leger every year, stood on a small section of the land where the Midland Hotel can now be found until it was demolished to make way for the Gentlemen's Concert Hall. The Midland Hotel replaced the concert hall in 1903, and on the Lower Mosley Street side carvings were inserted rich with reliefs including that of the mythical Wyvern beast, the Midland Railway Company logo.
west side
Gentlemen's Concert Hall, corner with Peter Street
The Gentlemen's Concerts were the forerunners of the concerts staged so successfully over the past 150 years by the Hallé

Orchestra. They were so called because women were allowed to attend only as guests of gentlemen members. During the concerts' mid-nineteenth-century heyday they attracted 600 subscribers and there was a four-year waiting list to join. One highlight was Mendelssohn conducting *Elijah* here only months before his death in 1847. Nevertheless the standard of the performances was not high when Hermann Leo, a German calico printer resident in Manchester, contacted a young pianist who had fled Paris for London during the 1848 revolution and told him that Manchester was 'ripe to be taken in hand' by someone who could 'stir the dormant taste for the art of music'.

The pianist was Karl (or Charles) Hallé. In Paris Hallé had played and associated with Liszt, Wagner and Chopin, and the idea of moving to this centre of industry, with its stinking rivers and smoking factories, was ridiculous. But Hallé came. His first visit to the Gentlemen's Hall was to hear Chopin give a recital, but he was unimpressed by those playing alongside. 'The orchestra, oh, the orchestra!' he later wailed. 'I was fresh from the concerts of the Conservatoire, from Hector Berlioz's orchestra.' After playing Beethoven's *Fifth Piano Concerto* at the hall Hallé was even more depressed: 'I seriously thought of packing up and leaving Manchester so that I might not have to endure a second of these wretched performances.' When Hallé's friends pointed out that that was exactly why he had to stay and 'accomplish a revolution', he did so.

In 1850 Hallé became conductor of the Gentlemen's Concerts. Eight years later he founded the orchestra that still bears his name, whose first concert took place not in the Gentlemen's Concert Hall but in the Free Trade Hall on 30 January 1858. The Gentlemen's Concert Hall was demolished in 1898 to make way for the construction of the Midland Hotel (p. 26).

east side
Bridgewater Hall

Manchester's main classical concert hall, designed by the firm of Renton Howard Wood Levin in 1996 as a new home for the Hallé Orchestra, was built after years of debate about the supposed inadequacies as a venue of the Free Trade Hall, the Hallé's historic home.

Those who wanted to move away from the Free Trade Hall could point to the rushed and uninspired rebuilding of the hall carried out by city architect Leonard Howitt after the wartime bombing. When the government gave a new quango, the Central Manchester Development Corporation, powers over Manchester's regeneration in the 1980s the campaign gathered pace. The council commissioned a new concert hall, which was built with £42 million of government and European money, and is mounted on 270 giant foundation springs to shield it from the noise of the nearby trams and railway. The hall was named to accord with nearby commercial developments, rather than for musical considerations, and so the popular choice of Barbirolli Hall, after the legendary mid-twentieth-century Hallé conductor, was dropped in favour of Bridgewater Hall.

Despite no end of plaudits for its design, it now appears that the praise was more for its status as a symbol of regeneration and urban confidence than for any architectural or acoustic qualities. The exterior of the building mixes glass and sandstone with battleship-grey stainless steel, a style already ubiquitous and as dated as the 1960s brick-faced block seen throughout council house Britain. The shape of the hall's façade, the prow of an ocean liner, is supposed to symbolize Manchester's marine mercantile past. Cynics have pointed out that the prow also faces the Town Hall, a constant reminder of the power behind the new Manchester.

Inside, the arena space exudes none of the warmth and sensitivity of the Free Trade Hall, pre- or post-war. Another shortcoming is the programming. The quantity of music offered at the typical concert falls far short of earlier programme lengths, a failing compounded by the high prices charged compared to those at the Free Trade Hall. Nevertheless the Hallé Orchestra has gone from strength to strength since moving to the hall, under first Kent Nagano and more recently Mark Elder.

► Free Trade Hall, p. 29.

Watson Street
Great Northern Railway Company's Goods Warehouse
A Victorian warehouse in which, uniquely, all three available transport systems – canal, rail, road – met, each on a different floor, is now a shopping and leisure centre. Its construction in the 1890s wiped out nine acres of streets with their cramped terraced houses, inns, burial ground and school. The new building was ingeniously designed. At the base was the waterway, a branch of the now disused Manchester and Salford Junction Canal; on the ground level, the road; and above that the rail tracks, which entered on a viaduct. After the warehouse closed in 1963 the building was left to rot. From the mid-1980s it was used as a car park for visitors to G-Mex, and it was refurbished into a shopping and leisure centre at the beginning of the twenty-first century, a move which had the contrasting effect of putting the building to some use while allowing the destruction of many of the most interesting brick features.

► Manchester and Salford Junction Canal, p. 105.

Windmill Street
There was a windmill here until the 1830s. The hustings from which Henry Hunt was meant to speak at what became the Peterloo Massacre of 1819 stood on Windmill Street.
south side
Manchester Central/G-Mex
What was Central station, the last of Manchester's railway termini to be built, opened in July 1880. The Midland Railway could now run a service to London via Chorlton, Stockport, a scenic route through the Peak

District, on to the east Midlands and arrive in the capital at St Pancras. A covered walkway connected the station to the luxurious Midland Hotel from 1903, so that guests would not get wet on leaving the station.

Some 300,000 Manchester United fans gathered in the station on 25 April 1909 to greet the team that had just won the FA Cup for the first time. While waiting they were entertained by a brass band playing 'See the Conquering Hero Comes'. The team later made its way to Albert Square for a civic reception at the Town Hall and then through the streets of east Manchester, where many climbed statues or perched on roofs, headed for the club's Clayton ground.

By the mid-twentieth century 400 trains a day were using Central station. Its future looked assured in 1960 when the new Blue Pullman service, a fast, air-conditioned diesel train, began running, enabling commuters to reach the capital well ahead of the four-hour steam service from Piccadilly to Euston. Then the latter line was electrified, with a new fleet of blue-and-grey InterCity trains travelling to London in just over two and a half hours, and British Rail deemed Central station superfluous to requirements. When transport minister Barbara Castle announced that the entire station could close provided the services could be accommodated at Piccadilly and Victoria, Central was doomed. Its Manchester to London line closed on 6 March 1967, and Central station shut in May 1969.

By then the station had achieved the awful notoriety of playing a key role in the Moors Murders. On 6 October 1965 Ian Brady picked up seventeen-year-old Edward Evans by the station milk-vending machine, took him home to Hattersley in a car driven by Myra Hindley and axed him to death. A few months later, detectives searching for evidence to link the pair to the disappearance of various local schoolchildren, discovered in a prayer book belonging to Brady a ticket for a left-luggage locker at Central station. There they found suitcases filled with sadistic paraphernalia and tape recordings of the couple torturing 10-year-old Lesley Anne Downey.

In the mid-1980s the disused station was converted into the G-Mex exhibition centre (now Manchester Central).

► Piccadilly station, p. 74.
► the Moors Murders, p. 154.

KNOTT MILL

Knott Mill is a heavily industrialized backwater at the south-west edge of the city centre, lying within a small rectangle bounded by the Bridgewater Viaduct, Whitworth Street West and the River Medlock. Here the warehouses and old mill buildings, smaller than those of Ancoats, are now being carefully restored to house new industries and well-designed apartments. Local legend claims that the name derives from Canute's Mill, a building owned by the pre-Norman king, but it is more likely that the source was John Knott, a late sixteenth-century merchant.

The area was an undeveloped suburb of Victorian Manchester until the railway line connecting Manchester with Altrincham was built in 1849. The new Knott Mill that sprang up was soon bustling with energy and industry, described by an unnamed contemporary commentator as being 'full of noisome courts and alleys, the view from the passing trains dismal and mournful'. Slum clearance took place in 1888 when the station was extended and a new wide thoroughfare, Whitworth Street West, now home to some of Manchester's most popular clubs and bars, was created. On Hewitt Street the iron columns that carry the railway have inspired generations of musicians seeking to capture the brutal reality of industrial Manchester.

Little Peter Street
north side: Deansgate to Albion Street
The Boardwalk (1984–99), No. 21
Manchester's most important venue for showcasing new bands at the end of the twentieth century was based in the former St Peter's school building, a bleak brick barn standing in an area that before the 1980s had been full of engineering firms and workshops buzzing with industrial activity.

Forty years before the Boardwalk became a rock venue the building was used for rehearsals by the Hallé Orchestra, who had been bombed out of the Free Trade Hall. The musicians nicknamed the place 'the Factory' in honour of its industrial setting, a name that coincidentally became central to a different kind of Manchester music thirty years later.

Leading the Hallé at that time was John Barbirolli, the conductor who came from New York to take over a ramshackle group of musicians he tirelessly moulded into Britain's most celebrated orchestra. Barbirolli arrived at Little Peter Street on his first day in a hat made by Borsalino of Rome, who had supplied them to Verdi, and helped the musicians get their heavy instruments to the large top-floor rehearsal room, insufficiently warmed by its measly coal fire, by means of a hoist. When a train from the nearby Manchester–Liverpool line thundered past for the first time Barbirolli beat his baton on the stand three times to stop the musicians. 'What was that?' he moaned. 'It's the free world outside,' came the reply from a trumpeter.

In 1986 Colin Sinclair converted the building into a venue aimed at promoting new bands. Those who took advantage included James, Inspiral Carpets, the Charlatans, Happy Mondays and Oasis, who played their first gig under that name on 18 August 1991. The venue closed in 1999 but reopened for one last night on New Year's Eve 2001. It has now been converted into flats.
► The Hacienda, p. 61.
T J Davidson's Rehearsal Studio, No. 35
Rehearsing in the disused warehouse that then stood on this site in 1978, Joy Division made the quantum leap from being an obscure punk band of little merit to one of the most extraordinary groups in rock history. In the group's early days the critic Paul Morley had described them as 'easily

Unknown pleasures – music in Manchester

Despite having no history of making memorable music Manchester became the most fêted music city in the world towards the end of the twentieth century, acclaimed for its role in nurturing groups such as Buzzcocks, the Fall, Joy Division, New Order, the Smiths and 808 State.

That Manchester would attain such elevated status looked unlikely in the 1960s when the city lived darkly in the long shadow cast thirty-five miles away in Liverpool by the Beatles, and it remained so in the 1970s with Manchester playing little part in prog rock. There was no indication that anything was to change when the Sex Pistols played two chaotic gigs at the Lesser Free Trade Hall in the summer of 1976. Yet out of those two nights came the first stirrings of a revolution that would soon make the city the most important in British music, and power the all-embracing cultural changes that have revived twenty-first-century Manchester.

Present that night were many of those who went on to dominate Manchester music for the next few decades, including Barney Summer (Joy Division, New Order), Mick Hucknall (Simply Red) and Morrissey. Some formed groups, while others set up from scratch a music industry infrastructure of promoters, songwriters, agents, designers, journalists and record-label owners.

The first true Manchester record, produced locally, not in London, about life in the area, was made by the two Bolton students, Howard Trafford and Pete McNeish, who promoted the Pistols' gigs. Renaming themselves Howard Devoto and Pete Shelley they formed their own band, Buzzcocks, and cut a low-budget EP, 'Spiral Scratch'. It revolutionized non-mainstream rock. The four songs sounded like the work of ordinary people concerned about everyday notions such as getting up late, shopping at the supermarket, hanging out with friends. They were catchy, pithy, funny, charming, irreverent and human. There was no whiff of glamour or showbiz escapism, and it had all been done independently of the established music business.

Soon there were more Manchester acts attempting to do the same. Although they were mostly inspired by the fast American garage rock style of the Stooges and MC5, each had its own peculiarly Northern outlook, able to craft well-constructed three-minute singles of surprising resourcefulness. The most interesting of the new groups was the Fall, led by the irascible and irredeemable Mark E. Smith, a mass of unresolvable contradictions and neuroses. An avowed anti-student, he named the group after a cerebral novel by

digestible, doomed maybe to eternal support spots [whose] instinctive energy often compensates for the occasional lameness of their songs'. How, within less than two years, Joy Division had become purveyors of a sound of brutal strength and blistering emotional depth, captured in songs such as 'Dead Souls' and their terrifying first album, 1979's *Unknown Pleasures* (recorded in Stockport), remains a mystery that continues to fascinate critics and music fans.

south side
Sun House, No. 2

One of central Manchester's most inspired recent conversions is an old mill redesigned in the 1990s by Ben Kelly into a *pied-à-terre* for local rock impresario Tony Wilson. Kelly, who was also responsible for the work on the Haçienda nightclub and Dry Bar, incorporated a polished antique floor and shelving made from industrial scaffolding. Wilson based his Factory Too label here briefly in the 1990s, continuing his Dadaist cataloguing system by ascribing serial that student favourite, Albert Camus. A vehement defender of Northern culture, he couched the group's sound in American rockabilly and later hired a dyed-blonde US glamour girl on guitar, Laura 'Brix' Salenger, whom he married. Smith's barbed songs, laden with esoteric, practically indecipherable lyrics and arch humour, were often aimed at unlikely targets – bingo callers, the *Observer* magazine, the naff singer Shakin' Stevens, Winston Churchill – who were wheeled on and slaughtered in turn. Under his tutelage the Fall continue to make records well into the twenty-first century.

With the new groups came new independent record labels, in particular Factory, founded by local TV presenter Tony Wilson. Although the Fall wouldn't join because Factory was based on the 'wrong', i.e. the southern/student, side of the city, nearly all the other talent in Manchester did, particularly Joy Division whose clipped rhythmic sound and apocalyptic textures, bracketing Ian Curtis's stark, expressive imagery, echoed the de-industrialization of the city.

In January 1980 Joy Division were featured on the front cover of *NME*, then the most influential cultural magazine in the country, walking along the southern bridge over the motorway running through bleak, hopeless Hulme. The

choice was apt. Manchester would be responsible for some of the most important music to emerge over the forth-coming decade, and Hulme's attuned population would be at the forefront of pushing it. But only three members of Joy Division would be involved, for Ian Curtis hanged himself a few months later. Remarkably, the remaining members prospered anew as New Order, veering from angst-ridden rock to up-tempo electro disco to *faux-naif* pop, culminating in unlikely fashion in the rousing 1990 England World Cup single 'World in Motion'.

Yet the most lauded Manchester group of the period was none of these but one entrenched in traditional rock ideology rather than the new avant-garde or electro sounds that defined the era. The Smiths were a revelation because they showed it was possible to frame the basic guitar-bass-drums rock format with sophisticated up-to-the-minute production values. Their songs were simultaneously foot-tappingly catchy and twisted with lyrical complexity, a combination perfected by guitarist Johnny Marr and singer/song-writer Morrissey. The Smiths' Manchester was a throwback to the days of Northern music-hall comics and dismally damp streets of brick terraces, set around Morrissey's twin obsessions of kitchen-sink films and the Moors Murders, where

numbers to hats and rucksacks, as well as records. The building now houses offices.
► Factory Records, p. 176.

PARSONAGE

North of Bridge Street the land between the River Irwell and Deansgate gradually shrinks until the two meet. Historically it was owned by the church, which is reflected in names of local streets such as College Land and Parsonage Lane.

Parsonage Gardens

The tiny green of Parsonage Gardens marks the site of St Mary built in 1756 on land given to the Church in the eleventh century and run by clergy from the St Mary's church that is now the cathedral. St Mary closed in 1890, as the congregation had dwindled away when the area became commercialized, and it was later demolished. Early in the twentieth century monolithic textile warehouses – Arkwright House and National Buildings – were built over-looking the site.

every Smiths song seemed to feature a new twist on these themes. It also meant that at last the Manchester music scene had a group to rival the Beatles.

Where the Smiths were a compendium of all that had gone before, 808 State were as technologically advanced as it was possible to be. Even their name came from a computerized drum machine. This was not a group as such but a collective of DJs, rappers, tape experts and computer buffs who melded rhythm, noise, bleeps, bloops, electro beats and lush synthetic orchestration into disarmingly beautiful soundtracks. Typical was 'Pacific State', a sublimely gorgeous mood piece which would have been the perfect theme tune for Manchester's Olympics bid of the time but was ignored in favour of a song performed by the St Winifred's Girls' School Choir.

By the mid-1980s Manchester could look proudly at a roster of acts that were defining the new era in music; at lyricists making up for the city's lack of a poetic history; at a record label whose back catalogue would rival that of Stax or Studio One. It was unlikely that the next wave of groups would be able to exhibit such cleverness and craftiness – and so it proved. The Stone Roses presented a potentially exciting blend of driving rock, psychedelia and dance beats but were lyrically inane, with no manifesto other than

drugs good; Thatcher/the Queen bad. Their debut album, lauded in the press in terms usually devoted to the Beatles' *Revolver*, was mostly empty bluster. Their turn-of-the-decade contemporaries, Happy Mondays, ne'er-do-wells from uninhabitable Little Hulton, wrote sharp songs of base crudeness, played with a funky edge, but suffered from a limited range of ideas and an out-of-tune singer. Both groups soon imploded under the weight of expectations and the greater weight of their ever-increasing drugs bills.

By 1993 it was clear that the Manchester music scene had passed its best days. The Smiths were no more and Morrissey was unreliable; the Fall were too inconsistent and New Order had ground to a halt. There were no new groups emerging with a unique vision as there had been ten years before. The last hurrah of Manchester's music scene came from Burnage's underclass. Oasis were unoriginal in their music, little more than Status Quo souped-up for the E generation, with a roguish image carefully manufactured by the band's PR team. Wallowing in boorishness and imitative attitudes, displaying little purpose other than hedonism, Oasis soon managed to rid Manchester of its reputation for producing literate and original music.

west side
National Buildings/(Century Buildings)
One of a number of huge local Harry S. Fairhurst constructions, National Buildings was built for the National Boiler and Generator Insurance Company in 1905–9 and given a buff terracotta façade typical of the time. It was reworked in the late 1990s as luxury apartments – Century Buildings – with a million-pound penthouse.
south side
Arkwright House
The English Sewing Cotton Company commissioned Harry S. Fairhurst in the 1920s to

design this huge neoclassical Portland stone office block with its gigantic three-storey Corinthian pilasters, naming it in honour of the eighteenth-century cotton-spinning pioneer Richard Arkwright. During the Second World War Arkwright House was the regional government headquarters, used by Winston Churchill when he visited the area.

Southgate
No. 7, rear of House of Fraser
Friedrich Engels, co-author with Karl Marx of *The Communist Manifesto*, worked for the

family's textile firm, Ermen and Engels, at
№. 7 Southgate in the mid-nineteenth
century. Engels first arrived in Manchester
in December 1842, aged twenty-two, to learn
the cotton trade. He left in 1844, but
returned in 1850 to work as a clerk for £100
a year and 10 per cent of the firm's profits.
Engels's father hoped that a spell in industry
would rid his son of his radical leanings.
Instead it reinforced them, for his income
meant he could finance the research work of
Karl Marx, whom he considered to have the
sharper analytical mind.

In Manchester Engels lived the dual life of
fiery socialist thinker and cultured German
merchant. Keen to study what was then the
world's leading industrial city, he spent
much of his time researching working conditions and scouring the streets of the
impoverished areas, guided by an Irish girl,
Mary Burns, with whom he enjoyed a
twenty-year relationship. He wrote for various socialist and radical papers, providing
articles on the Ten-Hour Bill for Robert
Owen's *The New Moral World*. He collected
most of his findings for his own *Condition of
the Working Class in England in 1844*, published at first only in German, and not
available in English for forty years.

But Engels was also a member of the
gentry. He joined the Albert Club, often
entertained what he called the 'Philistines',
who knew nothing of his extra-mural activities, and rode with the Cheshire Hunt.
There he met merchants whose views widely
clashed with his own. Typical was the
businessman who listened patiently as
Engels related the terrible plight of the poor,
only to respond: 'Yet there is a great deal of
money made here. Good morning, sir.'
Engels left Manchester for London in 1870.
► Engels and Marx at Chetham's Library,
p. 95.

PICCADILLY

Piccadilly is the main route for commuters
heading between the city centre and the
main railway station. To the east are streets
mostly filled with Victorian textile warehouses. These are smaller, less ostentatious,
less exclusive than those along Princess
Street or around Parsonage, the Italianate
detail almost absent, as the owners felt
there was little need to impress the type
of clients they were attracting, mostly
individual buyers rather than merchants.

In the eighteenth century the land
between Ancoats Lane (now Great Ancoats
Street) and the daub holes (now Piccadilly
Gardens) was owned by Sir Ashton Lever.
He sold it to a William Stevenson –
remembered in Stevenson Square – who
in turn sold the land plot by plot to individual developers. Some of them live on in
the names of the side streets.

Briefly this was a smart residential area,
but by the 1830s the growth in local industry
meant a heavy cloud of factory smoke made
it uninhabitable as far as those who could
afford to move away were concerned. There
was much small-scale industry as well, and
among the cotton warehouses and workshops were dry-salters, hat-block makers,
cork-cutters, tin-plate workers and clothes-
makers such as Flusheim and Hesse of Back
Piccadilly who in 1845 registered the patent
for a new collar, the following year for an
'Imperial Shirt' and in 1848 for a combination collar and necktie.

The area now accommodates a range of
twenty-first-century businesses and only the
smallest residential population. This is the
shabby, dishevelled and working side of
Manchester, but no less fascinating for
being so.

(i) between Oldham Street and the Rochdale Canal

Lever Street
A handful of remarkable original Georgian
properties remain on Lever Street, a traffic
choked route between Piccadilly and
Ancoats. Nos. 69–77, built in 1787 as work-
shops-cum-dwellings, are three-storey
merchants' houses which sport a short flight
of steps flanked by Tuscan pilaster door-

cases leading up to a main door decorated with fanlights. What makes them special is not just their unlikely survival but that their gardens still contain smaller three-room properties (one up, one down, one basement room), built there a few decades later in the desperation to use every inch of space in this part of Manchester for homes and workshops. They are the only examples of back-to-back houses still standing in the region and can be seen behind Lever Street on Bradley Street.

• Nos. 8–14 Lever Street are grander houses built in a similar Georgian style with doorcases sporting acanthus-leaf capitals and fluted entablature but without the back-to-backs.

Piccadilly

The thoroughfare linking Market Street with Piccadilly Station was Lever's Row until 1812 when it was incongruously given the name of a London location. Shops and large office blocks began to replace the first houses at the end of the nineteenth century. At that time the south side of Piccadilly, at the Market Street end, was still dominated by the biggest building in the area, the Infirmary (now Piccadilly Gardens), which was demolished early in the twentieth century, around the time that the last of the grand office blocks built in the baroque style were being completed further south towards the station.

Making its way along Piccadilly one day in October 1853 was a carriage containing the Liberal statesman Gladstone and the local merchant Robert Philips. A huge crowd had gathered, and as the vehicle turned into Piccadilly a cheer went up. Gladstone immediately put his head out of the window, removed his hat and waved it to the crowd. A moment later the noise abated and a solitary voice piped up: 'Put tha bloody 'ead in. It's Bob Philips we're shouting for.'

L. S. Lowry was asked in 1930 by the director of the City Art Gallery to produce some paintings of Piccadilly, but his work was

rejected and he was told to try again, which he refused to do. Ironically the City now owns a later, locally set Lowry painting, *Piccadilly Gardens* (1954).

▶ Reform Club, p. 58.

west side

Malmaison, north junction with Auburn Street

Mick Hucknall of Simply Red was part of the mid-1990s consortium that bought the disused Joshua Hoyle warehouse, a distinctive 1904 Charles Heathcote building with a brick, terracotta and green ceramic façade. In 1998–9 Darby Associates converted the warehouse into what is now one of Manchester's most popular hotels. To enable the work to proceed the adjacent Imperial Hotel, with its garish red and white painted exterior, where the Professional Footballers Association was founded in 1907, was demolished.

The name Malmaison comes from a château outside Paris bought by Josephine, wife of Napoleon, while he was away at war. When the emperor returned and found she had completed the deal without his permission he was so annoyed he promulgated a law stating that French women could not own property in their own name, a law not rescinded until 1960.

The Rochdale Canal runs underneath the building.

▶ Grand Hotel, p. 98.

east side

Ceylon Tea House, Nos. 7–9

A bizarre-looking 1910 building, designed in the style of an Indian palace, was the Ceylon Tea House during the early twentieth century, and enjoyed a variety of uses until 2002 when it was unexpectedly demolished and the original wood interior, panelling and elaborate decorative mirrors ripped out despite the intervention of the Manchester Civic Society and the Victorian Society. The site had previously been the town house of the Lever family of Alkrington, north Manchester, and had been converted into the White Bear coaching inn, which was itself demolished in 1906 to make way for the tea house.

Stevenson Square

Barely noticeable as a square and now little more than a mini-terminus for buses, Stevenson Square was until the mid-twentieth century a major site for street orators, demonstrations and public gatherings. It was also where locals would rally to learn the latest news in pre-radio days – cheaper and easier than buying a newspaper.

On 2 June 1841 a vicious battle took place in Stevenson Square between Chartists and anti-Corn Law campaigners. The Chartists, mostly working-class supporters of changes in the voting system, attacked the anti-Corn Law brigade for being middle-class dilettantes. But the latter were well prepared. They had hired a band of Irish toughs known bizarrely as 'the Lambs' and beat off the Chartists.

Two thousand people turned up in Stevenson Square on 16 October 1905 to cheer on suffragette Annie Kenney, who had just been released from prison after disrupting a Liberal Party meeting at the Free Trade Hall to promote votes for women. In 1911 a wave of strikes in Manchester in favour of increased pay led to a number of rallies being held at Stevenson Square. Speakers included Harry Pollitt, founder of the Communist Party of Great Britain, who saw himself surrounded by 'men for years underfed and underclothed living in hovels, having no chance to obtain normal physical fitness'.

On 8 August 1920 5,000 demonstrators crammed into the square to denounce government involvement in the attacks on Soviet Russia three years after the Bolshevik revolution. The speakers were led by Ellen Wilkinson, who later became a Labour cabinet minister and pushed the hire purchase law through Parliament. There were boos whenever the name Winston Churchill, then secretary for war, was mentioned. But not all the rallies held here were left wing. In the 1930s William Joyce, who went on to disseminate propaganda from Germany during the Second World War as 'Lord Haw-Haw', spoke for the British Union of Fascists.

In Howard Spring's 1940 novel *Fame Is the Spur*, Stevenson Square is where the hero, Hamer Shawcross, has his politics shaped at the end of the nineteenth century by the sight of hundreds of people waiting for the soup lorry, 'overwhelmed by [poverty], crushed, hopeless, utterly defeated'.

The square declined as a major Mancunian meeting place along with the demise of adjacent Oldham Street in the 1970s.

(ii) between the Rochdale Canal and the River Medlock

Here the lively office hours territory near Oldham Street gives way to an eerily quiet land of depots and small industrial estates at the back of Piccadilly station.

Berry Street

Berry Street, obscure and barely noticeable, is the home of the Davenports, poor cellar-dwellers, in Elizabeth Gaskell's 1848 novel *Mary Barton: A Tale of Manchester Life*:

> Berry Street was unpaved; and down the middle a gutter forced its way, every now and then forming pools in the holes with which the street abounded. Never was the old Edinburgh cry of 'Gardez l'eau!' more necessary than in the street. As they passed, women from their doors tossed household slops of every description into the gutter; they ran into the next pool, which over-flowed and stagnated.

Binns Place
Brownsfield Mill

Alliott Verdon Roe founded the world's first aeroplane manufacturing company – Avro – on 1 January 1910 in Brownsfield Mill, a seven-storey 1825 building off Great Ancoats Street. Seven years previously at Kitty Hawk in America, Orville Wright had made the first ascent in an aeroplane. In 1907 Verdon Roe had written to *The Times* bemoaning the British authorities' lack of interest in motor-driven aircraft, and had received a reply from the engineering editor explaining that all attempts at 'artificial aviation' were doomed to failure. However, a year later Samuel Franklin Cody made the first sustained powered flight in an aircraft in Britain (from London).

At first Verdon Roe received few orders, for most planes were built in France, so to stay buoyant the company specialized in making flying accessories. In 1912 Avro made the first plane with an enclosed cockpit, and as tests for new aircraft had to be conducted in the countryside he took the plane to the nearby London Road railway terminus (now Piccadilly) on a horse-drawn cart, the wings folded, a bizarre clash of medieval- and modern-age transport.

In 1914 Avro moved to a new site a mile north-west in Miles Platting, where it was soon involved in making bombers for the Allies' war effort. Ten years later the remains of a triplane were discovered in the attic at Brownsfield Mill and donated to the Science Museum.

▶ Aviation sites of Manchester, p. 178.

Ducie Street
The Place
Manchester's best surviving example of an early railway outhouse is a starkly beautiful, decoration-free, seven-storey brick block of 1867, built around a skeleton of cast-iron columns. It was originally joined to the station by a track that ran over Store Street, and to the Ashton Canal by a side arm of the waterway. Abandoned in the mid-twentieth century, the building became a car park, but has recently been converted into a hotel, The Place.

▶ Great Northern Railway Company's Goods Warehouse, p. 65.

London Road
The main road heading south from Piccadilly towards Ardwick is no longer a central part of Manchester life, having been mostly cleared in recent decades of all but the biggest office blocks.

In early Victorian times London Road was a lively place. Angus Bethune Reach,

writing in the *Morning Chronicle* in 1849, noted that while

> looking for the Apollo music saloon on London Road one Saturday night, itinerant bands blow and bang their loudest; organ boys grind monotonously; ballad singers or flying stationers make bold proclamations of their wares. The street is one swarming mass of people. Boys or girls shout and laugh and disappear into the taverns together . . . From the byways and the alleys and back streets fresh crowds every moment emerge.

Trouble broke out here at a well-attended demonstration against unemployment on 7 October 1931. When the crowd arrived at the junction of London Road and Whitworth Street, they found a triple row of police barring their way. The marchers at the front sat down, as did those grouped behind for 200 yards back, and there was a stand-off for fifteen minutes before the policemen drew their batons and charged. Hoses from the nearby fire station were turned on the marchers. Fighting broke out and several people were injured but there were no deaths.

Early in the twenty-first century the last remaining Victorian cottages on London Road facing Piccadilly station, which included a cosy pub and antiquated curry house, were wiped away to build speculative office blocks.

London Road fire station
Abandoned in the 1980s and still forlorn-looking at the start of the twenty-first century, the ornate terracotta London Road fire station is an Edwardian marvel, designed by the firm of Woodhouse, Willoughby & Langham, who formed solely to create the building and dissolved the partnership immediately afterwards.

The fire station was ingeniously planned. It contained working and living quarters for forty firemen, policemen and their families, and had its own library, stables, bank and gymnasium. To prevent noxious smells from the stables annoying the tenants, a sophisticated ventilation system was installed, whereby fresh air was drawn in through the main bell tower (cleverly disguised as an Italianate campanile) and pumped around the complex as foul air was expelled through the pillars of the stalls. Reports of fires were relayed to the station's marble and wood control centre from 200 Gamewell fire-alarm boxes spread throughout the city in what was then the largest fire-alarm network in Britain, used until 1959. The building's prominent position near Piccadilly station and its listed status have ensured it remains protected.

► More Edwardian terracotta buildings: St George's House, p. 28; Tootal, p. 18.

Piccadilly Station Approach

The slope from Ducie Street to the station is dominated by Gateway House, a huge serpentine office block of curtain wall-glass panels nicknamed 'the lazy S', which replaced railway warehouses. It was designed in the mid-1960s from a doodle drawn on a menu by Richard Seifert, Britain's leading architect of large-scale state-sanctioned projects, whom the government commissioned during the Cold War to construct blocks for secret strategic use. Gateway House has for many years housed the regional health authority, and is one of the main Manchester sites that would have been used as a regional HQ in the event of war.

Piccadilly station

Now Manchester's major terminus, the station was originally Store Street in 1842. Trains were soon running to London, a journey that revolutionized travelling for northerners. Instead of a twenty-four-hour stagecoach trip with an overnight stop, passengers could now take a nine-and-a-half-hour train journey. Soon there were 35,000 people a week using the route, with those going by coach down to 3,600.

Due to the hilly nature of the land by Piccadilly the station had to be built on high ground. Trains were thus spared the climb of a nasty gradient, while passengers were left to negotiate the slope from the centre of

town. In 1860 Store Street was renamed London Road, and by 1884 the journey to London was down to four and a quarter hours. Until use of the telephone became widespread, the station was often the first point in Manchester at which news arrived. For instance, during the Boer War at the end of the nineteenth century, a bulk of *Daily Mail*s put on the train at Marylebone by Alfred Harmsworth, the main newspaper baron of the period, provided eager Mancunians with their first news of the important battles of the conflict.

When John Barbirolli arrived at London Road on 2 June 1943 to take over the Hallé, he was met by a contingent of officials from the orchestra who whisked him away from the station doors by taxi 'so that I should see as little as possible of the city and [not] be dissuaded from taking up the post', he later mused.

When the lines were electrified and the station rebuilt as Piccadilly in 1966, the journey was cut to two hours and thirty-five minutes. Further improvements in the travelling time – if not the quality of the trains – have brought it down to just over two hours on some journeys.

The cast-iron and glass train shed of 1880 surrounding Platforms 1–12 survives but few of the once vast selection of goods buildings remain.

RIDGEFIELD

The narrow sloping streets west of Albert Square, such as Lloyd Street and Jackson's Row, built on land once owned by the Ridge family, are full of charm and character. They are also home to a number of small eighteenth-century pubs such as the Sir Ralph Abercrombie on Bootle Street, used as a makeshift mortuary after the 1819 Peterloo Massacre.

Bootle Street

The street has long enjoyed the nickname 'Brutal Street' on account of the tactics occasionally deployed by police stationed here at the force's Central Manchester headquarters.

north side

Police station

Brendan Behan, the writer and Irish nationalist, spent a night inside the police station in 1939 after entering Britain illegally. He had been banned from the country under the Prevention of Violence Act after shooting at three policemen, but having been released in an amnesty came to Manchester at the invitation of the local IRA cell, thereby reneging on the deal. In Manchester Behan was arrested by Robert Mark, then a detective constable in the Special Branch, who went on to become Commissioner of the Metropolitan Police. In court Behan had an extra four months added to his jail sentence, despite, or perhaps because of, the pleas of his lawyer who kept referring to the writer as a 'love choild of the Oirish revolution'.

The following year Robert Mark brought to the station Ernando Landucci, an Italian waiter arrested after Italy joined the Second World War because of prime minister Winston Churchill's edict that all Italian-born men in Britain should be detained. On being arrested at his home Landucci burst into tears and explained to Mark that he belonged to the Manchester branch of the Fascist party only because, as the owner of a small patch of land in southern Italy, he would find it impossible to deal with the authorities otherwise. Before leading him away from his house Mark allowed the waiter to open a bottle of wine and drink the toast 'Bugger the Fascio!' Landucci, like scores of his countrymen, was interned on the Isle of Man before being deported to Canada on the ship *Arandora Star*. At sea in the Atlantic a few days later the vessel was torpedoed by the Nazis, despite flying the swastika for protection, and nearly all lives, including that of Landucci, were lost.

During the 1960s the station's police liked to flex their muscles by dropping into Manchester's clubs to make drugs busts, especi-

ally if there happened to be a newsworthy musician in the crowd. One night in January 1967 they picked up Jimi Hendrix in the Twisted Wheel on Whitworth Street, hauled him into a van, and when they arrived at Bootle Street threw him against the railings to conduct a humiliating search.

The station was caught up in considerable controversy in the mid-1980s when a Manchester University student, Steven Shaw, claimed he had been assaulted by Bootle Street officers after being caught up in the demonstration against the visit of the Conservative home secretary, Leon Brittan, to the students' union.

► Manchester's IRA HQ, p. 135.

south side

Slack Alice/42nd Street, No. 2a

George Best took over what was the Costa Del Sol nightclub in 1972 and revamped it as Slack Alice, named after an imaginary character in Larry Grayson's television show. Despite the presence of the nearby police station, at a time when the force was keen to crack down on Manchester's nightlife, the venue was a success. Showbiz figures such as Jimmy Tarbuck, Bruce Forsyth and Dave Allen visited, and Best himself would patrol the queue, inviting inside those women he considered to be the most attractive.

In his history of the local music scene, *Manchester England*, Dave Haslam recounts the story of a man who took a girl with him one night to Slack Alice's and was personally invited in by Best. The three of them spent the evening chatting over the champagne and at the end the man left alone, the girl staying on with her host. Haslam asked the spurned boyfriend if he had minded being cuckolded so publicly. 'Not at all,' came back the reply, 'it was Bestie. It was an honour.' The venue later became 42nd Street.

Brazennose Street

Post-war plans to create a grand, tree-lined Processional Way through Brazennose Street, from the Town Hall to Deansgate and

Metrolink

Remarkably, for a city of its size, Manchester has no underground railway system. Instead it is partly served by Metrolink, tram-trains that run on three lines into the city centre. During the early twentieth-century tube boom in London there was much discussion locally about building an underground system. A group of influential Mancunians petitioned the government for a Manchester tube, and it was announced that a circle line would be built connecting the main termini of London Road (now Piccadilly), Oxford Road, Central, Exchange and Victoria. The scheme never got past the drawing-board stage, and although it was revived in 1912 it was soon shelved again because of the Great War.

In the 1920s the Manchester Corporation set up an Underground Railway Special Committee to look into a system that would link the suburbs in the south (around Stretford) with those of the north (around Prestwich). By 1928 this had been extended – on paper only – to thirty-five miles of track, including an inner and outer circle. This time the work was impeded by cost and bureaucracy, and it was abandoned when the Second World War started.

Another revival of the Manchester underground idea came in the 1960s, under the name the Pic-Vic line, its main purpose being to link the two termini of Piccadilly and Victoria. Scheduled to be built in the 1970s and open in 1978, it was shelved in 1976, when the government asked the local transport committee to look for a cheaper alternative. It was another lost opportunity.

Of the legion of unbuilt underground schemes mooted for Manchester the most inspired was the simplest: two tunnels, one from Salford station to Piccadilly, the other from Oxford Road to Victoria, crossing at a new station at the Royal Exchange. This would have allowed suburban trains using the various lines around the region to make journeys across central Manchester in a manner that is still impossible.

The one scheme that *was* implemented was the one that had been most denigrated by the experts and enthusiasts: Metrolink. At the end of the 1980s two popular suburban rail routes – Altrincham–Manchester and Bury–Victoria – were converted for new vehicles – part train, part tram – that ran on the old railway lines in the suburbs and in the city centre took new street-level tracks to Piccadilly. Bury–Altrincham Metrolink (via Piccadilly) opened in 1992. A third line from Piccadilly to Eccles later joined the network. But Metrolink has proved not to be the long-awaited solution to Manchester's incessant rail transport problems. It does little that wasn't previously available other than allow suburban rail passengers to arrive slightly nearer their city-centre destination. It has failed to link up the various suburban rail lines and to provide

beyond, finishing at a new Crown Square, were abandoned in the 1960s.

Twisted Wheel (1963–5), No. 26
Legendary among Manchester's legion of 1960s beat clubs was the Twisted Wheel where locals first heard the new black music that was then barely played on the radio – acts such as James Brown, Curtis Mayfield and Otis Redding. The venue had been a coffee bar, the Left Wing, where CND members met and danced to the house band Dean West and the Hellions, who later became Herman's Hermits. In 1963 it was renamed the Twisted Wheel, and at the opening night the Graham Bond Quartet and the Spencer Davis Group played till dawn. The club moved to Whitworth Street in 1965.
▶ Twisted Wheel on Whitworth Street, p. 42.

John Dalton Street

Driven through the slums as part of the street improvements of 1844, the street is named after the great scientist who discovered the nature of the atom in his rail transport for the huge swathes of south Manchester that have no railway. The only new track runs through obscure parts of Docklands, and even there the stops are far from the main busy areas, such as the Lowry Centre, and there is no service to the Trafford Centre. The vehicles are considerably smaller than the trains that preceded them, so that large numbers of commuters who would like to use Metrolink instead of their cars, particularly on match days, are discouraged from doing so. The trams are far too infrequent to be of practical use; they pale in comparison with the driverless vehicles of the Docklands Light Railway; fares are payable by machine only, which discriminates against the law-abiding majority in favour of the petty criminal; there are no tickets linked with the bus and rail networks; no smartcard as with London's Oyster; the station buildings have been abandoned and now look like slums awaiting demolition, a sight guaranteed to dissuade visitors to the city from returning; and there are few information boards announcing the time of the next tram. Consequently successive governments have been reluctant to support more extensions to the system and in the first decade of the twenty-first century the city was still waiting for a new link to the Trafford Centre and to the sports stadiums of east Manchester.

George Street, Manchester, laboratory in the first decade of the nineteenth century. William Morris opened a Manchester branch of his design outfit, the Firm – 'cabinet makers, upholsterers and general house furnishers' – at 34 John Dalton Street in 1883. A year later the shop moved to nearby Albert Square, but it closed down soon after as there was not enough interest in Manchester for Morris's florid designs.
► John Dalton's experiments, p. 54.

Manchester Academy of Fine Arts (early twentieth century), No. 16
Founded in 1859 on Brazenose Street following the highly successful Art Treasures exhibition in Old Trafford, the academy moved into Edward Salomons's Prince Chambers, built as furniture showrooms, in the early years of the twentieth century.

By this time the academy was in the doldrums, many of its best practitioners having moved to London, and when members debated whether only professional artists – no weekend enthusiasts – should be allowed to join there was an outcry. Eventually a compromise was reached: no white frames could be used. These new rules meant that Manchester's greatest amateur painter – L. S. Lowry – could now apply.

Lowry was accepted into the life class, but found it depressing compared to the classes he had attended at the Manchester School of Art in All Saints. And not all his fellow students were impressed with him. One of them, Bert Wilson, later explained how Lowry 'was lousy, he couldn't draw and we all used to laugh at him because he was so bad'.

As a member of the Academy Lowry now had the right to exhibit his paintings in the annual exhibition at Manchester City Art Gallery. He first took part in 1919 when his first name was misspelled as 'Lawrence'. On another occasion his surname was wrongly written as 'Lowrey', a mistake which, farcically, continued on the gallery's postcards until the 1980s. Lowry failed to sell any of his work at first but his *Portrait of an Old Woman* from the 1919 show, which displayed a 15 guineas price tag that enticed no one, now hangs in the Manchester Art Gallery.
► Lowry the rent collector, p. 56.

Mount Street
Looking north from Peter Street, one of the most striking architectural views in Manchester comes into play: the spire of the Town Hall, the gable of the post-Gothic Town Hall extension and the dome of the

classical revival Central Library set together. In 1894 a Gothic triumphal arch was erected at Mount Street's junction with Albert Square to greet Queen Victoria who had come to Manchester to officially open the Ship Canal. The processional route took her from London Road (Piccadilly) station to No. 1 Dock.

Friends Meeting House

Behind Richard Lane's Ionic façade, based on the Temple of Ilissus, is a Quaker meeting hall built from 1828–30 on the site of a building where those fleeing from the Yeomanry at Peterloo in August 1819 took shelter. Richard Lane was the main instigator of classical-style public buildings in late Georgian Manchester even though he once claimed that 'Manchester afforded little scope or encouragement for architectural display.' His other buildings include Chorlton-on-Medlock Town Hall, the façade of which remains; the former church of St George's by Chester Road roundabout; and the demolished Infirmary in Piccadilly Gardens. Past congregations have included the pioneering atomic scientist John Dalton; John Edward Taylor, founder of the *Manchester Guardian*; and the Town Hall architect, Alfred Waterhouse.

Mulberry Street
St Mary (The Hidden Gem)

Central Manchester's only Catholic church, built in 1794 to cater for local Irish immigrants, was the first erected in England since the Reformation. It acquired its popular name, 'the Hidden Gem', when Herbert Vaughan, Bishop of Salford, stated after a visit: 'No matter on what side you look, you behold a hidden gem.' In 1835 the roof collapsed, having been badly built by volunteers hired by the local parish priest, Father Henry Gillow. Its replacement, with its odd Spanish and Byzantine features, aroused fury in the great Catholic architect A. W. N. Pugin, who raged: 'it shows to what depths of error even good men fall when they abandon the true thing and go whoring after strange styles'. St Mary still

has one of the largest congregations in the north-west. Prints of L. S. Lowry's 1962 charcoal and chalk drawing of the church are sold inside.
▶ First Church of Christ Scientist, p. 173.

ST ANN'S

The intimate streets surrounding the eighteenth-century sandstone church of St Ann showcase Manchester at its best. Here can be found stylish shops adorned with the lavish architectural effects of the nineteenth century – much decorative brick, plaster, half-timbering and cast iron – and an enticing medieval passageway that takes the inquisitive from the back of the church, past King Street, Manchester's most attractive shopping avenue, towards John Dalton Street under three giant umbrellas which mock Dalton, the great Georgian scientist, who was never without shield from the rain.

Barton Square
Barton Arcade

A fine-looking, three-storey, cast-iron and glass Victorian shopping centre fills the land between Barton Square and Deansgate. Designed in the 1870s by the firm of Corbett, Raby and Sawyer, with the success of the original Crystal Palace in mind, Barton Arcade stands as one of the earliest examples of factory-built architecture. The Macfarlane Saracen Glass works in Glasgow produced the parts on site and shipped them to Manchester. Although many of the original shop fronts no longer remain, the interior layout is untouched.
▶ Arndale Centre, p. 11.

King Street, see also Financial District, p. 57
West of Cross Street, King Street contains Manchester's most exclusive stretch of shops, housed in antiquated buildings sporting effects such as the mock Tudor half-timbering at Nos. 15–17, which dates back only to 1902; a rare Georgian survival, built 1736, at No. 35; and ironwork arcades at Nos. 28 and 52. The popularity of King

Street suggests that the council's choice of regularly obliterating old Manchester in favour of characterless modern buildings has been misguided.

north side

The sign 'Old Exchange' halfway between Deansgate and Cross Street refers to the long gone Georgian assembly rooms established by Lady Ann Bland, founder of St Ann's church, which provided temporary accommodation for the Cotton Exchange around 1800.

Nos. 35–37

The oldest surviving property on King Street dates from 1736. It became a bank in 1788 and is of interest not for its architectural qualities – it is typical of the period, rather than unusual – but for its very existence: it is the only remaining Georgian house in Manchester with a central block and wings. There are steps leading up to the pedimented entrance flanked by stone walls and, rare for the city, iron railings. The ground floor is now a shop.

► Georgian 'back-to-back' houses on Lever Street, p. 70.

south side

No. 52

The Fall played their first gig on 23 May 1977 in the unlikeliest of locations, the basement café of the North-West Arts office on King Street. The audience consisted mostly of musicians from the Manchester Musicians' Collective, a body organized by Hallé percussionist Dick Witts which included Buzzcocks' Howard Devoto. Witts later remembered the venue as being like a 'fashionable restaurant with everything white. It was done out like a small white cave.' Mark E. Smith, the Fall's leader and vocalist, was uncompromising and visceral from the beginning, according to the Fall's guitarist, Martin Bramah. 'He just let fly with such venom. I remember he just sort of reached into the audience and virtually poked his finger up Devoto's nose.' Unusually for a new group the Fall's set contained all original material – no cover versions – which included agitprop rants

such as 'Hey Fascist' and 'Race Hatred'. They ended the evening with the two-chord dirge 'Repetition'.

► Morrissey meets Marr, p. 186.

St Ann's Square

Manchester's smartest square postdates the church of the same name and was built on the site of Acresfield, where an annual fair was held from 1222. When in 1823 complaints from shopkeepers about pigs and cows invading their premises became too numerous to ignore, the fair moved to Campfield, before being abolished in 1876.

On 28 December 1745 Charles Edward Stuart, the Young Pretender (Bonnie Prince Charlie), and his troops arrived at St Ann's Square looking to gain support for his bid to take the throne back for the Catholic Stuarts. Mancunians had been expecting their arrival for three weeks, and a crowd, spurred on by the promise of £5 each and a cockade they could wear in their hats in return for their support, cheered on the Jacobites, who in turn celebrated as if they had 'captured' the town. As news of Charles's arrival spread around Manchester Peter Mainwaring, a local JP and monarchist, ordered the town bellman to visit the homes of leading local figures, urging them to arm themselves with guns, swords and shovels to beat off the Jacobites.

Not everyone was hostile to the Pretender. One of those who came to St Ann's Square to greet the party was Elizabeth Byrom, daughter of the local poet and scholar John, who kissed the Pretender's hand. Byrom himself stayed at home. He had already incurred the wrath of the authorities on account of his support of the Jacobite cause and chose not to be caught in another controversy. Instead he wrote a notable epigram about the events which ran:

'God bless the King! I mean our faith's
    defender
God Bless – no harm in blessing – the
    Pretender!'
But who pretender is, or who is King,
God bless us all, that's quite another thing.

After the defeat of the Pretender's forces at Culloden there were reprisals against two local Jacobite leaders, Thomas Syddall, adjutant of the Manchester Regiment, and Thomas Deacon. They were executed in London, where their bodies were pickled in spirits before being sent back to Manchester so that the heads could be exhibited outside the Exchange. Four years later the skulls were removed by an eighteen-year-old medical student, Edward Hall, who buried them in his own garden.

Robert Owen, who became the main influence on the mid-nineteenth-century cooperative movement (p. 82), came to Manchester in 1779 to work in a St Ann's Square draper's shop. On 4 June 1792 a large crowd celebrating George III's birthday in St Ann's Square took support for the monarchy too zealously and became so intoxicated that they attacked two Dissenting chapels and any radicals they could find on the streets. News of the battle of Waterloo first reached Manchester at St Ann's Square in 1815, only eighteen hours after the victory. Around this time Manchester's first hackney coaches took people from this starting-point.

In December 1832 the square was the setting for the hustings for Manchester's first parliamentary elections, the town having had no MPs to represent it since 1660. Ballot was by a show of hands, not the secret vote of today, and Mark Philips and Charles Poulett Thompson were elected for the Liberals. By that time the square was home to Manchester's most fashionable shops, such as Miss Faulder's milliner's and dressmaker's.

In 1880 a St Ann's Square surgeon, Mr Mudd, was called out to a murder victim, Sarah Jane Roberts, to check whether the image of her murderer might have been captured on her retina. Mudd was taken to the body of the dead woman, peered at her eyes, but could find nothing of interest.

Mostly residential in the eighteenth century, St Ann's Square became commercialized in Victorian times and has remained one of Manchester's most elegant addresses.

clockwise from the north
Royal Exchange
See Cross Street, p. 5.
Old Bank Chambers, corner Old Bank Street/St Ann's Square
Manchester Liners, a local shipping company, occupied these offices, now a branch of Barclays Bank, for much of the twentieth century. That a city thirty-five miles inland had its own shipping line was thanks to the construction of the Manchester Ship Canal, which had made Manchester a port in the 1890s. Manchester Liners was formed that decade by Sir Christopher Furness, who had started up the Furness Withy line that sailed between Manchester and Montreal, and whose vessels regularly crossed to the ports of eastern Canada and the eastern seaboard of the USA.

The company moved to this city-centre location in 1921, and three years later became agents for a service linking Manchester to Vancouver via the Panama Canal. Before the St Lawrence Seaway opened in 1959 Manchester Liners ran a service to the Canadian Great Lakes, where its flag became ubiquitous. The company was buoyant enough in the 1960s to build stylish new headquarters in the docks area but containerization of goods around that time saw it leave Manchester, first for Ellesmere Port, then Liverpool. The last Manchester Liners vessel was sold in 1985 after which the company lost its Mancunian identity and became part of the Orient Overseas Container Line.
▶ Manchester Ship Canal, p. 105.
Royal Bank of Scotland, corner St Ann's Square/St Ann Street
One of Manchester's most elegant *palazzo* buildings, featuring a rusticated ground floor with arched pedimented windows, was built in 1848 by J. E. Gregan for Benjamin Heywood's bank. Adjacent, on St Ann Street, is the original manager's house in stripped down *palazzo* form, linked to the main block by a single-storey entrance.
▶ The Athenaeum, p. 40.

St Ann, south side

Built in 1709 on the site of a medieval fair by an unknown architect in the Christopher Wren style, the red sandstone massing of St Ann's church is the most picturesque feature in an area full of baroque office blocks. The church was named after both the mother of the Virgin Mary and Lady Ann Bland, then Lady of the manor of Manchester, who became its patron, and is the only survivor of nineteen churches built in central Manchester in the eighteenth century. Originally the tower, which is considered to be the exact centre of the city, featured a three-tier cupola, but this was replaced with a spire in 1777, which in turn was removed in 1800.

St Ann was run from its earliest days by those who considered themselves Low Church, free of quasi-Catholic rituals. They were also Whigs and supported the new Hanoverian kings in opposition to the clergy at St Mary's (now the cathedral) who were High Church, conservative and backed the Stuart line of succession. This explains why the grave here of Thomas Deacon, an eighteenth-century bishop of the so-called 'True British Catholic Church', describes him as 'the greatest of sinners and the most unworthy of primitive bishops'.

St Ann remained a society church, the best pews costing more than £100, throughout the eighteenth century. During the Victorian era the local population diminished in number as the area became commercialized. Nevertheless the church survived, probably because of the wealth of its congregation. Today it provides lunchtime services and recitals.
► Manchester Cathedral, p. 91.

No. 4, west side

This was the early twentieth-century office of the renowned architect Joseph Sunlight who came to work in St Ann's Square in 1907 when he was eighteen, and within three years was buying land, and planning and building estates such as the one in Prestwich where he erected 1,000 houses. One of his later works, the synagogue on Wilbraham Road, Fallowfield, was inspired not by Jewish religious buildings but by the church of St Sophia in Istanbul.
► Sunlight House, p. 47.

SHUDEHILL

To the north of the Arndale Centre, between Withy Grove and Miller Street, the streets are filled with dingy warehouses and venomous-looking oxblood brick factories that once served as jewellers' and watchmakers' premises, small workshops making boots, shoes, hats and what was known as 'Manchester smallwares' – braids and ribbons – and offices for produce merchants handling cheese, sugar, butter and eggs.

In an attempt to wipe out the shabbiness brought about by two centuries of commercialism the authorities began mass demolition at the end of the twentieth century. Consequently, what was once one of Manchester's main clothes-making areas is losing its character. Gone, for instance, is the premises where Joseph Mandleberg manufactured clothes stamped FFO ('free from odour') as opposed to the waterproof garments made by rivals which exuded an unpleasant whiff. Also demolished recently was the warehouse on Bradshaw Street that contained the Beach Club, mentioned by New Order in 'Blue Monday'. Between Corporation Street and Dantzic Street the land is dominated by a large collection of buildings housing various branches of the cooperative movement.

Balloon Street

In May 1785 James Sadler, an Oxford man, made three trips in a balloon from the garden of the Manchester Arms pub, a site now covered by Balloon Street, to the amazement of Mancunians. Sadler made his first ascent two years after the Montgolfier brothers had sent up a balloon in Paris containing a sheep, a cockerel and a duck. And it was almost 100 years after Moses Cocker, a Bolton farmer, leapt from the roof

Robert Owen and the cooperative movement

At the Corporation Street end of Balloon Street, at the edge of the estate of office blocks run by various wings of the cooperative movement, a statue of Robert Owen pays tribute to the cotton merchant whose philanthropic ideas of how workers should be treated inspired the movement.

Owen, who came to Manchester to work as a draper's assistant on St Ann's Square in 1779, gradually developed an ideal of society based on mutual cooperation and brotherhood rather than the pursuit of selfish interests. Many of Owen's views were utopian. For instance, he advocated monetary reform which he believed would 'put an end to unemployment and depressions', and felt that the existing system of money should be 'replaced by money representing units of labour time and issued freely concomitant with the production of goods'. He was also a passionate opponent of religion,

believing all religions to be 'based on the same absurd imagination' that made mankind 'a weak, imbecile animal; a furious bigot and fanatic; or a miserable hypocrite'.

Owen put his ideas into practice at his cotton mills in Lanark, Scotland, where he raised wages, shortened hours, improved housing and social conditions, and even refused to employ very young children, unlike other mill owners, instead opening facilities to educate them. He set up a cooperative shop which sold high-quality goods at a reasonable price but he was keener on 'villages of cooperation', where he believed the absence of competition and capitalism would lead to a classless society. Nevertheless such ventures in Orbiston in Scotland and Indiana, America, where workers tried to raise their income by growing their own food, making their own clothes and becoming self-governing, were not so successful, and it was the cooperative societies, particularly the one famously founded in Rochdale in 1833, that took up the cooperative cause.

of his barn using home-made wings and landed on the ground a few seconds later despite being buoyed by an unshakeable belief in his own aeronautical prowess.

The owners of the garden Sadler used charged 3s for a close-up look of the take-off and attracted 5,000 people who paid for the privilege of witnessing Sadler's attempts to fly above Manchester. He stayed afloat for nearly two hours – regulating the hydrogen in the balloon by means of a contraption that allowed iron filings to drop into a vat of sulphuric acid – before coming down near Bury. Sadler fell in a heap of manure and walked off with only minor injuries.

He went up a second time, also from the Manchester Arms, a week later. This journey was more dramatic. He rose 13,000 feet and travelled some fifty miles north-east to Pontefract in Yorkshire, but was dragged for two miles after landing and was badly injured.

Cannon Street

Named after the upturned cannons used to stop carts breaking up the pavement, the street was lined with cotton warehouses from the earliest days of Manchester's textile industry. It was here that Sam Bamford, the Middleton radical scapegoated at Peterloo, was a warehouse assistant in the late eighteenth century, his job being to carry batches of cloth on his shoulders, twenty pieces at a time, up to the first floor. Bamford was particularly wary of the buyers spotting him, for they would practically tear the pieces off his back in their desperation for the best items.

In 1938 the Corporation announced plans to upgrade Cannon Street into Manchester's version of Regent Street. It would 'rival London's magnificent street in dignity and uniformity, in architectural design and general lay-out', the Town Hall explained. Old warehouses were bought up and

Mules, jennies and water-frames – the machinery of Cottonopolis

The mechanical inventions of the late eighteenth century, many of which took place in the North-west, revolutionized the cotton industry which had relied on slow hand-spinning as the number of cotton-spinning spindles in Lancashire increased from 1.7 million in the 1780s to 4.5 million by 1812. The oldest surviving local mills of this crucial stage in industrialization are Murray's Mills (p. 148), opened in Ancoats in 1798.

● 1733, **John Kay** patents the flying shuttle
Handloom weaving had traditionally been carried out by passing the yarn slowly from one hand to the other. In 1733 John Kay, who came from Bury, five miles north of Manchester, devised a mechanical way of distributing the yarn which dramatically increased the speed of this process. The flying shuttle, as he called it, saved the weaver much time and effort, but was not used by local cotton weavers until around 1760, when Kay's son, Robert, improved the machinery with his drop-box.

● 1764, **James Hargreaves** invents the spinning jenny
Hargreaves was a Blackburn-based weaver who developed the idea for a new machine when his daughter, Jenny, accidentally knocked over the family spinning wheel and he noticed how the spindle continued to revolve. Hargreaves came up with the idea of a line of spindles that could be worked off one wheel: the spinning jenny. At first he produced the machine only for family use, but when he began to sell the machines local spinners, fearing the loss of their craft, gathered at Blackburn's Market Cross and marched to his house nearby where they smashed the frames of twenty machines. One of the rioters even placed a hammer in Hargreaves's hands and forced him to destroy his own machine. By the time Hargreaves died in 1778 over

20,000 spinning jennies were in use in Britain.

● 1769, **Richard Arkwright** develops the water-frame
Richard Arkwright, considered by many the world's first great industrialist, began as a Bolton barber and while travelling the North-west buying up hair to use in his wigs heard about the race to build the perfect spinning machine. In a Warrington tavern he plied the clockmaker and inventor John Kay with drink and persuaded him to build him two models of a spinning-jenny-style machine that may have predated Hargreaves's brainchild (see above). This became the Arkwright water-frame, a machine that used rollers to spin at increasingly faster speeds. Arkwright moved to Preston and then Nottingham to avoid the Lancashire machine-breakers, and in 1771 opened the world's first water-powered cotton-spinning mill at Cromford in Derbyshire where he developed the modern factory system. From then on the industry would no longer be family run, located in small cottages, but take place in big buildings – factories – that could house a large number of machines.

● 1779, **Samuel Crompton** invents the spinning mule
Crompton was a mill worker who, frustrated at how the spinning jenny kept breaking the thread, designed a new wooden machine at his Bolton home (now Hall i'th'wood Museum) that combined the best features of the jenny and Arkwright's water-frame. He called the crossbred machine the spinning mule, and it enabled him to produce a fine and even thread suitable to spin yarns for making muslin. The invention fired up local hand-spinners, who went on the rampage breaking the machines wherever they found them. Crompton was forced to dismantle his machine and hide the various parts in the attic until the trouble subsided.

destroyed, those lost including Cheeryble House, once the headquarters of the Grant Brothers, merchants on whom Dickens based the Cheeryble Brothers in *Nicholas Nickleby*. By the 1970s Cannon Street had indeed been transformed – into a cavernous bus route between two wings of the Arndale Centre. At the beginning of the twenty-first century the council wiped out the street to extend the Arndale.

Garden Street

Manchester's first synagogue opened in 1794 in a warehouse on a street described in James Butterworth's 1820s *Antiquities of the Town* as 'mean looking, the buildings chiefly ancient . . . unclean and disagreeable'. The local Jewish community soon moved north a mile to Cheetham where it flourished in the late nineteenth century (p. 158).

Miller Street

Richard Arkwright, whose name has become synonymous with northern industry and industriousness (see box on p. 83), opened Manchester's first water-powered mill here at the north end of town in 1782. Initially he incorporated a water-wheel which simply raised the water as he was not able to power his textile machinery by steam. But by the end of the decade mechanical improvements such as James Watt's invention of the steam engine saw fifty-two mills open locally using steam power. Manchester's mill owners were not initially popular for incorporating such machinery. For instance, when Robert Grimshaw opened a steam-powered weaving factory in 1790 in Knott Mill, on the other side of the town, in which he used the new spinning mules, the mob burned it to the ground. Arkwright's mill was destroyed during Second World War bombing in 1940. When Manchester University's archaeology department dug up the site, then covered by a car park, in 2006 they found the remains of the mill.

CIS Building

For decades the cooperative movement's twenty-five-storey flagship building of 1959–62 was the tallest building in Manchester, and a rare example of a successful early post-war skyscraper. The architects, G. S. Hay and Sir John Burnet Tait and Partners, copied the transatlantic look perfected by Mies Van Der Rohe and gave the main tower a steel frame covered with glass, aluminium and black enamelled steel. There is an adjacent service tower without windows.

Shudehill

Shudehill was traditionally the start of the main route from Manchester to Rochdale, and its unusual name may derive from 'shude', meaning husks of oats, or could be a corruption of 'shoot'. Before the improvements to the town's water supply in the late nineteenth century Manchester took its water from the Shudehill pits alongside the long vanished River Dene.

A food riot on Shudehill in 1757 was caused by 900 demonstrators who destroyed the corn mills in Clayton and headed for Manchester, where they battled with soldiers. Three people were killed and fifteen wounded. After dispersing, the mob returned later that night and tried to break open the dungeon on Salford Bridge.

In the first half of the twentieth century Shudehill was best known for its bustling Saturday market, which peaked in the evening with huge crowds, stalls and street entertainers. Towards midnight the price of the food dropped considerably. There was also a book market, which survives in the roadside shops that are now central Manchester's only remaining independent bookshops.

The street's demise since the 1960s can be blamed on the opening of the nearby Arndale Centre which led to shops closing and the premises decaying until they had to be demolished. Shudehill's deterioration has been exacerbated by the authorities' desperation to close down all the pubs on what was one of the most popular pub crawls in the city, a favourite of the Fall's Mark E. Smith, for whom the less inviting the premises the better. Those pubs that have recently disappeared include the Castle and Falcon, previously a lock-up for prisoners and later a chapel, which was threatened by the arrival of Metrolink, reprieved, but soon abandoned, and more recently the exquisitely tiled Lower Turk's Head at No. 36, which dated back to 1744. A large and ungainly transport interchange was built at the junction of Shudehill and Bradshaw Street early in the twenty-first century.

Rovers' Return, No. 16

A timber-framed pub that stood here for centuries advertised itself as 'the oldest licensed house in Manchester, AD 1306', but the date was probably fanciful, as were the many legends associated with the building. These included claims that Oliver Cromwell and Guy Fawkes drank here, that a ghost called Jeremy sometimes made banging noises in the cellar at 2 a.m., and that the building was connected by tunnel to Ordsall Hall, several miles away. After losing its licence in 1924 the Rovers' Return became a working-men's caff, and was demolished in 1957 after a fire. The makers of *Coronation Street*, first transmitted a few years later, borrowed the name for their now more famous establishment.

Withy Grove

Withies were willows woven together to support the clay filling used to secure timber-framed cottages. The rural nature of the street disappeared after Wythengreave Hall, home of the Hulme family, was offered for sale in 1763 with eight and a half acres of land that was soon covered with shops and properties. In the late 1960s the entire south side of the street was demolished to build the Arndale Centre.

north side

Printworks

For much of the twentieth century the Printworks, now an entertainments centre, was the largest newspaper office complex in the world, home to the *Manchester Evening Chronicle* and *Sunday Graphic*, and the northern offices of the *Daily Telegraph* and *Sunday Times*. Newspapers were first published here in 1873 when Ned Hulton, sacked from the *Manchester Guardian* for running his own horse-racing paper, launched the

Sporting Chronicle and built a publishing empire of titles mostly using the name 'Chronicle'. In 1937 Kemsley papers took over the plant and renamed it Kemsley House, and twenty-two years later it became Thomson House.

In 1985 the corrupt tycoon Robert Maxwell purchased the plant for £1 and renamed it, unamusingly, Maxwell House. Thoughts that the tycoon had bought the place to close it down were confirmed in 1986 when the last paper was produced here. For ten years the site was derelict – by which time Manchester had lost much of its newspaper industry – but after the 1996 IRA bomb it was bought by Richardson Developments of Birmingham for £10 million. They reworked it around the retained façade to incorporate a multi-screen cinema, bars and outlets for well-known chain restaurants based around recipes devised in London and the United States rather than Manchester. Even the launch, despite being hyped in the local press as a symbol of a revitalized Manchester, came with a large dollop of ersatz American schmaltz, courtesy of the singer Lionel Richie.

south side

Seven Stars, No. 16

Until the late 1960s the Seven Stars was one of the oldest pubs in Britain, having obtained its first licence in 1356. Inside was a rare one-finger clock and a cupboard that wasn't opened for 100 years prior to the Second World War. Troops serving the Young Pretender (Bonnie Prince Charlie) during his ill-fated 1745 campaign to seize the throne of England stayed here.

In the Harrison Ainsworth historical romance *Guy Fawkes* (1842) the would-be destroyer of the Houses of Parliament visits the pub, 'an excellent hostel, kept by a worthy widow, who, he affirmed, would do anything to serve him'. Uncertain whether Fawkes really had stayed there or whether Ainsworth was using poetic licence, the pub hedged its bets by promoting 'Ye Guy Faux Chamber'. In Mrs Banks's 1876 novel *The Manchester Man* Tom Hulme stays at the Seven Stars before joining the army.

SMITHFIELD

The area around the defunct and mostly demolished Smithfield Market still exudes a character that neighbouring parts of Manchester have lost since the building of the Arndale Centre. East of Church Street are tiny streets of early nineteenth-century brick cottages converted by Pakistani immigrants in the 1970s into cash-and-carry clothing outlets, and curry houses with amazingly low prices serving food more varied and interesting than their more lauded Rusholme counterparts.

The first traders at Smithfield Market appeared in 1822. They sold fish, fruit and vegetables under a huge iron-and-glass roof that was open to the elements. The market was expanded a number of times in the second half of the nineteenth century, especially after the newly formed Corporation bought the manorial rights from the Mosley family, and by the beginning of the twentieth century was the biggest market complex in Britain, with live birds sold as well as food. Much of the work at Smithfield took place around 6 a.m., and at the end of the day the left-over fruit and veg would be sold at knock-down prices to the poor of nearby Angel Meadow, although the less fresh produce was eventually given away.

The various markets closed in the 1970s, as the streets were deemed to be too congested, and most of the buildings were demolished. Attempts to revitalize the area in a style similar to London's Covent Garden have failed, and into the twenty-first century the area was still exuding an ungentrified, downhome feel that many locals find welcoming. However, the council wants to 'clean up' Smithfield, which is sure to rid the area of any lingering character. A worrying sign of the future for Smithfield came in 2006 with the removal of three 1770s weavers' cottages on Turner Street, taken down brick by brick to be rebuilt nearby on a different site.

Church Street

The church after which the road was named – St Paul's – was moved to New Cross in 1880. On the east side of Church Street are the last grocers' barrows, all that remains of Smithfield's pre-Arndale food markets. On the west side is Manchester's cultish shopping centre, Affleck's Palace. Church Street was the setting for Manchester's first Orange riot, which took place on 13 July 1807 when Protestants fought with Catholics at the junction with the High Street after troublemakers had daubed graffiti proclaiming: 'No Popery'.

Affleck's Palace, No. 52

Three floors packed with stalls selling second-hand clothes, jewellery, records and unusual gifts jostle for space inside a labyrinthine Victorian building. Affleck's Palace was opened by James Walsh in 1982, a decade after the area had begun to die commercially following the opening of the Arndale Centre, and showed how youth culture could revitalize the city despite the protestations of the old-school Labour-run council.

Affleck's soon became a setting for outré events. In the mid-1990s the complex's Oblong Art Gallery held an unusual exhibition called 'Stolen', organized by legendary local eccentric Edward Barton. It consisted mostly of items removed from various Manchester stores by a shoplifter Barton hired who brought back cans of lager, washing powder and toys. Once the story of how the exhibits had arrived at Affleck's appeared in the press the authorities lined up to denounce the show. 'Only lunatics would call it art. This person is openly promoting crime,' claimed Steve Murphy, chairman of the county police authority, with no hint of irony. 'It would make the artist an accessory to crime and I am sure the police will be most interested in talking to him.' Officers from Greater Manchester Police duly paid a visit, bringing with them notebooks and handcuffs, but not to add to the show's wares. Barton was arrested and 'Stolen' closed.

High Street

John Rylands, the city's most successful nineteenth-century textile merchant, opened his first Manchester shop at №. 11 High Street in the 1820s. Rylands was an indefatigable toiler who rose at 5 a.m. and began the day working in Wigan, arriving in Manchester at around eight. His speciality was attention to detail, and his motto 'small profits and quick returns'. By the 1840s Rylands was one of the most successful clothes-makers in the country, employing more than 1,000 workers across the area. Rylands was lucky as well as tireless. Coal seams were found on his land in Wigan which complemented his assets admirably. He later became one of the first financiers of the Manchester Ship Canal, opened the first library in Stretford, as well as a number of other institutions in that area, and amassed a major collection of religious works which formed the basis of the library bearing his name on Deansgate (p. 9).

Oak Street

Now home of the Manchester Craft Centre, Oak Street was where the dramatic events surrounding a group of Fenians or Irish nationalists who became known as the Manchester Martyrs began in 1867. The Fenians became marked men after shooting a policeman dead while springing associates from a prison van in east Manchester on 18 September that year. A week earlier four of their number had been arrested while loitering outside a tailor's on Oak Street. Two of the men escaped but two, Colonel Thomas Kelly and Captain Timothy Deasy, were hauled in and interrogated. They gave false names and claimed to be American citizens (both had fought in the American Civil War) but were sent to Belle Vue Gaol. Over the next week their supporters in the Fenian movement planned how to spring them. (See Hyde Road, p. 151.)

The Communist agitator and author Friedrich Engels, who spent much time in Manchester working for the family business while campaigning for left-wing causes, used to visit a leading Chartist, James Leach, at his bookseller's on Oak Street in the 1840s. Leach wrote unusual political pamphlets with titles such as 'Stubborn Facts from the Factories', and was one of fifty-eight Chartists arrested after the 1842 General Strike. Howard Spring worked the tale of Leach and his shop into his epic 1940 novel *Fame Is the Spur*, partially set in Victorian Manchester, in which Engels makes a cameo appearance.

Oldham Street

One of Manchester's most vibrant shopping streets till the building of the Arndale in the early 1970s, Oldham Street has enjoyed a revival of sorts in recent years as the centre of Manchester's youth/rock culture, thanks to ventures such as Dry Bar, Eastern Bloc records and the proximity of Affleck's Palace.

Oldham Street took its name from Adam Oldham, a mid-eighteenth-century felt maker and associate of John Wesley, the founder of Methodism, and was a private track until it was opened to the public in 1772. It soon became a major route, home in the early nineteenth century to Abel Heywood, a printer keen on educational works and political pamphlets, who produced a newspaper on which he controversially refused to pay stamp duty. Another resident was Isabella Linnaeus Banks, author of the celebrated locally set novel *The Manchester Man* (1876).

Around that time Oldham Street was preyed upon by a dangerous gang of ruffians known as the Napoo, made up of the sons of Irish stall hands at Smithfield Market. They dressed in red neckerchiefs and buckled belts, and took their unusual name from army slang meaning 'good for nothing', which itself came from the French *il n'y en a plus* ('There is no more').

It was here in the twentieth century that some of Manchester's best-known stores – Marks & Spencer, C&A – had their premises alongside smaller clothes shops, furniture stores and jewellers. Oldham Street as a major retail centre can be seen along with a number of other similar Northern streets in one of the most exciting shots in British cinema history, at the beginning of John Schlesinger's *Billy Liar* (1961), when Julie Christie is shown walking along the road, swinging her bag with carefree abandon to a brassy upbeat soundtrack supplied by Richard Rodney Bennett. 'She didn't just walk down that street,' the *Observer* noted, 'she floated, oozing happy self-confidence.'

After the Arndale Centre opened Oldham Street became a backwater. Revival began a decade later when the bohemian Affleck's Palace shopping centre opened nearby. This was boosted at the end of the 80s by Factory Records and New Order who converted an Oldham Street furniture shop into Dry, Manchester's first 'designer' bar. Meanwhile the Eastern Bloc record shop moved out of Affleck's Palace to premises on Oldham Street, other record shops opened nearby and ventures such as the kitsch 1960s revivalist Pop Inn and the Night and Day bar opened. Opposite Dry are loft apartments created by Stephenson Bell out of the old British Home Stores building.

Also on the west side of the street is a throwback to the old days of serious Manchester drinking – the City pub. But attempts to turn Oldham Street into a leading night-time venue have not fully succeeded, as the eastern/Ancoats end resists all attempts at improvement, the quality of the buildings deteriorating the further east one moves from Piccadilly.

east side: Great Ancoats Street to Piccadilly
No. 60
Michael Marks, founder of Marks & Spencer, opened one of his first penny bazaars at No. 60 in 1898, three years after the first 𝔐𝔞𝔯𝔨𝔰 & 𝔖𝔭𝔢𝔫𝔠𝔢𝔯 𝔰𝔥𝔬𝔭 opened on Cheetham Hill Road. Goods were sold cheaply under the slogan: 'Don't ask the price: it's a penny.'
► First Marks & Spencer store, p. 161.
Dry Bar, Nos. 28–30
Once the most exciting new bar in the country, but now run-down, Dry was

opened by Factory Records in June 1989 as somewhere discerning clubbers could congregate before the Haçienda opened. The stylish decor – lots of beechwood, marble, steel and egalitarian Japanese-influenced furniture – was the work of Ben Kelly, who had previously created the Haçienda nightclub's look. Or as Factory-owner Tony Wilson put it: 'Kelly is the man who gave Alvar Aalto stools to the kid in the street.' Dry's owners were inspired, they explained, by 'the bars of Europe, where café culture is ingrained as a part of society'. But they failed to take into account centuries of local socializing, which has never included cultured, continental-style eating. Consequently Dry, despite being encased in an exciting and uplifting building, quickly became just another stop on the Manchester binge-drinking circuit.

Eastern Bloc (1990s), 5 Central Buildings
The city's best-known record store has long specialized in US dance, hip hop and house, but is best known as the birthplace of the formidable electro outfit 808 State. It began as a cooperative in the 1980s in the nearby Affleck's Palace building and moved across Oldham Street to Central Buildings at the end of the decade. By this time store assistants Graham Massey and Darren Partington were experimenting with tape machines in the basement, releasing the results as 808 State, the name of a drum machine. So successful were their electro instrumentals that they were soon working with guest singers of the calibre of Barney Sumner of New Order and Björk. The store lost its iconic status in 1993 when it was bought by the impresario Pete Waterman.
► Manchester music, p. 67.

SPINNINGFIELDS

The area between Bridge Street and Quay Street bounded by Deansgate and the River Irwell was rebranded Spinningfields, Manchester's 'new business district', early in the twenty-first century when for the second time in little more than half a century it was subjected to mass demolition and redevelopment.

After the workshops and factories that filled it were destroyed in the Second World War, the entire area was cleared to make way for a series of public buildings – law courts and council offices – in the fashionable brutalist concrete style of the day, the anti-social effect intensified by the ferocity of the wind that whipped along the pedestrianized stretches. By the end of the twentieth century the entire area had been declared unfit for purpose, and the 1960s blocks, which had been disingenuously lauded at the time as symbols of a dynamic new modern Manchester, were demolished. Unfortunately mass rebuilding has again been wrapped up with pedestrianization and a mania for wind-strewn open spaces dictated by the latest architectural fashions, this time a vogue for sandstone, stainless steel and glass architecture copied from Manchester's Bridgewater Hall, which will doubtless attract the same brickbats in future decades as the demolished 1960s buildings.

An exception is the new Manchester Civil Justice Centre, the most exciting building to emerge in the city centre since Oxford Road station in 1960. Designed by the Australian firm Denton Corker Marshall, it is a vast multi-coloured glass construction, with sections that jut out in mid-air 'like pieces from the open drawers of a filing cabinet', as Aidan O'Rourke of *Eyewitness Manchester* has memorably described it.

Bridge Street

Bridge Street is one of the most interesting main roads in Manchester city centre, thanks to its varied architecture, which includes fake Tudor timber-framing (No. 69), the cottage-like Bridge pub, the gorgeous terracotta façade of the Manchester and Salford Children's Mission and the classical revival bulk of the Freemasons' Hall.

People's History Museum

A well-devised museum dedicated to labour history is set in a converted Edwardian pump house. It contains much of the National Museum of Labour History's collection that was formerly housed in the Manchester's Mechanics Institute (p. 40), the highlights of which are the many vintage and elaborately designed trade union banners. There are exhibitions on the 1819 Peterloo Massacre, the suffragettes, the cooperative movement, and life in the cotton mills and factories. Admission is free.

Hardman Street
Manchester Evening News (2006–)
Britain's best-known provincial evening newspaper, which moved into new premises in 2006, began publication in 1868 as a Liberal Party mouthpiece and was soon acquired by the *Manchester Guardian*. As a populist title, it was aimed not at the city's intellectuals and bohemians, like its revered stablemate, but at working-class Mancunians. This, the owners felt, would guarantee sales, which could then be used to prop up the elitist *Manchester Guardian*. It was a system appropriately explained in the 1930s by Malcolm Muggeridge, one of the great journalists of the age, who claimed the *Manchester Evening News* contained the 'ecstatic statements of charwomen who had won sweepstake prizes, rows of bathing girls, angelic film stars, turf lore, salacious seepings of the police courts and divorce courts'.

By the 1960s the *Manchester Evening News* was taking an increasingly uninformed line on the changes taking place in Manchester. The paper's journalists greeted outlines for the new anti-social architecture that would begin to disfigure Hulme, Ardwick and other inner suburbs with awe and reverence, rather than derision, blithely regurgitating press releases without question. After the paper became a tabloid in 1983 sensationalism replaced populism. Succinct news and well-researched articles on Manchester life soon gave way to an excess of features on

The Pink

From 1962 to 2005 the most interesting section of the *Manchester Evening News* was the Saturday *Pink*, a separate newspaper printed on tinted paper, published within an hour of the end of football matches. Regular readers joked that the paper's football subs only ever used a handful of headlines – mostly along the lines of 'United in 3/4/5/etc-Goal Thriller' or 'Away-Day Blues for City' – above match reports which inevitably had to be cobbled together as play proceeded, with little room for manoeuvre if there was a change in circumstances. Occasionally this would result in a report extolling the virtues of, say, Rochdale's easy 2–0 home romp, ending with an instruction for the reader to turn to the back page for the final score, only to find that Rochdale had lost 3–2 in the last minute.

In the 1960s the *Evening News* was

edited by Tom Henry, a fanatical Manchester United fan. On the last day of the 1967–68 football season only United or Manchester City could win the League. The subs on the *Pink* prepared two headlines: 'United Champs' and 'City Champs' and by 4.30 p.m., with less than a quarter of an hour to go at both matches, City were leading 4–2 at Newcastle, while United were losing at home to Sunderland. As it looked likely that City would be champions the sub-editors suggested that the *Pink* run with the 'City Champs' headline. However, Tom Henry wanted to hold out to the last second, even if it meant a late paper. The destination of the championship failed to change, and when Henry saw the compositor throw the 'United Champs' headline in the bin he fainted. For the only time the *Pink* hit the streets late.

celebrities, with a manic obsession for *Coronation Street*, and predictable 'lifestyle' spreads. At the same time the paper dropped its liberal position and began supporting the ruling Labour councillors rather than their challengers during the bitter party in-fighting, a stance as predictable as it was pointless. The 1980s also saw the paper give what most of its readers felt was excessive respect to the authoritarian antics of Chief Constable James Anderton during his tenure in charge of Greater Manchester Police. These factors plus the *Evening News'* inability to keep abreast of the dynamic new developments locally in music, fashion and design, and its refusal to comment analytically on the appalling social and architectural problems to be found in Manchester, cost it a vast number of readers.

As sales declined the owners realized they had to give the paper away to attract back readers. Consequently, early in the twenty-first century the *Manchester Evening News* began to adopt bizarre give-away schemes (a free chocolate bar with every copy sold, for instance), culminating in the decision to

make the paper a freebie in the city centre but with a cover price in the suburbs. Meanwhile, the *Guardian–Manchester Evening News* publishing group has voraciously bought up local titles, mostly to stifle any possibility of a vibrant independent voice commenting on city life.

▶ The *Manchester Guardian*, p. 12.

VICTORIA

Whereas Roman Manchester grew around the fort in what is now Castlefield, medieval Manchester developed around the parish church (now Manchester Cathedral) and manor house (Chetham's) near the modern-day Victoria station. Here the high ground by the confluence of the Irk and Irwell provided a natural vantage point for these two important local buildings, while the presence of the rivers contributed to the town's growth as a centre for trade in coarse woollen cloth. Commercialization arrived with the opening of Hunt's Bank (now Victoria) station in 1844, but by then some of

Manchester's worst housing could be found here, as noted by the pioneer of Communism Friedrich Engels. In *The Condition of the Working Class in England in 1844* Engels described how he found

> a degree of dirt and revolting filth, the like of which is not to be found elsewhere. The worst courts are leading down to the Irk, which contain unquestionably the most dreadful dwellings I have ever seen. In one of these courts, just at the entrance where the covered passage ends, there is a privy without a door. This privy is so dirty that the inhabitants of the court can only enter or leave the court if they are prepared to wade through puddles of stale urine and excrement.

The deprivation was cleared up by the end of the century, and as the population moved away Victoria became one of Manchester's busiest areas, dominated by two connected railway termini (Victoria and Exchange), smart hotels, imposing Gothic office blocks and a statue of Oliver Cromwell, which upset Queen Victoria. Second World War bombing was followed by random, unnecessary demolition (the Manchester Arms pub, the entirety of Long Millgate, the glorious Lancaster shopping arcade) and the demise of the stations as the authorities dithered over Victoria's future.

The IRA bomb of 1996, which exploded at the edge of the area, damaged many local buildings. But rather than taking the opportunity to demolish the partly wrecked Arndale Centre on the eastern side and restore to their former glory buildings such as the Corn Exchange, the authorities made the same mistakes as their 1960s predecessors, demolishing or ruining the good, patching up the bad, altering the road system and cluttering the site with the latest gimmicky design features. Major new developments such as the Manchester Evening News Arena, Urbis, the revamped Corn Exchange and Exchange Square have been trumpeted in the press as symbols of a dynamic new city but it appears rather that their admirers have confused lavish spend-

ing with aesthetic grandeur, and that the new Victoria will come to be seen as an aberration much as the once similarly lauded Piccadilly Plaza was within a few years of its 1960s creation.

Cathedral Gates

What looks like a pair of authentic medieval pubs is an illusion, for both Sinclair's Oyster Bar and the Wellington Inn (which falsely bills itself as 'Manchester's oldest building') date from only 1999, having been moved brick by brick from their medieval home in the 𝔐arket 𝔓lace (p. 95).

Cathedral Yard

Manchester Cathedral

Gothic in the Perpendicular style, and the widest church in England, Manchester Cathedral is a relatively new creation, upgraded from a parish church in 1847. Its origins were in a charter that Thomas de la Warre, Lord of the Manor of Manchester, obtained from Henry V in 1421 to found a church with an attached college of priests (what is now nearby Chetham's). The new church, dedicated to St Mary, St George and St Denys, was built out of local Collyhurst sandstone between 1422 and 1458. Its best features are the misericord carvings under the choir stalls, which include the figure of a hunter cooking a rabbit, men playing backgammon, and a family of piglets dancing to a tune played by the mother pig. After the church became a cathedral more work was carried out by J. S. Crowther and Basil Champneys, architect of the John Rylands Library on Deansgate, who coated it in Derbyshire grey stone. Wartime damage led to a gorgeous rebuilt East Window by Hubert Worthington.

Corporation Street

A major traffic route cut through the late medieval slums in 1846 to connect the city centre with Cheetham Hill, Corporation Street serves as a buffer between the Co-op buildings to the east and the medieval area around the cathedral and Chetham's. The street acquired a grisly place in Manchester history in 1996 when the IRA's powerful bomb exploded in a van parked on Corporation Street outside Marks & Spencer.

west side: Market Street to Miller Street
Location of the 1996 IRA bomb
The IRA's Manchester bomb, the largest ever detonated in peacetime in Britain, exploded at around 11.15 a.m. on 15 June 1996. An hour previously a man with an Irish accent had telephoned Granada TV calmly announcing that a bomb placed in a vehicle on Corporation Street would go off at that time. The man made similar calls to North Manchester General Hospital, Sky TV, Salford University and the Garda in Dublin. Police knew it wasn't a hoax as he used a codeword known only to Special Branch, and CCTV footage showed that a white Ford Cargo van, its hazard lights flashing, was illegally parked outside Marks & Spencer. Suspecting correctly that the bomb was in the van, the police began evacuating 80,000 people from the city centre.

When the bomb went off no one was near enough to be killed. Nevertheless the power of the device sent out a shockwave travelling at 2,000 yards per second that was enough to hurl people along the road a quarter of a mile away and send a huge shower of glass and debris across the city. More than 200 people were injured, parts of the Arndale Centre destroyed, and the Corn Exchange and Royal Exchange damaged. The vehicle itself landed on the roof garden of the second floor of a nearby Co-op building. The site where the bomb exploded can easily be identified by the pillar box which remained relatively undamaged despite being next to the detonated vehicle.

Corn and Produce Exchange/The Triangle, between Exchange Square and Fennel Street Remodelled into a bland shopping centre of dull, chainstore outlets at the beginning of the twenty-first century, the Corn Exchange was one of the major casualties of the 1996 IRA bomb, its role as home to a much-loved flea market destroyed by both the explosion and unsympathetic regeneration.

A Corn Exchange has stood here since 1837. The first was a classical-style building created in homage to Ceres, goddess of crops and vegetation, and was home to large numbers of grocery traders, at one time attracting around 1,000 dealers a week. In 1839 an Anti-Corn Law League meeting held at the Exchange ended in disarray after a fierce row raged between those who ran the League and the Chartists, a radical pressure group also opposed to the Corn Laws but hostile to the League. The Chartists, who had denounced the League as too middle class, controversially proposed the roguish Pat Murphy – 'Honest Pat Murphy' as he was known – for chairman. As the radical journalist Archibald Prentice later explained: 'Whatever his honesty might be, he was not very clean and very far from being sober.' Murphy climbed on the top table, ruining it with his clogs, and when challenged to come down replied in the vernacular: 'Damn they een, if theau spakes to me aw'll put my clogs i' thy chops,' which swiftly resulted in a chair fight and the end of the meeting.

In 1904 the little-known firm of Ball & Elce designed a new Corn Exchange in the characteristically flamboyant Edwardian baroque style. The first conference of the Irish Race in Great Britain group was due to be held here in 1919 but the group was banned at the last minute by the police, who, fearful that Irish nationalism would raise its head in Manchester, arrested a number of would-be speakers leaving Ireland on the ferry. The ban succeeded only in driving the meeting underground and it took place at a secret location – secret, that is, until the *Daily Sketch* newspaper printed a photo of delegates entering another building.

After the Exchange ceased trading in the 1960s there were the inevitable threats of demolition, but instead the new Royal Exchange Theatre Company temporarily moved in. In 1981 the period lifts and staircases featured in the TV adaptation of Evelyn Waugh's *Brideshead Revisited*.

Within a few years the Corn Exchange had become home to an exciting flea market with tarot-card readers, New Age mystics, book and record sellers, and second-hand clothes merchants. Upstairs in the maze of corridors with their ornate panelled offices could be found a variety of small firms, among them private detectives, theatrical agents and the poetry publishers Carcanet. All this changed in June 1996 when the explosion of the IRA bomb destroyed all the glass, damaged the roof and ruined much of the building. To widespread disappointment the authorities rebuilt the Exchange as a shopping mall, the Triangle, the character of the building and its inhabitants lost in the process.

Urbis

A monumental glass façade with an impressive angular shape houses Urbis, a 2002-built museum of urban life. Designed by Ian Simpson Architects as part of the regeneration of the Victoria area following the 1996 IRA bomb, it occupies a site that had stood vacant for twenty years since the demolition of the Lancaster Arcade, a galleried Victorian shopping centre. Although the building is exciting as a piece of architecture, Urbis's purpose has never been clear, the need for the museum compromised by the existence of the Museum of Science and Industry in Castlefield. Soon after its opening, the contents were changed and the admission price scrapped.

Exchange Square

Despite being promoted early in the twenty-first century as a major new Manchester centre alongside Piccadilly Gardens and Albert Square, Exchange Square, at the crossroads of Corporation Street and Cateaton Street, is an architectural mess of over-elaborate features: concrete terraces, stepping stones, the usual predictable fountains (in a city with an excess of water) and naff metal windmills.

Long Millgate

From the street's barely noticeable presence – empty lot after empty lot on a meander-

ing route south of Victoria station – it is impossible to believe that in medieval times this was Manchester's most important throughfare. Long Millgate was built as a route connecting the parish church (now the cathedral) and manor house (Chetham's) with the long gone Market Place. It was lined on the east side with a cluster of timber-framed buildings that always looked as if they were on the point of collapsing into the road. These included the Sun Inn – known as Poet's Corner after a group of nineteenth-century writers who drank there – which also served as the tuck shop for the nearby Manchester Grammar School.

It was on Long Millgate in 1788 that the first Jewish presence in Manchester was recorded: Hamilton Levi, a flower dealer, was listed in that year's trade directory. Manchester's first Jewish community which settled around here mostly consisted of German hawkers and peddlers, and they built their first synagogue in 1794 on what is now Garden Street. There was also a Jewish burial ground, paid for by Samuel Solomon, a well-known quack doctor, responsible for the supposed cure-all 'Balm of Gilead', which was mostly intended to discourage masturbation. As the Jews prospered economically they moved north, away from medieval Manchester, first to Cheetham Hill (p. 16), and more recently to Prestwich and Whitefield.

By the beginning of the twentieth century the centre of Manchester had moved away from the cathedral area to Piccadilly Gardens and Albert Square, but Long Millgate was still full of character, a busy if dilapidated thoroughfare lined with basement cafés, offices, shops and pubs catering for those using or working at Victoria station. The street was gradually cleared, decade after decade. Poet's Corner partly collapsed in 1914 and was later demolished, rather than repaired. Less antiquated but as popular was the Manchester Arms pub from whose gardens James Sadler made his famous ascent in a balloon in 1785 (p. 81).

It lasted until mid-1970s demolition, by which time it had become one of the most riotous pubs in Manchester, infamous for its lewd strippers and lewder crowd of leering railway porters.

Since the 1996 IRA bomb the council has spent much energy debating ways of regenerating this area while systematically continuing to allow the destruction of this ancient route; early in the twenty-first century the last remaining buildings closed.

west side

Chetham's

Manchester's fifteenth-century manor house and surrounding Tudor structures, set in the typical late-medieval courtyard style, have somehow survived and are now the oldest and most unusual set of buildings in the city. They have been used as religious college and civil war armoury, and now contain Chetham's music school and Chetham's Library, the oldest public library in continuous use in Britain.

Chetham's stands on an outcrop at the confluence of the Rivers Irwell and Irk. It dates back to 1421 when Thomas de la Warre, Lord of the Manor of Manchester, gained permission from Henry V to convert the nearby parish church, of which he was rector, into a collegiate foundation with warden, fellows, clerks and choristers. De la Warre donated his baronial hall to the new college, which was built around it using stone from a quarry in Collyhurst transported along the river Irk which runs to the side of the building.

Edward VI dissolved the college in 1547 on religious grounds – it leaned too heavily towards unreformed Catholicism – and the buildings then came into the possession of the Earl of Derby, who converted them into his town residence. During Mary Tudor's reign the college was refounded as a Catholic establishment but was changed back to Protestant as Christ's College, under Elizabeth I in 1578.

Two decades later, in 1595, John Dee, one of the era's greatest scholars, became the college's warden. An expert in mysticism,

magic and mathematics, he had been a member of Elizabeth I's inner circle. Given that Manchester was then an obscure village, the college in a bad state of disrepair, and Dee not a Calvinist like the college fellows, it is possible that he came here deliberately to get away from opponents in London. In 1597 Dee described the college affairs in a letter as 'intricate, cumbersome and lamentable'. He returned to London in 1605, distraught after his wife and three of their daughters died in the Manchester plague.

During the English Civil War of the 1640s the buildings were used as an arsenal. By the time Oliver Cromwell had replaced Charles I as head of state in 1649 the premises had been abandoned. It was then that Humphrey Chetham, a Manchester merchant, bought the former college so that it could be converted into a school and library. Chetham died in 1653 before his plans could be completed. However, the executors of his will carried out his wishes, and Chetham's Hospital, a school for the 'maintenance and education' of forty-four poor boys (never a medical institution, despite the philanthropic name) opened in 1656. The uniform, which pupils wore until 1969, consisted of a blue frock coat, a yellow undercoat and a blue pancake cap. The library (see p. 95) was established in the same year. In 1969 Chetham's Hospital became a school for musically gifted children.

There has been considerable renovation and rebuilding on the site over the centuries but most of the fifteenth-century features remain. These include the baronial hall, cloisters, fellows' dormitories and the Audit Room, with its original moulded beams and bosses, where the feoffes who run Chetham's meet. Their survival is a remarkable occurrence in this most urban and overdeveloped of cities.

● The medieval buildings can be visited on occasional term-time days following a concert given by the pupils.

Chetham's Library

In his will Humphrey Chetham stipulated that funds be used to found a library 'open to scholars and others well affected'. He also instructed the librarian 'to require nothing of any man that cometh into the library', which is why today Chetham's Library is still free and open to the public, and particularly useful to those studying local history.

The original stock was bought in London, and by 1684 there were 3,000 volumes. Many of the original seventeenth-century books are chained to the stacks, as Chetham himself decreed, surrounded by the original period furniture. Early users of Chetham's Library included Daniel Defoe, who commented on the 'competent stock of choice and valuable books', and Karl Marx and Friedrich Engels, who came to Chetham's in 1845 to research what became *The Communist Manifesto*. Engels lived in Manchester for some time but Marx was only an occasional visitor.

When Marx returned to Manchester in June 1852, staying with Engels at nearby No. 70 Great Ducie Street, they returned to Chetham's to work on the final draft of *The Great Men of the Exile*, a satire on those who had split the Communist league in 1850. Marx told his wife: 'the process of curing these stock fishes makes us laugh till we cry.' Many years later Engels wrote to Marx: 'During the last few days I have again spent a good deal of time sitting at the four-sided desk in the [library] alcove where we sat together twenty-four years ago. I am very fond of the place. The stained-glass window ensures that the weather is always fine there. Old Jones, the librarian, is still alive but he is very old and no longer active.'

New Cathedral Street/Market Place

A new twenty-first-century-built street links St Ann's Square and the cathedral. It runs through the site of Manchester's medieval Market Place (The Shambles), where the medieval cross stood until 1752, and where the stocks and pillory were situated until 1815. Here was Manchester's first public building, the Boothes, a fifteenth-century courthouse and town hall outside which public proclamations were made.

It was in the Market Place in 1729 that Sir Oswald Mosley, Lord of the Manchester Manor, built the town's first Exchange. Unlike the current building on Cross Street this was a simple classical building, with a Roman-style open-air ground-floor space and a single room upstairs for conducting important business. It was also where Manchester's first recorded theatrical performance – Farquhar's *The Recruiting Officer* – took place in 1743. Later Exchange buildings were constructed further south on the present Cross Street site (p. 5).

Market Place was a major setting for political rallies. Here on 11 December 1790 Robert Peel Snr addressed a meeting of royalists at which the Manchester Association for Preserving Liberty was formed. The crowd, having drunk too much ale, then marched through the streets of central Manchester carrying placards emblazoned 'Church and King', headed for the offices of the radical paper the *Manchester Herald*, which they attacked.

For hundreds of years the site was lined with black-and-white timber-framed buildings such as the Fish and Game Market, but in the 1820s many stalls were moved to the new, covered Smithfield Market. Its original purpose gone, the Market Place became Manchester's main drinking spot, home of pubs that included the Slip Inn, a favourite of Charlie Chaplin and other theatricals.

The area was heavily bombed during the Second World War, and only two pubs survived – the Olde Wellington Inn and Sinclair's Oyster Bar. Around them was created a shopping precinct of horrific ugliness in smooth grey concrete beset by ramps, hidden entrances and service roads. Greater change came at the end of the twentieth century when the square was wiped out.

Olde Wellington Inn

What was Manchester's oldest pub, lucky to escape Second World War bombing, was physically moved from the Shambles to a new site nearby in 1999 at the behest of Marks & Spencer, who demanded the land for a new extension. The Wellington was of uncertain antiquity, but may have dated back to the 1550s. For much of its life the building was not a pub. In the sixteenth century it was a draper's shop, with attached living quarters, and for the next 250 years was owned by the well-known local family the Byroms whose best-known member, John (see box, below), may have been born here on 29 February 1692. It wasn't until 1830 that it became a pub, the Vintners' Arms, later known as the Kenyon Vaults after the landlord, 'Old Kenyon', whose ignored cries of 'time please' would be complemented ten minutes later by warnings of 'the bucket, Jim'. From 1865 the building was the Wellington Inn, the upstairs serving as an optical-instrument maker's workshop, easily identifiable by an enormous pair of glasses in the gable. In the pub there was also a brass plate to a silent drinker who sat

in the same seat for twenty years and spoke to no one.

Following considerable wartime damage to the old Market Place there were calls to demolish the two surviving pubs – the Wellington and Sinclair's. Instead, when the site was rebuilt in the early 1970s, the two buildings were hoisted five feet up so that an underground slip road could be installed below. Damaged in the 1996 IRA bombing, the two pubs were repaired and then dismantled, brick by brick, beam by beam, bolt by bolt, stored away at a secret site, and then reassembled fifty yards to the north.
► Seven Stars, p. 85.

Sinclair's Oyster Bar

Although Sinclair's looked like an authentic medieval pub at its Shambles Square location, and still does, though to a lesser extent, in its new Cathedral Gates home, the building dates back only to 1720. In 1738 it became a pub-cum-gentlemen's club, John Shaw's Punch House, which was closed promptly at 8 p.m. every evening by a landlord who would punish slow drinkers by pouring water into their boots. By 1845 it was Sinclair's Oyster Bar, and along with the Wellington Inn was moved nearer the cathedral in 1999.

Todd Street

A barely noticeable part of the street that links Victoria station to Corporation Street has one of the most detailed etymologies in Manchester. Previously Crooked Lane and New Street, in the seventeenth century it was T'owd Lane (the old lane) and later went through several changes, going from Towd Lane to Toad Lane, Todd Lane and Todd Street.

It was here that Ann Lee, founder of the religious cult the Shakers, was born in 1736. A cook at Manchester Infirmary, she believed God was punishing her following the deaths of four of her children in infancy and left her husband to form a religious group whose members stood up and trembled in church in fear of the supposed imminent second coming of Christ, which

---

John Byrom – inventor of shorthand

John Byrom (1691–1763), poet, Jacobite and inventor of one of the first forms of shorthand, was probably born at the Wellington Inn, when it was a draper's shop owned by his family and stood in the Market Place (now New Cathedral Street). Byrom became a Fellow of Trinity College, Cambridge, in 1714 and four years later was offered the post of Chetham's Library Keeper, which he declined. He was the first Mancunian to be fêted by the Royal Society, the country's foremost intellectual group, and along with contemporaries such as Isaac Newton, and the architects Christopher Wren and Nicholas Hawksmoor, dabbled in ancient mysticism, forming the Kabbalah Club in 1725 to examine the numerical pattern of the universe.

earned them the name the 'Shaking Quakers' or 'Shakers'.

Lee claimed to be 'the counter-Eve and counterpart of Jesus', and was nicknamed 'the woman clothed with the sun', a line taken from the book of *Revelation*. After being imprisoned for disrupting a service in the Collegiate Church (now the cathedral) she and her followers decided to emigrate to America and left Manchester in 1774. The ship nearly sank during the rough voyage, but they eventually landed in New York State, where they were branded as spies in the days leading up to the American War of Independence.

Nevertheless the Shakers continued to promote their beliefs – the cult of the Messiah, common ownership of property, the sanctity of labour and isolation from the outside world. To supplement their incomes they began to specialize in making an austere style of furniture. By the time Ann Lee died in 1784 she had established a community of 'around 1,000 souls', according to her modern-day biographer, Richard Francis. Because the Shakers advocate celibacy their numbers have dwindled.

Victoria Station Approach
Victoria station

What was for more than 100 years Manchester's most handsome station has recently been reduced and ruined by insensitive rebuilding and interference, leaving it a forlorn shell, though still in use.

Victoria opened as Hunt's Bank, the terminus of the Manchester and Leeds Railway, in 1844. Of the original George Stephenson buildings, only those which lie perpendicular to the modern station, around the bend in the roadway, survive. The station was soon linked to the Liverpool line and began to serve all the main routes north, west and east from Manchester. Abutting Victoria on the Salford side from 1884 was the London and North Western company's terminus – Exchange – built after the two companies failed to agree terms over using Victoria.

When they were later joined the result was the world's longest platform at 2,194 ft.

Victoria's demise came in the 1980s after plans were announced to link the station with Piccadilly via the new Metrolink system. British Rail's response was to reroute many of the services away from Victoria to Piccadilly, thereby emasculating the station, crippling Piccadilly with an excess of commuters that has made it unbearably congested and negating one of the main purposes behind Metrolink.

Many of Victoria's platforms were then uprooted, the space they had occupied left blighted and the Metrolink lines inserted with no thought for the appearance of the station. The final blow came when the northern side of the station was obliterated for the monstrous new Nynex Arena concert hall (now the Manchester Evening News Arena). Some features remain untouched, however, including the names of the European cities served at the continental end of the boat-train route emblazoned on the façade, and a wall map drawn on the tiles by the main entrance, which omitted lines run by rival companies, thereby misleading travellers into making labyrinthine journeys.

Victoria Street
east side
Hanging Bridge

Still visible within the precincts of Manchester Cathedral is the medieval Hanging Bridge of 1425, the third oldest surviving structure in central Manchester after the Roman remains off Collier Street (c. AD 200) and Chetham's (1421). Hanging Bridge – the term Hanging comes from 'hangan' or hollow bridge – was built of red sandstone quarried nearby in Collyhurst and spanned the now dried up Hanging Ditch, filled in in 1770. After being mostly hidden by Victorian improvements the bridge was partly uncovered in 2002. It can best be seen from the refectory of the Cathedral Visitors' Centre café.

THE VILLAGE

Just as a drab estate of textile warehouses around George Street was saved from decay in the 1970s by being reborn as Chinatown, so the commercial buildings on the southern side of Portland Street found a new lease of life in the late twentieth century as home to Manchester's gay community.

Although many of the area's pubs had long attracted a gay clientèle, it was only in the 1980s when clothes shops, cafés and other establishments came out in their choice of target market that the area began to be dubbed the Gay Village, and more recently simply the Village. After Russell T. Davis's 2000 *Queer As Folk* TV series used village locations it lost its exclusivity, and became the magnet for raucous hen parties. It is now one of the city's liveliest neighbourhoods at night, but no longer mainly gay.

Aytoun Street

Roger Aytoun was a mid-eighteenth-century Scottish soldier, known by the unfortunate nickname 'Spanking Roger', who married a wealthy local, Barbara Minshull, but wasted her fortune. By the middle of the twentieth century Aytoun Street was lined with major civic and corporate buildings: the Crown Court, the Employment Exchange and the Grand Hotel. The former was insensitively redesigned at the end of the century, the second was abandoned, a huge empty building in so central a location at odds with Manchester's regeneration, while the latter closed down in the 1980s and has since been converted into private flats.

Grand Hotel

Collie & Co's 1867 warehouse, built in Darley Dale stone by the firm of Mills & Murgatroyd, became the Grand Hotel in 1880. An early attraction was the telegraph connection with Liverpool and Leeds. The hotel was not only a destination for wealthy visitors to Manchester, it also became a major location for key commercial events. For instance, it was here in 1896 that Sir

Humphrey de Trafford, owner of the then rural Trafford Park, sold his estate by auction. De Trafford had grown tired of waiting for Manchester Corporation to decide whether or not they wanted to buy his land, and now he had a rival private prospective buyer. The Derby-based businessman Ernest Terah Hooley was the successful bidder at the auction, and within a few decades Trafford Park had become the world's first industrial estate.

In 1904 the players and officials of Manchester City, including Billy Meredith, the greatest footballer of his day, were questioned at the Grand Hotel by the FA over receiving illegal bonuses. City's directors were suspended and the players were barred from playing for the club again. Yet Meredith, who later starred for Manchester United, managed to return to City to end his career. The hotel closed in the 1980s and the building was abandoned, but it was converted into flats by Ian Simpson Architects in the early twenty-first century. The apartments are arranged around the former ballroom.

▶ Midland Hotel, p. 26.

Canal Street

What as recently as the 1980s was a nondescript city-centre street devoid of interest and night-time visitors is now central to Manchester's social life, the heart of the Village and the nearest thing in the Northwest to London's Old Compton Street. One of the main springboards for change was the opening of the swish Manto's Bar at No. 46. Soon there were smart restaurants, nightclubs and a regular presence of curious 'straights', keen to check out media interest in the place especially after it featured in the television series *Queer As Folk*.

Manto's, No. 46

Along with Dry on Oldham Street, Manto's was one of Manchester's pioneering chic 'designer' bars. Originally Unity House, a workingmen's reading room, it was redesigned in 1989 by Caroline Benedict-Smith, who gave the building full-height glazing on both levels, a mezzanine and a balcony to show that the gay scene had nothing to hide. The bank that financed the venture didn't know they had funded a gay bar until it opened. Manto's soon became the first stop on the gay nightlife circuit and was profitable within two years.

▶ Dry Bar, p. 88.

Chorlton Street

Best known as home of the city's coach station, Chorlton Street was where Sir Joseph Whitworth, philanthropist and engineer, set up his first workshop in 1833. Here Whitworth made machine tools accurate to one ten-thousandth of an inch, at a time when his rivals were producing theirs only to one-sixteenth of an inch, and also devised standardized sizes and threads in machine screws – the 'Whitworth Thread' – used by industry before metrification.

Whitworth's inventions helped make Manchester one of the world's great engineering centres and his premises attracted hosts of visitors. Jane Carlyle, wife of the celebrated essayist and historian, Thomas, visited the factory in 1846 and described colourfully how 'Whitworth, the inventor of many wonderful machines, has a face not unlike a baboon; speaks the broadest Lancashire; but has a talent to drive the genii to despair.' In 1871 Whitworth lost a court action brought by the clergy of St Augustine's Church, Granby Row, who sought by legal means to restrain him from using the steam hammer at his works. His name lives on in nearby Whitworth Street and the Whitworth Art Gallery, Chorlton-on-Medlock, by Whitworth Park.

Granby Row

Many of Manchester's busiest textiles mills were based here in the early years of the nineteenth century when working conditions were at their most desperate. For instance in the Medlock New Mill on Granby Row children were employed from the age of five and the working day was fourteen hours long – summer and winter.

Around the mills at that time was open land, and it was on Granby Row Fields on 11 August 1842 that some 15,000 gathered to protest against wage cuts. The demonstrators had pulled the plugs from the factory boilers to prevent any work taking place – in what became known as the Plug Riots. At the rally Chartist leaders joined the mob and urged them to stay out until demands to extend the vote were met. This alarmed the Manchester magistrates who sent in a company of the 60th Rifles, fifty artillerymen and 400 special constables. At their arrival the crowd fled, and the Plug Riots were ultimately unsuccessful.

Over the next 100 years more and more mills were built around Granby Row until only the land by the junction of Sackville and Whitworth streets remained open. It was in one of these mills, at 49 Granby Row, in 1908 that the soft drink Vimto was first produced. Around that time the first buildings accommodating UMIST, the science and technology institute now part of Manchester University, were built here by the north bank of the River Medlock. These college buildings now dominate the southern tip of the area.

Orient House, Nos. 65–66

A packing warehouse built for the Barlows firm by Henry Goldsmith from 1912–16 was one of the first city-centre office blocks converted into exclusive flats in the 1990s. As with many of these large early twentieth-century warehouses the front is grand and elaborate, covered in faience, huge fluted and decorated columns separating the nine bays, but the rear is drab and dismal. Also converted in similar fashion was the less ostentatious Granby House to the east.

Major Street
York House

While much of the traditional look of the Village has survived, the area is dotted with random empty lots that suggest haphazard demolition. One of these open spaces, on Major Street, marks the site of the remarkable York House, Harry S. Fairhurst's masterpiece, a 1911-built warehouse which featured a unique rear wall of cascading glass that allowed maximum light into the show-rooms. When it was earmarked for demolition to make way for a new road scheme in 1967 there was an outcry led by Walter Gropius, founder of the Bauhaus. A plan to convert the building into a museum of science and technology was rejected and 𝔜orʇ 𝔥ouse was pulled down in 1974. The road scheme never materialized and the site is now a car park.

Minshull Street

Manchester Crown Court

Thomas Worthington's Italianate court of 1871 remains one of Manchester's most impressive sights, its setting alongside the Rochdale Canal an assured Venetian touch. Worthington won the competition to design the building soon after the disappointment of losing the commission to build the new Town Hall to Alfred Waterhouse. His use of red brick ensured that the courts would stand out from the sooty skyline of industrial Manchester, while the addition of ferocious-looking gargoyles to collect the rain was another playful architectural joke – either a nod to the courts' likely users or a warning to those passing by.

Before 1971 the building was used as a magistrates' court. After reorganization it reopened as the new Crown Court, dealing with overflow cases from outside the city.

Police marksmen patrolled the roof during the 1985 trial of three Libyan terrorists. Renovation in the 1990s saw an unsightly extension in an unsympathetic style built alongside.

Thomas Worthington – Gothicist supreme

While it is Alfred Waterhouse who receives the accolades for Manchester's Victorian Gothic face, thanks to immense projects such as the Town Hall and the main university building in Chorlton-on-Medlock, Thomas Worthington's Venetian Gothic style is a more common city sight. Worthington came from a Manchester cotton family who owned premises on the High Street. At the age of twenty-two he left for a tour of Italy – ironically he never reached Venice, the city that most inspired him. In 1849 he opened his own architectural practice on King Street, where he remained, astonishingly, for fifty-seven years. Most of Worthington's buildings were churches or used for some social purpose. They were small-scale and intimate, the exquisite stone decoration applied to brickwork coloured in the Venetian manner, as can best he seen in the Albert Memorial on Albert Square (p. 2) and the Overseers and Church-wardens Office at 46 Fountain Street.

Rivers and Waterways

the first half of the twentieth century, was the Manchester Ship Canal. It mostly follows the course of the river Irwell.

Following a decline in usage during the twentieth century there was serious discussion about filling in the canals, but instead they were revived for leisure and tourism from the 1980s, while the land alongside soon became some of the most valuable real estate in the region.

Nearly 200 miles of rivers, streams and canals flow through Manchester within ten miles of the city centre. Some waterways, such as the Dene, Tib and Corn Brook, have long been forced underground, although their names live on in roads and places, while four rivers flow visibly through the city: the Irk, Irwell, Medlock and Mersey, with all but the Mersey found in the city centre.

Of greater importance to Manchester's history are its canals. The city played a key role in developing man-made waterways for industrial use. The Bridgewater Canal, the country's first, was built in the 1760s to transport coal from the mines of Worsley to central Manchester, and had its eastern terminus in Manchester at Castlefield. The Bridgewater was soon joined by the Rochdale Canal and the Ashton Canal which still dominate the landscape to the east of the city centre. The greatest Manchester canal, which buoyed its economy for

ASHTON CANAL

Built in 1796 to transport coal from the pits around Oldham to the Ancoats mills and factories, the Ashton Canal comes no nearer to central Manchester than its junction with the Rochdale Canal near Piccadilly station, a site that stubbornly refuses all attempts at gentrification. After side arms, such as the Hollinwood branch and the Stockport branch, closed in the mid-twentieth century, the Ashton Canal became virtually unnavigable. However the founding of the Peak Forest Canal Society in 1964 led to a huge campaign to restore the waterway. In 1968 600 volunteers cleared 2,000 tons of rubbish from the section east of Manchester, and three years later restoration was officially approved by the British Waterways Board.

BRIDGEWATER CANAL

The single most important factor in Manchester's industrial development was the 1764 opening of the Bridgewater Canal, the first man-made waterway with a route independent of rivers. The canal was financed by Francis Egerton, 3rd Duke of Bridgewater. Needing to find a way of reducing flooding in his Worsley mine, his engineers proposed channelling the water underground and taking the coal out along it. When the Duke realized he had enough coal to supply the needs of Manchester and Salford he decided to build a canal across the land so that his supply could reach those towns. Once it opened the price of coal locally dropped, as it was cheaper to transport it by water than road, and new industries started up in mills and factories.

Work on the new canal, with John Gilbert as resident engineer and James Brindley as consulting engineer, began in 1758. As there were to be no locks the two engineers built an aqueduct to take the waterway forty feet above the River Irwell; one on this scale had never been constructed before in England. Although the canal cost the Duke £200,000, it was soon returning profits of £80,000 a year, thanks to the money charged to the barges carrying food, cotton, salt, timber and stone, as well as coal. Even the opening of the Manchester–Liverpool railway line in 1830 didn't dent its profitability, and when sterner competition arrived in 1895 in the form of the Manchester Ship Canal, the Bridgewater's owners simply joined forces with those who ran the new waterway.

During the twentieth century the canal ceased to have much industrial use, and from 1952 leisure craft were allowed to use it. The closure of the Lancashire coal fields in the 1980s brought the end of the canal's working days.

Worsley to Castlefield
Worsley Delph, north bank
Coal was first mined in Worsley in the Middle Ages, but every time a seam was

exhausted deeper pits were sunk, which became increasingly prone to flooding. In the 1750s Gilbert and Brindley constructed an underground canal as a way of taking the coal out, and by the end of the century miners had cut around fifty miles of underground canal, stretching as far north as Farnworth. The coal was carried out on special boats four and a half feet wide with protruding sides known as 'starvationers' that were loaded at the coal face and hauled up an inclined plane into the open. Since the mines closed, the Worsley Delph tunnels have been shut for safety reasons. The canal's orange colour in Worsley is caused not by pollution but by iron ore deposits in the rock.

Worsley Packet House, north bank
Outside this elaborately designed black-and-white property the world's first steamboat was built in 1780, around thirty years before the better-known New Orleans vessels that cross the Mississippi first appeared. Regular passenger services left Worsley from here en route to Manchester until the mid-twentieth century.

Barton Swing Aqueduct
Two different but equally ingenious aqueducts have crossed the Irwell/Ship Canal at this point. The first, by James Brindley, was one of the great engineering feats of the Georgian period. When Brindley first announced he intended taking the canal thirty-eight feet over the river on an aqueduct held up by three sandstone arches, he was greeted with incredulity. The Duke of Bridgewater himself muttered: 'I have often heard of castles in the air, but never before saw where any of them was to be erected.'

To prove how the aqueduct would work, at the parliamentary hearing Brindley unwrapped a large cheese which he carved out till it resembled his planned design. He then explained that he would make the aqueduct watertight using clay-puddling – placing several layers of clay, sand and water on the floor of the waterway – demonstrating the idea in front of MPs with buckets of water and wet clay. Indeed so fond was

Brindley of the system, his dying words were 'puddle it, puddle it'.

Brindley's bridge was demolished when the Manchester Ship Canal was created in the 1890s. It was replaced by an equally remarkable structure which allows the canal to run through a steel trough that can be sealed at each end and swings to one side when ships need to pass underneath.

Trafford Centre, south bank

The Trafford Centre, one of Britain's largest shopping malls, stands half a mile south of the aqueduct. It opened in 1998 on land that had been part of the Dumplington sewage works earmarked in the early 1990s as the setting for the Olympics if Manchester were chosen. The architects jokingly designed the main building in the form of a cathedral dome to highlight the idea of shopping as the new religion.

Trafford Park, south bank

The factories of the world's first industrial estate are mostly screened from the canal by trees. (For the full story of Trafford Park, see p. 190.)

Taylor's Bridge

Here the Worsley arm of the canal meets the Runcorn branch. The north bank of the canal near the bridge offers many views of the intense industrialization that powers this part of Trafford Park and of the endless procession of lorries delivering goods to the Euro freightliner terminal on a road lined with ancient disused railway goods tracks which run on street level without being separated from the traffic. From here heading east there are few access points to the canal until the area beyond the football stadium is reached.

Old Trafford, south bank

The canal runs alongside the back of the north stand of English football's biggest club ground. All access points here have been blocked off, probably to stop supporters falling into the water. There is also a sign, barely legible, warning 'no berths here'.

Throstles Nest Bridge

A rare remaining vestige of rural Old Trafford in name only. There was also a

Throstles Nest ford on the nearby Irwell. To walk from here into Manchester it is necessary to cross the bridge and take the towpath on the south side.

Pomona station, north bank

The Metrolink station is built on the site of the Ship Canal's 𝔓omona 𝔇oᴄᵗs (p. 110), opened in the late nineteenth century on what had been the 𝔓omona 𝔊ardens. Despite being some of the busiest docks in Britain they closed in the 1970s, and all the dock warehouses have been demolished.

In transport terms this is one of the most exciting points on the canal. Not only do the Ship Canal and Bridgewater Canal almost meet but four different means of transport – waterway, rail, tram and road – all run extremely closely together here.

Pomona Lock

New lock gates connect the Manchester Ship Canal and the Bridgewater Canal near the point where the Metrolink viaduct crosses the waterways.

Cornbrook

Cornbrook, the local area, is named after the stream that rises in Gorton and runs west, flowing under Manchester University, joining the Ship Canal near Cornbrook Metrolink station. By 1763 the canal had been built as far east as Cornbrook, allowing barges bringing coal to Manchester to get within a mile of the town centre. A year later the canal was extended east to Castlefield in the heart of Manchester.

St George's Island, north bank

On the north bank, near St George's church, stands a large estate of new tower blocks which the developers, Dandara, were optimistically advertising as a desirable and exciting address in 2006. The site is almost an island, for on the north side is the Hulme junction side arm of the canal.

Timber Wharf, south bank

Well-appointed flats of glass, concrete and stone were built in the 1930s modernist style early in the twenty-first century for developers Urban Splash by Glenn Howells Architects.

Hulme Locks, north bank
A tiny stetch of water links the Bridgewater
Canal with the Manchester Ship Canal
through the now unusable Hulme Locks
near the A57. Before the locks were built in
1838 those piloting vessels on the Bridgewater Canal who wanted to reach what was
then the River Irwell had to travel the long
distance to Runcorn to find a link with the
river system. Hulme Locks were last used by
ships carrying goods for Kellogg's.

Interarms, south bank
Until the late twentieth century the bleak
and well-secured factory of the gun manufacturers Interarms stood on the canal by
busy Egerton Street. Interarms' presence in
the city shocked the liberal consciousness of
Manchester citizens, for this was a weapons
outfit owned by Sam Cummings, a one-time
CIA agent. The building was mostly demolished when the road was widened in 1997
and rebuilt as flats. There is an inlet that
allowed boats to load the arms as close to
the building as possible for security reasons.

Worsley Mill, south bank
On the Castlefield side of Egerton Street is
the renovated Worsley Mill, an enormous
block designed with distinctive Italianate
flourishes in 1896 by William Waddington
for the Canal Flour Mills company. It even
had its own canal basin. It was converted
into flats at the end of the twentieth century.

Castlefield Canal Basin
Four waterways meet at this impressive
canal crossroads, a sight made more spectacular by the various overhead railway lines
that dominate the view to the north. The
waterway meeting the junction from the
north is the Staffordshire mini-branch of
the Bridgewater Canal, named after the long
demolished Staffordshire Warehouse. To the
east, opposite the main branch of the
Bridgewater, is the Rochdale Canal, which
drops into the basin through Lock 92. To
the south is the continuation of the
Bridgewater Canal.

The nearest railway viaduct, with its eye-
catching red brickwork, is that of the
Manchester–Liverpool line. Beyond are the

fat, cast-iron columns that hold up the now
disused lines into Central station (G-Mex)
and the modern-day Metrolink tracks.
Beyond that is the disused branch that once
ran into the Great Northern Goods Warehouse. In the distance can be seen the railway line that takes trains to and from
Salford Crescent.

The arrival of the Manchester end of the
canal here in Castlefield in the 1760s by the
site of the old Roman fort led to an outbreak of industrial activity. The first wharf
was built in 1765, and was soon followed by
buildings such as the surviving Merchants
Warehouse of 1827. Others, like Potato
Wharf, survive only in the names of roads.

Barca, north bank
A Spanish-themed bar and restaurant, built
into the arches of the railway viaduct, was
opened in 1996 by Hale Leisure and So
What Arts, managers of Simply Red.

Merchants Warehouse, north/east bank
The oldest existing warehouse in Castlefield
dates from 1827 and has two shipping holes
which allowed boats to enter the building
and unload directly from the canal. After
being damaged by fire in 1971 the run-down
warehouse was bought by bookmaker Jim
Ramsbottom and redesigned by Ian
Simpson. It is now up-market offices.

Middle Warehouse, south bank
Another restored Victorian warehouse, it
houses offices for the Key 103 radio station.

Quay Bar (by Deansgate), east bank
Stephenson Bell created a white 'living stack'
alongside a stainless-steel stair tower, influenced by 1930s modernism (a style which
barely features in Manchester), for the Quay
Bar in 1998. Despite the undoubted quality
of the architecture, it closed in 2005 and in
its derelict state was taken over by squatters
and drug addicts who set it on fire three
times in September 2006, thereby ruining
Stephenson Bell's work.

Castlefield Coal Wharf, north bank
Opposite the Middle Warehouse stood the
most significant early industrial site on the
local waterways network – the Castlefield
Coal Wharf where, from 1765 until the mid-

twentieth century, coal mined at the Duke of Bridgewater's Worsley mine was unloaded. To make it easier to get the coal up to the road the canal was extended into the rockface where a water-wheel powered a hoist that allowed the crates of coal to be raised some forty-five feet. In 1780 the Duke of Bridgewater's Warehouse opened alongside and was demolished in 1914.

Knott Mill Packet Station, north bank
To the immediate east of the coal wharf was the landing stage used by the Knott Mill passenger service that took passengers on Fly Boats to Runcorn at the other end of the canal.

Grocers Warehouse, north bank
Here in the 1770s James Brindley constructed the five-storey brick and timber Grocers Warehouse, the first warehouse on the new Bridgewater Canal. Inside the building a forty-seven-foot shaft enabled goods unloaded from the canal to be taken up to street level by crane and water-wheel. The warehouse was partly demolished in the 1960s, at a time when Manchester was not interested in preserving its heritage, but has since been partly reconstructed as an outdoor museum piece.

Congregational Chapel, 378 Deansgate, north bank
A rare church by Edward Walters, architect of the Free Trade Hall and a number of *palazzo* warehouses in Chinatown, which dates from 1856 and has a fine Romanesque tower. Disused by the 1990s, it was briefly transformed into a recording studio by Pete Waterman.

Canal terminus
The eastern end of the Bridgewater Canal can be found near the Knott Mill side of the quiet stretch of Deansgate, past the station. Beyond this point the water belongs to the River Medlock.

MANCHESTER AND SALFORD JUNCTION CANAL

Central Manchester's forgotten waterway, only a tiny section of which is visible, was built in 1839 to link the Rochdale Canal with the River Irwell. It runs under G-Mex, the Great Northern leisure centre, Camp Street, the set of *Coronation Street* and the Granada TV building where a locked door in the basement leads to a staircase that runs down to the tunnel containing the waterway. A few hundred yards to the west, beyond Water Street, the canal can be seen joining the River Irwell.

The canal was expensive to build but its opening meant that boats wanting to journey from Castlefield to the river could avoid Hulme Locks and the excessive charges. However, it was always short of water so it wasn't economic to run and closed in 1936. The canal was then mostly filled in, but in the late 1990s, during the construction of the Bridgewater Hall, ambitious plans were unveiled to reopen the waterway and bring patrons to the venue by waterbus. The southern section was rebuilt and, even though the waterbus plans came to nothing, it now provides the area around the hall with an attractive water feature.

MANCHESTER SHIP CANAL

The canal era staged one grand last hurrah after the coming of the railways – the Manchester Ship Canal. A remarkable feat of Victorian engineering, linking the city with the Irish Sea at Liverpool, the Manchester Ship Canal resurrected the city's dormant economy and resulted in Manchester becoming one of Britain's biggest and busiest ports, despite being thirty-five miles inland.

The idea for the canal had long germinated, and engineers had already tampered with the course of the local waterways. A company was formed in the 1820s to investigate the idea of a ship canal but it was subjected to public ridicule, and hostile songs were even aired in local music halls. Parliament rejected the proposal, while approving by one vote the building of a railway along the same route. However, the canal's supporters weren't dissuaded, and their campaign gained ground in the 1870s when economic depression in Manchester saw industries fail, mills shut and workshops close. They knew they needed a way round the charges imposed by the Port of Liverpool for allowing cotton imports, charges that were so high it was cheaper for companies to bring their goods into England at Hull on the east coast and pay rail freight charges across the Pennines to reach Manchester.

The main drive for what became the Manchester Ship Canal came from engineer Daniel Adamson. He invited more than seventy local dignitaries – politicians and businessmen – to a meeting at his Didsbury home in June 1882 to 'consider the practicability of constructing a tidal waterway to Manchester'. Adamson told them: 'If the Suez Canal, situated in a barbarous country and where for fifty miles there was a solid cutting of the depth of twenty-six feet, could be carried out, there ought to be no engineering difficulties to stand in the way as far as the Mersey is concerned.'

The meeting decided to commission a detailed survey, but again the idea was ridiculed. 'Real salt water could not come to Manchester,' claimed the *Manchester Guardian*, which wondered whether the city would turn into Amsterdam 'with its smells'. More worried, understandably, was Liverpool, where one newspaper commented: 'Meddling with the river would be an act of felony.'

The Ship Canal Bill received Royal Assent on 6 August 1885, prompting the *Liverpool Post* to mock Manchester for planning to 'throw £10,000,000 into a big ditch'. Unperturbed Manchester celebrated mightily. On

Saturday 3 October 1885 around 30,000 people marched from Albert Square to Belle Vue Gardens excited at the prospect of more jobs, better wages and the imminent sight of steamships gliding along a canal only yards from the smokestack chimneys. So large was the triumphant throng that when the front section reached Belle Vue the back was just leaving Albert Square. One visitor to the city that day, who arrived knowing nothing of the festivities taking place around him, was the Africa explorer Henry Morton Stanley. Alighting from his train he thought revolution had broken out.

Work began on the canal in 1887 and lasted six years. Seventeen thousand navvies were taken on. They were known only by their nicknames, and were paid once a month, usually in the nearest pub. They wore, as Terry Coleman noted, 'moleskin trousers, double canvas shirts, velveteen square-tailed coats, hobnail boots, gaudy handkerchiefs and white felt hats with the brims turned up'.

The canal builders were hampered by problems with the terrain, particularly the boggy ground, bad weather and flooding. In November 1890 locomotives, rolling stock and workmen's materials vanished in a deluge as six miles of the canal and its bridges were washed away. A year later a train of twenty-three wagons was sent through the wrong points and fell directly on top of a team of twenty navvies.

The canal opened to traffic on New Year's Day 1894. Manchester was now a customs port. But Daniel Adamson, who had done so much to catalyse the project, was not around to see it. He had died in January 1890. So too had Thomas Walker, the main contractor, which caused a loss of confidence in the company and the withdrawal of some financial backers. The company was rescued by the Manchester Corporation, which took over 51 per cent of the Ship Canal Company shares.

In its first year the canal handled nearly one million tons of cargo, but it wasn't a financial success until the twentieth century.

Manchester Ship Canal – facts and figures

• The 35½ mile-long canal begins at the sea end by Eastham, Cheshire, where the company chairman, Lord Egerton, cut the first sod on 11 November 1887, the earth ceremoniously wheeled away in a silver barrow.

• The course of the waterway mostly follows that of the adjacent River Mersey, west of the confluence with the River Irwell, after which it merges with the latter river. The canal officially ends a mile west of city-centre Manchester by Hulme Hall Road/Woden Street.

• There were 39,000 shareholders when the Manchester Ship Canal Company was formed, the largest number any company had ever gathered.

• The cheque with which the company bought the navigation rights in 1886 was then the largest ever signed at £1.7 million.

• The depth of the canal is twenty-six feet, the same as the Suez Canal, and four times that of the Irwell.

• There are five sets of locks: at Eastham, Latchford, Irlam, Barton and Mode Wheel.

• Stanlow oil refinery, at the western end of the canal, where the smell of petrol hangs in the air, was built in 1922 on the site of a Cistercian monastery riddled with underground passages only discovered during construction of the canal.

• Passenger ships plied the canal in its early days but they stopped in 1896 as by then there was no room for non-industrial activity.

Many ship owners continued to use the established ports, and rumours that the new canal wouldn't be able to handle large vessels meant traffic remained light. A lead was taken by North-east firms, who used the canal for importing raw cotton. This, and the exporting of finished cotton goods, buoyed the company.

By 1903 Manchester was the fourth largest port in the country. It was no longer reliant on the cotton industry for its economic strength for the canal had brought new and different industries – cars, food, paper – to Manchester, particularly at Trafford Park (see p. 190). The canal continued to prosper until the 1950s when the importing of cheaper foreign textiles, made, ironically, on machines produced in Manchester, brought misery to the local textile industry and led to a decline in the use of the canal. The following decade saw the introduction of containerization – the packing of goods into huge containers which were unloaded from the ferries nearer the sea – which made the Manchester Docks and much of the Ship Canal redundant.

When the Ship Canal Company began contemplating closing the upper reaches a private company, Peel Holdings, stepped in and assiduously bought shares. On gaining control, it turned the Manchester Ship Canal Company into property developers and began to regenerate the now derelict ex-industrial land on the canal's banks.

The twenty-first-century Ship Canal is symbolized not by ocean-going vessels, bringing the world's produce to the city on its waterway, but by giant corporate projects located along the water's edge – the Trafford Centre shopping mall, the Lowry Centre arts complex, the Imperial War Museum North, and most of all the corporate skyscrapers of Salford Quays. The lower reaches of the canal are still busy with shipping, particularly around the Queen Elizabeth II Dock at Eastham and the Stanlow oil refinery, carrying some 7 million tonnes of cargo, mostly oil, chemicals and grain. The sighting of a cargo ship in the old Manchester Docks area is now a rarity.

north (Salford) side: Barton Aqueduct to Woden Street, Ordsall

Following the course of the canal on foot is practically impossible west of Salford Quays. East of the Quays it is possible to walk along the canal to its unnoticeable terminus by Woden Street, Ordsall.

Barton Swing Aqueduct

The swing bridge that allows the Bridgewater Canal to cross the Ship Canal replaced James Brindley's 1770s aqueduct, which was found to be too low to accommodate the ships that would be using the new Ship Canal. (See also Bridgewater Canal, p. 102.)

Irwell Park Wharf

Large ships discharged coal (from America), sulphur and lampblack iron ore at Irwell Park Wharf, just south of Eccles town centre. Lampblack, a fine black powder used for making rubber, came in awkward paper bags which if held in the middle would double up and split, spewing clouds of black dust everywhere. Before handling the stuff the dockers would prepare by donning a boiler suit, scarf, cap and gloves, leaving only the face uncovered. At the end of the shift they would take a shower, but on the bus home would invariably find their faces suddenly going black again.

Cold Air Stores

The warehouse for storing frozen bacon, butter and cheese was so cold the men could only work there in twenty-minute shifts.

Mode Wheel Locks

South of Weaste Cemetery are the most easterly locks on the Canal, Mode Wheel, which control the amount of water in Salford Quays. In Mode Wheel's heyday there was one large lock for big ships and one small one for tugs and boats. The sluice gates were raised and lowered by men using hand winches, and the signals were operated by a system similar to that used on the railways.

Salford Quays/Manchester Docks

What is now Salford Quays was the location of Manchester Docks (Nos. 6–9) for nearly 100 years and is now once again a centre of activity thanks to the Lowry Centre and the nearby shopping precinct.

The Manchester Docks (technically in Salford, not Manchester) opened in 1894 and were used for unloading ships arriving from across the world. (Pomona Docks on the southern bank were mostly for British coastal vessels.) At first only members of the public management deemed to be 'respectable' were allowed to wander through the area. However, the Ship Canal Company's private police force soon ended even this privilege. High walls were built to protect the area from the curious, and officers were stationed at obvious entry points to ward off trespassers. There was no shortage of miscreants. The surrounding area, Ordsall (p. 184), soon became one of the most aggressive communities in Britain, rife with casual violence and political corruption.

The dockers who worked here were chosen from the mass of men who stood outside the gates by a ganger or 'bummer' who would pick ten or fifteen from the several hundred who turned up. Of the tens of thousands who worked at the docks over the decades the most famous are probably Ewan MacColl, the folk singer who wrote 'Dirty Old Town' about Salford; George Best, who briefly worked here as a tea boy when he first joined Manchester United in the early 1960s, a time when footballers' wages were low and the club ensured that apprentices had a trade to go to if their career stalled; and Mark E. Smith of the Fall, who was a clerk in an import–export business in 1976. During breaks from work Smith would tap out short stories and poems on a typewriter. The early Fall song 'Rowche Rumble' recalls the arrival at the docks of large amounts of drugs – 'it's valium, valium,' for 'wives [who] need their pills' – sent by the pharmaceutical company Roche AG.

With the demise of the Manchester Ship Canal as a working waterway in the early 1980s, the land alongside became a prime site for regeneration. That decade Salford council, in partnership with the Ship Canal Company, drew up plans to redevelop the area for business and leisure under the name Salford Quays. The site was cleared of industry and cleaned up, and alongside the old docks cottage-like 'executive' homes were built. To the east skyscraper office blocks coated in coloured glass fill the sky-line. The centrepiece of the new Salford Quays is the Lowry Centre and the shopping mall by the former No. 9 Dock. Despite the lavish public spending Salford Quays remains an artificial construct, lacking human warmth and a sense of community.

No. 9 Dock/Huron Basin/Erie Basin

Half a mile long, with room for ten ships, No. 9 Dock, opened by Edward VII in July 1905, was the largest and deepest (at twenty-eight feet) of the Manchester Docks. It was the waterside home of Manchester Liners, the shipping company created to take advantage of Manchester's remarkable conversion into a port, which worked with the Canadian-Pacific Railway to bring Manchester grain, timber, wood pulp and apples.

The company's first vessel was the 460-foot-long *Manchester City*, built on Teeside and launched in 1899. It had large refrigeration facilities and telescopic masts that allowed it to navigate bridges easily. When the ship's quadrant broke during a gale in the Pentland Firth it made its way back to Britain zigzagging across the North Sea without a rudder.

Another line which ran ships from No. 9 was Strick & Ellerman, whose vessels left for Aden and the Gulf States laden with an eclectic mix of goods – Corn Flakes, Guinness and sewing machines, which the crew gave to their wives (most of the Lascars operating the vessels had four wives each), who used them in their burgeoning textile industries.

The north side of the dock was for timber storage; the south side was ribbed with numerous railway tracks. At the eastern end, where Anchorage Metrolink station can now be found, from 1915 was Grain Elevator No. 2. A ferro-concrete eyesore, it was capable of storing 40,000 tons of grain discharged from ships by four little floating pneumatic grain elevators that sucked and siphoned. The grain that was stored here attracted an inordinate number of rats, said to be the best-fed specimens in the region. So robust was the building it did not

completely fall at first when demolition explosives were detonated in 1983.

During the creation of Salford Quays the rail swing bridge was moved here from Trafford Road to be used as a footbridge.

Lowry Centre

Striking geometric metallic shapes proclaim the Lowry, Salford's boldly designed new cultural centre, home to L. S. Lowry's locally set paintings. It contains two theatres and stands on the site of what had been No. 9 Dock, itself built on land previously occupied by a racecourse so marshy a punter once complained that 'the going was so rotten as to be absolutely dangerous'. The Lowry Centre opened in 2000 and was the last work designed by the acclaimed modernist architect James Stirling, who died suddenly in 1992 during the planning stages. Despite the building's bold façade, the inside is a disappointment. The colour scheme is nauseous, the theatres claustrophobic and the café a poor attempt at aping those similarly overpriced inside London theatres. Alongside is the Lowry Outlet shopping mall, the Red Cinema and new flats which provide excellent views of the waterside.

No. 8 Dock/Ontario Basin

The dock that could house as many as eight ocean-going liners is now Ontario Basin where model-yacht racing and water sports take place. No. 8 Dock was used by such vessels as *Pacific Unity* and the *Pacific North-west* that sailed regularly to Texas and on through the Panama Canal.

When the ships returned they would be unloaded with the help of a floating crane that removed the bulk of the goods from the vessels. Often this included vast quantities of whisky, which the dockers would tap by whacking the bottom of the carton with a hook, draining the liquid from the bottles at that end. When customs officials opened the top of the cartons they would find nothing amiss. In its heyday No. 8 Dock was surrounded by cotton warehouses, built to store the raw material imported from the United States before it was taken to east

Manchester or the various local mill towns
to be made into clothes.

No. 7 Dock/South Bay

Ships journeying from Manchester to
western Europe used No. 7 Dock. Now, as
part of Salford Quays, it has been replen-
ished with fish. On the north bank are
quaint new cottages.

No. 6 Dock

The smallest dock, No. 6, was the setting
for a bitter labour dispute in its early years
when the canal company hired experienced
dockers to oversee what for Manchester was
new work. Hundreds of dockers marched
here threatening to throw what they called
'foreigners' in the canal. The dock was
partly filled in during the making of Salford
Quays, when it became home to Manchester's first and shortlived cineplex.

Trafford Road swing bridge

When the docks were busy the swing bridge
on Trafford Road opened to allow ships to
pass along the canal. The result was that
many a worker would arrive late, having
been 'bridged'. When Edward VII opened a
new Salford Dock in 1905 the triumphal
arch on Trafford Road contained the motto
'Wake Up, England! Trafford Park is
Awake!' The bridge no longer swings at
right angles to the road line to allow ships
through but the old mechanism can be seen
from the towpath underneath.

Throstles Nest Lock

Despite the antiquated rural name this was a
lock for the Irwell Navigation, built in 1734
on the site of an ancient ford. When the
ford was removed the owners of the Navigation were obliged to provide a free ferry.

No. 5 Dock

Though No. 5 Dock was planned for Ordsall,
opposite Docks 1–4, work on it was started
but never completed. The site was then built
over.

Tea Warehouses

By a remarkable coincidence one case of tea
from each load arriving at the docks was
usually found to be 'damaged', leaving the
dockers no alternative but to brew its
contents instead of throwing it away.

Ship Canal eastern terminus

The footbridge leading from Woden Street,
Salford, to Hulme Hall Road, Cornbrook,
marks the eastern end of the Ship Canal.
Beyond this arbitrary point the waterway is
the River Irwell (p. 112).

*south (Trafford) side: Cornbrook to Barton
Aqueduct*

Pomona Docks

Little remains of the docks on the south side
of the Ship Canal where, because of the proximity of the Bridgewater Canal, there are
fewer possibilities for regeneration. Pomona
Docks were built at the end of the nineteenth
century over what had been Pomona
Gardens, a site now dominated by Pomona
Metrolink station. The gardens featured
exhibition halls, one of which was the
largest in the country, and a sports ground
that staged one of the first floodlit football
matches.

The Gardens were also the setting for
public meetings. When, in 1874, local agri-
cultural labourers demonstrated over pay
and in favour of a twelve-hour day, they
marched from Albert Square to Pomona
Gardens and there sang a rebel song to the
tune of 'Rule Britannia' which ran: 'Rule
Britannia, Britannia rules the knaves . . .'

The Gardens closed in 1888, a year after
an explosion at a nearby chemical works. By
then the intrusion of industry on a mass
scale was threatening the last remaining cultural pleasures in Old Trafford. Pomona
Docks can be seen in their early 1960s incar-
nation in a scene from the Tony Richardson
film *A Taste of Honey* in which Rita Tush-
ingham walks along the quayside by the ship
Manchester Pioneer.

No. 1 Dock

This was the only dock partly located within
the City of Manchester. The warehouses
built alongside were used for storing sand
and gravel by the firm William Cooper &
Sons which brought the material from the
Mersey bed near Liverpool for Manchester
house builders on ships known as sand-
hoppers. Cornbrook Metrolink station now
stands on the site.

No. 2 Dock

Where boats bearing cargo from ports on the south English coast such as Whitstable and Falmouth berthed.

No. 3 Dock

This was used by Irish ships. Modern roll-on-roll-off facilities were installed in the 1970s for vessels capable of handling loads of 300 tons.

No. 4 Dock

London ships belonging to the Fisher Renwick and Coast Lines used No. 4 Dock. Here Guinness had their warehouse, with company workers wearing a uniform that included underwear with the Guinness logo. The firm was a popular employer thanks to working conditions which stipulated that employees were entitled to two pints of Guinness a day, one at lunchtime, one at the end of the shift.

Trafford Wharf

The long stretch of waterside west of the Trafford Road swing bridge was initially used by ships bringing timber, usually from Norway. These ships carried a small rowing boat, often stolen from the main vessel by canal company apprentices who would make off as the powerless sailors threw curses their way and return it later unseen, they hoped. Robert Casey, a self-styled sea captain, used to ferry workers from Trafford Wharf around the docks in his small boat in the early years of the twentieth century, saving them lengthy walks. He also gave waterborne tours to visitors.

For much of the twentieth century Trafford Wharf was dominated by the wide, wooden Grain Elevator No. 1, built by a Chicago firm whose staff came over especially for the job, and later connected to Hovis by underground conveyor belts. The building was overrun with rats plump from gorging the produce. The incessant work carried out within meant that the entire vicinity was covered with a thin choking layer of dust that penetrated everything and everyone. Elevator No. 1 was destroyed, along with 30,000 tons of grain, during the Christmas 1940 Blitz. The mounds of grain

remained red hot for a year, during which time the contents would catch alight if a shovel was dug into them and turned them over.

Imperial War Museum North

Daniel Libeskind's striking metallic building for the Imperial War Museum of the North fills part of the former Trafford Wharf. (See also p. 193.)

Trafford Park

Several miles of the south side of the canal, between Mode Wheel Locks and Barton Aqueduct, are taken up by the companies located on the northern fringes of the vast Trafford Park industrial estate (p. 190). These used to include Manchester Lairages, where cattle were discharged from Canadian ships. Of all the trades taking place on the banks of the various Manchester canals only the handling of cattle required state legislation to function, in this case the Contagious Diseases (Animals) Act of 1878.

Barton Aqueduct/Bridgewater Canal

See p. 102.

RIVER IRK

Rising in the Pennine foothills near Oldham, the Irk makes its way through the northern Manchester suburbs of Middleton, Blackley and Collyhurst, dives under Victoria station, flows directly below the nearby road of Walker's Croft, and meets the Irwell by the junction of Victoria Street and Chapel Street, the confluence visible only at the far end of the car park that used to be Exchange station.

The Irk was the setting for some of Manchester's earliest industries. From 1282 its banks were used for fulling – cleaning and thickening cloth – although nearly 200 years later, in 1440, the river was still being celebrated for the 'exquisite flavour' of its eels, according to an unnamed commentator. By the mid-nineteenth century the river was ruinous. In 1844 a visitor to Manchester, Léon Faucher, described the waters as 'black and fried'.

Around the same time the Communist agitator Friedrich Engels stood on Ducie Bridge over the river near the cathedral and noted a 'narrow, coal-black, foul-smelling stream, full of debris and refuse, its banks full of the most revolting blackish-green puddles of slime from the depths of which bubbles of miasmatic gases create a stench which is unbearable', a description he included in his *Condition of the Working Class in England in 1844*.

The Irk regularly flooded in the days when its banks were industrialized. In 1921 a baby was found floating Moses-like in its basket on the flood waters. In August 1953 Manchester's worst railway disaster resulted in ten people being killed and thirty-four injured when two trains collided on the viaduct over the Irk in Collyhurst. One carriage, full of holidaymakers, plunged ninety feet into the water.

In the opening of Isabella Linnaeus Banks's *The Manchester Man* (1876) the infant Jabez Clegg is rescued from the Irk. When he becomes a pupil at the nearby Chetham's school he is thrown back in by Manchester Grammar School boys.

RIVER IRWELL

Manchester's main river, which divides the city from Salford, rises as a spring in Irwell Farm, near Bacup in Lancashire, and takes a meandering course towards the two city centres. It arrives in Manchester by Victoria station, after which it runs in a relatively consistent westerly direction between the two cities. A few hundred yards west of the St George's roundabout, between Woden Street, Ordsall and Hulme Hall Road, Cornbrook, the Irwell officially ceases to be a river and becomes the Manchester Ship Canal, mostly flowing with the canal until the original confluence with the Mersey near the edge of the county boundary.

Engineers had long considered ways of converting and improving the river so

that it could be used to bring goods to Manchester. In 1714 the Mersey and Irwell Navigation Company was formed and parts of the river were straightened to help craft. Wharves and quays appeared along its banks, but when the Duke of Bridgewater opened a canal that by-passed the Irwell in bringing coal to Manchester river trade plummeted.

In 1840 the Irwell in Manchester was deepened to take vessels of up to 300 tons, but the main change came in the 1890s when the lower stretches of the river were reworked as the Manchester Ship Canal. This made the Irwell, not the Bridgewater Canal, the main industrial waterway.

Until recently the Irwell would often flood in the winter. In November 1866 heavy rains and the narrowness of the course in central Manchester and Salford caused the river to overflow into Lower Broughton and much of the central area, filling the cellars of the poor. Louis M. Hayes in *Reminiscences of Manchester* recalled 'a huge lake of turbid water rushing irresistibly along carrying on its course everything which it was capable of uprooting. It was truly a magnificent sight to those who could from some point of safety stand and take in the panorama of seething waters . . .'

Alongside the flooding there was a major problem with the stench and quality of the water. In 1790 local historian Dr Aikin complained that the river was 'destitute of fish, the water being poisoned by liquor flowing in from the dye-houses'. Hugh Miller, the early nineteenth-century Scottish novelist, described the Irwell as 'a flood of liquid manure in which all life dies whether animal or vegetable'. And when the Suez Canal opened in 1869 locals quickly dubbed the Irwell the Sewage Canal in response. Late-Victorian sewerage improvements cleaned the river of the worst pollution.

As a city-centre river the Irwell is barely used; an almost forgotten amenity. Whereas the Thames in London and the Seine in Paris act as a focus, drawing in the life of the city through their power and presence, the

Irwell has long been something of an embarrassment to both Manchester and Salford, tucked away behind monolithic buildings, with no waterside boulevard to attract the public. There was even a scheme outlined in 1963 to cover the Irwell completely from the cathedral to Pomona, with roads and railway lines placed on top.

Two reasons are behind the Irwell's lowly status: northern rivers run through rugged landscapes, winding and twisting in a manner that mostly precludes development. But mainly it is because of their traditional role for industry. Only in the twenty-first century has that started to change as the authorities have begun to clean up the rotting metal machinery alongside and treat the Irwell as an asset not a sewer.

River Irk confluence to Manchester Ship Canal

Although it is now becoming increasingly possible to walk alongside the Irwell in Manchester and Salford city centres, west of Quay Street the path has fallen into disrepair and is almost unusable until Regent Road.

Salford Bridge

Chapel Street's barely noticed arrival at Victoria ends on a bridge over the Irwell that is featureless apart from a decorative plaque.

Victoria Bridge

Originally it was Salford Old Bridge, the first built over the Irwell in this area, dating from 1365, and the last heading upstream before the river becomes too shallow for craft. Half way across there was a chapel so that travellers could stop and pray for a safe journey – not across the rest of the bridge, but through the wastes of Broughton and Crumpsall. In the fifteenth century the chapel became disused and served temporarily as a jail. During the English Civil War of the 1640s heavy fighting took place by the bridge after Lord Strange besieged Parliamentarian Manchester for a week, but his Royalist forces were unable to take the city for the Crown.

Sam Bamford, the early nineteenth-century radical, claimed after Peterloo that Salford Old Bridge should have been renamed the Bridge of Tears – an echo of Venice's Bridge of Sighs – for it was across the bridge that many of the wounded on the day of the 1819 massacre made their way home. Richard Wright Proctor in *Memorials of Bygone Manchester* described a walk across it in 1879: 'The bridge was thronged with traffic including groups of street singers warbling "Home Sweet Home", a melody then just composed.' In the early twentieth century it was renamed Victoria Bridge. Local legend claims that a boggart or supernatural dog is buried underneath.

Highland House, south bank

Leach, Rhodes and Walker's tower block, one of the most depressing sights in the area, stands as a supreme example of the redundancy of 1960s corporate architecture. It was built as cheaply and quickly as possible by means of a tower crane that enabled concrete to be poured continuously as reinforcements were put in place, with no need of scaffolding. Farce followed, for some of the wacky, funnel-like window frames fell on to the bus station one night soon after. The building's first use, aptly, was as the local tax office. It is now a block of flats with the seediest looking of hotels at the base.

Blackfriars Bridge

Originally built in 1760 by a theatre company who were performing in Salford and wished to help patrons reach their venue. They chose a name associated with London as Blackfriars Bridge was being built there at the time. The wooden bridge was dismantled in 1817.

Blackfriars House, south bank by Parsonage

Built in 1923 for the Bleachers' Association, this is architect Harry S. Fairhurst's worst building, an ungainly mix of ashlar and rustication.

National Buildings, south bank

Harry S. Fairhurst's monumental 1909 warehouse blocks views of the river from Parsonage Gardens.

Lowry Hotel, north bank

Salford's first five-star hotel, built on waste ground at the beginning of the twenty-first century, is a dramatic and bold construction with a curved, glass-fronted façade, even if the choice of name shows an alarming absence of imagination, as does the decision to design the rooms in the style of New York lofts. Confusingly the Lowry Centre is more than two miles away.

Trinity Bridge

Built in the shape of a sail to the designs of the revered Spanish architect Santiago Calatrava, it links Quay Street on the Salford side with the Parsonage area on the Manchester bank.

Albert Bridge

The bridge was built in 1844, replacing a toll bridge that led to New Bailey prison. Sixteen years earlier, in 1828, the site had been the setting for the worst incident in the history of the river. *Emma*, the biggest vessel ever seen on the Irwell at the time, named after the builder's daughter, was launched near the toll bridge in front of a huge crowd of dignitaries and members of the public. A brass band played as the boat set off, but the festivities turned to disaster within seconds as the vessel careered to the other bank, throwing people into the water, and capsized. Twenty-two people died, while some of the injured were treated with transfusions of dogs' blood. One Scottish man who dived in to rescue people came ashore to find his clothes stolen, and died later that day from hypothermia.

People's History Museum, south bank, west of Albert Bridge

A museum devoted to labour history based in an old Edwardian pump house. The extraordinary new Manchester Civil Justice Centre now overlooks the site.

The Old Quay, south bank, west of New Quay Street

Goods brought into Manchester on the Mersey and Irwell Navigation were unloaded here at the first quay built by the river. Quay Street was later built from the quay towards St Peter's church (now

replaced by St Peter's Square). The Victoria and Albert Hotel, converted from an old warehouse, fills the site today.

Manchester and Salford Junction Canal, south bank

To the west of the Victoria and Albert Hotel is a small inlet for the mostly disused Manchester and Salford Junction Canal. The canal runs under Granada Television's studios towards the Bridgewater Hall where it now forms part of a water feature, joining the Rochdale Canal a little further south.

Mark Addy, north bank

The pub was opened in 1981 by well-known local entrepreneur Jim Ramsbottom, and is based in an old boat passengers' waiting room by what used to be the busiest spot on the river. It was named the Mark Addy after a local man who used to jump into the Irwell to rescue people from drowning. Addy died in 1889 from accidentally swallowing contaminated water while engaged in saving lives. He was the only civilian to receive the Albert medal from Queen Victoria.

Prince's Bridge

Opened in 1842, it was blocked off when the ring road was built at the end of the twentieth century.

Manchester, Bury and Bolton Canal, north bank

Only a short but deep section of the canal that ran from the Irwell to the two northern towns remains in this part of Salford. It is fenced off on overgrown and derelict land barely accessible from the Irwell towpath amid signs warning off the public. The canal was used mainly for taking coal from Agecroft Colliery and other nearby pits to the local mills. Once the pits were run down in the mid-twentieth century it had little use and was mostly filled in, particularly the sections close to Manchester.

Regent Road Bridge

Opened in 1808 to link Hulme and Salford, it has also been known as Quaker's Hall Bridge.

Railway bridges
Of the three railway bridges that cross the river by Granada Television the most westerly connects Deansgate and Salford Crescent stations, the middle one takes steam trains along the original Liverpool–Manchester line on a short stretch of track from and back to the museum, and the most easterly is a disused goods line that is now part of the *Coronation Street* set.
River Medlock, south bank
The Medlock, the river that forms the southern boundary of Manchester city centre, meets the Irwell in industrial land at the edge of Castlefield at some distance from any roads.
Woden Street/Hulme Hall Road
A footbridge linking Woden Street in Ordsall to Hulme Hall Road, Cornbrook marks the point where the River Irwell, heading west, becomes the Manchester Ship Canal. Upstream of this site only barges – no ships – can use the water. The footbridge used to be known as Mark Addy's Bridge, after the Victorian man who rescued people from the water. It became Woden Street, the name recalling the ancient Great Ordsall cave which the Romans may have used as a place of worship for the God Mithras, and which was later a Saxon temple for the Norse God Woden. The cave later became home to a colony of medieval monks and was still called Woden's Cave into the nineteenth century when it was filled in.

RIVER MEDLOCK

Only the most intrepid explorer, equipped with stout boots, detailed maps and infinite patience, would attempt to trace the path of the Medlock through Manchester city centre. Centuries of intense industrialization have seen the Medlock polluted, re-routed and mostly hidden away. The river disappears into sewers or threads its way between forbiddingly high walls, emerging in the unlikeliest locations, often behind a rotting factory, or is glimpsed through the

trees over a bridge, which only makes the search for its ghostly presence in central Manchester the more rewarding.

The Medlock rises east of urban Manchester, flows through Clayton, Philips Park (where floods in July 1872 lifted some fifty coffins out of Manchester City Cemetery and swept them along the swollen river), Bradford, Ancoats and into central Manchester, where it forms the boundary between the city centre and Chorlton-on-Medlock, and further west, Hulme. The river meets the Irwell a few hundred yards north-west of the St George's roundabout.

By the early nineteenth century the Medlock was being used in Manchester as a water supply for the new mills, and to carry the waste away. It was soon so full of detritus that many wondered how it managed to flow at all. Archibald Prentice in the *Manchester Times* in July 1830 memorably called the Medlock a 'nasty, inky stream'. It continued to be little more than a sewer until the mid-twentieth century. Even now, despite the massive improvements made to the local canals, the Medlock remains a forgotten backwater.
Ancoats Bridge to River Irwell: east to West
Pin Mill Brow to London Road
After the river flows past the site of the long-demolished Ancoats Hall, for centuries the home of the Mosley family, who owned Manchester, it heads towards central Manchester south of Fairfield Street through what is the most featureless part of the city centre, an area entirely filled with inconsequential light-industrial buildings.
London Road to Princess Street
Practically no sign of the river can be seen around what was until recently UMIST, the institute of science and technology that has now merged with Manchester University. The river was culverted here when UMIST expanded after the Second World War.
Princess Street to Oxford Street
At 118 Princess Street a tumbledown eighteenth-century riverside cottage almost collapsing into the water stands as a unique survivor of the kind of shabby properties

that would have lined the Medlock before mass commercialization. Beyond Princess Street the river meanders alongside impressive and glamorous Edwardian textile warehouses built by the water to aid transportation. At one of these, India House on Whitworth Street, is the entrance to a long obsolete tunnel that took coal by barge to a wharf by Piccadilly station.

Oxford Street to Cambridge Street

Much of the river is buried underground around Oxford Road station, partly through Manchester's desperation to remove all traces of the Victorian community of Little Ireland that stood by its banks here (p. 60). The river reappears by Cambridge Street where, remarkably, there are still some old mill buildings involved in waterside industrial activity.

Cambridge Street to Albion Street

The Ganthorn gasworks were built here in the nineteenth century, forcing the river underground. The site is now mostly taken up by the former British Council building.

Albion Street to the Castlefield Canal Basin

A rare, visible, open-air, city-centre stretch of the river runs through Knott Mill. West of Deansgate the river again plunges underground, diverted under the Castlefield Canal Basin and reappearing north of Potato Wharf.

Castlefield Canal Basin to confluence with the Irwell

The last few hundred yards of the river became accessible in the early twenty-first century after years of being hidden by factories in one of the most industrialized parts of Manchester. Off the road called Potato Wharf is James Brindley's ingenious Giants Basin, a huge weir constructed to regulate the water level in the canal by taking the overflow into the Medlock, and one of the great, obscure sights of Manchester.

RIVER MERSEY

Nearly ten miles of the world-famous river runs through Manchester thanks to the Corporation's decision to buy a chunk of land in Cheshire for its new Wythenshawe estate in the 1920s. The name Mersey means boundary water – traditionally it was the boundary between Lancashire and Cheshire. Because of the river's propensity to flood in the Manchester area its banks in Didsbury, Northenden and Chorlton are meadowland, devoid of buildings.

ROCHDALE CANAL

The main canal running through Manchester city centre was completed in 1804. Its opening considerably reduced the journey time from the east coast to Liverpool, and meant that factory owners in Yorkshire now had access to the ports on the west and east coasts. The downside was the need for ninety-two locks between Sowerby Bridge in Yorkshire and Castlefield, Manchester. At its busiest the canal was carrying up to fifty fully laden barges a day, but the growth of the railways from the mid-nineteenth century on saw a decline in usage. The Rochdale Canal took its last full load in 1937 and was abandoned in 1952.

In the early 1970s the section from the junction with the Ashton Canal to Newton Heath was almost filled in, leaving only six inches of water in some parts. The land on its banks became covered with broken glass and other debris, the locks in Manchester city centre were broken, and vessels abandoned. Revival came through the determination of several canal pressure groups, well-known supporters such as the folk singer Mike Harding, and the efforts of local councils such as Manchester city council and the now defunct Greater Manchester county council. The current healthy state of the Rochdale Canal in central Manchester is one of the city's greatest recent regeneration stories. Even the once abandoned stretches north-east of the city are now being cleaned up.

Great Ancoats Street to Castlefield Canal Basin

Junction with Ashton Canal

Wharves and warehouses once surrounded the junction of the two canals off Ducie Street near Piccadilly station. Long-running plans to gentrify the area along the lines of its Castlefield equivalent were still in its infancy at the beginning of the twenty-first century, and the area remains a wasteland.

Dale Street

The castelled entrance to the canal junction is a rare example of Victorian pop architecture. The Salt Warehouse next to the canal company offices has an external hoist on one side, but the bays which allowed boats to be brought inside the building for loading and unloading have long been bricked up.

111 Piccadilly

At Piccadilly the canal passes under Rodwell House, an ungainly 1966 tower block used by News International papers. The long undercroft taking the canal below is the most unpleasant spot in central Manchester. Dark, dank and eerie, it is riddled with metal cages used by prostitutes.

Auburn Street, south bank

As the canal emerges from the gloom of the Piccadilly undercroft the north bank contains views of the easily missed, delicate brick scroll of the former employment exchange on Aytoun Street. The more imposing Venetian massing of the Crown Court is apt for a waterside setting.

Canal Street, north bank

Canal Street, lined with smart bars built into the old warehouses, provides the towpath through the heart of the Village. At the Princess Street end of the road is the quaint lock-keeper's cottage, which stands above the canal.

Central House, south bank

One of Manchester's few Scottish-style buildings stands by the canal on Princess Street.

Bridgewater House, south bank

The rear elevation of Harry S. Fairhurst's imposing warehouse dominates the south bank east of the Palace Theatre. Opposite is the unexpected sight of a power station chimney.

St James's Building

A vast Edwardian office block, built for the Calico Printers' Association, stands over and to the sides of the canal. From a distance it looks as if the canal is coming to a halt at the building, however a lock takes the water down.

Tootal Building, north bank

Past Oxford Street, to which there is now street-level access, is the sturdy terracotta shape of the former Tootal Building.

Lee House, north bank

At the Castlefield end of the three buildings set close together just beyond Oxford Street is the back of Lee House, an exceptional 1930s office block, originally intended as a skyscraper, designed by the master of Manchester commercial buildings, Harry S. Fairhurst.

Manchester and Salford Junction Canal, north bank

A well-restored section of the Manchester and Salford Junction Canal leads off the canal by Lock 89 (Tib Lock) towards the Bridgewater Hall.

Lock 89 (Tib Lock)

On the north bank by the lock was Haveloct Mill where silk parachutes were made during the Second World War.

Former Hacienda nightclub, south bank

The metalwork of the apartment block that has replaced the famous nightclub commemorates episodes in the club's history. Opposite are the remains of four classical pillars, all that is left of Albion Wharf.

Lock 91

The canal once ran through the Deansgate Tunnel, cut out of the sandstone rock, from this point west for about 100 yards. The tunnel was built by Irish and Scottish navvies known only by their nicknames, such as 'Banjo Jack' and 'Roaring Tommy', who lived in shanty towns on the site.

Pioneer Quay, north bank
Its name came courtesy of a radio competition held to find a title for an unnamed
quay.

Disused canal, north bank
Between Deansgate and the Castlefield
Canal Basin are the remains of an under-
ground canal constructed by James Brindley
to link this part of the waterway with the
Grocers' Warehouse on Castle Street.

Manchester–Liverpool railway bridge
This part of the railway was cut through
the site of the Roman fort.

Eastgate Offices, south bank
Gail House, an 1860s ragmop factory,
became one of a number of Castlefield buildings bought by bookmaker Jim Ramsbottom
in the early 1980s, at a time when a rejuven-
ated Castlefield was a pipe dream. It was
redesigned in 1992 by Stephenson Bell as the
first local building to be part of the new
regenerated Castlefield. The name Eastgate
was chosen in honour of the east gate of the
Roman fort which stood here. Opposite in
industrial days was the Castlefield coal
wharf.

Lock-keeper's Cottage, north bank
What looks like a country retreat with an
immaculately kept garden nestles brazenly
in this most industrialized and urbanized of
settings. The cottage was deliberately placed
at an angle so that the lock-keeper could see
the basin and look along the canal for some
distance. Here the lock-keeper would collect
tolls from barges using the waterway.

Lock 92
The last lock on the Rochdale Canal, where
it meets the Bridgewater Canal, was given
the number 92, rather than 1, as the Yorkshire builder refused to have the first lock in
Lancashire. Because the lock is so close to
the bridge, there isn't enough room for
normal-length lock arms. The lock can be
opened by a system of chains and wheels.

Duke's 92, south bank
By Lock 92 is the smart Dukes 92 pub,
designed in 1991 by Stephenson Bell from
old stables which housed the horses used
for transporting goods from the nearby
Merchants' Warehouse. Stephenson Bell
introduced a variety of stylish effects, such
as a black metal spiral staircase leading to a
balustraded upper level, and luxurious furniture bought on a trawl of antiques shops.

Castle Street Bridge
The bridge taking Castle Street over the
water marks the Manchester terminus of the
Rochdale Canal, whose waters drop into the
Castlefield Canal Basin here.

Central South Manchester

CHORLTON-ON-MEDLOCK 119

(i) Oxford Road 120
Oxford Road 120

(ii) Chorlton Row 124
Cambridge Street 124

(iii) All Saints 125
Cavendish Street 125
Grosvenor Square 125
Mancunian Way 126

(iv) around the hospitals 126
Grafton Street 126
Nelson Street 127
Upper Brook Street 127

HULME 128

Royce Road 131
Stretford Road 132

MOSS SIDE 132

(i) around the brewery 134
Gretney Walk/Lingbeck Crescent 134
Princess Road 134

(ii) Greenheys 135
Lloyd Street 135

(iii) around Alexandra Park 136
Bedwell Street 136

(iv) around Claremont Road 137
Lindum Street 137
Maine Road 137

CHORLTON-ON-MEDLOCK

What used to be Manchester's most successful working-class inner suburb was systematically destroyed from the 1960s as the Corporation and various academic institutions colluded in demolishing streets, shops and homes to create the Manchester Education Precinct, the largest collection of colleges and halls of residence in Europe.

Land on the south side of the River Medlock was known in pre-industrial times as Chorlton Row. It became urbanized early in the nineteenth century when large mills were built by the river and simple brick terraced houses went up further south. In the 1870s Owen's College (later Manchester University) arrived in Chorlton-on-Medlock to occupy what was at first a small site by the junction of Oxford and Burlington roads. After the Second World War, extension after extension of the university swallowed up vast chunks of the area. This empire building was part of a scheme – the Manchester Education Precinct – outlined by the Corporation in its 1945 Manchester Plan, a grandiose project to destroy Victorian Chorlton-on-Medlock and rebuild it in zones, neighbourhoods and precincts. According to the Plan's instigator, city surveyor Rowland Nicholas, the Manchester Education Precinct would be a community where 'Manchester's artists, writers, dons, students, Continentals [sic], journalists, architects, actors, musicians, engineers . . . should find dwellings to cater for their personal and professional needs. In such an environment cultural societies would flourish as never before . . .'

With the firm of Wilson and Womersley, architects of the Hulme Crescents and the Arndale Centre, as consultants, work began on clearing Chorlton-on-Medlock in the late 1960s. Street after popular neighbour-hood street around the university was wiped away or radically altered. These included Butler Street, where Karl Marx lived in the autumn of 1855, and Ackers Street, where *Fame Is the Spur* novelist Howard Spring lodged in theatrical digs in the early years of the twentieth century.

Their replacements were not the bohemian enclaves optimistically envisaged by the authors of the 1945 Manchester Plan but landscaped zones dotted with ugly laboratories and admin buildings set on windswept grass verges. Typical of these was the Maths Tower on Oxford Road, an ungainly skyscraper, access to which demanded advanced algorithmic analysis, as there was no obvious entrance. It lasted thirty years before being demolished as unus-able. Similar absurdity was soon evident at the nearby University Precinct Centre, designed, it seemed, to dissuade all but the most perverse from entering, and where landlords had difficulty finding tenants to take the retail units and shoppers to negoti-ate its obscure paths and bridges. Criticism that Wilson and Womersley had not per-formed the most admirable of jobs was reinforced in 1978 when Manchester city council sacked them as consultants to the MEP following criticism of their work on Hulme and the Arndale Centre.

In recent decades the area between the new extended Manchester University and the city centre has become further colonized by students and academics as the new Metro-politan University competes with the older university to build ever more halls, annexes and wings.

(i) Oxford Road

Oxford Road
The main route south of the city centre via the two universities was created in 1790 to link St Peter's Square with Rusholme Lane. By the mid-nineteenth century Oxford Road was home to some seventy types of occupa-tion, including watchmaker, surgeon and tea dealer. It was also an unhealthy place. G. J. Holyoake noted in 1848 that 'as you enter Manchester from Rusholme the town at the lower end of Oxford Road has the appearance of one dense volume of smoke, more forbidding than the entrance to Dante's Inferno'. By the twentieth century Oxford Road was lined with small shops such as the Pan-African Federation book-shop at No. 58, where Jomo Kenyatta, who became the first president of Kenya, worked in the 1940s. The growth of the local colleges since the Second World War has led to many of these shops being replaced with college buildings.

west side: Moss Lane East to the River Medlock
Whitworth Art Gallery, Oxford Road at Denmark Road
This well-kept art gallery, set in pleasant grounds just south of Manchester Univer-sity, was founded in 1889 and has been owned by Manchester University since 1958. It was named after Joseph Whitworth, the pioneering nineteenth-century engineer who bequeathed large sums for the benefit of local causes. The Whitworth's textiles collection rivals the scope of London's Vic-toria and Albert Museum, and the gallery also has works by Henry Moore, Eduardo Paolozzi, Francis Bacon and David Hockney.
► Manchester Art Gallery, p. 17.
Manchester University, between Burlington Street and Bridgeford Street
The university, one of Britain's most pres-tigious outside Oxford and Cambridge, is the largest in the country, with 35,000 full-time students, and occupies the biggest single-site campus in Britain. Founded in

1851 as Owen's College (the university now wrongly proclaims itself on the area's advertising hoardings as having been established in 1824), it was based on Quay Street in the city centre until the 1870s when it moved to Chorlton-on-Medlock.

New buildings were designed by the great Gothic stylist Alfred Waterhouse, architect of Manchester Town Hall, and they are now the university's administrative headquarters. In 1880 the college received a Royal Charter and became a university. In the early twentieth century Manchester University scientists achieved considerable success in various fields. They included the philosopher Ludwig Wittgenstein; the chemist Chaim Weizmann, who became the first President of Israel; and Ernest Rutherford and Neils Bohr, who conducted pioneering work on the nature of the atom. In 1948 a university team led by Tom Kilburn and Fred Williams was responsible for developing the first programmable computer.

Notable alumni include the comedians Ben Elton, Rik Mayall and Ade Edmondson, and the novelist Anthony Burgess, taught history by the legendary A. J. P. Taylor, who wrote on one of his essays: 'Bright ideas insufficient to conceal lack of knowledge', and who in Latin classes was given the task of translating into the Roman tongue the well-known lyric from a Fred Astaire musical that runs 'you say "potatoes" and I say "potahtoes" . . .' which he expertly rendered as *Dico ego 'pomum', dicis tu 'phomum'*.

Recent decades have seen the university maintain its high standards while devouring vast swathes of Chorlton-on-Medlock to build a giant campus – the Manchester Education Precinct – the largest of its kind in Europe. In 2003 the university merged with nearby UMIST to form an even larger institution.

Ludwig Wittgenstein in Manchester and on the moors

Of the formidable array of talent that worked at Manchester University in the early twentieth century, few people were more remarkable than Ludwig Wittgenstein, considered by many to be the greatest philosopher of the twentieth century. Wittgenstein arrived at Manchester University in 1908, when he was nineteen. He was studying for his doctorate in engineering, but he also began conducting research into aeronautics which was then considered the most primitive of sciences and was regularly derided in the press, this being only five years after Orville Wright had become the first man to stay airborne for several hours.

On the moors east of the city, near Glossop, Arthur Schuster, who had recently retired as a professor of physics (his name endures in several campus buildings), had set up an 'Upper Atmosphere' station. There Wittgenstein studied the flight of kites and balloons, staying at the Grouse Inn, where he complained about the incessant rain. That autumn Wittgenstein enrolled as a research student in the university engineering department, dividing his time between debates about logic and mathematics and attempts to construct an aircraft engine similar to those later used in Second World War helicopters.

Dancehouse Theatre, No. 10

The tragic downfall of the mathematician and computing pioneer Alan Turing, who helped break the Nazis' Enigma code during the Second World War, began outside what was then the Regal Cinema, one evening in 1951. As Turing walked out of the building, a boy caught his eye. He was Arnold Murray, an unemployed nineteen-year-old from Wigan. The computer expert approached him and asked where he was going. When Murray replied 'Nowhere special,' Turing invited the malnourished-looking teenager to have lunch with him in the café opposite. There he fascinated Murray by telling him he was a lecturer at the university working on the 'electronic brain', and then invited him to his Wilmslow home. There they ended up in bed together. Before leaving, the boy took the opportunity to steal some money from Turing's wallet.

Turing wrote to Murray to end their relationship, but the boy returned to the house to ask for more money. Some weeks later Turing's home was burgled and he called the police. He also wrote to Murray, whom he believed was responsible, asking for his possessions to be returned, but the boy threatened him with blackmail.

But Turing had made the mistake of telling the police a bogus story, and his

Chaim Weizmann and the war effort

Chaim Weizmann came to be Manchester University's best-known early twentieth-century scientist, not through his research but because of his political campaigning for Zionism. Weizmann arrived in Manchester in 1904 as a chemistry researcher and was put in a windowless basement laboratory. Barely able to speak English, he taught himself by reading the speeches of the Liberal statesman William Gladstone. The future President of Israel was unimpressed by those he met in Manchester – 'a very stupid rabble . . . covered with soot, like the city itself', he once declared – and immersed himself in his work. In 1915 Weizmann was encouraged to steer his research towards the war effort. Invited to the Admiralty, he was asked by Winston Churchill, a member of the War Cabinet, 'We need 30,000 tons of acetone. Can you make it?' Weizmann obliged with a new process that used vast quantities of horse chestnuts, willingly collected by eager schoolchildren. The British government's thanks was to take Weizmann's push for a homeland for Jews in Palestine more seriously.

Splitting the atom

The first major breakthrough by a Manchester University scientist came from Ernest Rutherford, a New Zealand-born physicist who in Manchester in 1917 split the atom for the first time, in a room that is still unusable. At the physics building on Coupland Street he and William Kay, using a huge stash of radium on loan from Austria, bombarded nitrogen atoms placed in a glass chamber with alpha particles emitted by the radium. This caused the nitrogen atoms to disintegrate into oxygen and other subatomic particles. It wasn't exactly lead into gold – the alchemists' age-old dream – but it did win Rutherford a Nobel Prize.

With a team that included Hans Geiger, after whom the Geiger counter that monitors the amount of radioactivity in the air is named, Rutherford also discovered that atoms were not the most basic form of matter, but consisted of smaller particles. He developed the idea of the 'solar system' atom, with a nucleus like a sun at the centre around which the considerably smaller 'planet' electrons orbited.

Despite developing these startling new ideas Rutherford was not aware of the implications of his discoveries. When he first split the atom he claimed his achievement had no practical application. It would be twenty-eight years before the technique would be used for setting off two atom bombs in Japan.

homosexuality became known. He was prosecuted and convicted for acts of gross indecency, and the authorities tried to 'cure' him with drugs. In June 1954 he killed himself at his Wilmslow house by taking a bite out of an apple laced with cyanide. Thirty years later Apple Mac used a partly eaten apple as their company logo in an allusion to Turing's suicide.

A statue of Turing can be found in Sackville Park in the Village.

Birth of the computer

Before the Second World War a computer was not the machine that aided the calculations but the person doing them – a clerk who computed – much in the same way that a typewriter used to be the person who typed. This changed in the 1940s thanks to the maths department at Manchester University.

During the Second World War a department professor, Douglas Hartree, created what he called the 'differential analyser' to perform the most complex calculations. When the Germans' magnetic mines were discovered the analyser was the only machine that could help unravel the mechanism. Although officials from the ministry came to the university to meet Hartree and discuss its operations, for security reasons they were not allowed to see the machine itself, which was stored below the physics department building.

In 1946, with the war over, Tom Kilburn and Fred Williams from the university maths team based on Bridgeford Street built a machine made of war surplus materials that could perform calculations from a stored program, what is now recognized as the first computer, which they called 'Baby'. They first used it on 21 June 1948, running a program written by Tom Kilburn, the world's first and the only one he ever wrote. As Fred Williams later recalled: 'The start switch was pressed, and immediately the spots on the display tube entered a mad dance. It was a moment to remember. Nothing was ever the same again.'

One of the computer's first tasks, which demonstrated its scope and originality, was to find the factors of an enormous number, 2^{18}. This took it fifty-two minutes, which compared favourably with the several hours an individual might have taken. A month later a different program was introduced by a then unknown member of the department, Alan Turing, who had been involved in the breaking of the Germans' Enigma code. He later achieved notoriety due to the circumstances of his unfortunate demise (p. 122).

The first commercial use of a computer was taken up by a local firm, Ferranti. However America's IBM also began making interested noises, and they invited Professor Fred Williams on an all-expenses-paid, two-week visit to the USA in 1949 to discuss business. As Williams sat on the ship taking him across the Atlantic – the *Queen Mary*, no less – a phone call came from the government's Lord Halsbury ordering him, in the nicest possible terms, not to succumb to any offers from the Americans and take up an alternative British-based offer instead. Although Williams went to IBM's headquarters in New York, where no one could believe that a small team from 'Manchester, England' [*sic*] had made so startling a technological breakthrough, he kept to his word and worked solely for the British. He and Kilburn went on to produce a machine that could process a million instructions in a second, but it was American rather than British companies that forged ahead with computing science. Though the Ferranti plant in Gorton became the largest computer plant in the world, Manchester is no longer the world's main centre for computing science.

► John Dalton and the atom, p. 54.

The Dancehouse had previously been a ballet club where lectures were given in the 1940s by Marie Rambert and even Jomo Kenyatta, the future African statesman, on tribal dance. The ballroom scene from the 1961 film *A Taste of Honey* was filmed inside using cameras positioned on the balcony taking shots of the dance floor, where patrons were unaware they were being filmed.

► Royal Exchange, p. 5.

east side
Church of the Holy Name of Jesus, north of Ackers Street
This imposing Gothic church, one of south Manchester's best-known landmarks, was built from 1869–71 by Joseph Aloysius Hansom, famous for designing the hansom cab. The architect incorporated typical four-teenth-century French Gothic features, such as slender piers supporting a rib-vaulted roof, and a profusion of side chapels, but the spire originally planned for the tower failed to materialize, and it wasn't until 1928 that Adrian Gilbert Scott's octagonal tower was completed.

A young Anthony Burgess, who attended the Holy Name in the 1920s, described the priests as 'steely-eyed and blue-jawed' and called the church 'a stronghold of the British Jesuit [which] would soon have to be deconsecrated for a lack of sufficient congre-gation. Islam was growing, Irish Catholicism disappearing.' His father once entered the building for a service still absent-mindedly wearing his bowler hat and smoking a Three Castles roll-up. A priest doused the cigarette with a spray of holy water but took more offence at the bowler, hissing at Burgess Snr, 'This is not a synagogue.'

Although the church was scheduled for demolition during the great post-war rebuilding boom to make way for a new medical school, a campaign led by the architectural historian Nikolaus Pevsner suc-ceeded in saving the Holy Name, and the medical school was built a few yards further south. Despite the dwindling local congre-gation the church survives thanks to the wor-shippers who travel from afar to keep this iconic building in its intended use.

Given its central position, the church, unsurprisingly, has many connections with Manchester life – and death. The funeral of Charles Hallé, founder of the orchestra of the same name, took place here in 1895, as did that of the much-loved *Coronation Street* actress Pat Phoenix, in 1986. The mourners at her funeral included the then unknown Tony Blair, whose wife, Cherie, is the daughter of Pat Phoenix's partner, the actor Tony Booth.

It is from the roof of the Church of the Holy Name that Morrissey absurdly and hilariously imagines himself lifting the lead when he spies a vicar in a tutu in the 1986 Smiths song of the same name.
▶ St Mary (The Hidden Gem), p. 78.

(ii) Chorlton Row

Cambridge Street
Macintosh Village
This formidable complex of early nine-teenth-century mills, situated between Oxford, Cambridge and Hulme streets, is now student accommodation.

The first mill, which is set back from the building line on the east side of Cambridge Street, was built in 1814 by the Birley family, a member of which, Hugh, was one of the commanders of the Manchester and Salford Yeomanry at the Peterloo Massacre. The next phase came in 1818, creating a complex that was the most technologically advanced in Manchester in that it used gas lighting and incorporated cast-iron columns. The Birleys then went into partnership with the Scottish merchant Charles Macintosh who patented his waterproof clothing – soon to be known as 'macs' – in the 1820s.

After Macintosh's death in 1843 the works were run by Thomas Hancock. He patented a new type of rubber production called vulcanization, which added to the findings made by Charles Goodyear in America. This new substance wasn't affected by the weather and would snap back to its original shape if stretched. The site continued to be extended, and by 1850 more than 2,000 employees were producing life belts, military equipment, era-sers, and waterproof knapsacks and saddle bags from three mills, a warehouse, a vulcan house and gas holders, the site easily identifi-able by its two lofty chimneys. There were even tunnels in the basement with rail tracks that connected different buildings.

The Dunlop rubber company took over the mills in 1923, and rubber products con-tinued to be manufactured here until

February 2000. Despite the closures the crumbling Dunlop buildings still stand on the west side of Cambridge Street.
▶ The mills of Ancoats, p. 141.

(iii) All Saints

As Manchester spread south over the River Medlock at the end of the eighteenth century into what is now All Saints, developers gave the new estate grandiose names such as Grosvenor Square and Cambridge Street to attract well-to-do residents. However, it was a working-class community which grew around the 1819 church of All Saints. After the Second World War the church was destroyed and the area was taken apart as pubs, churches, corner shops – even whole streets – were swept aside in preparation for the extravagant schemes (new cultural centre, civic theatre and grand assembly hall) outlined in the 1945 Manchester Plan, none of which ever materialized. The cleared area did, however, provide ample space for the ever-expanding Manchester Polytechnic (now Manchester Metropolitan University) and the Mancunian Way motorway.

Cavendish Street
Oxford Road to Higher Ormond Street
Chorlton-on-Medlock Town Hall
The fifth Pan-African Congress, one of the most significant events in shaping recent African history, took place in Manchester in October 1945. The venue was Chorlton-on-Medlock Town Hall, an austere, 1831-built Richard Lane block of which only the Doric façade remains, and the congress was organized by the International African Service Bureau, founded by the historian and cricket writer C. L. R. James in 1937. The eighty-seven delegates included William Du Bois, the veteran American sociologist; Kwame Nkrumah, then a lawyer, and who, in 1957, became the first president of Ghana; Hastings Banda, who became the first president of Malawi in 1963; and Jomo Kenyatta, a part-time lecturer who ran a restaurant on Oxford Road. Kenyatta, who used to 'strut

in his full regalia with his swat, swishing about as he walked along Oxford Road', as a colleague remembered him, called the conference 'a landmark in the history of the African people's struggle for unity and freedom'. In 1964 he became the first president of Kenya.
▶ West Indian Moss Side, p. 132.

Art College/Grosvenor Building
Adolphe Valette, the French Impressionist painter, Ossie Clark, the fashion designer and Manchester's best-known painter, L. S. Lowry, all had connections at the neo-Gothic art college at the corner of Cavendish Street and Oxford Road, now part of Manchester Metropolitan University. The French-born Valette, whom pupils nicknamed 'Mr Monsieur', taught here from 1906–20, his teaching style of sitting and painting with his students then unknown in Britain. The Frenchman was puzzled by one strangely quiet and introverted pupil, L. S. Lowry, who studied here from 1905–6. A contemporary, Bert Wilson, later recalled how 'Valette used to roll his eyes at Lowry and shake his head' when examining his work. Valette himself left a series of mesmerizing Impressionist paintings inspired by the city's hazy industrial atmosphere, which the *Manchester Evening News* once described as showing a Manchester of 'strange subdued colourings, of blues, of mauves and of Turneresque greens, all lurking in its shadows'. Although Valette's work is barely known now outside Manchester, his paintings are more highly regarded than Lowry's by art critics, if not by the Manchester public.
▶ Lowry at the Manchester Academy of Fine Arts, p. 77.

Grosvenor Square
Naming a new late eighteenth-century development, built at the edge of industrial Manchester, Grosvenor Square was an optimistic attempt to create an estate in the style of the smart London square of that name and attract the town's wealthiest residents. The development was slow to take off and

by the end of the century only one house had been built. Even the construction of railings around the central grassed area, in the London style, failed to catch the eye of prospective buyers, and it wasn't until 1819, once the end of the Napoleonic Wars had eased people's fears about the future, that more houses followed.

In 1819 came All Saints church, which eventually gave its name to the locale. The church was the brainchild of the Revd Charles Burton, who predicted that Christ's millennium would take place in 1868, but failed to foresee that the church would burn down in 1850, only hours before a wedding was due to take place. Restored, it remained a focal point for the community, but was not a popular place of worship with everyone. 'God's most gloomy tabernacle . . . so filthy it appeared to be carved out of charcoal,' the prolific Manchester novelist Howard Spring called it.

In October 1931 during a demonstration against unemployment the vicar, Etienne Watts, offered sanctuary to those trying to avoid the clutches of the authorities, and refused to allow the police access. Ten years later the church perished in the Blitz. The square has continued to decline, despite the well-designed 1960s St Augustine's church on the west side of the square. The last vestige of genteel respectability – the ornate Victorian drinking fountain – was removed in 1982. Pleasant gardens surrounded by what are mostly hideously designed 1960s college buildings fill the site.

Mancunian Way
The city's first motorway, officially the A57 (M), was built between 1964 and 1967 to link St George's with Ardwick. The name Mancunian Way was suggested by Manchester schoolchildren, invited by the Corporation to come up with a title for the new road. Thoughts that the Mancunian Way was built for perfunctory rather than practical reasons became evident once locals noticed that one of the slip roads near Brook Street ended in a stump in mid-air and has

remained so, to Manchester's embarrassment, since.

(iv) around the hospitals

The Infirmary's move from what is now Piccadilly Gardens to Chorlton-on-Medlock at the beginning of the twentieth century started a fashion for building medical institutions in this part of Manchester. Consequently, the area to the south-east of the main university campus is now home to not only the Manchester Royal Infirmary, but St Mary's and the Royal Eye Hospital as well as the university medical school.

Vera Millward, the ninth victim of Peter Sutcliffe, the Yorkshire Ripper, was found dead in the grounds of the Manchester Royal Infirmary on Tuesday 16 May 1978. Millward, a forty-year-old prostitute, had left her flat in Greenham Avenue, Hulme, to buy cigarettes and painkillers but was unfortunate enough to come across Sutcliffe, who was looking for a likely target. They went off to the hospital area for sex, and once there he struck her on the head three times, undressed her and slashed her so violently across her stomach that her intestines spilled out. Somehow Millward's screams for help were ignored by a man and his son who were in the hospital grounds at the time. She was found dead at 8.10 a.m. the following day, her arms folded, legs straightened and shoes placed neatly on her body.
► The Yorkshire Ripper and Lingbeck Crescent, p. 134.

Grafton Street
Grafton Hotel, No. 56
Len Johnson, one of Manchester's most successful boxers, who fought in the 1920s when black fighters were ostracized by the sports authorities, opened the New International Club at that time to promote his Communist and anti-racist beliefs. It was here a decade later that Mancunians who wanted to fight for the Left in the Spanish Civil War signed up to go to the continent.

During the Second World War Johnson was engaged in war work locally at the ARP centre on Claremont Road. Resources were a fleet of single-decker buses which were used to carry all manner of tools – ropes, axes, crowbars, jacks – around the city to free people trapped in their houses after bomb damage. In 1949 Johnson stood for election to the council in Moss Side East ward as a Communist under the slogan 'Houses, hospitals, schools, not tanks, planes, warships'. He lost. Around that time the premises became the West Indian Colonials' Club, used by the earliest immigrants to the city from the Caribbean. It is now a hotel.

► Moss Side's West Indian community, p. 132.

Nelson Street

The Pankhurst Centre, No. 62
Emmeline Pankhurst and her group of suffragettes founded the Women's Social and Political Union (WSPU) on 10 October 1903 at 62 Nelson Street, the house where Emmeline and her family then lived, to further the campaign to win women the vote. The WSPU initially limited its membership to women only, despite the support of politicians such as Keir Hardie of the Independent Labour Party, noting how even within the Labour Party 'the help of women is welcomed in the work of elections, but when leaders and men members of the party are asked for efforts to be made to secure the enfranchisement of women they express at best vague sympathy'. Weekly meetings of the new body were held in the Nelson Street drawing room ('very artistically furnished', as leading member Annie Kenney later described it) where the group's famous slogan, 'Votes for Women', was coined.

To explain the suffragette cause to a wider audience, Rachel Scott, the body's secretary, wrote to the left-wing newspaper the *Clarion*, outlining how the WSPU wanted to 'secure for women complete equality with men, both social and political'. The movement was soon involved in a series of high-profile campaigns of civil disobedience. Spurred on by Emmeline Pankhurst's insist-

ence that 'deeds, not words, were to be our permanent motto', the WSPU hit the headlines in 1905 when two members, Christabel Pankhurst (Emmeline's daughter) and Annie Kenney, deliberately caused a disturbance at the Free Trade Hall (p. 30) during which Christabel spat in the face of two policemen. By then the Pankhursts were national figures.

The vote was extended to women in 1918, with certain conditions, and fully, ten years later. When the regional health authority threatened to demolish the building in 1979 a trust was formed to save it, and with the money raised it opened as a museum in 1987.

► Political turmoil at the Town Hall, p. 3.

Upper Brook Street

Plaza, (1970s–90s), No. 267
No Manchester restaurant has ever attained the legendary status of this pioneering and much mourned curry cafe, established by a group of Somalis in the early 1970s. At that time the Plaza was one of the few places in Manchester open till the early hours of the morning, and because of its location on the edge of the university campus was always filled with hordes of students enticed not by the richness and quality of the menu but by its very frugality.

Instead of the usual list of kormas, madrases and rogan joshs, there was only one dish, a huge biryani, enough for three people, sprinkled with meat which was allegedly chicken, but looked like no chicken that existed elsewhere. Sightings within the premises of a greyhound, and even a stricken seagull caught in the extractor fan, fuelled a thousand pernicious rumours and served to stoke the legend further.

With the biryani the Plaza waiters served up one of five sauces: mild, medium, hot, killer and suicide – differentiated inevitably by the amount of chilli. But patrons were not allowed to choose their own sauce. They had to start on mild and were served something more challenging only when they had proved to the management they could handle the existing chilli content. Understandably, few were allowed to reach 'killer' or 'suicide' level; another equally pernicious rumour spread about a crazed diner who had drunk the suicide sauce in one draught, and expired on the spot.

It was only after the café closed following the owners' decision to return to Somalia to fight in the civil war of the 1990s that it emerged that all along there had been six sauces. The sixth was the hottest of all. Unknown to nearly all customers and served only to the most privileged cognoscenti, it rejoiced in the deliberately pedestrian but wonderful name of 'English gravy'.

HULME

Slum Manchester, demolished, destroyed and rebuilt twice in the twentieth century, Hulme stands alone as the most notorious housing estate in the city's history – perhaps even in British history, *pace* the Gorbals – a template for every half-realized, underfinanced, ill-conceived, town hall-driven social-engineering project.

Hulme grew as a working-class suburb on the edge of central Manchester in the nineteenth century. Its population increased at a phenomenal rate as people came from the country towns to work in the nearby factories and waterways. By the beginning of the twentieth century the population density was around 150 people per acre, at a time when the Manchester average was only 34 per acre. The housing in Hulme was basic and brutal: two-up, two-down brick boxes with next to no sanitation – what the suffragette Sylvia Pankhurst described as 'endless rows of smoke-begrimed little houses, with never a tree or a flower in sight . . . how bitterly their ugliness smote me!'

With its lack of railways, Hulme was never as industrialized as the suburbs of east Manchester, where the heavy metallic work took place. Instead it was dotted with small workshops such as that run by Rolls and

Royce, who made their first internationally famous cars here. Unlike nearby Chorlton-on-Medlock and Ardwick, Hulme never had a resident middle-class community – there were no desirable squares or attractive villas – and so in 1934 Manchester Corporation chose it for slum clearance, the largest such site in Britain at over 300 acres.

Now the 'black fortress', as Howard Spring described it in his 1938 novel *My Son My Son*, would go. Although the press sided with the Corporation in citing Hulme as a good-for-nothing slum, there were many dissenting voices, including local architects, who pointed out that the housing stock was mostly sound, but what gave the area its depressing veneer were the social conditions all around; that few of the properties had a tap or sink, which were mostly found in the yard at the back, and that drainage was poor. There were also many crumbling walls, leaky roofs and a lack of doors on the bedrooms. A sensible and cheaper solution than total demolition would have been installing inside taps, sinks and improved drainage, repointing the walls, securing the roofs and adding doors, but these ideas were discounted. During the Second World War slum clearance halted; there was still time to reconsider. Instead, after the war ended, demolition recommenced and continued until 1960 under the manic eye of the Corporation's chief public health officer, Alf Young, who decreed that anything built before 1919 had to go.

Rather than provide high-quality brick council houses along the lines of those that had been built in Old Moat and Wythenshawe, the Corporation told residents that such properties were dated and that the way forward was system-built, deck-access flats. 'Progressive' architects – Hugh Wilson and Lewis Womersley – were commissioned to provide a radical rebuilding programme. Wilson had been responsible for part of Cumbernauld New Town in Scotland, voted Britain's ugliest town in a television programme at the beginning of the twenty-first century. Womersley had worked on the

Park Hill flats in Sheffield; gruesome, inhuman, inexcusable, but not as bad as Cumbernauld. In Manchester the partnership would also be behind the Arndale Centre.

The centrepiece of their new Hulme, begun in 1968, consisted of four immense, low-lying, concrete crescents of maisonettes, each overlooking a dismal grassed area. With tongue firmly in cheek, Wilson and Womersley claimed the Hulme Crescents were based on the revered Georgian crescents of the late eighteenth century, and named each after a period architect – Robert Adam, Charles Barry, William Kent and John Nash. 'By the use of similar shapes and proportions and open spaces, and, above all, by skilful landscaping and extensive tree-planting,' Wilson and Womersley explained, 'it is our endeavour at Hulme to achieve a solution to the problems of twentieth-century living which would be the equivalent in quality of that reached for the requirements of the eighteenth century in Bloomsbury and Bath.'

Yet whereas those Georgian properties are still standing over 200 years later, with million pound-plus valuations, their supposed equivalents in Hulme lasted barely twenty-five years and were worthless when demolished. The Georgian terraces of Robert Adam and Co. were carefully built: they were made of brick and stone, natural materials. They were set on streets which linked directly with the rest of the area. They could be entered from the street up a few steps. In contrast, the Hulme Crescents were built shoddily as pre-fabricated, machine-made housing units rather than through personal craftsmanship. They were made from concrete covered with a coating of glass-reinforced plastic – Resiac – at John Laing's Heywood factory and slotted together on site. The Hulme Crescents were not placed on roads but dumped on land-scaped sites accessible only along windswept open paths. Nor could the maisonettes even be entered easily. Access was up flights of stairs, or reliant on lifts that never worked,

and connected by high-level concrete walk-ways – streets in the sky – that filled the horizon with ugliness.

The Corporation and press drooled over the proposals, but later claimed 'in hindsight' that Wilson and Womersley were misguided. Yet it was obvious from the beginning that the new Hulme would be a disaster. The Town Hall would now decide where locals would live without consultation; people were uprooted en masse without debate. Nor were the existing residents moved back into Hulme, but sent to the new out-of-town overspill estates such as Partington and Hattersley. Consequently those who were transplanted into the new Hulme had no feel for the area and no wish to promote it, and the place soon began to decline. Whereas in the condemned houses every housewife washed down her step each morning, or risked being ostracized, now no one cleaned the vast publicly owned spaces – least of all anyone from the Corporation – and these spaces rapidly became permanently encrusted with litter and infested with the stench of urine.

It was soon apparent that little thought had been put into the quality of the building work. The bolts and ties that held the panels in place hadn't been fitted properly. The rain began to seep in, just as it had done in the old houses. The low-quality ventilation meant that the blocks were rife with condensation. There was a major problem with vermin. The heating, serviced by huge fans on the roof, sucked in air and blew a large amount of asbestos around the flats with it. Sewage smells were pervasive.

Only some people spoke against the new estate. The *Architects' Journal* described Hulme as 'Europe's worst housing stock . . . hideous system-built deck-access blocks'. Colin Buchanan in *The State of Britain* (1972) talked about the way the authorities had changed people's lives for the worst with such developments:

Often when I am travelling by train I look at the rows of fairly poor houses that back on to the railway lines . . . but I see bits tacked on. I see flowers in the garden, little patches of mown grass, greenhouses, pigeon lofts and of course sheds, and I feel that those houses, miserable though they may be in many respects, provide a creative outlet for the occupants in a way that a flat in a tower block never can provide.

And so it proved in Hulme, where the council failed to provide the new occupants with anything that might have smacked of individuality. All the public spaces were owned by the Corporation, and were unavailable to individuals; and there were no greenhouses, pigeon lofts or sheds, as the council feared that if people were left to run their own lives they wouldn't be able to cope. To make matters worse, along with the vast stretches of old housing, Hulme's shops, nearly all its pubs, churches and social clubs, and most of the old streets were torn down as well, with the construction of the Mancunian Way and Princess Road motorways cutting the area off from the rest of the city.

Life on the new estate was unbearable for many from the first. The elderly and families with young children had been put on the top decks of the blocks. Crime became a major problem as the police would not patrol the long dark decks, the excuse being that officially they were not streets. Muggings and burglaries could be carried out in almost total privacy. Design flaws resulted in people either having permanent free heating or freezing in poorly insulated damp homes. Tenants were telling journalists that they preferred the old slums. By 1978 the *Manchester Evening News*, which had done so much to proselytize the Corporation's pro-Hulme propaganda, describing the proposals as worthy of a new Bath, was now casting Hulme as the new Colditz.

Yet by the mid-1980s Hulme, despite its tortuous birth, social problems and architectural inadequacies, was beginning to work. Whereas a 1975 survey had found that 96.3 per cent of Hulme tenants wanted to leave, ten years later it was clear that people were *choosing* to live in Hulme. The families that

the council had moved in to fill the new blocks had by now left, and their place had been taken by single people, groups of friends and public sector employees working for the ever-expanding Manchester municipal sector.

The largest demographic group was students, for whom Hulme was ideal, being close to the colleges and the perfect two-year bohemian bolt-hole between hall of residence and well-paid job. The students clearly didn't mind living in such squalor; many revelled in it. Yet there was much resentment between them and long-standing locals, the two sides easily identifiable through a simple shibboleth: the students pronounced the name of the area 'Hyoom', the locals 'Ooom'.

In the 1980s Hulme was the centre of a lively political scene based around a myriad of esoteric and cryptic quasi-Trotskyite organizations: Socialist Action, the International Marxist Group, Socialist Organizer, the Workers Revolutionary Party – anything as long as it was not the Communist Party – and an equally vibrant, thriving music scene which few areas so small could match. Hulme groups of the 80s making inspired music included the Inca Babies, Big Flame, Skol Bandaleros, Dub Sex, the Ruthless Rap Assassins, the ingeniously named Tools You Can Trust and best of all the cryptically named A Guy Called Gerald who provided an iconic and mesmerizing Hulme signature tune, 'Voodoo Ray', composed and produced in his own Robert Adam Crescent bedroom, that attained international success.

Then there was Edward Barton. The most outré and left-field resident in an area full of such characters, Barton rented two adjacent flats on Charles Barry Crescent and knocked through the adjoining wall to form one huge apartment which he furnished with wooden railway sleepers. In the middle of the room he planted a tree that he decorated with babies' dummies and shoes. Inside this grotesque creation he wrote songs for Kylie Minogue, the Inspiral Carpets and his *pièce de résistance*, an autobiographical piece of Dada whimsy entitled "I've Got No Chicken But I've Got Five Wooden Chairs', which he performed live on *The Tube* TV programme.

Those looking for an exciting nightlife didn't even need to head for city-centre Manchester, even though it was little more than a mile away. Pubs such as the Junction, Grant's Arms and the Henry Royce (named ironically after the teetotal car manufacturer) were patronized by a mix of aesthetes, intellectuals, drug dealers and retired Ship Canal workers. The 𝕬𝖆𝖇𝖊𝖓 cinema featured mouth-watering rep double bills, and at the end of the 1970s Tony Wilson's Factory nights at the 𝕽𝖚𝖘𝖘𝖊𝖑𝖑 𝕮𝖑𝖚𝖇 showcased some of the most exciting music acts on the planet, with patrons still gushing over the performances of Joy Division, the Pop Group, Pere Ubu and Magazine.

It couldn't last. The city council decided in the 1990s that Hulme would have to be rebuilt, despite being barely twenty years old. It was not the horrendous state of the housing that motivated them but the idea of a mini-society run according to its own rules – what local writer John Robb called 'a virtually independent freak scene run by the freaks for the freaks' – when the whole point of Hulme had been to create a community entirely run by the Town Hall.

In the 1990s Hulme was demolished for the second time in thirty years. A street party to celebrate the demise of the Crescents in 1993 was thrown with 'skeletons', bonfires and inflatable giant cockroaches (the area's most conspicuous inhabitants). It was duly rebuilt amid yet another PR campaign extolling the virtues of the 'new Hulme'. This twenty-first-century Hulme is a land of brick houses rather than concrete/plastic deck-access flats. However, many of the same mistakes have been made again: the same manic desperation to knock everything down, even the bits that work; the same culs-de-sac and blocked roads that encourage ghettos and dereliction; the same blight caused by needless land-clearance

policies; and the same level of ugly, anti-social architecture.

Royce Road

All traces of Cooke Street, where Charles Rolls and Frederick Henry Royce made the first Rolls-Royce cars, have gone although both men are commemorated in the names of nearby streets. Royce, who set up an electrical firm in Hulme in 1884, was not a popular employer. 'Everything had to be perfect. I've never worked for such a good engineer,' recalled one anonymous employee, 'but he would not hesitate to sack a man for using the wrong file or faking a job.' On 1 April 1904 Royce drove his first car out of the Hulme workshop. News reached Charles Rolls, a London-based car agent, rally driver and aviator. He came to Manchester, met Royce at the Midland Hotel, and formed a partnership that within two years had produced the first Silver Ghost Rolls-Royce.

▶ Ford's in Trafford Park, p. 192.

𝕽𝖚𝖘𝖘𝖊𝖑𝖑 𝕮𝖑𝖚𝖇/𝕿𝖍𝖊 𝕵𝖆𝖈𝖙𝖔𝖗𝖞, Royce Road at Clayburn Street

A small, nondescript, box-like building by the Hulme Crescents became the most revered night-time venue in Britain in the late 1970s after it was taken over by Granada Television's Tony Wilson for his 𝕵𝖆𝖈𝖙𝖔𝖗𝖞 nights. Known both as the 𝕽𝖚𝖘𝖘𝖊𝖑𝖑 𝕮𝖑𝖚𝖇 and the ℙ𝕊𝕍, as it catered for public service vehicle workers, it was owned by the colourful Don Tonay who ran a strict 'no hats' policy, despite the surfeit of local rastas, and posted a sign near the stage which proclaimed: 'No Tams Allowed'. At 1 a.m. most nights Tonay would be collected by a van containing two seductive prostitutes, an occurrence recalled in the 2002 film of the era, *Twenty Four Hour Party People*, in which Tonay was played by Peter Kay.

𝕵𝖆𝖈𝖙𝖔𝖗𝖞 opened in May 1978. The poster for the opening night was given a Factory Records Catalogue Number – Fac 1 – thereby making it an instant collector's item. It was, however, practically uncollectable given that it appeared *after* the gig. Yet soon 𝕵𝖆𝖈𝖙𝖔𝖗𝖞, was hosting the best up-and-coming groups during the golden era of rock music: Joy Division; the Pop Group; Pere Ubu; the Undertones; the early UB40, when their sound was fresh and exciting; even Iggy Pop. The Factory nights ended in the early 1980s but the concept reappeared, invigorated and updated, at the Hacienda in 1982.

▶ The Hacienda, p. 61.

Stretford Road

The main road running through pre-slum clearance Hulme was a vital link between All Saints and Old Trafford, and a typical bustling working-class high street with useful small shops, clubs, churches, pubs and Hulme Town Hall.

In the 1960s Stretford Road, along with other local streets, was declared passé by the Corporation, and flattened. Even so the Corporation was unsure whether it had made the right decision and so, while the section between All Saints and Chorlton Road was wiped out of existence, the part further west was retained, even if most of the buildings were demolished, leaving it bereft of life, the cluster of pubs – including the Flatford and Three Legs of Man – left high and dry, a surreal sight.

By the 1990s the council was admitting it had been a mistake to tinker with Stretford Road, and plans were made to rebuild it. However, the job was only half done. Despite the construction of the graceful Hulme Arch Bridge in May 1997 the council refused to reconnect the road with All Saints, thereby rendering all its good work pointless.

south side

Hulme Town Hall, No. 223

The largest hall in the area was the setting for a number of major local meetings during the middle years of the twentieth century. More than 3,000 Manchester United supporters crammed into the hall on Friday 17 October 1930 to pass a motion of no confidence in the club's board after a dismal set of results including a 6–0 defeat to Huddersfield and a 7–4 loss to Newcastle.

They also voted to boycott the following day's game against Arsenal at which the attendance slipped to just 23,000. Worse was to come, and for the last game of the season, against Middlesbrough, by which time United were relegated, there were only 3,900 at the ground. In 1936 a meeting of Oswald Mosley's British Union of Fascists was cancelled after a crowd of thousands surrounded the building and pushed a tram over. Hulme Library now covers the site.

▶ Manchester United, p. 189.

MOSS SIDE

Where Hulme is notorious for the bizarre municipal housing experiments foisted on it by the Town Hall, Moss Side, the adjacent district to the south, derives its infamy more through the behaviour of its citizens and visitors, who rioted in 1981 and have made the neighbourhood one of the most trigger-happy in the UK in subsequent years. Though it is often lumped with Hulme, there are few similarities between the two areas. Moss Side's houses in red glazed brick were more spacious than those of Hulme, as they were built later in the nineteenth century when controls on building work were tighter, and even contained gardens. And where Hulme was solidly working class, Moss Side cultivated a lower-middle-class gentility away from the main roads.

What changed everything was black immigration after the Second World War and the Corporation's fear that because of that influx Moss Side was becoming a black ghetto. The first black settlement locally had appeared as early as the 1930s. Although there had been black communities in Manchester before thanks to trade with Africa created by the opening of the Ship Canal, they were mostly near the docks. After the war West Indians were encouraged to come to Britain to take jobs in the expanded public sector. In Manchester they found a relatively tolerant indigenous population. As one of those who arrived in Britain on the

Empire Windrush ship, Euton Christian, explained: 'We had no difficulty in going about in Manchester. [People] were quite helpful and willing to give you any assistance.' There were some problems, however, and a colour bar operated in some Moss Side pubs and clubs. A well-known story tells of a West Indian entering the Denmark Hotel soon after arriving in the area and being asked by the publican, 'Do you believe in the colour bar?' When the man replied: 'No, of course not,' the publican retorted, 'Well we do, so off you go.'

Gradually the local demographics changed. West Indian families would club together to rent, or sometimes even buy, one of the larger houses at the Chorlton-on-Medlock end of Moss Side. A house would become home to three or four groups of friends from the same island, the over-crowding mitigated by the conviviality. However, after the original Caribbean tenants left, these properties often became lodging houses, and with no stable community the area declined.

In the press, antipathy to the new Moss Siders was blatant. All misdemeanours committed by a black immigrant were magnified, with particular attention paid to prostitution, as if there were no white girls on the streets of Manchester. For instance in 1957 the *Evening Chronicle* dubbed Moss Side 'Little Harlem – a hot bed of vice and corruption [where] God-fearing people have to live next door to blackguards, pimps, prostitutes and thieves.' But not all the newcomers to Moss Side in the 50s were black. One Scottish arrival who went on to achieve considerable infamy for his Manchester exploits was Ian Brady, the Moors Murderer.

As recently as the mid-1960s Moss Side was a successful working-class community. There was employment at the bus depot on Princess Road, small shops and businesses set around the main junction of Princess Road and Moss Lane East, a pleasant park – Alexandra Park – and well-used clubs, pubs and societies all around. But in April 1967

Manchester Corporation announced plans for a new-look Moss Side. Its population would be reduced by a quarter through deliberate and forced relocations to break up the West Indian community. 'Moss Side will lose its ghetto status,' announced the housing chairman, Richard Harper. Over the next two decades those parts of Moss Side set around its main junction were wiped out and replaced by bottom-of-the-range council houses built with the smallest possible windows, standing away from the main road behind grass verges and set in labyrinthine culs-de-sac. Also demolished were scores of small shops which were replaced by a covered shopping precinct serving one of the poorest populations in the city. (By the 1990s the council had changed its mind, and it destroyed the shopping centre. By then it was too late to reinstate the corner shops.)

The residents' revenge for the state-sponsored devastation of Moss Side were the 1981 riots during which disaffected youths besieged the police station which they claimed, with some justification, was home to a particularly nasty brand of racist officers, and burned down the few remaining shops on the main Princess Road. Just as the council had responded to the problems of 1950s Moss Side by trying to wipe out the area, they responded to the riots with the wrecking ball. The demolition of pubs such as the Big Alex, and night-time venues such as the Nile and Reno, put an end to the harmony that existed locally between poor young blacks and slumming whites. And rather than eradicating the violence, it coincided with a sharp increase in local gun crime as warfare raged between rival gangs such as the Gooch and the Pepperhill.

A police crackdown on these new local crime spots simply led the gangs to regroup under different names. The police picked off the ringleaders in 1990 but that left a power vacuum soon filled by new contenders intent on carrying out even wilder shootings and more witness intimidation. The latest Moss Side crime scene is fuelled by nastier drugs – heroin and crack, not cannabis – and violence played out to a misogynist gangsta rap soundtrack which has replaced the uplifting soul, reggae and jazz of earlier decades.

(i) around the brewery

Gretney Walk/Lingbeck Crescent

In an area dominated by ugly, barely inhabitable concrete council flats, Lingbeck Crescent and its neighbour, Gretney Walk, were the worst of all. Two blocks of low-rise, deck-access flats off Princess Road, they were infested with mice and rats, their lifts never worked and the dustbins were never emptied. The flats had bubbles of mould on the walls and the warped wood was often soaking, dystopian conditions emphasized by the conspicuous graffiti on one wall which read 'Join the Housebreakers' Association – cost: one TV'.

In the late 1970s Lingbeck Crescent was home to prostitute Jean Jordan – 'Scotch Jean' – victim number six of Peter Sutcliffe, the Yorkshire Ripper. Jordan was killed on 1 October 1977 after Sutcliffe drove from Bradford to Manchester to test out his new car. Cruising the red-light district of Moss Side, he picked out Jordan and took her to a location further down Princess Road, near Southern Cemetery, where he hit her with a hammer eleven times. As he crouched over the dying woman, Sutcliffe saw a car's headlights and quickly hid the corpse near some bushes. He then drove back to Bradford, but on the way realized he'd left incriminating evidence on the body, which meant he had to return to the scene of the crime. Jordan's common law husband, Alan Royle, failed to report her missing. He assumed she had taken off without warning to visit relatives in Scotland, and so her body wasn't discovered for over a week.

The two blocks were demolished in the 1990s.

▶ The Yorkshire Ripper at Southern Cemetery, p. 167.

Princess Road

The main road south out of central Manchester is still Moss Side's highway, even if its decline over recent decades is symbolic of the area's greater demise. The stretch to the immediate south of Moss Lane East, now just empty grass, used to be occupied by a number of businesses and venues, including the Reno and Nile clubs, and the tobacconist's at No. 21 where the young Anthony Burgess briefly lived. The Burgess family also lived nearby at No. 261 Moss Lane East, now demolished, which the author later visited and claimed had been turned into a shebeen, and at No. 47 Princess Road, now a Rastafarian gift shop.

Reno/Nile, No. 3

Moss Side's most famous West Indian venues in pre-riots time were the Reno and the Nile, the latter a drinking club based above the former. The Reno was opened in 1962 by Phil Magbotiwan as a Salvation Army hostel for African seamen. It was a relaxed place which the local black community saw as their only haven from a hostile society, one where they could smoke, drink, listen to music and gamble. Music at the Reno was initially provided by calypso bands featuring musicians such as Granville Edwards, a carpenter and tenor sax player also known as Lord Kitchener, while in the Nile the 1960s house band included on trumpet the revered Nigerian Fela Kuti.

Both venues soon began attracting a smattering of white bohemians who were at first scorned but later tolerated. During the 1970s the clientèle included the leading West Indian cricketer Clive Lloyd, who played locally for Lancashire and whom George Best remembered passing round the Cockspur rum, but by the end of the decade both venues were caught up in the local drugs industry. Much dealing took place in the alley behind the building, which led to the police putting pressure on the council to demolish the block and expose the pushers. The site was duly bulldozed in the mid-1980s. Unsurprisingly, local drug dealing has continued elsewhere.

(ii) Greenheys

A pleasant suburb named after the ancient house of Greenhay grew in late medieval times to the north of Moss Side. Greenhay stood in three acres of land, the Corn Brook flowing outside the main door, and was the boyhood home of the early nineteenth-century author Thomas de Quincey, best known for *Confessions of an English Opium Eater* (1821). Later it was home to Robert Owen, often known as the 'father of British Socialism'.

In the opening of her 1848 novel *Mary Barton*, Elizabeth Gaskell describes the area as having a 'charm about it which strikes even the inhabitant of a mountainous district'. Greenhay and a number of other substantial properties such as Pepperhill Farm also featured in the same novel, but these, together with the house where orchestra leader Charles Hallé lived in the mid-nineteenth century, were swept away by the next century in the desperation to cover this part of Manchester with workers' houses. Local history has been dutifully remembered in the names Pepperhill Road, further south in Moss Side, and Charles Hallé Road to the east of the brewery.

Lloyd Street

Paddy O'Donoghue ran the Manchester branch of the IRA from a long demolished grocer's shop on Lloyd Street in the early years of the twentieth century. O'Donoghue was a good friend of Michael Collins, the leading Irish nationalist of the era, who was best man at his wedding. In February 1919 he helped spring Eamon de Valera, who later became President of Ireland, from Lincoln Jail where the statesman had been imprisoned after a British swoop on Irish nationalist leaders they suspected of collaborating with Germany during the First World War. O'Donoghue was later arrested for shooting a policeman at the Bridgewater House warehouse in Manchester city centre.
▶ Fenian ambush on Hyde Road, p. 151.

(iii) around Alexandra Park

Bedwell Street
Former Pepperhill pub/Saltshaker

As the Pepperhill pub in the late twentieth century the building, now the Saltshaker community centre, was central to the wave of violent gun-related crime that spread through Moss Side and other run-down parts of Manchester. Gun crime, linked with the city's growing drugs industry and protection rackets involving nightclub bouncers, first hit the headlines in an article in the *Guardian* of 7 June 1988 in which Clive Atkinson, deputy head of Greater Manchester CID, explained: 'We are dealing with a black mafia which is a threat to the whole community.'

After a series of shootings in the early 1990s Manchester earned the unfortunate nickname 'Gunchester' in the press. By then gangs such as the Pepperhill and their rivals the Gooch, from Moss Side's Gooch Close, were using young children as foot-soldiers and runners, paying them sums their peers could only dream about. This, of course, came with the risk of being at the end of a bullet. But it was not just teenagers on mountain bikes who were caught up in the violence. Typical was the story of a local woman, Erinma Bell, who, arriving at a party with her husband in 1999, saw a friend gunned down by three hooded youths. Bell later discovered that the friend was not the target but his half-brother. The gang had reasoned that if they shot the man dead there would be a funeral which the half-brother would attend, where he in turn could be killed. Their scheme foundered half way through, but it was typical of the new crime pattern of Moss Side.

Following a spate of shootings and tit-for-tat killings in the 1990s – twenty-seven over one five-year period, with 250 people injured – the Pepperhill was closed down. But the gang simply reformed on a nearby estate, Doddington Close, and called themselves the Doddington. The decline of Moss Side as a community reached a new nadir in

The 1981 Moss Side riots

The 1981 Moss Side riots – echoed in similar disturbances in other parts of Britain around the time – centred on the local police station, long a butt for the local black community's grievances about supposedly racist policing.

The year had started badly for Britain's black community. In January 1981 thirteen young blacks died in London's New Cross fire. In April an intensive stop-and-search police exercise in nearby Brixton led to riots, and a few weeks later Toxteth in Liverpool went up in flames. In Manchester many wondered when, not if, Moss Side would erupt, and they cited the police station as an inevitable target. That June the Black Parents Association claimed that the station had 'long been regarded by the black community as the operational base of a racist army in occupation'.

On 8 July 1981 more than 1,000 mostly young people besieged Greenheys police station on what is now Charles Hallé Road and tried to batter their way inside before being repelled. At the same time a group of officers drove up and down Moss Lane East shouting, 'Nigger, nigger, nigger, oi,

oi, oi.' Meanwhile, a mob went on the rampage along Princess Road, the main route through Moss Side, wrecking and ransacking shops, finishing off, some cynics noted, the council's systematic, if legal, wrecking and ransacking of the area over the previous few decades.

The next afternoon crowds gathered on Quinney Crescent in the heart of council-estate Moss Side waiting for something to happen, served by conscientious ice-cream salesmen and hot-dog sellers who realized they had a captive audience. In the evening officers in riot gear appeared. They were attacked with missiles while a mob besieged the police station. Again shops on Princess Road were attacked, with little police intervention because, cynics alleged, the police wanted to see Moss Side burn down.

After the riots were over, retribution – mostly verbal – was swift. Community leaders raged against the local schools' low expectations of their pupils, the lack of facilities provided by the council and other authorities (failing to add that most of Moss Side's problems had been caused by public sector involvement in the first place), and the shortage of jobs. The

1993 with the shooting of fourteen-year-old Benji Stanley, who was gunned down outside Alvino's Pattie and Dumplin Shop on Great Western Street despite having no connection with the local drugs industry.

The following year a supposed truce between the Moss Side gangs was heralded in the *Manchester Evening News* alongside a visit by members of Los Angeles' Bloods and Crips gangs. The truce ended within a year, following the killing of the Doddington leader, Raymond Pitt, after which his brother, Tommy, took over what became known as the Pitt Bull Crew and the violence continued. In January 2002 Pitt was found guilty of murder, three attempted murders, and various drugs and firearms offences. The gangs are still constantly re-

forming under different names, centred around different Moss Side venues, attracting a never-ending roster of ever tougher opponents from Manchester's many sink estates.

In 2004 the city learned of the rivalry between Moss Side's Gooch Close Gang and the Longsight Crew from two miles east when gang members clashed at the Manchester Royal Infirmary, chasing each other on mountain bikes down the hospital corridors as staff tried to barricade doors and protect patients. Twelve months later, in July 2005, the Gooch and Doddington gangs fought hand-to-hand, and let off gunshots in Manchester city centre on a Wednesday afternoon. A year later the slaying in the street of fifteen-year-old Jessie James in the police, led by the deliberately controversial chief constable James Anderton, spoke of Trotskyite *agents provocateurs* travelling to Moss Side from afar to cause trouble, while neglecting to mention the role of plain-clothes police *agents provocateurs* in fomenting trouble among volatile locals.

Although Anderton insisted his force was innocent of any anti-social behaviour, his opponents were proved to have been correct all along when a decade later the police made an embarrassing volte-face and began to deploy the kind of progressive policies they had been urged to adopt all along. 'When you look back and ask, did we provide policing to meet the needs of the community then, we clearly didn't,' Chief Superintendent Dave Thompson, late twentieth-century commander of Manchester metropolitan division, explained. 'The way policing was conducted then is almost alien at times to how we police now.'

Unfortunately for the neighbourhood, while policing has improved beyond all recognition in Moss Side, crime – gang warfare, if not small-scale villainy – has spiralled out of control in the twenty-first century.

early hours of the morning showed that little had changed despite some £400 million of investment in the area since the 1981 riots.

(iv) around Claremont Road

Lindum Street

During the Second World War this small street was home to Robert Winstanley, the so-called 'King of the Forgers'. Winstanley rented two rooms in a terraced house, convinced the landlady to forgo the cleaning, and spent many months inside engraving copper plates and etching blocks of stone to produce banknotes which he dried on a newspaper-covered coat rack. For six years Winstanley used the notes for placing bets at racetracks, but he was caught at the Albion

Stadium in Salford when two of his notes – one real, one fake – were spotted with the same serial number. Winstanley willingly invited detectives back to Lindum Street where he showed them his collection of 8,730 forged £1 notes. He received a ten-year sentence.

Maine Road
Manchester City, (1923–2003), south of Claremont Road
Whereas the story of Manchester United represents everything about Manchester at its best: dynamism; energy; glory; fierce independence and loyalty; style with swagger, Manchester City symbolize everything about Manchester at its worst: managerial incompetence; victim mentality; cheap, quick-fix solutions regretted at length; and over-confidence bordering on woeful arrogance that soon gives way to hand-wringing and greying hair as defeat is snatched from the jaws of victory generation after generation.

Founded in Gorton, east Manchester, in 1880, the club joined the Football League as Ardwick in 1892, moving to this former clay pit at the southern edge of Moss Side in 1923. Here Charles Swain, whose other best-known Manchester building is the frosted glass Cornerhouse extension on Whitworth Street, built a new stadium which became one of England's most popular. Limited success for the next decade culminated in 1937 in that unlikeliest of football phenomena: Manchester City – champions. Remarkably, a year later the club was relegated, despite scoring the most goals in the division that season.

The early post-war period climaxed with another trophy – the FA Cup in 1956 – however, at the time the Busby Babes-era Manchester United were winning the League in consecutive seasons. A slump saw City drop to the Second Division in 1963, and at the end of the 1965 season only 8,015 saw them play against Swindon. That game ended with fans demonstrating and smashing boardroom windows, just as

United were about to win the championship again.

Within months two saviours arrived to revive the club and bring about City's most successful era. They were an unlikely couple: Joe Mercer – genial 'Uncle Joe' – a former championship-winning captain at Arsenal, an icon of what was increasingly looking like old-fashioned, gentlemanly football, and the tactically astute, flamboyant, young coach, Malcolm Allison. A year later City were promoted as Second Division champions. Two years later they were League champions, even if their achievement was overshadowed by United's winning of the European Cup. The FA Cup followed in 1969, and a year later came the cup double of League Cup and European Cup-Winners' Cup. City had arrived as a major club on a continental scale.

Would the club continue to prosper and begin to rival Europe's greats or would they be unable to cope with success? The bare facts are that since their 1970 European triumph City have won just one trophy; United twenty. The main reason for this decline was the appointment of TV sales-man Peter Swales as chairman in 1973. Swales soon began to implement measures that would have given City prizes for self-destruction. After the club narrowly missed out on winning the League in both 1977 and 1978 he 'promoted' manager Tony Book to general manager and invited Mal-colm Allison to return as coach. Allison, by now a fedora-wearing, cigar-munching par-ody of himself, systematically dismantled a great side studded with quality inter-nationals and replaced them with a suc-cession of increasingly desperate and costly flops.

Relegation followed in 1983, and City then began yo-yoing between the top two div-isions (still their current default position). However, they have compounded their prob-lems with more self-inflicted disasters. After Peter Reid had guided the club to two suc-cessive seasons in fifth position in the early 1990s, Swales sacked him for reasons still

unclear. Yet the chairman couldn't even bring himself to carry out the deed. He hired a local journalist, John Maddock, as chief executive, who promptly embarrassed himself by announcing: 'I am the supremo now.'

Under Reid's inferior replacement, Brian Horton, City continued to flop. But this time Swales was forced out. His replacement in February 1994 was former star striker Francis Lee, whom fans heralded as a saviour. When Lee took his seat in the direc-tors' box as chairman there was a surge of excitement through the ground. Thousands of blue and white balloons soared to the sky and a banner read 'Welcome Francis'. But the honeymoon didn't last long, for Lee appointed the incorrigible serial relegation achiever Alan Ball as manager.

In one of his first acts Ball met the squad in Fallowfield and tore into the players, explaining that he had drunk in better bars than them, danced in better clubs than them and earned more respect than them. The speech fell flat. Towards the end of the season City faced relegation again, and with a week to go Peter Swales died. Even his last words directed at the club were disastrous. Fans are still uncertain of the meaning behind the statement: 'Tell them that the last thing I want is for them to go down.'

Then came another avoidable calamity. City needed to win their last match of the 1995–96 season against Liverpool *and* hope for favourable results elsewhere to stay up. News came through while they were draw-ing that that result would be enough, thanks to events elsewhere. Consequently Steve Lomas took the ball to the corner flag to waste time and the game ended in a draw. But City were relegated nonetheless; the incoming news had been wrong.

Surely the club would quickly bounce back? Unfortunately Alan Ball had dis-mantled a Premiership-standard line-up and replaced it with second-rate journey-men. Despite being promotion favourites they were soon struggling even at this level. Ball's response was not to blame his own shortcomings but to cite *Manchester Evening News* reporter Paul Hince as the culprit for stirring up the supporters against him. Ball didn't last much longer, and his replacement, Steve Coppell, was there only thirty-three days. Eventually Frank Clark steered the club to safety for the 1996–97 season. The end of the season highlight was when Ball, as a TV pundit during a City match, dismissed the team and performance out of hand – only to be reminded by his fellow guests that they were players he'd brought to the club.

A year later City suffered their greatest humiliation – relegation to the third tier of the League. Despite regaining Premiership status since, City always appear to be a club a couple of results away from a crisis. Only Manchester City could allow themselves to be bought by a foreign politician wanted back home for alleged criminal charges who to add to the farce was then banned. Even a multi-million pound cash injection of Abu Dhabi money in the summer of 2008 that made City the richest club in the world and saw the arrival of the lauded Brazilian striker Robinho failed to improve results, while excited talk from club executives of Top Four finishes and Champions League football was quickly followed by a suc-cession of defeats that saw the club slip into the relegation zone. Much of the blame for their second-club status lies with the fans. One group, refusing to acknowledge the 1958 Munich air disaster that killed half the Manchester United team, refer to the event as the 'Frank Swift tragedy', as their former goalkeeper also died in the crash. And to many Manchester City fans the highlight of the season is not the possibility of winning a trophy but beating United. As long as such a state of mind exists City look likely to remain in the shadow of their illustrious neighbours, no matter how many Brazilians the club's plutocratic owners buy.

● In 2003 the club left Maine Road, one of the largest and best-attended grounds in the country (since bulldozed), where the crowd of 84,569 for City *v* Stoke in March 1934 is still an English club record. Although the ground's architectural development over the decades was ill-considered, piecemeal, unplanned, ungainly and unrelated to what had gone before, Maine Road, at its best in the early 1970s, when thousands stood safely on the Kippax, had what the club's new City of Manchester Stadium will never have: soul and style.

► Queen's Hotel, p. 38.

East Manchester

For two centuries east Manchester was home to some of Britain's noisiest and nastiest industries, with power stations, coal pits, locomotive depots, engineering works, chemical factories and cotton mills filling the landscape, shaping what became known as 'the workshop of the world'.

The development of the mill system in the Industrial Revolution of the late eighteenth century shaped east Manchester. Previously local industry, mostly textiles, had taken place mainly in the workers' own homes. After John Kay invented the flying shuttle in Bury, a few miles north of Manchester, in 1733, it made more sense economically to house a number of workers in one building. The use of the flying shuttle and other new machines, particularly the steam engine, gave rise to the birth of the factory or mill system which overtook east Manchester by the end of the century. Ever-increasing numbers of people were drawn to the city, and the east side of town became one of the main centres not only for manufacturing cotton but also for making the machinery used in the factories.

Work took place in horrific conditions. Angus Bethune Reach of the *Morning Chronicle* described it for his London readers in the 1840s: 'The Manchester Operative is up and stirring before six. The factory bell rings from five minutes before six until the hour strikes. Then the engine starts and the day's work begins. Those who are [late] are fined two pence.' He could have added that the fourteen-hour day ended at eight in the evening.

For over 100 years east Manchester remained an economic and industrial powerhouse. As well as textiles there were power stations such as the huge Stuart Street site in Bradford, a nearby colliery, two of the world's greatest railway engineering works and the Clayton Aniline Company. Decline came gradually after the Second World War, with firms hampered by retrograde labour relations and poor training, and increasingly unable to cope with economic changes. Closure after closure turned its communities – Ancoats, Bradford, Gorton and Newton Heath – into ghost towns, and now little industry remains.

In the twenty-first century there has been minor regeneration around the twin themes of sport and leisure. The land above the closed-down Brabford Colliery now holds the City of Manchester Stadium, home of Manchester City Football Club, with other sports venues nearby. Nevertheless east Manchester remains one of the most depressing sights in the civilized world, a barely inhabitable and mostly desolate landscape of rotting industry, shuttered, vandalized buildings peopled by a demoralized older generation, their lives scarred by drudgery, and a lawless younger element responsible for some of the worst school results and the highest truancy rates in the country.

ANCOATS

> ... Ancoats, that teeming, squalid quarter which lies but a stone's throw from the principal thoroughfares of Manchester –
> *The History of David Grieve*, Mrs Humphry Ward (1892)

Ancoats was the world's first heavily industrialized suburb. Between 1790 and 1820 it was transformed at a frightening rate from farming country into a land of factories, ramshackle terraced houses and cotton mills, with not a patch of greenery in sight, just brick, stone and soot.

The immensity of the new factories and mills shocked Manchester, but problems of size were nothing compared to the monstrous working conditions, the noise of thundering machinery, the smell of belching smoke, the suffocating air and the high accident rates. These factories were run under the most notorious employment practices,

horrors as damnable as they are now clichéd – an emaciated, underpaid workforce slave-driven for unsustainably long hours amid disease, darkness, damp and desperate heat.

Child labour was prevalent. As one Ancoats mill owner explained to the early nineteenth-century poet laureate Robert Southey, when he visited Manchester in 1808, 'You see these children, sir. By the time they are seven or eight years old they are bringing in the money. They come at five in the morning, they leave at six and another set relieves them for the night; the wheels never stand still.'

Alongside the smoky, blackened and hellish mills, mean, dingy streets of tiny workers' houses were erected: jerry-built, two-up two-down brick boxes standing back-to-back to squeeze as many properties as possible into the smallest of spaces. All around was poverty, a new kind of mass poverty that festered alongside the untrammelled riches of the mill owners. Unsurprisingly, Ancoats also had the highest death rate in a city which itself had the highest death rate in England; half the local children died before they were five years old. All around was the nauseous stench of industry, or as Thomas de Quincey put it in *Confessions of an English Opium Eater* in 1821: 'Gloomy the streets of Manchester were at that time, mud below, smoke above . . .'

Commentators came from afar to see the horrors first hand. In 1838, a time when industry in Ancoats was at its most manic, Thomas Carlyle, one of the great commentators of the age, visited from London. He rose early in Manchester to note how 'at five in the morning all was still as sleep and darkness. At half-past five all went off like an enormous mill race or ocean tide. Boom-m-m, far and wide. It was the mills that were all starting then, and greasy drudges by the millions taking post there. I have heard few sounds more impressive to me in the mood I was in.'

As the century proceeded Ancoats became ever more industrialized. Foundries, dyers, glass works and timber-yards added

Made in east Manchester

In its industrial heyday east Manchester was one of the world's great centres for manufacturing heavy machinery for engineering, locomotives and even cars. Of the scores of firms based here the most important were:

● 𝔄𝔳𝔯𝔬, Briscoe Lane, Newton Heath. What had been the world's first aircraft makers, originally based near Piccadilly station (p. 72), moved further east after the Great War, where it manufactured a number of famous aircraft including the Avian, designed by Roy Chadwick, and later components for the Lancaster bomber. The building is still used as a warehouse.

● 𝔅𝔢𝔶𝔢𝔯 𝔓𝔢𝔞𝔠𝔬𝔠𝔨, Bessemer Street, Gorton. Begun by a German, Karl Beyer, and the Englishman Richard Peacock, the firm made locomotives that were used throughout Africa and Australia, and engines for many of the London Underground tube trains prior to early twentieth-century electrification.

● 𝔊𝔩𝔞𝔶𝔱𝔬𝔫 𝔄𝔫𝔦𝔩𝔦𝔫𝔢, Croft Street, Clayton. The company, which ran the single biggest manufacturing plant in Manchester and recently announced plans to close,
specialized in lubricants, printing inks, plastics and colour pigments. Because of the dyes the snow that fell outside the plant in winter would occasionally turn purple after settling.

● 𝔊𝔯𝔬𝔰𝔰𝔩𝔢𝔶 𝔐𝔬𝔱𝔬𝔯𝔰, Pottery Lane, Openshaw. East Manchester was a centre for the manufacture of early motor vehicles thanks to Crossley Brothers who set up their firm in 1867 and two years later acquired the world rights (except in Germany) to the patents for the new gas-fuelled atmospheric internal combustion engine. The Crossleys were teetotallers who refused to supply breweries and committed Christians who adopted the symbol of the Coptic Cross as the emblem for their vehicles. Decline set in after the Second World War and in the 1960s the company called in the receivers, later becoming part of Rolls-Royce. Engines are still made at the Pottery Lane factory, although the Crossley name no longer appears on the products.

● 𝔉𝔢𝔯𝔯𝔞𝔫𝔱𝔦, Wenlock Way, West Gorton. In the late 1950s and 1960s 𝔉𝔢𝔯𝔯𝔞𝔫𝔱𝔦's east Manchester site was the biggest computer plant in Europe, but it sold the computer division in 1963 to ICT,

to the busy intensity, especially around the Ashton and the Rochdale canals. The population rose accordingly, from 11,039 in the 1801 census to 53,737 in 1861. Many of the new residents were Irish, escaping poverty on one island for drudgery on another. A smaller number were Italians who roamed the streets as itinerant musicians accompanied by monkeys clinging to their necks.

By the twentieth century Ancoats was no longer a novelty, more of an embarrassment for Manchester, which saw it as a lawless, dirty, dangerous place where the sun never shone, where everyone wore clogs and the women black shawls, where public money need not be spent on maintaining the fabric of so unwelcome an area. Slum clearance began in the 1930s, when tenants
were moved to the new soulless suburban estates of Old Moat and Wythenshawe, and the area suffered considerable wartime damage the following decade.

The aftermath of the war brought more devastation, dereliction and slum clearance. Landlords were wary of carrying out repairs to houses for fear that the properties would soon be demolished. By the 1960s the library and museum had closed, and there was no resident doctor, home helps, meals-on-wheels service or child welfare clinic. Ancoats, according to social workers at the Manchester University Settlement on Every Street, was 'the lost suburb'.

The decline was exacerbated by mass factory closures in the 1970s and de-industrialization the following decade.

which was later bought out by the Japanese.

● Gorton Locomotive Works, Cornwall Street, Gorton. Here Eric Laithwaite conducted pioneering work on magnetic trains in the 1960s but saw his findings ignored by successive governments only to be taken up by Germany and Japan.

● Johnson and Nephew Wire Works, Forge Lane, Beswick. In the mid-nineteenth century Johnson and Nephew made the first transatlantic cable from its Ancoats factory. The firm later moved to Beswick, where it won the contract to manufacture barbed wire during the Great War. Manchester City's stadium covers the site of the plant.

● Laurence Scott Electromotors, Louisa Street, Openshaw. One of Manchester's bitterest and longest strikes took place at the plant in the early 1980s after the owners announced plans to transfer all work to Doncaster and Norwich, and pay minimum redundancy.

● Mather and Platt, Acres Lane, Newton Heath. Originally based in Salford, Mather and Platt moved to the edge of Philips Park, Newton Heath, early in the twentieth century and soon expanded to include a research laboratory, iron foundry and

sports ground. The company specialized in fire sprinklers and dominated the market until its patent rights expired in the 1970s. It was then taken over by the Australian-based Wormald International. The foundry and main office building have survived.

● Murray's Mills, Redhill Street, Ancoats. Along with the adjacent McConnell and Kennedy complex Murray's were one of the world's leading cotton spinners during the nineteenth century peak years of the industry. Using raw cotton imported mostly from America, they turned out finished cloth, much of which was exported, often via wholesale warehouses such as Cook and Watts (now the Britannia Hotel) on Manchester's Portland Street. Some cloth went straight to drapery businesses both fashionable, such as those on St Ann's Square or the Kendal Milne department store on Deansgate, and high street, such as Lewis's store on Mosley Street and Rylands (now Debenham's) on Market Street.

Only since the late 1980s have there been any voices suggesting that there is anything in Ancoats worth preserving. At first these were mostly just industrial archaeologists and historians, but slowly others have caught on that close to the heart of Manchester is one of the most remarkable industrial landscapes in the world. Now the battle is on between conservationists and developers, between those who want a new Ancoats to come alive alongside the preserved remains of the great mills and those who want to knock it all down and build flats on a virgin landscape.

Every Street

The strange name, which launched a thousand music-hall jokes ('I say, I say, I say, did you know there's a church on Every Street

in Manchester?' 'Why, a church and a pub to be sure'!) should be Yvery after Baron Yvery, whose daughter married into the landowning Mosley family.

By the end of the nineteenth century Every Street was at the heart of respectable working-class Ancoats. Home to shopkeepers and artisans earning relatively high wages for the area, it was safer, friendlier and more prosperous than the western end. It was also the most important street in Ancoats culturally, with meeting halls, a library and an art gallery. But its decline since the mid-twentieth century neatly encapsulates the demise of working-class Manchester. Gone is the library designed by Alfred Waterhouse. Gone is Ancoats Hall, the Mosleys' stately home, where Bonnie

'Useful Work Versus Useless Toil' – the Ancoats Brotherhood

Ancoats in the nineteenth century was prime territory for middle-class philanthropists concerned about the moral and economic problems found locally and the lack of aesthetic nourishment for the soul. In 1889 the engineering magnate Francis Crossley gave up his mansion in salubrious Bowdon to live among Ancoats' poorest in an old music-hall building he had converted into a temperance mission. But a bigger contribution was made by Charles Rowley, a local picture-frame maker, who in the 1880s founded the Ancoats Brotherhood to bring high culture to Ancoats.

Rowley, who was once described by a colleague as a 'romantic anti-capitalist', had grown up in a radical household, his father having been at Peterloo. Rowley hated industrialization, as it created urban squalor, and believed that music, literature and art would civilize the working classes and stave off drunkenness. He decided to put on concerts and talks in Ancoats for locals. At one of these the Pre-Raphaelite artist Ford Madox Brown, creator of the murals on Manchester history that embellish the Town Hall, lectured on *Possible Aesthetics in Manchester*, which he summarized as 'simple directions to simple folk on how to look beautiful for ever'. On another occasion the playwright George Bernard Shaw spoke on the Ten Commandments and later recalled: 'No matter on what spot of the globe you may happen to be, you are never safe from a summons to come to Ancoats and speak for the Brotherhood.' William Morris, the great designer and thinker, also came north, lecturing at the Churnet Street Hall on 21 January 1884 on 'Useful Work Versus Useless Toil'. The programmes for these events, printed at Morris's Kelmscott Press, contained translated quotes from Plato or Milton, and the membership cards were designed by a different leading graphic artist each year.

The lectures, which were free, attracted crowds of nearly a thousand, but few of the audience were Ancoats workers, who had little spare time to enlighten themselves nor the education to have even the most basic understanding of the topics Shaw or Morris were talking about. Occasionally, however, the audience did contain the people Rowley was trying to reach. Eva Gore Booth, a friend of the Pankhursts, recalled how she used to read Shelley at the Ancoats Brotherhood to what she described as 'a group of extremely rough girls'.

Prince Charlie stayed in 1745, and which later became an art gallery. Gone is the monument to Peterloo speaker 'Orator' Hunt. Gone is the quaint Round House where the philanthropic University Settlement began. In their place are empty lots, slum housing and dereliction.

east side: Tutbury Street to Great Ancoats Street

Henry Hunt monument, south of Tutbury Street

A statue to Henry 'Orator' Hunt, the main speaker at Peterloo, set on a slender 32-foot obelisk, stood from 1842–88 in the burial ground of the Bible Church on Every Street. The land was donated by James Scholefield, who had built the adjacent Round House

chapel (see p. 145), and he toured the area to win support for the idea following Hunt's death in 1836, urging people to 'remember the foul deeds of Peterloo'.

The foundation stone was laid on Good Friday 1842, when some 16,000 people lined the half-mile route from Stevenson Square to Every Street. Presiding over the ceremony was Feargus O'Connor, the Irish radical MP and a leading member of the Chartists, the body that wanted to change radically the British voting system. During the proceedings a fifteen-year-old boy from the Manchester Youth Chartist Association made a speech warning O'Connor that the young people of Manchester would have little time for the Charter 'unless it would give them a

Government based on the principles of Republicanism'. This call to replace the monarchy with a presidency alarmed the authorities. Worried at the prospect of a large unruly mob assembling, they cancelled the official unveiling of the monument, set for 16 August 1842, the anniversary of the Peterloo Massacre. Prime Minister Robert Peel told Queen Victoria that he planned to send 'a battalion of Guards by railway . . . it is feared that there may be a great assemblage of persons riotously disposed on that day'. The government also published a Royal Proclamation, threatening action against 'lawless and disorderly Persons assembled in a riotous and tumultuous manner'. The day passed off peacefully.

By the 1880s the monument's stone work had rotted away due to pollution and it was demolished. Surprisingly the stone itself was sold for only its market price, with no value put on its associations with Peterloo. The site, including the burial ground, was listed in 1974 but razed in 1988, as it was said to be unsafe.

The Round House, north of Ancoats Grove
The unusual circular brick building that stood behind 20 Every Street until 1986 was founded as a 'democratic' chapel in 1821 by James Scholefield, a Chartist and quack doctor. Locals dubbed it the 'Pork Pie Chapel'. Nevertheless the Round House became one of the best used buildings in the area, hosting recreational events, lectures and exhibitions for the Manchester Settlement next door. An L. S. Lowry show held here in March 1930 was then the artist's most successful, for he sold every picture.

In the 1960s there were reports that a new road was to be built through the site, and the Round House fell into disuse. It was sold, first to Manchester city council, then in 1974 to the Greater Manchester council, but in its derelict state was vandalized, and deteriorated into such a state of disrepair that there was no alternative but to demolish it, to the dismay of locals who saw it as yet further evidence of how the authorities were allowing Ancoats to die.

Ancoats Hall/Ancoats Museum, between Ancoats Grove and Great Ancoats Street
One of the homes of the Mosley family, who owned the Manchester manor before the town's mid-nineteenth-century incorporation as a borough, Ancoats Hall was a spacious Tudor building on the banks of the River Medlock just over a mile from the centre of Manchester. It was there that Oswald Mosley secretly entertained Charles Edward Stuart (the Young Pretender) when he came to Manchester in 1745 looking for support to seize the English throne from George II. In 1800 the incumbent Mosley sold the property to local mill owner George Murray, who demolished Ancoats Hall and built a smaller Gothic structure in its place.

The new hall was bought by T. C. Horsfall, an art collector, in 1876. Keen to show how the study of art might help people understand natural history and human nature, Horsfall had written a letter to the *Manchester Guardian* explaining that he wanted to 'alleviate the miserable dullness and emptiness of the life lived by a very large proportion of the inhabitants of Manchester'. He won support from Manchester worthies and figures from the arts, such as William Morris and the great art critic John Ruskin, who wrote back: 'You can't be wrong in getting good and beautiful things put anywhere within the sight of numbers of people.'

Horsfall eventually secured the lease of Ancoats Hall from the Midland Railway Company at a low rent, and opened a museum there on 7 October 1886. William Morris helped Horsfall with wallpapers and textiles, which went up alongside engravings of Pre-Raphaelite works, and paintings by G. F. Watts and Turner. But the museum was not just a gallery. It was home to the Manchester Settlement charity and was promoted as a 'People's Parlour' for music and other entertainment. Two thousand people attended on average each week, and only children with a clean face were allowed entrance. Ownership transferred to the council in 1918, and it continued as a museum until 1953 when the lease reverted to the landlord, British Rail. Following its closure, the collection was dispersed among the other Manchester museums. Soon after, the 'secret' tunnel beneath the hall, linking it with Clayton Hall, two miles east, collapsed, causing subsidence in Every Street. The building was demolished in the 1960s.

Great Ancoats Street

The main road bridging the city centre and Ancoats is now largely featureless thanks to continual road-widening over the years and redevelopment. Ancoats Lane in medieval times, it was a cart track leading from Shudehill to the cattle drovers' highway, Ashton Old Road, and was renamed Great Ancoats Street in 1788, around the time that industrial development hit the area.

Gradually the houses gave way to factories and businesses. At No. 49 James Wroe ran the radical *Manchester Observer*, and nearby was the Griffin Inn where the Chartists founded their Manchester branch in 1840. Commercial activity along the street increased in the twentieth century, and in the late 1920s Great Ancoats Street became home to the huge modernist glass and black vitrolite *Daily Express* building, where the newspaper was printed until the 1980s. At that time the street was still lined with a hotch-potch of greasy-spoon cafés and eccentric pubs, their clientèle as colourful as their names – Land O' Cakes, the Dargan Arms, the Cotton Tree and the wrongly spelt Ancoates Hotel.

However, the authorities' desperation to remove every last vestige of old industrial Ancoats has meant that almost all the pubs and cafés have been forced out, mostly on spurious grounds of imminent redevelopment, leaving a blighted, ugly, useless environment shorn of character.

east side: Oldham Road to Ashton Old Road
New Cross
The junction of Oldham Road and Great Ancoats Street, first recorded under the name New Cross in 1787, became a major centre of Irish immigration in the nine-

teenth century, where the Irish would gather to hear news from home. But as Leon Faucher explained in his book *Manchester in 1844*: 'The Irish are perpetually in a state of agitation. Often they assemble by hundreds at the corner of Oldham and Ancoats Street. One of their number reads in a loud voice the Irish news . . . and afterwards the whole is commented upon without end and with great clamour by the closely pressed crowd.'

Whenever there was political agitation in Manchester, New Cross often seemed to feature. On 9 August 1819, a week before the Peterloo Massacre, a spontaneous protest about social conditions degenerated into three days of rioting at New Cross as hundreds fought the police. There was also trouble here on the evening of Peterloo. A rumour spread that a grocer named Tate had captured one of the demonstrators' flags as a souvenir. A crowd gathered outside his shop and destroyed it. The story caught the imagination of the *Manchester Guardian* journalist and novelist Howard Spring who incorporated it into his best-known work, *Fame Is the Spur* (1940).

A month after the massacre a special constable called Campbell was murdered at New Cross by a mob who attacked him for being one of 'Nadin's men' – in the pay of the hated deputy chief constable Joseph Nadin. Four years later nothing had changed as far as the *Manchester Chronicle* was concerned, a report noting that it was dangerous to walk around the area in the evening because of the 'groups of Irish ruffians who appear to feel no interest but in ill-treating the peaceable and unoffending inhabitants'.

New Cross improved as the population moved away and it is now mostly commercialized, although there are pockets of dereliction. Victoria Square council flats nearby stand as a remarkable Victorian survival.
Crown and Kettle
Until the 1990s the pub, situated on the corner of Oldham Road and Great Ancoats Street, was furnished with wooden panelling looted from the wreckage of an airship.

Caught up in too many battles between football hooligans, it closed towards the end of the twentieth century. It has recently reopened but with little of the earlier atmosphere or decor.

Daily Express (1927–89), between Luna Street and George Leigh Street

One of three nearly identical glass and black vitrolite modernist newspaper buildings that Owen Williams designed for Lord Beaverbrook, owner of the *Daily Express*, in the late 1930s, it served as the newspaper's home for over sixty years, and meant that at night passers-by were greeted with the sight of the presses, easily visible through the glass façade, churning out thousands of copies of the paper.

The paper's employees were zealous and thorough. When Beaverbrook visited the plant one day the commissionaire on the door refused to allow him into the building. 'But this is Lord Beaverbrook,' insisted the proprietor's secretary. 'Oh aye,' replied the commissionaire, 'and I'm Cecil Parkin [Lancashire cricketer].' Quick as a flash, Beaverbrook, who had never heard of Parkin, responded: 'Give Parkin a bonus to reward his vigilance.'

The newspaper magnate was serious about making the northern edition a success and moved the celebrated journalist Arthur Christiansen to Manchester. Christiansen, the only Fleet Street editor to star in a major film (he played himself in the Cold War classic *The Day the Earth Caught Fire*), was not happy about leaving for the north. 'Manchester can be a pretty awful town at any time of the week,' he wrote in his memoirs.

Derelict throughout the 1990s, the building was recently converted into up-market offices.

No. 29

A slender corner building of 1899 designed by William Sharp, with distinctive mock-Tudor black-and-white weatherboarding on the top floor, was a Methodist-run women's night shelter until 1960 when the *Daily Express*, based next door, took it over for offices. Like its larger neighbour, it too is now enjoying a new commercial role as Ancoats splutters into life after years of neglect.

Redhill Street

Running alongside the Rochdale Canal east of Great Ancoats Street is Redhill Street, which features the best stretch of cotton mills in Manchester. Formidable palaces of work by day, they were lit up like the churches of Mammon at night, the setting made more dramatic by the presence of the Rochdale Canal on the south side of the street. Twenty-first-century renovation has seen these unique buildings cleaned up and restored for commercial use after years of inactivity and near dereliction, and the street now attracts tourists from afar who come to marvel at Manchester's legacy of industrial buildings. Redhill Street was cast as Broadbent Street in Howard Spring's 1940 novel *Fame Is the Spur* and is where the hero, Hamer Shawcross, in his childhood imagines himself to be in Venice 'when [he] shut [his] eyes to everything else and concentrated upon the flow of water under the smooth round arch of the humped-back bridge'.

north side: Great Ancoats Street to Radium Street

McConnel and Kennedy's mills, between Henry Street and Murray Street

> See Kennedy's stupendous structure joined
> to thine McConnel – friends of human kind!
> Whose ready doors for ever wide expand
> to give employment to a numerous band
> – 'The Family Economy of the Working
> Classes in the Cotton Industry',
> Frances Collier (1965)

One of Manchester's largest mill complexes – there are seven blocks on the site – was founded by James McConnel and John Kennedy, who came to Manchester from Scotland in the 1780s. Kennedy originally made textile machinery, and teaming up with McConnel in Manchester became a cotton spinner, installing the world's first steam-powered cotton-spinning mule in 1797. They soon overtook nearby Murray's as the biggest cotton-spinning firm in the area, and were employing 1,500 workers by 1835.

That year the French historian Alexis de Tocqueville visited the site and described the mills as 'a place where some 1500 workers, labour 69 hours a week, with an average wage of 11 shillings, and where three-quarters of the workers are women and children'. A year later the firm was commended by the factory inspector for the way they treated staff and for the 'neat condition of the rooms, and the attention to cleanliness and ventilation'.

The two original mills no longer survive. The oldest existing section is Sedgwick Mill, the eighteen-bay eight-storey block on Redhill Street, just west of Murray Street. It was built 1818–24, and is made of cast-iron beams and columns which support brick-vaulted ceilings. To the west is the recently renovated Royal Mill, built in 1913 on the site of Old Mill, the company's first Ancoats building.

Murray's Mills

Murray's Mills, which date back to 1798, are the oldest surviving mill buildings in Manchester. They were opened by two Scottish brothers, Adam and George Murray, who came to Manchester in the 1780s to make textile machines. The Murrays were the first mill-owners brave enough to withstand Luddite attacks on workplaces using new machinery that reduced the need for manpower. The Murrays also took advantage of the latest developments in steam power to operate spinning rollers and spinning mules which surpassed in power the old-style water-wheel contraptions that had been driven by fast-flowing rivers.

As this new machinery could now be used in urban centres such as Manchester, the only water needed was that of a canal to transport the goods away, in this case the Rochdale Canal (opened 1804), an arm of which linked the site to the waterway and allowed the raw cotton to arrive and the finished goods to depart easily. Throughout

the nineteenth century the Murrays continued to expand and update their machinery, building a complex of mills around a quadrangle that became the largest in Manchester, employing over 1,000 people. Workers had to arrive before 7 a.m; late arrivals were locked out and lost a day's wages.

The oldest Murray mill is the six-storey eleven-bay Old Mill of 1798 on the corner of Murray Street and Redhill Street, itself the oldest cotton mill in Manchester. It was built of load-bearing brick with cast-iron columns that support wooden floorboards, and is typical of mill buildings of the late eighteenth–early nineteenth century in that it is wide enough for two spinning mules to be worked back to back. The firm closed in the 1950s and the buildings are now being converted for mixed use – leisure, retail and accommodation – after years of neglect.
Waulk Mill, west corner Redhill Street and Bengal Street
Two structures in one, a doubling mill of 1842 and the attached Fire Proof Mill, are both part of the expansion of the A. & G. Murray firm. The building was recently renovated amid some controversy for the roof was changed without planning permission or listed building consent.

Victoria Square

Manchester's oldest surviving municipal estate is an antiquated-looking five-storey block of flats, built of red brick around a central square, with striking ironwork balconies and a pitched slate roof. It was created in 1889 to provide room for 848 people in 237 double tenements and forty-eight single tenements. Rare for the time, the flats even had internal bathrooms, and the common areas had laundries with drying facilities in the top rooms of the corner towers that reduced the risk of bronchial problems in notoriously damp Manchester. The property now provides accommodation mostly for the elderly.

Nearby, similarly sturdy working-class housing was built on Sanitary Street. A 1950s campaign by locals to get the name changed led the Corporation ingeniously to knock off several letters and end up with the more wholesome Anita Street.

ARDWICK

Ardwick takes its name from *Ard*, an abbreviation of King Aethelred, and *wic*, a farm or small hamlet. To the north the border is the River Medlock; to the south the now culverted Corn Brook. A prosperous late Georgian/early Victorian middle-class suburb situated barely a mile south-east of central Manchester, Ardwick was home to the cotton king John Rylands; the engineer William Fairbairn, who conducted pioneering work on metal fatigue; and the banking family patriarch Nathan Meyer Rothschild, who lived in a smart villa on Downing Street, now the main traffic route away from Piccadilly.

Industry arrived with the building of mills on Union Street, a lime works alongside the Medlock, and ironworks, boilerworks and brickworks all around which removed the last remaining vestiges of rural Ardwick, and led locals to call the Corn Brook the 'Black Brook' on account of the pollution. The early firms were soon joined by Chapel Fields works ('India-Rubber Manufacturers'), Jewsbury & Brown's (purveyors of 'Oriental Tooth Paste'), and biggest of all, Great Universal Stores, still one of the country's main mail-order firms.

With its hotch-potch of industrial zones and railway lines, Ardwick was a prime target for the German bombing planes of the Second World War. Nevertheless in the 1950s it was a thriving working-class community. The main roads were lined with popular shops, and there were theatres and cinemas by the junction with Hyde Road, of which only the Apollo, once one of the biggest cinemas in the country and now a rock venue, survives. Then came unsympathetic town-planning policies from the Corporation and architectural experimentation.

Ardwick soon became a no-man's land of boarded-up units and sink estates, epitomized by 'Fort Ardwick', an early 1970s estate whose hideousness was mitigated only by the knowledge that the Hulme Crescents were just over a mile away. Despite the demolition of Fort Ardwick and the reversal of the urban clearances, the kind of improvements that have recently made other similar inner suburbs of Manchester more amenable have not come to Ardwick.

Ardwick Green

The most prestigious address in the area in the early nineteenth century, Ardwick Green has somehow survived in shape if not in status following 150 years of decline. First mentioned in 1685, it soon became an attractive residential location with fine Georgian houses and a neo-baroque church set around a railed-off grassed area containing a lake.

That this was one of the most desirable addresses in Manchester a century before that accolade moved south to Didsbury, can be gleaned from the arrival of John Rylands, the cotton magnate, at No. 24 (later a school) on the north side in 1850, before he moved to his better-known residence, Longford Hall, Stretford.

The inclusion of the south side of Ardwick Green in the main traffic route southeast of the city centre led to its decline. Manchester Corporation bought the land in 1867 for its public park, but this only hastened its demise for now only the Corporation could spend money on it and the Corporation, predictably, was permanently cash-strapped. Soon the lake, which featured in the ice accident scene in Isabella Banks's 1876 novel *The Manchester Man*, was converted into ponds with a fountain. It was later filled in.

Little of the once elegant green now remains. St Thomas's church of 1740, though still standing, has been turned into offices. One of the few remaining quality houses is No. 31, a detached brick villa depicted as the home of Lawrence Aspinall, one of the murderous Manchester

Yeomanry, in *The Manchester Man*, and
which Affleck and Brown, the department
store, used for boarding employees early in
the twentieth century. What was Ardwick
Barracks and is now Territorial Army premises on the north side makes the most
imposing local site with its rooftop crenella-
tions like those of a medieval castle.
*east side: railway bridge to Ardwick
roundabout*
Coverdale Crescent
'𝕱𝖔𝖗𝖙 𝕬𝖗𝖉𝖜𝖎𝖈𝖐', east of Devonshire Street
A fearsome-looking 1970s-built estate of 537
flats, made of rough concrete and looking
like Second World War anti-invasion forti-
fications, stood off Hyde Road just east of
the Apollo throughout the 70s and 80s. The
blocks were fronted by a vast landscaped
grassed area on which ball games were forbidden; residents had no gardens (although
they could look out on a useless communal
space); and there were no worthwhile shops,
for only the intensely masochistic would
contemplate opening premises in this
dystopia.

Locals were perplexed and soon nicknamed the development 𝕱𝖔𝖗𝖙 𝕬𝖗𝖉𝖜𝖎𝖈𝖐. 'They
really are a visual abomination,' said one
man interviewed by the *Manchester Evening
News*, while another remarked that the place
was 'grey, grim and totally uninviting'. Local
MP Gerald Kaufman was equally scathing,
calling it 'an excrescence in my constitu-
ency, which looked like a French foreign
legion fort'. Within little more than a
decade the estate was riddled with damp,
the steel fixtures had corroded and the concrete was crumbling. It was soon demolished and later replaced with small brick
houses, which left locals even more puzzled
as to why the original houses were demolished in the first place.

Hyde Road
*west side: Ardwick roundabout to railway
bridge*

𝔐𝔞𝔫𝔠𝔥𝔢𝔰𝔱𝔢𝔯 𝔈𝔦𝔱𝔶 (1887–1923), Hyde Road at
Bennett Street
Manchester's second most successful football club, but the only one located within
the city boundaries, was founded in 1880 by
wardens of Gorton's St Marks church, and
originally played in scarlet and black,
unusual colours occasionally seen now in
Manchester City's away strip. Sometimes
their jerseys bore a white cross, influenced
by the Christian White Cross movement,
which was active locally in the 1880s and
campaigned for 'purity' and chastity in
sport.

In 1887 the club moved to a new ground
on Hyde Road and became Ardwick. The
opening fixture here should have been held
on 10 September 1887, but when Salford
failed to turn up it had to be rearranged for
the following week. Early matches were
marred by crowd disturbances and a
number of opposing teams were stoned off.

Ardwick became founder members of the
Football League's Second Division in 1892
and re-formed a year later as Manchester
City, following financial troubles. The club
made steady progress, secured promotion to
the First Division in 1899, and five years
later won the FA Cup for the first time. But
the joy was not to last for long. Within a
fortnight the FA, suspicious that the club
had broken association rules in making
excessive payments and offering bonuses,
arrived in east Manchester to inspect the
books. City were found guilty and the
ground was closed. The fans had commited
no crime, however, and *Athletic News* voiced
the views of many when they ventured that
'the mistake was ever to pass such absurd
rules. Would Parliament ever pass a law forbidding any English worker from receiving
more than £4 a week?'

It was to get worse. In August 1905 star
player Billy Meredith was accused of offering an Aston Villa player a £10 bribe to
throw a match and was suspended for
twelve months. Meredith continued to draw
his wages but his relationship with the club
became ever more acrimonious, and he

began to disclose salacious pieces of gossip to the Football Association about illegal payments the club were still making. When City placed Meredith on the transfer list he admitted his guilt over the bribe but explained that he had been forced to approach the player by the City manager.

The FA conducted further investigations and found several players guilty of receiving illegal payments. Seventeen current and former City players were fined a total of £900, suspended from football for seven months and forbidden to play for the side again. Almost the entire Cup-winning squad was subsequently put up for auction at the Grand Hotel in central Manchester. The highly rated full-back Herbert Burgess went to United, whose directors had hidden him away before the auction at an address unknown to City's board. Astonishingly, Meredith himself was transferred to Manchester United where he continued to prosper . . . on the pitch. Even more surprisingly he later returned to City for another successful spell.

A fire at Hyde Road destroyed the main stand in 1920 and three years later the club moved to Maine Road, Moss Side (p. 137). **Location of 1867 'Fenian outrage'**, Hyde Road railway bridge
Irish nationalists, or Fenians as they were then known, sprang two prisoners from a police van under the Hyde Road railway bridge on 18 September 1867. In the mêlée a policeman was shot dead. Three supporters who were later hanged for their part in the events have since become known as the Manchester Martyrs.

The two freed prisoners, who had both been involved in the Fenian uprisings of the mid-nineteenth century, were Colonel Thomas Kelly and Captain Timothy Deasy. The pair had fought in the American Civil War and had been sent to Britain to rally support for the Irish republican cause. However, they were arrested in Manchester on 11 September 1867 while loitering in Smithfield, and taken to Belle Vue gaol.

Fellow republicans immediately began

plotting to free them. As a horse-drawn police van taking the men to court on 18 September made its way along Hyde Road, a man appeared from under the railway arch brandishing a revolver. He called on the police to stop, and shot over their heads. At the same time some thirty men, who had been hiding, stormed to the scene and attacked the van with hammers to free the prisoners.

Inside the van was a Sergeant Brett, who made the mistake of looking out of a keyhole and was shot in the head. A woman prisoner, Ellen Cooper, then seized his keys and thrust them through the grating. Soon the door was unlocked, and Kelly and Deasy were off, fleeing over the fields, taking refuge in St Wilfrid's church in Hulme, and eventually escaping to America.

Manchester police swarmed through areas with a large Irish population and arrested many, filling the jails with hapless Irish nationals. Soon there were twenty-nine people in prison accused of murdering Sergeant Brett. Five men were eventually charged, and there was uproar when they appeared in court in manacles. Although two were cleared, three Fenians – William Allen, Michael Larkin and William O'Brien – were tried, convicted and hanged at New Bailey Prison, Salford, on 23 November 1867, in what proved to be the last hangings to take place in public locally.
▶ New Bailey Prison, p. 182.

BRADFORD

This was Manchester at its most industrialized throughout the nineteenth and twentieth centuries. For here was a coal mine only two miles east of Manchester city centre, the enormous Stuart Street power station (target of an unsuccessful IRA terrorist attack in the 1920s), huge gasometers (near the present-day home of Manchester City) and a host of engineering companies such as Johnson and Nephew's wire works.

In medieval times Bradford was Broad

Ford, a rural suburb of no consequence until the coming of the Industrial Revolution and the opening of the colliery. During Bradford's industrial heyday the area suffered from the highest fall of soot in the world, or as the *City and Suburban News* put it, 'Its trade mark is an obnoxious smell which pervades the area and haunts its long-suffering residents by day and night.'

Economically, the community was buoyant until the 1960s, when Manchester Corporation announced plans to drive out privately owned homes and small shops, and replace them with council houses and shopping centres, as part of their post-war social engineering project. Residents were horrified at the prospect of being forced to move away from where they had lived for decades. When they complained to councillors at a public meeting, the chairman of the housing committee snubbed them, insisting they submit points or questions on a sheet of paper with their name and address at the top. He promised that some of the points would be answered at a forthcoming meeting. But this was simply a time-buying device to diffuse the tension without solving the problem. Those tenants who refused to go quickly were encouraged to think again in 1969 when a series of underground explosions in the middle of the night, supposedly part of vital repair work on the sewers, also managed, coincidentally, to cause maximum discomfort and convince stallers of the benefits a move would bring.

Since the beginning of the twenty-first century post-industrial Bradford has been rebranded 'Eastlands', an uninspired choice of name reeking of 'Wastelands', which perhaps is not incongruous in an area where there has been a population drop of 13 per cent in recent years. The old industrialized landscape has been uprooted for first-rate new sports facilities – the City of Manchester Stadium (now home of Manchester City FC), the Velodrome National Cycling Centre, the Manchester Tennis Centre, the National Squash Centre – all promoted under the incongruous American-style

name Sportcity. Renovations to the local housing stock have not been so successful, however, and properties have been known to change hands in pubs for £500. Despite multimillion-pound redevelopment Bradford remains a semi-derelict wilderness, dotted with state-of-the-art sports facilities but devoid of shops, pubs, desirable houses and pleasant society.

Ashton New Road

Manchester City (2003–), west of Alan Turing Way

Built for the 2002 Commonwealth Games, the stadium has been the home of Manchester City since 2003. In the mid-1990s, before it was built, the site was put forward as a contender for a new national football stadium to replace Wembley, but it was rejected owing to the lack of local public transport, which would have caused gridlock on match days.

Although enormous sums of money were spent on the design of the stadium and its facilities the preponderance of steel rather than brick and cement-washed stone – typical of so many of the soulless concrete bowls erected throughout England since the closure of the football terraces in the 1990s – has created an arena devoid of the romance, chaos and warmth of Maine Road.

Manchester City have a 250-year lease on the ground – the time, detractors claim, the club's long-suffering fans will have to wait before they win their next championship.

Forge Lane

Bradford Colliery

Running east of Manchester city centre is Britain's second-deepest coal mine, which opened in the 1840s and was later connected to the nearby Stuart Street power station by underground conveyor belts which took 30 per cent of the colliery output in exchange for free electricity. Despite yielding high-quality coal the mine closed in September 1968, for supposedly being uneconomic, and more than 1,000 men lost their jobs. The pit-head which stood between Mill Street and Forge Lane, just north-east of land now

occupied by Manchester City's ground, was
demolished in 1970.

CLAYTON

Working-class Manchester *par excellence*,
Clayton has been less spoilt by municipal
interference than neighbouring communities, such as Bradford and Newton Heath,
even though it too was industrialized in the
nineteenth century, being perfectly positioned alongside the Ashton Canal and only
three miles from Manchester city centre.
Manchester United played locally at the end
of the nineteenth century and the first few
years of the twentieth in a ground opposite
the Clayton Aniline Company, the area's
main employers until recently. Surprisingly,
Clayton still has its medieval hall – Clayton
Hall – seventeenth-century home of Humphrey Chetham, who gave his name to the
well-known school and library near Victoria
station. Alongside the hall is the church of
St Cross, one of Manchester's few Grade I
listed buildings, designed by the master of
elegant Gothic ecclesiastical revivalism, William Butterfield.

Bank Street
Manchester United (1893–1910)
Founded as the works team of the Lancashire and Yorkshire Railway Company, Manchester United were still known as Newton
Heath when they moved to Clayton in 1893.
Despite having won election to the newly
enlarged First Division the club struggled,
because of its proximity to the Aniline
chemical works, some detractors claimed.
Others argued that the plant's owners would
ensure that noxious fumes to which Newton
Heath were immune would exude to annoy
away teams.

The decade and a half spent in this part of
east Manchester were not successful for a
team that would later dominate the game –
second only to Liverpool in the number of
trophies won – and they spent much of the
time in the Second Division. With cash

short in 1901, the club held a four-day
bazaar to raise funds. One of the items on
sale was a St Bernard dog which ran off with
a collection tin and made its way to the
home of businessman John Henry Davies.
His daughter was so taken with the beast
that he made some enquiries about its
origins, and ended up meeting the team captain, Harry Stafford, and saving the club
from ruin. When he became president in
1902, Davies changed the club's name to
Manchester United, resisting options to call
it Manchester Celtic or Manchester Central.
He also changed its colours to red and
white.

Results improved and the club won promotion back to the First Division in 1906.
Two years later United were champions for
the first time, profiting considerably from
the turmoil at Manchester City which had
led the Football Association to order City to
put all their players up for auction. The best,
such as Billy Meredith, then joined United.
The following year Manchester United won
the FA Cup for the first time and were
greeted by some 300,000 fans who lined the
streets of east Manchester to cheer them
back to the stadium, where they drank champagne out of the trophy but lost a league
game to Arsenal.

A year later United moved across town to
Old Trafford.
▶ Manchester United at Old Trafford,
p. 189.

GORTON

First mentioned in 1237, Gorton, three miles
east of Manchester city centre, became
heavily industrialized in the mid-nineteenth
century when a number of railway lines
were cut through and attracted two firms
that went on to become major locomotive
manufacturers worldwide: the Gorton Locomotive Works and Beyer Peacock.

What was until the 1960s a lively if impoverished working-class suburb of Manchester, housing those who worked in the

The Moors Murders

The Moors Murderers – Myra Hindley and Ian Brady – became Britain's most notorious and reviled serial killers due to the sadistic nature of their crimes. The murders took place from July 1963 to October 1965 at locations in Hattersley, an overspill council estate on the fringes of east Manchester, and in the moors beyond. Ian Brady, who had moved from Glasgow to Manchester when he was seventeen in 1955 to live with relations in Moss Side, worked as an errand boy at Smithfield Market in the city centre until he was imprisoned at Strangeways for stealing lead seals. In 1959 he joined Millward's Merchandisers on Levenshulme Road, Gorton, as a clerk. Two years later the firm took on a new secretary, Myra Hindley, who had grown up at 20 Eaton Street, Gorton. A year later they began a relationship, and they were still working at Millward's at the time of their arrests in late 1965.

Victim No. 1 – Pauline Reade

Brady and Hindley snatched their first victim, sixteen-year-old Pauline Reade, on the night of 12 July 1963 as she made her way to the Railway Workers' Social Club in Crumpsall. Reade was unaware that she was being followed, not by Brady and Hindley, but by two friends who were worried that she was walking alone, but soon tired of the chore. She was then stopped by Hindley, who slowed down in her van and asked the girl if she would help her look for a glove she'd lost on Saddleworth Moor in exchange for some records. A few hundred yards behind Hindley's vehicle was Ian Brady on his motorcycle. As the girl helped Hindley with her supposed search on the moors, Brady pounced, smashing Reade's skull with a shovel before slitting her throat with a knife. He buried her in a three-foot-deep grave that was not discovered until July 1987.

Victim No. 2 – John Kilbride

Twelve-year-old John Kilbride disappeared without trace on 23 November 1963, the day after the assassination of John F. Kennedy. He had gone to Ashton-under-Lyne market to earn some extra pocket money by helping the stallholders pack up, but never made it home. A major search yielded nothing, for Brady had whisked Kilbride away to the moor, where he sexually assaulted the boy, attempted to slit his throat with a knife, and strangled him with a piece of string. He then buried the body in a shallow grave.

When Brady was eventually arrested for killing Edward Evans in October 1965, police searched Brady's home and came across a list of names he had written down, which included Kilbride's. They also found out that Hindley had hired a car on the day of the boy's disappearance, returning it in a muddy state, and that Brady and Hindley regularly shopped at Ashton market.

Victim No. 3 – Keith Bennett

At the beginning of the twenty-first century still no trace had been found of Keith Bennett, who went missing aged twelve on 16 June 1964. Bennett vanished while travelling between his mother's house in Chorlton-on-Medlock and his grandmother's home a mile away. In 1987 Myra Hindley confessed to abducting, sexually

local heavy industries and also home to the exciting Belle Vue entertainments complex, is still trying to recover from the discovery that two seemingly nondescript Gorton office workers, Myra Hindley and Ian Brady, were responsible for the most notorious killing spree in twentieth-century British history – the Moors Murders.

Few parts of Gorton remained untouched by the story. Even the revered monastery, now a world heritage site in its dilapidated state, features, for it was here that Hindley was baptized and confirmed, and briefly toyed with the idea of becoming a nun in 1958. As the community struggled to make sense of the awful revelations, Gorton assaulting and strangling the boy, and even drew a map showing where on the moors the body might be found. Digging has been undertaken at several places on the moors, to no avail.

Victim No. 4 – Lesley Anne Downey

The most shocking of the Moors Murders was that of ten-year-old Lesley Anne Downey, who disappeared on 26 December 1964 from the Hulme Hall Lane fair in Miles Platting. After Brady and Hindley were arrested for the murder of Edward Evans, a police officer took a prayer book down from a shelf and out fell a left-luggage ticket for two suitcases locked away at Manchester's Central station. Inside were photos of Lesley Anne naked and gagged, and tape recordings of her being tortured. A dig of the moor on 16 October 1965 yielded the body.

Victim No. 5 – Edward Evans

The final Moors Murder took place on 6 October 1965 after Brady and Hindley invited seventeen-year-old Edward Evans to their address at 16 Wardle Brook Avenue, Hattersley. Evans had had a dramatic evening. He had arranged to meet a friend at Aunty's Bar, 73 Oxford Road, to go and see Manchester United play Helsinki in the European Cup at Old Trafford. When the friend failed to arrive, Evans went to the match by himself. Feeling alone in the large crowd, he left at half-time and went to the Barrowford Hotel, a homosexual bar on Sackville Street, near Piccadilly station. Also there was Ian Brady. The two men had a brief conversation before Evans left for a drink in the buffet at Central station (now

G-Mex). At the milk-vending machine Evans felt a tap on his shoulder. It was Brady again, who recognized Evans from the Barrowford and invited him home for a drink courtesy of a lift from his 'sister' – Hindley – waiting in the car outside.

Back at Hattersley, Brady attacked Evans with an axe for no reason other than to watch 'the look on his face'. But Brady brought about his own downfall by inviting Hindley's brother-in-law, David Smith, to help him 'finish Eddie off'. A terrified Smith thought he was watching a grim practical joke until he saw the dying Evans writhing on his stomach as Brady brought the axe down time and again on Evans's neck. Hindley's grandmother slept upstairs through the whole thing, completely unaware.

In shock, Smith agreed to help tidy up the mess but later went to the police. A search of the house yielded Evans's mutilated body in a polythene bag. Brady and Hindley were arrested, but initially only Brady was charged with murder. However, when a notebook containing a 'murder plan' was found in Hindley's room four days later, she was also charged.

Once Smith told police that Brady and Hindley had boasted about killing people and burying the victims on the moors, officers began a search of the area where they soon recovered the bodies of Lesley Ann Downey and John Kilbride. The couple were convicted of murder at Chester Assizes in April 1966, escaping the death penalty only through a recent change in the law.

coincidentally began its inexorable economic decline. Long-standing factories and workshops closed; even Beyer Peacock, whose railway engines travelled the world's tracks on five continents, collapsed. Meanwhile, streets and homes were wiped away as part of so-called slum clearance, and sturdy brick houses set in traditional road patterns

were replaced by glorified rabbit hutches located in culs-de-sac. The main road was cleared of shops which were replaced by grass verges, and the major local amenity – Belle Vue leisure park and zoo – closed down and was demolished.

Bessemer Street
Beyer Peacock Locomotive Works/New Smithfield Market

Karl Beyer, a German, and Richard Peacock founded one of the world's most successful railway locomotive firms in Gorton in 1854. They soon had orders from the East Indian Railway, the Royal Swedish Railway, the Lombardo and Venetian Railway and scores of others across the globe. During the Great War Beyer Peacock was a major manufacturer of armaments, but by this time its German founder was long dead. In the 1950s the company had so many orders for locomotives and engines that it was having to sub-contract work to rivals. Yet once British Rail switched from steam to diesel in 1955 Beyer Peacock wound down most of its production and closed its Gorton foundry in 1966.

Cornwall Street
Gorton Locomotive Works

Close to Beyer Peacock was another locomotive works which also provided engines for the world's railways: the Gorton Locomotive Works. Here in 1962 Eric Laithwaite, a professor at Manchester University and consultant to British Rail, carried out pioneering work on a new form of railway transport – magnetic trains. Laithwaite believed that he could generate magnetic fields on which an object could travel without being slowed by friction. He took out a patent in 1948 and fourteen years later at the Gorton works succeeded in accelerating a plate-layer's trolley to 30 mph within thirty yards. Little came of the developments, however, thanks to the apathy of British Rail. Nevertheless Laithwaite managed to convince the government to invest more than 30 million pounds in his

Hovertrain, a high-speed train without wheels resting on a cushion of air and driven by magnets, but the project was cancelled in 1973. The ideas were later picked up by the Japanese and Germans.

Gorton Lane
St Francis of Assisi

The largest new parish church in England built since the Reformation when it opened in 1872, this example of E. W. Pugin's carefully detailed Gothic revival architecture is now on the World Monuments' Watch Fund for endangered buildings. Three huge brick buttresses provide a sense of enormity on the western side, contrasting with the slender bell tower, and there is an adjacent monastery, a remarkable site in an urban church despite its dilapidated state. In its heyday the church was the major focus for local social life, and the monastery meant that anyone in Manchester considering taking holy orders could enter St Francis to try the experience. One local who did so in the late 1950s, while considering becoming a nun, was the future Moors Murderer, Myra Hindley.

Following 1960s slum clearance there was a severe decline in parish numbers. The last mass was held in November 1989 and the church was then deconsecrated. As the monastery was left unprotected, it was regularly vandalized, and twelve six-foot-high sandstone statues of saints belonging to the church spent a year in a Longsight junkyard before turning up at Sotheby's as garden ornaments. At this point the city council belatedly took an interest, spending £25,000 on retrieving the statues. A number of projected redevelopment schemes are now vying for the site.

North Manchester

ANGEL MEADOW

A small section of north Manchester near the city centre, set between Rochdale Road and Cheetham Hill Road alongside the river Irk, Angel Meadow was mostly open land dotted with farms and the occasional smart villa until the early nineteenth century when a glut of factories – tannery, dye works, iron foundry, brewery, tripe works, engineering depots and timber yards – turned the locale into an unpleasant neighbourhood.

To service these industries the larger houses on Angel Street, the main route running through the area, became workers' hostels. Nearby speculative builders put up hundreds of small cramped dwellings, which turned into a breeding ground for disease. It was here that cholera hit Manchester first in 1832, and soon there were more than 600 dead from the disease. By then Angel Meadow had acquired a fearsome reputation, not just for its appalling living conditions, but for the number of violent attacks taking place there. It gained the unwelcome nickname 'The Place of Terror'. Even teachers at the ragged school needed a police escort out of the area until the 1850s.

Dr James Phillips Kay, researching Angel Meadow in 1832 for his now famous pamphlet *The Moral and Physical Condition of the Working Classes Employed in the Cotton Manufacture in Manchester*, blamed the appalling living conditions on drink, substandard houses and the feckless behaviour of the Irish – a regular target at that time, thanks to the English's hostility to Catholicism.

Angus Bethune Reach, writing in the *Morning Chronicle* in 1849, could find nothing good about the place. Angel Meadow was 'the lowest, most filthy, most unhealthy, and most wicked locality in Manchester . . . full of cellars and inhabited by prostitutes, their bullies, thieves, cadgers, vagrants and tramps'. He noticed that conditions for the immigrant Irish were worse than for the natives, for they

> lived in more wretched places still – the cellars. We descended to one. The place was dark, except for the glare of the small fire. You could not stand without stooping in the room, which might be about twelve feet by eight. There were at least a dozen men, women, and children, on

stools or squatted on the stone floor round the fire, and the heat and smells were oppressive. This not being a lodging cellar, the police had no control over the number of its inmates, who slept huddled on the stones, or on masses of rags, shavings and straw, which were littered about.' He failed to mention the rats, which would emerge brazenly at night before venturing off to the cheese cellars of nearby Hanging Ditch.

Yet, according to the Communist agitator and commentator Friedrich Engels, writing around the same time, Angel Meadow was an improvement on nearby Red Bank (p. 162). 'Here there is somewhat better order. In place of the chaos of buildings, we find at least long straight lanes and alleys or courts, built according to a plan and usually square.'

The centre of Angel Meadow was St Michael's church, its burial ground the largest in Manchester until the twentieth-century growth of Southern Cemetery, where some 40,000 people were interred from 1787. Burials initially involved the digging of a large pit, into which coffins were thrown and then covered with planks so that more coffins could be added – a process which continued till the pit was full.

Improvement to Angel Meadow came about gradually. The worst houses were patched up, the newer ones of the late nineteenth century were better built than those that had been erected before, and free education in the form of ragged schools provided basic lessons in reading, writing, arithmetic and religious studies. By the end of the century the death rate had improved to 50 per 1,000 a year (compared with 19 per 1,000 nationally).

As the twentieth century proceeded so the population numbers in Angel Meadow dwindled till it was barely noticeable, and the area became almost entirely full of depots, warehouses and office blocks. There was some limited regeneration towards the end of the twentieth century, when one of the larger blocks, 23 New Mount Street,

became a popular choice for counter-culture businesses, and several nearby pubs began to attract a discerning crowd of real-ale lovers. However, in the twenty-first century the closure of these pubs and the decline of 23 New Mount Street meant Angel Meadow became one of Manchester's eeriest locales.

CHEETHAM

One of the great tragedies of Manchester is that the city council and other powerful local bodies have allowed the ring of inner suburbs surrounding the city centre such as Ardwick, Cheetham and Hulme to sink into deprivation and destitution.

Once a desirable and successful area but now a savage, mean, lawless inner-city suburb of stupefying decrepitude, before the Second World War, Cheetham had a healthy social mix and a varied range of clubs, societies, shops and institutions. It had changed from farmland to built-up Manchester after a new bridge was constructed over the Irk in the early nineteenth century. The new bridge came with a new road: York Street, now Cheetham Hill Road, the main route north out of central Manchester. Here were built Cheetham Town Hall and the Assembly Rooms (south-west corner of Cheetham Hill Road/Derby Street), buildings which spoke of Victorian self-satisfaction and confidence.

Jewish immigration in the nineteenth century brought synagogues and institutions to the main road, and factories and sweatshops to the side streets. The Jewish community was beginning to gain acceptance among the indigenous gentiles when the arrival of thousands of refugees fleeing persecution in eastern Europe after the pogroms of 1881 horrified Manchester's Jewish community. They saw the impoverished, dishevelled, Yiddish-speaking Jewish newcomers as a threat to their growing position within English society and encouraged them to move on – to Liverpool – with the enticement of half a crown. Meanwhile, they forced those who stayed to anglicize, banning the speaking of Yiddish in Jewish schools, clubs and other institutions, and giving alms to the poor only if they tried to speak English.

By the 1920s there were 40,000 Jews in Cheetham. As Howard Spring noted in his 1934 novel *Shabby Tiger*: 'the writing on the shop windows is Hebrew. [There are] synagogues and Talmud Torah schools; kosher meat shops; wizened little bearded men with grey goat's eyes and slim olive children with heifer's eyes.'

The two communities – Jew and gentile – lived together in reasonable harmony, as Louis Golding described in his 1932 novel *Magnolia Street*. Golding set the book in Cheetham's Sycamore Street, where he lived, which featured gentiles on one side and Jews on the other. But the 1960s TV version of the book angered locals with its avoidable mistakes: the Jewish children were wrongly given Manchester accents and there was too much emphasis on the (rare) antagonism between the two groups.

Some of Cheetham's Jews were particularly enterprising. For instance Michael Marks (with the gentile Tom Spencer) opened the first Marks & Spencer shop at 20 Cheetham Hill Road in 1893. On the other side of the road, at No. 97, the leading Zionist Chaim Weizmann had his headquarters in the early twentieth century, where many of the ideas realized by the founding of the state of Israel in 1948 were formed. Later came novelist Howard Jacobson (born 1942), who once explained that even though he was 'Oxbridge-educated [his] imaginative world was still the market stall and the Dormobile packed with avid Jewish boys on the razzle, racing up and down Cheetham Hill Road'.

After the Second World War Cheetham's Jews gradually moved away, mostly further north to Prestwich and Whitefield. Not one house they previously occupied now survives, not even the Cheetham Hill Road address of Michael Marks. At the same time, the larger clothing businesses shut, and in

the 1960s Cheetham began its monumental decline as an acceptable neighbourhood when the Corporation began knocking down the Victorian infrastructure and replacing it with houses of the lowest-quality legally possible, setting them on culs-de-sac in new estates. The dispersal of those living in the established structured communities, and their replacement with problem families imported by the council, provoked an atmosphere of hostility that soon made Cheetham infamous in the region.

In recent decades Cheetham has seen immigration from south Asia and east Africa that has paralleled the Jewish influx of the late nineteenth century. The shops on Cheetham Hill Road north of Waterloo Road teem with spices, halal meat and saris by day, while further south there is still healthy trade in the textile cash-and-carry warehouses and jewellery outlets. Yet all around casual violence, blight and shabbiness prevail, especially at night when the gangs and drug dealers take over the mostly deserted streets.

(i) Cheetham Hill

Cheetham Hill Road
Cheetham Hill Road is one of two main roads running through Cheetham, and its decline symbolizes the area's demise since its late nineteenth-century heyday. Few of the once important buildings which gave the community a sense of pride remain, and the surviving Town Hall is now a curry house.
west side: Trinity Way to Bury Old Road
Central Synagogue (1894–1928), Cheetham Hill Road at Park Street
Because the synagogue was on the west side of the road but the ark, which the congregation must face, had to be on the east side, facing Jerusalem, the builders were obliged to place both ark and entrance together, which made the internal layout look absurd.

In the early twentieth century the rabbi I. J. Yoffey used to give his sermons in Yiddish, which only a fraction of the congregation could understand. A later minister,

Louis Jacobs, was involved in one of the bitterest conflicts in modern Judaism. He suggested in a 1957 book, *We Have Reason to Believe*, that the Jewish laws might be man-made, rather than the work of God. He was soon ostracized by the Jewish establishment, and at one stage the Chief Rabbi withheld his licence to occupy a United Synagogue pulpit. Jacobs responded by opening his own synagogue in St John's Wood, north-west London, run along orthodox lines but outside the remit of the Chief Rabbi, and this later spawned its own wing of Judaism, the Masorti. Jacobs even won the *Jewish Chronicle*'s 2006 survey to find the greatest British Jew since the return of 1656.

The Central Synagogue moved to the northern end of Cheetham, at the junction of Heywood Street and Bellott Street, in 1928, but when the community later headed further north that too closed down.
► Manchester Jewish Museum, below.
No. 97
The Manchester Zionist Association was based at 97 Cheetham Hill Road in the early years of the twentieth century, its ranks boosted ironically by the tragedy of the pog-roms that followed the first Russian Revol-ution of 1905. Soon its leading campaigner was Chaim Weizmann, a research chemist at Manchester University, who went on to become the first president of Israel. Few of the association's archives remain as they were thrown out by an over-zealous care-taker while clearing up one day. The build-ing is now a clothes shop.
► Weizmann at Manchester University, p. 121.
east side: Bury Old Road to Trinity Way
Manchester Jewish Museum, No. 190
Manchester's Jewish Museum opened in 1984 in this small 1889-built former Spanish and Portuguese synagogue, designed by Edward Salomons in a style he described as 'Saracenic' – the use of arabesque styles of geometric patterns like those of the religious buildings of Moorish Spain. The museum was not without its detractors when first mooted. 'We need a Jewish museum like we

need a ham sandwich,' was the response from one Jewish newspaper. Nevertheless, the historians behind the project persevered without council or government help. In con-verting the building they changed little, and the long wooden pews remain on the ground floor; those upstairs in the women's gallery were stripped out to house exhibits. Sharp-eyed visitors will notice a mistake in the ironwork over the main exit. It is deliber-ate and acknowledges the imperfection of man in the house of worship of a perfect God. The museum organizes regular walks from the synagogue taking in Cheetham sites relevant to local Jewish history.
► Edward Salomons's Reform Club, p. 58; Edward Salomons's Lawnhurst, p. 169.
The Great Synagogue (1858–1986), No. 140
Although the Manchester establishment treated those who worshipped at the Great Synagogue as 'orthodox', the building, with its huge Corinthian columns and pilasters, looked like an Italian church. English, rather than Yiddish, was the predominant lan-guage. Indeed the real devout Cheetham Jews, those who worshipped at home in unfussed *steibels*, treated the Great Syna-gogue members with barely restrained con-tempt, deriding them as 'the English Shool'; much in the same way as those who ran the Great Synagogue despised their brethren at the New Synagogue (p. 161).

The most powerful figure in the early days of the Great Synagogue was Nathan Laski, a cotton magnate who became the first northern-based Jew to serve as an offi-cer on the national Board of Deputies of British Jews. Laski was keen to distance him-self from Manchester's immigrant Jewish community despite having been born in Poland, although when he became President of the Great Synagogue in 1896 he would hold court at his home on Smedley Lane. Over the years some 70,000 people came to see him to seek advice on a variety of matters.

Laski's judgement was often flawed, especially on major issues. For instance, he initially opposed the building of the

Manchester Victoria Jewish Hospital on the grounds that it might impede immigrant Jews from integrating into British society, but when the hospital went ahead he became chairman and, ironically, died there in 1941. Laski also opposed Zionism initially, but changed his mind after Chaim Weizmann won support from influential politicians such as Arthur Balfour.

After the building closed in the 1980s vandals wrecked it and it had to be demolished for safety reasons in 1986.

New Synagogue (1889–1980s), No. 122
The newly enriched north Manchester Jewish entrepreneurs of the late nineteenth century opened the New Synagogue after they were refused admission to the nearby 𝔊reat 𝔖ynagogue (see above). They were soon being mocked by the majority of the Jewish community, those who couldn't compete with them financially, as 'the alrightniks'. Following a financial scandal here the elders of the nearby 𝔊reat 𝔖ynagogue, by then their main rival, voted not to allow moneylenders – i.e. the kind of people found at the New Synagogue – into their congregation. Consequently the New Synagogue voted that each of their committees had to have at least one money-lender on it.

After its closure, the synagogue was converted into a lampshade factory, and is now a clothes shop. The central circular window still features the Star of David.

𝔉irst 𝔐arks & 𝔖pencer, No. 20
The first permanent Marks & Spencer shop opened at 20 Cheetham Hill Road in 1894, nearly twenty years after Michael Marks arrived in Britain from Slonim, Russia, unable to speak a word of English. Marks's first English home was not in Manchester, but in Leeds, where he joined the firm of Barran, who were happy to take on Jewish refugees. There in 1884 he met warehouse-owner Isaac Dewhurst and began buying goods from him to sell on. Soon Marks had enough money to set up a stall in the new Leeds market. There he sold his wares under a sign which read: 'Don't ask the price. It's a penny,' a clever way of getting around the

fear that his English wasn't good enough to barter. Before asking Tom Spencer to join him in business Michael Marks sought a partnership with Dewhurst, who twice rejected him, turning down the opportunity to form what would have been the less smooth-sounding Marks & Dewhurst.

Derby Street
After Cheetham Hill Road, Derby Street, which runs perpendicularly to it, was the main street of Jewish activity in late-Victorian/early twentieth-century Manchester. Few signs of that Jewish world remain, but the street is still a centre of textile industry.

north side: Waterloo Road to Cheetham Hill Road
Manchester Ice Palace, west of Woolley Street
Once the leading ice-skating venue in the country, and in Europe second only to the Berlin Eispalast, the building is a remarkable survival, even if in a state of disrepair. The Ice Palace opened in 1910 as the largest indoor rink in Britain, and a year later hosted the World Ice Skating Championships. For many years it was *the* place to socialize in Cheetham. Despite being used for munitions production during the Great War, it soon regained its status in the 1920s and continued to be at the heart of north Manchester life until 1960, when Lancashire Dairies took over the premises.

One of the Ice Palace's last regulars was the celebrated footballer Duncan Edwards, who died in the 1958 Munich air disaster.
Marks & Spencer's (early twentieth century), No. 46
What now looks no different from so many large red-brick Cheetham properties was Marks & Spencer's first warehouse when it opened in 1901. It served as the company's headquarters before the move to London in the 1930s.
▶ Marks & Spencer on Oldham Street, p. 88.

south side: Cheetham Hill Road to Waterloo Road

Manchester Jews' School (1869–1941), east corner with Camberwell Street

The playwright Jack Rosenthal and local author Louis Golding were among the alumni of the school that used to occupy this now dilapidated Edward Salomons building. Most of the school's early intake was the children of immigrants from eastern Europe. They spoke only Yiddish but were forcibly anglicized by the school authorities, who would try to rid them of all traces of their native customs, even going as far as to change their names.

Typical was the story of a pupil who gave her name on the first day as 'Tauber Goodman' and was informed by her teacher that although she could keep Goodman, as it sounded English, she would have to lose the Tauber, which means 'dove' in Yiddish. She was then given a list of English girls' names and told to select one if she wanted to return to the school. Choosing between 'Agatha', 'Evelyn' and 'Mathilda', she went for the latter and lived the rest of her long life, into her nineties, as Mathilda Goodman.

The building was abandoned during the Second World War, when many of the children were evacuated, and later became the successful King David school on a new site further north. The Derby Street building now houses a number of small businesses.

Jacob Cohen's (early twentieth century), No. 36

Opposite the former Marks & Spencer head office was a factory run in the early twentieth century by Jacob Cohen, a little-known entrepreneur. Cohen would have remained in obscurity but for a discovery made by historians from the Manchester Jewish Museum in 2005. A stash of period documents sent to the museum yielded a batch of sheet music captioned 'Published by Marks & Spencer, originators of the Penny Bazaar' and another proclaiming 'Published by Jacob Cohen, originator of the Penny Bazaar'. Further research unearthed the story that Cohen, a brother-in-law of Michael Marks, founder of Marks & Spencer, had tried to claim inheritance to the family name but had failed, dying in obscurity.

Nathan Hope's cloth cap factory, west of Blacklock Street

A typical example of the scores of Jewish-run textile firms in pre-Second World War Cheetham was Nathan Hope's cloth cap factory, which opened in 1890. With an almost entirely Jewish workforce, Hope made a style of headgear that all Jewish men then wore. The working conditions were appalling, especially in summer when the noxious smells were particularly acute. Employees would be fined for the smallest misdemeanour – a broken needle had to be paid for out of their wages – and if they objected they were sacked, for there was a plentiful supply of Jewish immigrants arriving at Victoria station eager to take their place.

Torah Street

The only street in the English-speaking world named after the Hebrew name for the first five books of the Bible is evidence of the one-time Jewish presence in Cheetham. On the side of Torah Street is a dilapidated building, now 11 Bent Street, which was a Talmud Torah, a boys' after-school learning centre where Hebrew and Judaism were taught. When the Jewish authorities in the 1930s asked the Corporation for permission to call the two side mews Torah Street and Talmud Street the Town Hall rejected Talmud Street but allowed Torah Street. The nameplate was duly stuck on to the neighbouring building – a bacon-curing factory – whose occupants took great delight in taunting the Jewish boys coming out of the school, occasionally hauling in a passing dupe whom they would smear with bacon fat.

(ii) Red Bank

The main route north from Manchester until the mid-nineteenth century was the Red Bank Highway – rather than Cheetham

Hill Road – a street whose surroundings ranked alongside Little Ireland and Angel Meadow as the worst of the early Victorian slums. The cellars of the properties near the River Irk were a couple of feet below the waterline, the houses had no water supply or sewerage system, just an open drain from an ashpit running down the middle of the street. Unsurprisingly cholera was rampant in the nineteenth century.

Friedrich Engels described the area vividly in *The Condition of the Working Class in England* (1844):

Right and left a multitude of covered passages lead from the main street into numerous courts . . . the most horrible dwellings which I have yet beheld. In one of these courts there stands directly at the entrance, at the end of the covered passage, a privy without a door, so dirty that the inhabitants can pass into and out of the court only by passing through foul pools of stagnant urine and excrement. This is the first court on the Irk above Ducie Bridge – in case anyone should care to look into it. Everywhere heaps of debris, refuse, and offal; standing pools for gutters, and a stench which alone would make it impossible for a human being in any degree civilized to live in such a district.

Many of the first Jewish immigrants from eastern Europe settled in Red Bank in the late 1840s. They found work in the small workshops that manufactured cloth caps, waterproof garments and furniture, and lived a life similar to the one they had left behind – speaking Yiddish and worshipping in small, home-based synagogues – but free from the threat of pogroms.

Some of the *ad hoc* synagogues were rather basic: one comprised two backyards under a roof of corrugated iron. As the Jews prospered they moved further north, away from the ravages caused by industry, first to the upper reaches of Cheetham – the *Manchester City News* of 1914 described it as the 'Jewish invasion of an English suburb' – and

after the Second World War to Prestwich and Whitefield, further north, in Bury.
▸ Little Ireland, p. 60.

Scotland

A road simply called 'Scotland' was named in honour of the Scottish cattle that crossed the river Irk at this spot when Smithfield Market was in use. The road was downgraded to a path early in the twenty-first century and the street sign was removed, thereby ruining a long-standing practical joke in which naïve visitors to Manchester were told they were going to be taken on a quick tour of 'Scotland'.

(iii) Strangeways

Southall Street
Strangeways Prison

A prison whose grim lofty walls, gruesome history and very name have the power to horrify has stood here since 1869. It replaced the demolished 𝔑ew 𝔅ailey 𝔓rison in Salford and was designed by Alfred Waterhouse, architect of Manchester Town Hall. His choice of a lofty minaret to crown the structure wittily implied an all-seeing eye sweeping across the city tracking wrongdoers, even if its real purpose was simply to improve ventilation.

Strangeways took over from the 𝔑ew 𝔅ailey the role of Manchester's chief place of execution. From 1869 to 1964 100 prisoners were hanged within its precincts, the last being Gwynne Owen Evans on 13 August 1964 for the murder of laundryman John West. At the same time as Evans dropped, Peter Anthony Allen was hanged in Liverpool's Walton Prison for his part in the same crime. The authorities chose to hang both men simultaneously to prevent either of them becoming famous as the last man to be hanged if, as seemed likely and indeed proved to be the case, these were the last hangings to be carried out in Britain.

Better known are some of the ex-inmates who didn't hang. The suffragette leader Christabel Pankhurst was held here for seven days in October 1906 after disrupting a Liberal Party meeting at the Free Trade Hall. Moors Murderer Ian Brady spent three months at Strangeways in the 1950s after stealing lead seals. And Harold Shipman, the serial killer doctor, was on remand here in the 1990s while awaiting trial.

In 1919 the IRA successfully sprang a number of prisoners from Strangeways after they had been transferred here from Belfast. The escape plan was hatched by the O'Donoghues – Paddy and Violet – the former the leader of the IRA cell in Manchester (p. 135), the latter in charge of smuggling in messages and maps secreted in cakes and sandwiches. The Irish prisoners overcame the prison warder, rushed into the yard, and found the rope that had been thrown over the wall for them. They thoughtfully left behind a note explaining that the warder was not to blame.

In January 1956 Albert Pierrepoint, Britain's most famous hangman, was due to hang a Thomas Bancroft, who later that day was reprieved. Pierrepoint claimed the full £15 fee but was offered just £1 expenses. He appealed and was eventually sent £4. Taking this as an insult, he resigned his post.

The worst riot in British prison history took place at Strangeways in April 1990 in response to overcrowding. Parts of the original building were destroyed, 147 warders and forty-seven prisoners were injured, and one prisoner was killed. The prison was later officially and anodynely renamed Her Majesty's Prison, Manchester.

▶ New Bailey Prison, Salford, p. 182.

South Manchester

CHORLTON

Chorlton is Manchester's most popular suburb, a land of attractive houses, well-stocked food shops and lively bars, closer in spirit to a chic London neighbourhood such as Clapham or Stoke Newington than a Northern suburb. Chorlton's exclusiveness stems partly from its proximity to the meadows of the Mersey Valley, away from the urban sprawl that is much of Manchester, and partly to the untrammelled growth of the universities and colleges which has provided it with a ready-made influx of bohemian residents.

The name Chorlton probably comes from *Ceorla-tun*, settlement of the *ceorls*, a low rank of Saxon freemen. In medieval times the area was the home of two aristocratic families – the Barlows and the Mosleys – the former, residents of Barlow Hall, which partly survives as a golf club-house, the latter, living at Hough End Hall, now function rooms next to Chorlton High School.

By the mid-nineteenth century the area was known as Chorlton-cum-Hardy, the smaller village of Hardy being south of Chorlton Brook. (The Hardy suffix has now been mostly dropped.) The railway arrived locally in 1880, and a station now earmarked for a potential new Metrolink stop stood by the junction of Wilbraham Road and Albany Road on the Midland Railway's line to London. It closed in 1967 without affecting Chorlton's popularity, even though the journey into central Manchester would now become tortuous.

In 1964 the station was depicted as 'Chorltonville', a Mississippi Delta-style halt, for a one-off Granada TV music programme featuring authentic US blues singers such as Muddy Waters, who sat on a straw-covered platform alongside 'Wanted' posters, wandering roosters and a tethered goat, and performed to a group of goggle-eyed youth stationed on the opposite platform. The event is still fondly recalled by locals, probably because Chorlton has little other interesting history to its name, and although barely 100 people were present thousands now claim attendance.

Chorltonville is also the name of Chorlton's garden suburb, built in 1911 according to the then fashionable utopian ideas that proposed the working-class should live in comfortable spacious houses surrounded by greenery and by amenities such as tennis courts and bowling greens, rather than the grime of Ancoats or Hulme. Despite the good intentions Chorltonville soon became a middle-class enclave, and few members of the working class have ever set foot there, other than to clean or mend. As recently as the 1980s the estate housed mostly retired members of the clergy and the army. It has since caught up with the prevailing make-up of south Manchester and now has its appropriate share of social workers, council officials and Labour Party stalwarts.

Between Chorltonville and the centre of Chorlton lies Beech Road, the processional way of bohemian Chorlton. Here are expensive gift shops, overpriced cafés (but no chain outlets) and chic bars. However, the recent closures of its butcher, post office, greengrocer and bookshop, and their replacement with estate agents and yet more cafés and wine bars has resulted in the loss of the street's character just when a surge in local house prices has sent all but the most generously waged into other neighbourhoods in search of affordable housing.

Aycliffe Avenue
No. 9

When George Best arrived in Manchester for the first time in July 1961 to become an apprentice footballer with Manchester United he was put into digs here at the edge of Chorlton. The landlady was a Mary Fullaway, and her first sight of the footballer who would become Britain's greatest player led her to claim later that he looked 'more like a jockey than a footballer', for Best was then only five foot tall and weighed just eight stone.

Best was initially consumed with home-sickness, having never left Northern Ireland before, and he and housemate Eric McMordie, another trainee from Belfast, locked themselves in their room after dinner on the first night. Knowing nobody, having little money, and with no TV or radio for company, they were at a loss to know what to do. After some discussion they decided there was only one course of action available: to return home. They took the night ferry back to Ulster, but when Best knocked on the door his father was horrified. The next morning Best Snr phoned Manchester United, and manager Matt Busby convinced him that Best Jnr should try again, even adding that if George failed to make it as a footballer United would find him a job.

Best returned to Manchester and began his mercurial career. Before his wages reached the superstar bracket he would spend many nights playing cards with the Fullaway family, and occasionally visit the snooker hall in the centre of Chorlton (now the Sedge Lynn pub) to play John Spencer, who later became a world champion. Spencer would give Best a 50-point start but always beat him, often only on the black. Returning to his digs after the 10.30 p.m. curfew, Best would use next door's ladder to enter via a bedroom window left open in advance.

He was still living at Mrs Fullaway's as late as 1965, sharing the digs with team-mate David Sadler, despite having been part of United's Championship-winning team.

Even at the height of his Man U fame Best would still use the place as a retreat, the local children zealously guarding his E-type Jaguar parked outside.

▶ Best's Slack Alice nightclub, p. 76.

Barlow Moor Road
Southern Cemetery

The largest municipal cemetery in Europe opened in 1879 and is the burial place of John Alcock, the pioneering airman who jointly made the first transatlantic flight in 1919 and died later that year in a test crash; the painter L. S. Lowry (died 1976); and the Manchester United manager Sir Matt Busby (1994).

Peter Sutcliffe, the Yorkshire Ripper, murdered Jean Jordan close to Southern Cemetery on 1 October 1977, and buried her in the undergrowth. When he was driving back to Bradford, he realized he had left incriminating evidence with the corpse – a £5 note he had taken from his wages to pay her for sex. Over the next few days Sutcliffe became increasingly tormented at the prospect of the body being discovered and the note being traced back to him. When after a week there was still no mention of the murder in the papers Sutcliffe decided to chance a return and retrieve the incriminating banknote.

He drove over in the early hours of the morning, at the end of a housewarming party he was hosting that would provide him with an alibi, and found Jean Jordan. Unable to find any trace of the handbag, he began mutilating the corpse in his rage by repeatedly stabbing it, even going as far as attempting to cut off her head, though unsuccessfully.

Jordan's body was eventually found by a passer-by, Bruce Jones, an aspiring actor who later became a *Coronation Street* regular. He called the police and they discovered the bag inside which was the rogue £5 note, which they traced to the payroll of several Yorkshire firms including the one for which Sutcliffe worked. The police interviewed him but found nothing suspicious and

believed the party alibi. Emboldened, Sutcliffe continued his murderous spree. He was caught in 1981 after killing thirteen women.

▶ The Yorkshire Ripper at the MRI, p. 126.

DIDSBURY

What was until the end of the twentieth century the most desirable suburb in Manchester is now being shorn of character and appeal thanks to overdevelopment, piecemeal destruction and an outbreak of rough pubs and tacky restaurants in the village centre.

In ancient times Didsbury was a farming community on the north bank of the Mersey, six miles from Manchester, with the village green set at some distance from the river due to persistent flooding. Gradually it began to take the form of a typical north Cheshire village rather than a Manchester suburb, with its quaint cottagey dwellings and roads evoking a semi-rural presence – Elm Road, Pine Road, Lapwing Lane, The Beeches.

Didsbury grew apace in the late nineteenth century, and after the railway arrived in 1880 as part of the new suburban network connected to Central station (now G-Mex), merchants and professionals began to fill the well-built, spacious, red-brick houses and rococo Gothick villas. Artists and writers took the smaller cottages, enticed by the villagey pubs, remoteness from industrial Manchester, proximity of the Mersey and the wild open land in the floodplain.

After the Second World War Didsbury also attained popularity with the better-paid ex-Manchester University students, whose numbers rose with the massive growth of local academia. Recent years, however, have seen Didsbury's influence on Manchester decline. Where its grand houses were once home to wealthy patrons of the arts, *Manchester Guardian* journalists and members of the Corporation's arts committee, they are now company offices, student halls of residence or care homes. Since the 1970s Didsbury's character has also been eaten away by waves of insensitive development, while councillors and the local civic society battle to fend off the unimaginative planners, despoilers and bar owners intent on wiping out the relaxed nature of the area.

Wimslow Road
west side: Kingsway to Barlow Moor Road
The Towers (Shirley Institute), opposite Wingate Drive
A Gothic palace built by Thomas Worthington (p. 100) in the style of a French château has earned the nickname 'Calendar House' as it has twelve towers, fifty-two rooms and 365 windows. The Towers is situated at the end of a long drive off Wilmslow Road and was commissioned in 1868 by John Edward Taylor, owner and editor of the *Manchester Guardian*. It later became the home of the engineer Daniel Adamson, who on 27 June 1882 convened a meeting here of some seventy prominent locals that led to the creation of the Manchester Ship Canal. By the end of the Great War there was no Mancunian merchant grand or arrogant enough to run the property and it was bought by the British cotton industry's research association. It has been used as textile offices since.

Old Parsonage, north of Stenner Lane
A sprawling mid-seventeenth-century cottage, one of the oldest properties in the city, stands in a sumptuous rock garden open to the public which is entered through a grand archway known as the Gates of Hell. The Old Parsonage, which was once part of the now demolished Spread Eagle Hotel on city-centre Corporation Street, has enjoyed a varied history. In the eighteenth century it was home to the Revd W. J. Kidd. His servants quit one day, claiming the property was haunted, and spread rumours that ensured no replacements became available. Investigations showed that the night-time noises, mostly servants' bells suddenly ringing in the small hours, were the work of rats using the wiring as a tightrope.

From 1865–1919 the Old Parsonage was home to Fletcher Moss, local historian, politician and prolix wordsmith, who once described himself as an 'astonishingly attenuated alderman and absurdly antiquated author'. Moss sat on Withington Urban District Council. He was the driving force behind the opening of libraries in south Manchester, seeking funds from the Scottish philanthropist Andrew Carnegie, and left his own literary legacy in the seven-volume series *Pilgrimages to Old Homes*. He could be disconcertingly picky with his generosity. Just before his death he was asked by Didsbury Cricket Club if he would like to make a donation and met the club's representatives for an hour only to tell them: 'I am now going to give you something far more valuable than money – my good wishes.' In his will Moss bequeathed his house, and its contents, to the Corporation, who used it as an art gallery from 1914 until 1978. It is now offices.

Also in the grounds is the eighteenth-century croft used as a café and storeroom by the parsonage gardeners, where in 1889 Emily Williamson formed the Plumage League to campaign against the slaughter of birds for the millinery trade. It later became the Royal Society for the Protection of Birds.

Village Green
Didsbury's Village Green by St James's church and the bend in Wilmslow Road is one of the best-preserved traditional sites in Manchester, overlooked by a Georgian cottage which has long been an exclusive restaurant, and two well-run pubs: Ye Olde Cock Inn and The Didsbury. It is thought that the troops who came to Manchester with Bonnie Prince Charlie (the Young Pretender) in 1745 stayed at the Cock Inn before raiding the town centre (p. 79). The Didsbury, where residents once elected the local constables, has more contemporary associations. Here the comic Steve Coogan took inspiration for his gross creation Paul Calf in the 1980s after watching the anti-

pathy of the pub's regulars towards its student clientèle.

Philip Godlee Lodge (formerly The Elms), north of Stenner Lane

As the Elms this substantial property, built by Manchester's foremost classical revivalist Richard Lane, was home to William Romaine Callender, a well-known Victorian cotton spinner and Liberal who was behind the election of Manchester's first MPs – Charles Poulett Thompson and Mark Philips – in 1832. Manchester and Salford corporations bought the house in 1955 to provide accommodation for the elderly, with funds provided from the estate of Philip Godlee, former chairman of the Hallé Orchestra.

Broomhurst Hall, north of Stenner Lane

One of the few high-quality Manchester buildings from the early 1960s is this seven-storey student hall of residence of 1962, an elegant block with a steel frame built in glass and multi-coloured vitrolite, a style Manchester soon dropped in favour of monolithic brutalism.

▶ Owen Williams's *Daily Express* building, p. 147.

Lawnhurst, south of Ford Lane

An immense, sprawling red-brick mansion, Lawnhurst was built in 1894 by Edward Salomons, architect of the city-centre Reform Club, for Henry Simon, founder of Simon engineering. Simon was one of the most successful of the large group of German Jews powerful in Manchester society in the late nineteenth century that also included Karl Beyer, founder of the important Beyer Peacock firm (p. 141). Simon was born in Breslau, Prussia (now Wroclaw, Poland) in 1835. He came to Manchester in 1860, and after forming his company began to play a prominent role in local affairs, co-founding the prestigious Withington School for Girls. While living at Lawnhurst Simon saw his milling operation take control of around two-thirds of London's flour. He died here in 1899. During the First World War his widow, Emily, made the property over to the authorities so

that it could be used as a hospital for wounded soldiers.

▶ Edward Salomons's Reform Club, p. 58.

The Limes, No. 816

Now a nursing home, this substantial villa provided the model for the Artingsall family home in Howard Spring's 1940 novel *Fame Is the Spur*. The grounds contain a cottage where the comedians Rik Mayall and Ade Edmondson shared student digs in the 1970s, its bohemian anarchy providing the inspiration for the hellish flat in the well-known sitcom *The Young Ones*.

east side: School Lane to Kingsway

Broome House, No. 779

This substantial cream-coloured Georgian villa was owned by textile magnate Joseph Birley in the early nineteenth century. Birley's brother, Hugh Hornby Birley, was one of the commanders of the Manchester and Salford Yeomanry at the Peterloo Massacre, who were responsible for the indiscriminate violence.

The Grove, south of Didsbury campus

A cluster of picturesque houses, built by the Watts family for their farm managers in the 1870s and also known as Watts' Folly, somehow survives despite the ever-encroaching college.

FALLOWFIELD

What for a hundred years was an inconsequential south Manchester suburb became a student city in the 1970s with the creation of the massive Owens Park halls of residence complex. Fallowfield is centred around the junction of Wilmslow Road and Wilbraham Road. Half a mile north, running across the area east–west, are the remains of the ninth-century Nico Ditch, one of Manchester's oldest constructions. An earthwork feature stretching from Stretford to Ashton-under-Lyne, it acted as a crude protection against invading Danes, and local legend claims that it was dug over one day, each man excavating a length of earth equal to his own height. In Fallowfield Nico Ditch is visible in Platt Fields, and further east between Mount and Wembley roads in Levenshulme. A number of nearby thoroughfares – Brantingham Road in Whalley Range and Old Hall Lane, Birch-fields – follow its course.

Fallowfield was the unlikely setting for the 1893 FA Cup Final, held at the recently demolished 𝔉𝔞𝔩𝔩𝔬𝔴𝔣𝔦𝔢𝔩𝔡 𝔖𝔱𝔞𝔡𝔦𝔲𝔪, which was located in a verdant setting off Whit-worth Lane. Because the facilities were inadequate and the crowd invaded the pitch before the match (Wolves beat Everton 1–0) the FA vowed never to hold another final in Manchester – and never has. After Wolves won the trophy, their supporters produced mock mourners' cards proclaiming 'In memoriam of Everton football team who departed from the Cup competition through a severe attack of Wolves. And those hopes were interred at the football cemetery the same day.'

▶ Manchester City, p. 137.

Whitworth Lane
The Firs, south-east end

A country villa dating back to 1850, and prac-tically the only substantial Victorian build-ing remaining in Fallowfield, the Firs was designed by Edward Walters, also respon-sible for the Free Trade Hall, for the pion-eering engineer Joseph Whitworth, who worked on improving the accuracy of rifles in the grounds' shooting gallery, a feature paid for by the War Office.

In 1882 C. P. Scott, editor of the *Man-chester Guardian*, moved to the Firs. Because Scott hated motorized transport he biked from here to his Cross Street office regard-less of the weather. Five years after moving in Scott donated the building to Manchester University, who leased it back to him, and he lived there for the rest of his life. During the Boer War of 1899–1902 Scott, who opposed Britain's involvement, was put under police protection at the Firs. After his death the property became home to Man-chester University's vice-chancellor. It is now part of a hotel.

▶ The *Manchester Guardian* on Cross Street, p. 6.

RUSHOLME

A once quiet middle-class suburb, Rusholme has been severely urbanized since the 1960s by mass Asian immigration and because of its location on the main south Manchester student route leading from the university to Owens Park. The stretch of Wilmslow Road between Whitworth Park and Platt Fields is Manchester's 'Curry Mile', lined with scores of curry houses which open and close with bewildering speed but are never short of custom. As with London's similar Brick Lane, the enjoyment stems from the socializing rather than the eating, for the food is dearer and less imaginative than that found in the less ostentatious curry cafes of city-centre Smithfield.

Dickenson Road
𝔐𝔞𝔫𝔠𝔲𝔫𝔦𝔞𝔫 𝔉𝔦𝔩𝔪 𝔖𝔱𝔲𝔡𝔦𝔬, west of Hythe Close

Manchester's only major film studio, popularly known as 'Jollywood', opened in a former Wesleyan chapel on 12 May 1947. A sizeable crowd turned out to see the comic Frank Randle, one of the studio's backers, arrive in his blue Mercedes accompanied by the better-known ukulele-playing comedian George Formby, the guest of honour.

In Randle 𝔐𝔞𝔫𝔠𝔲𝔫𝔦𝔞𝔫 had the greatest northern comic of the era, whose act centred around such catchphrases as 'I'll splificate the lot of you', 'Geroff mi foot' and 'Bah, I've supped some ale tonight', as sent up by Ricky Gervais in the show within a show *When the Whistle Blows* from *Extras*. Randle also had a remarkable imagination. He once advertised in the *Manchester Evening News* for a chauffeur/bricklayer, and when asked by a colleague why he would want someone who specialized in two such unrelated tasks he explained that six nights a week he liked to be driven to the best pubs and clubs but on Saturday would drive himself. Unfortunately, after a few pints his driving would become so erratic he would invariably drive into the garden wall when he returned home and therefore needed a bricklayer to rebuild it in the morning.

The studio's first Rusholme-made feature was *Cup-Tie Honeymoon*, filmed locally at a Manchester City *v* Aston Villa match with the penalty scenes re-shot separately outside the studio using extras. Its cast included a young Pat Pilkington, later to become world-famous as the formidable Pat Phoenix, playing Elsie Tanner in *Coronation Street*. Her screen debut consisted of what studio owner John E. Blakeley described as 'two lines, a cough and a spit'. Also in the film was another later *Coronation Street* regular, Bernard Graham, who later changed his name to Bernard Youens to play the bumbling, lovable idiot Stan Ogden.

Press reaction to *Cup-Tie Honeymoon* was unanimously awful. 'This is hardly the stuff to make Hollywood take notice,' wrote the *Manchester Evening Chronicle*, while the *Manchester City News* described a 'mere stringing together of comic situations to suit the backgrounds of Oswaldtwistle and other remote places'.

The main problem was that the 𝔐𝔞𝔫=cunian films were uncinematic. They were staged, rather than filmed, churned out as if on a production line, some taking only five weeks to be produced, the dialogue often made up on the spot. Scripts had pages blank save for the term 'bus.', standing for 'business' – the actor's business or trademark music-hall routine.

Nevertheless the public flocked in large numbers to see 𝔐𝔞𝔫cunian's films. However, in 1953 Blakeley sold the studio to the BBC. He assumed that cinema had run its course and that television was the medium of the future. Scores of TV shows were then produced from Rusholme including *Grandstand* and on 1 January 1964 the first *Top Of The Pops*. By 1967 the studio was deemed to be too small, and production moved to

London. The building was demolished in 1974. Nearby is the Welcome Pub, festooned with pictures of early TV stars such as Eamonn Andrews and Wilfred Pickles, who probably drank there.

VICTORIA PARK

A luxurious, tree-lined estate of villas was created two miles south of the city centre in the 1830s for Manchester's burgeoning middle class and is still the most attractive suburb in south Manchester. It is also the location of the city's most remarkable-looking building, Edgar Wood's expressionist First Church of Christ Scientist.

The area, which was named in honour of the new Queen, was first outlined in 1836 in newspaper advertisements asking the public to buy sites on 180 acres of land between Chorlton-on-Medlock and Longsight in what would become an exclusive landscaped estate. A company was formed, an Act of Parliament passed, and Richard Lane, the Greek revivalist architect responsible for a number of major Manchester buildings, was invited to design the new Victoria Park.

Lane built the first houses around Oxford Place, at the Moss Side end, including a substantial property for himself in 𝔒𝔵𝔣𝔬𝔯𝔡 𝔏𝔬𝔡𝔤𝔢. But no sooner was the scheme underway than an economic recession led to the company's collapse. The scheme was revived in 1845, and Victoria Park began to take shape around two crescents: Park Crescent and Hanover Crescent. (A third crescent around what is now Laindon Road never materialized.) Soon scores of spacious properties brimming with character and charm, ornamented with classical or Gothic effects, topped with lofty chimneys, set on wide, gently curving tree-lined roads and backing on to rambling gardens, filled Victoria Park. There were toll gates all round to thwart undesirables, no pubs were allowed, and the police had only limited powers of arrest within, owing to an anomaly in the by-laws that wasn't changed until 1935 which fuelled rumours that you could commit any crime inside the estate, except murder, with impunity.

By the late nineteenth century Victoria Park had become what the great *Manchester Guardian* journalist Neville Cardus once memorably described as a 'sequestered purlieu'. A number of the wealthy residents were German-Jewish merchants who owned businesses in town, men such as Maurice Spiegelberg and Schill Seebohm. There was also a smattering of prestigious figures from the arts and politics: Charles Hallé, founder of the Hallé Orchestra (on Daisy Bank Road's Addison Terrace), the 'Manchester School' political leader Richard Cobden (Crescent Gate) and the Pankhurst family (Buckingham Crescent).

Not all its well-heeled residents were satisfied with their lot. The young Sylvia Pankhurst, who went on to become one of the leading socialist campaigners of the early twentieth century, later wrote that

many a time in spring I would ask myself whether it could be just that I should live in Victoria Park, and go well fed and warmly clad, whilst the children of these grey slums were lacking the very necessities of life. The misery of the poor, as I heard my father plead for it, and saw it revealed in the pinched faces of his audiences, awoke in me a maddening sense of impotence; and there were moments when I had an impulse to dash my head against the dreary walls of those squalid streets.

In the 1880s the new Manchester University began buying up some of the larger houses for halls of residence, a move that characterized the future direction of the estate. After the Great War it became clear that successful Mancunians, the kind who once vied for the best houses, were now preferring Bowdon or Didsbury. Properties were left empty or turned into flats, more and more buildings were taken over by academia, a main road (Anson Road) was cut through the area, and in 1938 the toll gates were removed, resulting in a Victoria Park with little permanent community and few willing to care for it.

Surprisingly decline and demolition have not been as rampant here as in other parts of Manchester, despite the departure of its once affluent residents. Many of the most imposing properties still stand and the nineteenth-century street pattern remains, leaving Victoria Park as one of the least Manchester-like areas of the city.

Conyngham Road

Linking the east end of Oxford Place with Dickenson Road is Conyngham Road. It features a number of monumental buildings including, at the junction with Anson Road, the church of St Chrysostom, begun in the 1840s, the work abandoned incomplete soon after and built anew from 1874–6 by G. T. Redmayne, and the vast Dalton-Ellis Hall, an 1881 university hall of residence built for Quakers, also designed by Redmayne.
▶ John Dalton's scientific discoveries, p. 54.

west side: Dickenson Road to Oxford Place
Arden Lea

The first property north of Denison Road was the 1880s home of Rose Hyland who became one of the leading Manchester suffragettes.

Lane Court

Opposite Dalton-Ellis Hall stands the white-washed villa Lane Court, now luxury apartments. It was designed in the 1840s, probably by Richard Lane, the vehemently classical architect in charge of Victoria Park's overall early look, and for decades had no name or number, being known simply as 'Mr Hadfield's in the Park' after the original owner, George Hadfield, co-founder of the Anti-Corn Law League.

Ashburne House, corner with Oxford Place Ashburne House flats stand on the site of Ashburne House, a substantial detached classical-style property of 1849, typical of the high-quality residences that once filled Victoria Park. A generation later it became home to William Romaine Callender Jnr, son of the Liberal MP for Stockport but himself a Tory, who outraged his father by entertaining the Conservative statesman Benjamin Disraeli here in 1872 after the politician had made a three-hour speech at the Free Trade Hall. In 1918 the owner gave 𝔄𝔰𝔥𝔟𝔲𝔯𝔫𝔢 ℌ𝔬𝔲𝔰𝔢 to the university for use as a student hostel. When the hall moved a mile south to Fallowfield, the property became 𝔈𝔤𝔢𝔯𝔱𝔬𝔫 ℌ𝔞𝔩𝔩, a theological college. It rotted away through neglect when the college moved out and was demolished in 1970.

east side

Dalton-Ellis Hall

The hall was founded by the Quakers as Dalton Hall in 1876 to provide student accommodation and was named in honour of the great scientist John Dalton who conducted so much pioneering work in chemistry in Manchester. The site includes the substantial Gothic house Sunnyside, designed by Richard Lane (also responsible for the Friends Meeting House), which was home from 1875–89 to Charles Sacre, the chief mechanical engineer of the Manchester, Sheffield and Lincolnshire Railway.

Daisy Bank Road

The longest and most interesting street in Victoria Park features the extraordinary sight of the First Church of Christ Scientist, Edgar Wood's Arts and Crafts-inspired masterpiece, and a number of listed houses, including those on Addison Terrace (Nos. 84–106) and Buckingham Crescent (Nos. 108–120). The mansion Summerville (now accountants' offices) was the mid-nineteenth-century home of military campaigner Sir Harry Smith. Harrismith, a town in South Africa, is named after him, while Ladysmith, another South African town, is named after his wife.

north side: Upper Brook Street to Plymouth Grove

No. 114

Also known as 4 Buckingham Crescent, this was home from 1894–8 to the suffrage campaigners the Pankhursts, where life, according to the young Christabel Pankhurst, who became one of Britain's leading campaigners

for votes for women, was 'nothing but politics and silly old women's suffrage'. Visitors to the property during the Pankhursts' tenure included Eleanor Marx (daughter of Karl), Keir Hardie, the first leader of the Labour Party, and Tom Mann, secretary of the Independent Labour Party, who jumped out of the ground-floor window when the young Christabel slipped a grass snake around his neck.

▶ The Pankhurst Centre, p. 127.

No. 102

The house was occupied at different times in the nineteenth century by the orchestra leader Charles Hallé (in 1848) and the Pre-Raphaelite painter Ford Madox Brown (1883–7). Brown stayed here while working on his series of frescoes for the new Manchester Town Hall, and was visited by leading figures from Manchester society, including *Manchester Guardian* editor C. P. Scott and Henry Roscoe, the pioneering chemist. The property is also No. 3 Addison Terrace, part of a stretch of whitewashed houses with Tudor-style façades, built 1848–50.

No. 86

Also part of Addison Terrace (at No. 11) is this house, twice burgled by Charles Peace, the infamous mid-Victorian musician and Sunday School teacher who taught by day and burgled by night. Peace was caught in the garden on the first occasion, having scratched his trademark sign 'farewell' on the window-pane.

south side

First Church of Christ Scientist (1908–71)

An astonishing sight, Edgar Wood's First Church of Christ Scientist of 1903–8 blends Art Nouveau, expressionism and the traditional rural vernacular of the English Arts and Crafts movement in what is one of Britain's most exciting buildings. Entrance is through a lych-gate leading to the main block which is in the shape of an upside-down V and covered in white rendering. It is flanked by a small brick bay with a pitched roof on one side and a graceful brick tourelle with a conical roof on the other. Behind the tourelle is a Venetian chimney similar to those used in the mills that line the Bridgewater Canal in Castlefield. Two wings stretch out from the entrance – one originally a reading room, the other a meeting hall.

Wood, whose work can be seen mostly around Middleton in north Manchester, was the master at freely uniting disparate styles into an individual whole, and for Edwardian Manchester it was a shock to see a church built in a style other than the Gothic that had dominated local nineteenth-century architecture. Inside, the pattern is complex and mesmerizing, with piers of green Norwegian marble, a reredos panel in quartered marbles, and a bas-relief of the Christian Science emblem of a cross and crown. One of the anterooms contains a fireplace of astonishing ingenuity made of glazed green tiles set in an unusual vertical pattern.

The building was deconsecrated in 1971, quickly stripped by vandals of its lead, but restored for use as an annexe by Elizabeth Gaskell College in 1976. After lying empty for the first few years of the twenty-first century, it has recently been restored for use by the United Reformed Church.
► Harry S. Fairhurst's Lee House, p. 63.

Lower Park Road

Xaverian sixth-form college occupies a sprawling site on this short road, having taken over many of the substantial Gothic buildings.

west side: Kent Road West to Oxford Place
Firwood

An austere Catholic teaching order, the Xaverian Brothers, bought the Italianate Firwood villa on the west side in 1905 and the adjoining Sunbury three years later, and merged them into a preparatory school called Xaverian. According to local legend it was here that the leading Irish nationalist Eamon de Valera was hidden by priests after he escaped from Lincoln Jail in February 1919. Xaverian's most famous alumnus was Anthony Burgess who in 1928 won a scholarship to come here and in his memoirs

described the Xaverian Brothers as men who 'dressed like priests but were little more than glorified laymen who knew they were a fair cut above Paddy Stink and Micky Mud of the Christian Brothers'. A major influence on the burgeoning writer was his history teacher, Bill Dever, who shockingly gave Burgess a copy of James Joyce's *Ulysses*, banned everywhere apart from Paris, which he had smuggled out of Nazi Germany.

In the 1950s the Xaverian buildings often appeared as backdrops to films shot nearby at the 𝔐ancunian 𝔉ilm 𝔖tudio (p. 170). By the following decade the studio was being used to film *Top Of The Pops*, and Xaverian pupils were often used as extras to make up the crowd of dancers. Since 1977 Xaverian has been a non-denominational sixth-form college. The last brothers left in 1993.
► Chetham's school, p. 94.

Marylands

A vast Gothic mansion of 1870 built as Regent House for Henry Roscoe, the pioneering chemist who worked at Owen's College (later Manchester University) and built the first modern-style chemistry laboratory in Britain. In 1858 Roscoe created the world's first flash photo. The house contains some features introduced by Roscoe, such as a set of antique Germanic door handles donated by Robert Bunsen, after whom the Bunsen burner is named. The building is now part of Xaverian.

east side
Ward Hall, No. 3

An 1840s villa used as a camp for deserting American servicemen during the Second World War and now part of Xaverian. To the north is another substantial property, Greygarth Hall, now a university hall of residence.

Upper Park Road

Spoiled by insensitive rebuilding but still inspiring a sense of awe in the casual visitor is Upper Park Road in the heart of Victoria Park. Half way along the east side is Gartness, an 1865 mansion which for much of the twentieth century was the local headquarters of the Christian servicemen's Toc H organization. No longer standing is ₱efing Billa, an enormous Gothic monstrosity, as close as Manchester has come to the mansion of the reclusive in the film *Sunset Boulevard*, where the equally reclusive Dorothy McGill wallowed in a blissful romantic bohemia until her death at the age of eighty-nine in 1962. When auctioneers arrived to catalogue her estate they found a vast trove of Oriental artefacts including some dating back to 2,000 BC.

WHALLEY RANGE

Caught between desirable residential Chorlton and no-go Moss Side, Whalley Range has been on the cusp for several decades: parts have been reclaimed by families – who can't afford Chorlton but want to live close to its organic food shops and expensive cafés – while parts are still dominated by huge crumbling Gothic villas turned into squats, crack houses and student bed-sits, where the lawless streets have attained the sinister aura of Moss Side without the brutal architecture.

Whalley Range was created in the 1830s by Samuel Brooks, a native of the Lancashire town of Whalley, as a 'desirable estate for gentlemen and their families'. Building plots were sold with the proviso that development followed Brooks's ideas, one of which was temperance – hence the almost complete absence of pubs within the area's three square miles – and large houses were built on tree-lined avenues. The biggest properties, now rarely used as family homes, were those by Alexandra Park, while nearer Chorlton the houses, built later in the nineteenth century and beyond, are more modest.

Along Alexandra Park Road South, the main street that connects Moss Side with Hough End, are a succession of grand institutional buildings epitomized by St Bede's College, a Catholic school built in the Italian Renaissance style around an unsuccessful 1874 aquarium, memorable for the majolica reliefs on its bright red-brick façade. The area's most remarkable building is Irwin and Chester's monumental Gothic Lancashire Independent College, renowned for its striking octagonal tower, which for much of the twentieth century was a trade union centre but now faces an uncertain future.

Whalley Range's days as a desirable suburb for those wealthy enough to live close to town on the clean, south, side of the city, but not among the poor of Hulme and Moss Side, and who probably couldn't afford Victoria Park, declined in the 1970s. The growth of the university saw enterprising landlords buy up the larger properties and convert them into student accommodation, which frightened the long-term residents into leaving. Whalley Range became classic bedsitter land, its romantic architecture lending it an air of melancholia admirably summed up by Morrissey on the early Smiths track 'Miserable Lie' in which he wails: 'What do we get for our trouble and pain? A rented room in Whalley Range' in reference to 35 Mayfield Road, the early 1980s home of his muse, Linder Sterling.

Manley Hall

Sam Mendel, a vastly wealthy mid-Victorian merchant, whose Manchester offices were at Chepstow House, built himself a fifty-room Italianate hall, decorated with paintings by Landseer and Millais, surrounded by grounds filled with game, stables, fountains and a lake, in the heart of what is now suburban Whalley Range. Mendel's wealth came from trade with India and China, but his business was ruined when the Ship Canal opened, leaving his ships stuck in the southern seas.

In March 1875 Mendel organized what was heralded as the sale of the century, a three-day auction held on the premises during which he divested himself of the contents of Manley Hall, although his collection of silver, plate and gold went to Christie's to be auctioned. Mendel moved to London but attempts to turn the building into an entertainments complex along the lines of

Belle Vue flopped and the estate was destroyed, the land incorporated into the new residential Whalley Range.

▶ Samuel Mendel at Chepstow House, p. 63; ▶ Sale of Trafford Park, p. 98.

WITHINGTON

A suburb once covering a vast swathe of south Manchester, Withington is now limited to the streets converging on the parade of shops along Wilmslow Road, between Mauldeth Road and Burton Road. It has been vacated in recent decades by the middle class that was its main body of inhabitants throughout the twentieth century thanks to the relentless growth of the universities which has turned what were pleasant streets into bedsitter land. The closure of the White Lion pub and the Cine City cinema in the centre of the village are evidence of the area's decline.

Palatine Road

Created in 1862 following the sale of the nearby Lum Farm, it was soon lined with 'fine, rich houses', as William Essex explains in Howard Spring's *My Son My Son* (1958), home to the 'kings of cotton'. Early in the twentieth century Palatine Road attracted so many middle-class Jews that locals mockingly nicknamed it Palestine Road. The most famous of these, although he lodged here only briefly, was the novelist Elias Canetti (later a Nobel Prize-winner) who stayed with his uncle at the Rossett, No. 123, for a short time in 1912.

An unlikely non-Jewish resident in 1918 was Admiral Karl Doenitz, who succeeded Hitler as German Führer in 1945. Doenitz, a submarine commander, had been taken prisoner of war and sent to Manchester to build a water tower at Withington Hospital. He was granted parole, which meant he could settle in his country of captivity provided he promised not to escape. After the war he returned to Germany.

west side: Lapwing Lane to Burton Road
Factory Records (1979–90), No. 86
Tony Wilson set up Factory, Manchester's most important record label, at the Palatine Road home of colleague Alan Erasmus in 1979 with £3,000 his mother had left him. The label was created mainly to release albums by the mood music group Durutti Column, whom Wilson managed, but it was soon making records with the cream of the burgeoning Manchester music scene: A Certain Ratio; the Distractions; and Joy Division, whose contract Wilson wrote on a table napkin that generously gave them an 18 per cent royalty rate instead of the usual

---

Factory – the barely collectable first ten releases
To prevent fans from collecting everything the label issued Tony Wilson deliberately gave catalogue numbers to events, posters, ephemera and oddities. For instance, Fac 15 was the Leigh summer festival, inevitably impossible to 'collect', and Fac 51, the Ḥacienda nightclub. The first ten 'releases' were as follows:

Fac 1: Poster advertising gigs held at the Russell Club in Hulme in 1978 which didn't appear until after the concert.

Fac 2: 'A Factory Sampler': two 7″ singles showcasing Factory bands.

Fac 3: Poster advertising a gig by Cabaret Voltaire, Joy Division and the Tiller Boys.

Fac 4: Poster publicizing Factory's 1978 Christmas party.

Fac 5: 'All Night Party' single by A Certain Ratio.

Fac 6: 'Electricity' single by Orchestral Manoeuvres in the Dark.

Fac 7: In-house stationery. Only the envelopes bear the catalogue number 'FAC 7'.

Fac 8: Linder Sterling's menstrual egg-timer.

Fac 9: *The Factory Flick*, a film of Joy Division rehearsing.

Fac 10: *Unknown Pleasures* album by Joy Division.

industry 12–15 per cent. One group who didn't sign was the Fall who refused because Factory was based on the university side of town.

▶ The Hacienda, p. 61.

Holly Royde, No. 30

A Victorian mansion in a dense verdant setting was partly destroyed in the 1990s, its grounds of mature trees and orchard ruined, by its custodians, Manchester University, who allowed it to be converted into a so-called 'executive' housing estate, despite much local opposition. Holly Royde was the home from 1894–1944 of Gustav Behrens, shipping merchant, one of Manchester's wealthiest Jews, who entertained Charles Hallé, founder of the Hallé Orchestra, and Edvard Greig, the Norwegian composer, here. When Behrens died aged ninety in 1936, his family presented the house to Manchester University. At first the university authorities maintained the property and its gardens, converting the building into the extra-mural department. However, in March 1997 the university announced plans to sell the site, and applied for planning permission to demolish the property so that it could be replaced with housing, which gave rise to a mostly unsuccessful campaign to preserve the property as it was intended.

WYTHENSHAWE

The largest council housing estate in Europe is a product of pre-war social engineering by Manchester Corporation, conceived on a scale that rivalled anything created by the Soviet Union during Stalin's heyday. Wythenshawe was built in the 1930s as a new town for a population of around 100,000, to be run entirely by Manchester Town Hall, nearly ten miles away. There would be eight neighbourhoods, with a density of twelve people to an acre, each containing its own school, church, clinic and shops. Industry would be segregated into zones, and it would be linked to Manchester by a

new four-lane highway (there were few local railway lines) designed in the American Parkway or dual carriageway style – Manchester's first.

The inspiration for Wythenshawe came from the Manchester politicians Ernest and Shena Simon. Ebenezer Howard's 1902 book *The Garden Cities of Tomorrow* had convinced the Simons that a bright new, enlightened, progressive society would develop if you took working-class Mancunians out of the inner-city slums of Ancoats, Gorton and Hulme, away from the smog, blackened skies, roar of industry and casual violence, and put them in Arts and Crafts cottages with inside toilets, gardens and clean air, set in landscaped surroundings.

When the plans for Wythenshawe were conceived in the 1920s the land belonged to the Tatton family. After T. E. Tatton died in 1924 his heir was prepared to sell to the Corporation, but they voted narrowly in 1926 *not* to buy. Then Ernest and Shena Simon stepped in. They bought Wythenshawe Hall and 250 acres of surrounding land, and donated them to the city 'as some return for all that we owe to Manchester'. An Act of Parliament was needed to transfer the parishes of Northenden, Baguley and Northen Etchells, which lay south of the Mersey, from Bucklow into Manchester, but despite opposition the plans proceeded. When Wythenshawe joined Manchester on 1 April 1931 the headline in the *Evening Chronicle* read: 'Lancashire Bigger Tonight. Wythenshawe Coming In At Midnight'. Manchester had few problems acquiring more land.

The architect Barry Parker, whose deft touch had created a well-crafted idyll in London's Hampstead Garden Suburb, was brought in to oversee the plans. For Wythenshawe he designed semi-detached brick houses in the neo-Georgian style which still exhibit sturdiness and solidity. However, he ruined his work by setting the properties in culs-de-sac, rather than traditional roads, linked to other similar 'neighbourhood units' by serpentine lanes. And there were

Major aviation sites of Manchester

Ashburton Road, Trafford Park. The first designated airfield in the Greater Manchester area opened in 1911 in what had been the deer park of Trafford Hall. It closed during the Great War.

Barton Aerodrome, Liverpool Road, one mile west of the M60. Britain's first municipal airport opened here in 1930 but was soon deemed unsuitable for expansion. Eight years later major services were transferred to a new site at the southern end of Wythenshawe at Ringway. Barton remained a private aerodrome, and when its existence was threatened in the late 1990s by redevelopment of the land near the Ship Canal the listing of several aviation buildings warded off the wrecking ball. The 1933 control tower is believed to be the oldest of its kind in the world.

Brownsfield Mill, off Great Ancoats Street. Some of the world's earliest aeroplanes were made in Alliott Verdon Roe's mill near Piccadilly station.

Eccles Cricket Ground, Boardman Street. The first plane ever seen in the Manchester skies, made at Alliott Verdon Roe's factory, took off from the cricket ground in June 1912.

Hough End, Withington. The first airfield within the City of Manchester was constructed in 1917 near the junction of Princess Road and Mauldeth Road West by fifty Portuguese workmen brought to Manchester especially for the job. Hough End was the destination of the first domestic flight into Manchester, which arrived from Cricklewood in London on 1 May 1919, a journey of three and a half hours. On 25 May that year the Avro company began Britain's first domestic air service, its three-seater planes heading for Southport and Blackpool. The service ran for four months without mishap. When the Manchester Corporation chose this site for a proper airport in 1923 Lord Egerton of Tatton refused to sell the land. It is now sports fields.

Manchester airport Now among the world's twenty busiest airports, its first service, to Liverpool, began in June 1938.

Paulhan Road, Didsbury. In winning the *Daily Mail*'s 1910 London–Manchester air race, Louis Paulhan landed in Pytha Fold Farm, off Fog Lane, at 5.32 a.m. on 28 April. He beat Claude Grahame-White who failed to complete the race for mechanical reasons. Paulhan Road, appropriately, has since been built on the site.

---

no shops near the houses, for shops could be located only in designated shopping centres. Consequently tenants had annoyingly long walks to bus stops to get basic provisions. As for work, the industrial units were not finished until the 1950s. So much for planning . . .

By the 1970s Wythenshawe had become a no-go zone for aspiring Mancunians; a vast, crime-ridden slum bereft of amenities, attractive shops, friendly pubs and restaurants, as depressing and deprived as the communities it was meant to replace; a desert of isolation, boredom and unemployment, incorporating large stretches of dysfunctional estates.

Critics are still torn over who has been to blame for Wythenshawe's failures: the tenants who, despite being transported into houses with bathrooms and other mod cons, did not soften their personalities to fit in with their new green environment and within a generation had turned the garden village into a suburban slum, or the increasingly uninterested Corporation who left them to rot in a bleak, isolated, lonely, soulless, culture-free landscape cut off from the city centre, with few shops, social facilities, and rail and bus links.

Wythenshawe remains a prime example of how a community devised by

Town Hall committee rather than through organic human development can never work.

Terminal Road South
Manchester airport

In, but not of, Wythenshawe, Manchester airport has become one of the city's great economic success stories in recent decades, a major local employer and one of Europe's busiest airports. The airport was originally planned for Barton, west Manchester, but while work proceeded a temporary site was found in Wythenshawe, off Sale Road. It was from there on 29 April 1929 that the Lord Mayor of Manchester flew to London to collect from the air minister a licence to open the new airport. He returned to Manchester with the wrong piece of paper, which he nevertheless brandished to the waiting crowd.

Once Barton had opened, the authorities soon realized the site was not suitable for expansion and so a new location was found in Wythenshawe at Ringway. The airport opened here in June 1938 but within eighteen months had been commandeered for war work, and the name 'Manchester' in the landing area was masked throughout the hostilities to foil enemy bombers. It was at Ringway that agents from the Special Operations Executive, hired to engage in sabotage overseas, were trained in parachuting.

Civil flying resumed in 1946, and the first jumbo jet was seen here in 1970. Five years later Ringway became Manchester International Airport and has since expanded considerably.

Salford

A separate city occupying the north bank of the Irwell, Salford predates Manchester but has long lived in the shadow of its more illustrious neighbour. In early industrial days Salford was a centre of progressive ideas. The strongest campaigns for the abolition of child labour, against capital punishment, for temperance, against smoking, for vegetarianism all came from here, particularly from the circle around the pastor Joseph Brotherton whose wife, Martha, wrote the first vegetarian cookery book in 1812, and who became Salford's first MP in 1832, helping to pass laws to set up municipal libraries and art galleries.

Then came industrialization. Here in Salford it was dirtier and noisier than in much of Manchester. As factories replaced home-based work, the population shot up from 12,000 in 1812 to 70,000 by 1840. At the end of the century it stood at 220,000. Robert Roberts explained the workings of Salford

society of that time in his 1971 volume of reportage *The Classic Slum*:

> The social standing of every person within the community was demonstrated by their material possessions. Pictures, in a society far from wholly literate, were especially esteemed. Other articles longed for were pianos, sewing machines, bicycles, gramophones, gold lockets and watches and chains. Curtains had high significance, the full drape if possible, lace being a necessity for any family with pretensions to class.

Salford officially became a city in 1926 when it was still buoyant, but its post-1960s economic demise has left a legacy of poverty and squalor which will be hard to overcome. The old city centre around the cathedral and edges of central Manchester offers some of the most run-down urban stretches in England. The northern suburbs such as Broughton, once as desirable and salubrious as Didsbury, are now mostly decrepit, with little other than crumbling villas too cut off from Manchester life to attract wealthy residents. To the immediate west are inner-city slums – Pendleton, Ordsall, Irlam O' Th' Heights – of unimaginable bleakness; the highest concentration of dystopian high-rise wastelands in Europe full of boarded-up shopping precincts and pubs rife with violence.

CITY CENTRE

Chapel Street

Historically part of the ancient route linking St Alban's to Carlisle (now the A6), Chapel Street is traditionally regarded as the main road through Salford, home of the city's cathedral and first town hall, but is now a mostly derelict blight-ridden eyesore, lined with crumbling buildings.

With the advent of the Industrial Revolution mills for spinning and weaving cloth were built here near the factories making the machines that serviced them. At No. 19 in the early nineteenth century lived Reginald Richardson, printer, bookseller and leading radical. Believing that the Reform Act of 1832 had done little to help the poor, Richardson ran an unsuccessful campaign to allow people to own weapons, producing a pamphlet called 'The Right of Englishmen to Have Arms' which asked 'Dear brothers! Are your arms ready? Have you plenty of powder and shot? Do you intend to be freemen or slaves? Remember that your safety depends on the strength of your own right arms.'

Until the Second World War part of Chapel Street by Sacred Trinity church was home to the Flat Iron Market, ideal, according to the *Manchester Guardian* of 26 May 1906, for buying 'a rusty old cavalry sword, a pair of skates, a bunch of curtain rings, a pair of half-Wellington boots, a pair of cork soles, a bunch of old keys, an old rusty lock or a pink ice-cream'.

With the decline in local manufacturing at the end of the twentieth century came the closure of many Chapel Street buildings. The lavish regeneration of Manchester that has brought money and media attention to the city has yet to hit this part of Salford.

north side: Adelphi Street to Victoria Street
St Philip, north end of St Philip's Place
Robert Smirke, architect of the British Museum, designed St Philip's church in the early 1820s in the popular classical revival style of the time. It was one of the so-called 'Waterloo churches', built in the slums in thanksgiving following the Battle of Waterloo, amid fears voiced by Parliament that a 'godless people might also be a revolutionary people'.

Salford Cathedral, west of Great George Street
The Catholic church of St John the Evangelist, built by Matthew Hadfield in the decorated Gothic style between 1844 and 1848, became Salford Cathedral in 1890. Hadfield borrowed heavily from existing architectural features in creating the church. For instance, the west door is a copy of the west front of Howden Church in Yorkshire, the choir and sanctuary are a replica of Selby Abbey's, and the tall spire is similar to that of Newark Church.

Old Town Hall, north end of Bexley Square
The small and elegant paved area between the former Salford Town Hall (now a court) and Chapel Street was the setting for a violent demonstration on 1 October 1931 which came to be known as the Battle of Bexley Square. That day around 10,000 people marched to the Town Hall to protest at the 10 per cent cut in unemployment benefit introduced by the new National Government – many armed with placards proclaiming: 'Down down down with the National Starvation Government'.

At the end of the march a huge crowd gathered in Bexley Square. It included Walter Greenwood, who wrote the well-known Salford novel of the time, *Love on the Dole*, local trade union activist Eddie Frow (described by Greenwood in the book as a 'finely-featured young man with long hair') and the folk singer Jimmy Miller, who later changed his name to Ewan MacColl. Police charged and arrested Frow who, according to Greenwood, was 'set upon by a couple of constables savagely' and had his nose broken in the mêlée. Frow served five months in Strangeways Prison for assault and inciting the crowd. In his reminiscences Miller described the 'crush of shouting, screaming, angry and bewildered men and

women. They were pushing, pulling, trying to avoid the swinging batons of the police and the terrifying hooves of the horses.'
▶ The Frows' Working Class Library, p. 188.

Caxton Hall, Nos. 88–92

Caxton Hall, a stone building of 1907, fronted by an elegant Dutch gable, was built for the Typographical Society, one of a myriad of print unions that ran the industry until the late twentieth century. It was used for decades by various socialist and trade union groups, and was where the newly formed and short-lived British Socialist Party held its first conference in 1911. It now contains shops on the ground floor.

Sacred Trinity, east of Gravel Lane

Originally a wooden chapel built by Humphrey Booth in 1635 as a chapel of ease to Manchester Cathedral, it was where John Wesley preached in 1733 but on his return fourteen years later was refused admission and chased out of town. The church was nearly obliterated by the extensions to Victoria station at the end of the nineteenth century. Even though it won its right to survive after discussions that resulted in the railway company being forced to re-plan its route, one platform was built only a few feet from the building.

Exchange Station, at Greengate

The London and North Western company opened Exchange as a railway terminus in 1884 after failing to agree terms with rival lines over sharing the adjacent Victoria station. After nationalization in the 1940s Exchange was joined to Victoria, with the result that one platform, at 2,194 feet, was now the longest in the world.

Bobby Charlton was shocked at the grime all around when he arrived in Manchester for the first time in the summer of 1953 and got out at Exchange station. 'I saw all the buildings completely covered in a thick layer of black. There was so much smoke belching out of all the factories and mills that it clung to the buildings,' he later recalled. When George Best arrived in Manchester for the first time as a raw fifteen-year-old in July 1961, never having left Northern Ireland

before, he requested the taxi driver outside the station to take him to Old Trafford and was amazed to be asked 'Which Old Trafford?' Best was unaware that Lancashire cricket club's stadium shared the same name as the nearby Manchester United football ground.

In the mid-1960s, when plans were announced to close Exchange, the architect Lewis Womersley, co-creator of the Hulme Crescents and the Arndale Centre, outlined a scheme to convert the site into homes with a motel, shops and car park. Although the station closed as long ago as 1969, at the beginning of the twenty-first century it still lay derelict, apart from the predictable car park.

south side: Victoria Street to Oldfield Road

Copperheads/Brown Bull, No. 187

A hulking Victorian pub in the shadow of the railway line became an unlikely popular socializing venue in the 1960s thanks to George Best, who treated the Brown Bull as a home from home, spending more time inside it than he ever did on the football field. The landlord, Billy Barr, even gave Best a key so that he could let himself in and lock up when the last of his friends had left. Best, who once described the Brown Bull as a 'hard-drinking pub in a hard-drinking town', used to bring into the pub in his wake a number of media figures from Granada TV, based nearby, including Michael Parkinson, Germaine Greer and Clive James, who were then unknown researchers.

New Bailey Prison (1790–1868), west of New Bailey Street

On a huge site near where Salford station can be found stood the New Bailey Prison, the area's main jail before Strangeways. New Bailey was where the Blanketeers (demonstrators who wanted to extend the vote and who carried their blankets on their marches) were incarcerated in January 1817. A revolutionary mob planned to free them by taking over the army barracks, burn down the houses of those opposed to reform, and storm the New Bailey. The plot was revealed to Samuel Bamford, the well-known Middleton radical, by a man who arrived at his door and explained how the mob was planning to make a 'Moscow of Manchester' – to burn it down like the townspeople did to stop Napoleon taking that city. However, Bamford assumed the man was an *agent provocateur* sent by the government – a regular occurrence in those days – and refused to go along with the plan. He himself was briefly incarcerated in the New Bailey that March for helping a fellow radical flee Manchester after attending an illegal political meeting.

In August 1819 *The Times*'s reporter at Peterloo, John Tyas, wrote his report of the events after placing himself in protective custody at the New Bailey following the massacre. His piece was published on 19 August, three days after, but he had been beaten to it by John Edward Taylor, whose article had already gone into *The Times*. Taylor went on to found the *Manchester Guardian*.

William Allen, Michael Larkin and William O'Brien, Irish nationalists, or Fenians, who became known as the Manchester Martyrs, were hanged on 23 November 1867 for their alleged involvement in the springing of prisoners from a van in Ardwick and the murder of a policeman. The executions were watched by a large jeering crowd that gathered at daybreak alongside extra police and soldiers from the 72nd Highlanders who had occupied positions in the surrounding streets with field guns in case there was any attempt to rescue the men. Their last words before being hanged were 'Lord Jesus have mercy on us.' The drop failed to break the necks of Larkin and O'Brien and the hangman had to descend into the pit to finish the job. He killed Larkin, but was prevented from killing O'Brien by a priest who cradled the dying man in his arms for three-quarters of an hour until he expired.

► The springing of the Fenians, p. 151.

The Crescent

Salford's most elegant street, begun in the 1820s, retains much of its Georgian splendour, with a row of handsome brick-built properties by the River Irwell, even if the effect is somewhat spoiled by the roaring traffic of the A6. Here is the Peel Park museum, home of the city's collection of Lowry paintings until the recent opening of the Lowry Centre; the Frows' Working Class Library, which has moved from its original home in their Trafford semi; and Joule House, nineteenth-century home of the great physicist James Prescott Joule.

Friedrich Engels, pioneer of Communism, chanced upon a battle between brickmakers and their bosses at the western end of the Crescent, by the junction with Cross Lane, on 16 May 1843. The company owners wanted the workers to make bigger bricks, which would lower their output and lose them income, and when the workers demanded an increase in wages to make up for the shortfall, the bosses refused to agree and a strike was called. The dispute didn't last long, for when a group of brickmakers stormed the works at ten o'clock on the first evening they were easily outmanoeuvred by the militia.

north side

Salford Art Gallery and Museum

Britain's first free, council-run public library opened here in 1849 on land that had been part of Lark Hill Mansion and is now Peel Park, named after the Conservative statesman Robert Peel, who contributed to the subscription fund. A year later a museum opened alongside. It is now best known for its reworked Victorian street – Lark Hill Place – imbued with a cloying sentimentality about the past that contrasts sharply with Salford council's determination to wipe out all traces of the pre-1960s city in its desperation to modernize.

south side

Working-Class Movement Library, No. 51, junction with Acton Square

The vast collection of socialist tracts and publications accumulated during the twen-

tieth century by local activists Ruth and
Eddie Frow has been kept in Jubilee House,
a former nurses' home, since the late 1980s.
The library contains material on the
Chartists, early trade unionists, suffragettes,
Communists, assorted demonstrations,
strikes and campaigns, right up to the
present day.
► Working Class Library, Trafford, p. 188.

ORDSALL

Crammed with houses built in the
nineteenth century for workers at the new
factories, Ordsall later became home to
many of the men working at the nearby
docks and has remained a solidly working-
class, no-frills community since, with few
amenities beyond the pub and the bus to
Old Trafford.

Even by Manchester standards Ordsall
has long had a reputation for untrammelled
violence. In May 1889 John Rowlands,
sixteen years old, challenged 'any lad of his
own size' at the local glassworks to fight
him. Arthur Jones took up the gauntlet, and
the two youths went to open land opposite
the works where they took off their coats
and fought intensely, watched by work-
mates. After a few moments Rowlands
struck Jones several times on the head,
knocking him to the ground. Jones had a fit
and died soon afterwards. When the police
arrested Rowlands, he told them: 'I will give
myself up; but it was a fair fight. We shook
hands before we fought.' He was convicted
of manslaughter at Liverpool assizes and
sentenced to one day's imprisonment.

The 1960s saw Ordsall suffer twice: from
the closure of the docks and from the
Corporation's decision to knock down the
brick terraced houses and their streets, and
replace them with mean rabbit-hutch
properties set in culs-de-sac by waste
ground. The authorities refused to allocate
funds to maintain Ordsall's housing on the
grounds that it was relatively new; in the late
70s the steel window frames buckled, part-

ing from the walls, leaving inch-wide gaps
to let in the howling winter wind. Now, with
the jobs in the docks long gone and little to
replace them, the area has become a no-go
zone for all but the criminal youth who
prowl its dilapidated streets.

Coronation Street
Despite the name and proximity to Granada
studios the street was only a nominal inspiration for the long-running Granada soap,
the houses on the real Coronation Street
being more substantial than those on the
TV set, and the location, close to a busy
main road, bearing no comparison. The
main inspiration for the programme was
𝔄rchie 𝔖treet (p. 185).

Coronation Street is home to Salford
Lads' Club, which since being featured on
the sleeve of the Smiths' 1986 *The Queen Is
Dead* album has drawn in visitors from
across the world to pose for a photograph
outside the premises. Local youths remain
unimpressed by the connection and tourists
paying tribute are usually met with hostility.

Ordsall Lane
Ordsall Hall
The stately home nearest to Manchester
city centre, its grounds running down to
the Irwell in medieval times, and now a
museum, was the home of the Radclyffe
family, who brought the first Flemish
weavers to England until the late
seventeenth century, and later passed to
the better-known Egertons of Tatton. The
novelist Harrison Ainsworth, a close friend
of Charles Dickens, claimed in his 1875 novel
Guy Fawkes, on the slenderest of evidence,
that the Gunpowder Plot was hatched here.
That year Ordsall Hall became a working-
men's club and gym.

Salford Corporation bought the property
in 1959 from the trustees of the Tatton
Estate, and spent £42,000 on repairs, but
decided to abandon the project as the
continual upkeep would prove too costly.
Cleverly, they then threatened to demolish
the property. The blackmail worked, for the
government soon stumped up the money to

have the hall reopened as a museum in 1972.

St Clement's Drive

St Clement's Drive is built over 𝔄𝔯𝔠𝔥𝔦𝔢 𝔖𝔱𝔯𝔢𝔢𝔱, real-life inspiration for *Coronation Street*, which is filmed barely a mile away at Granada Television's headquarters. Archie Street was chosen after the soap's production team toured Manchester in 1959 looking for a real street they could evoke in the studio. The choice was perfect for this was the archetypal, self-sufficient, close-knit community, epitomized by the two-up two-down home of the Manchester United footballer and 'Busby Babe' Eddie Colman, killed in the Munich air disaster the previous year. It was where many of the players, including Bobby Charlton, would begin their Saturday-night socializing, as the Colman family sent for a jug of beer from the off-licence on the corner. Pictures of 𝔄𝔯𝔠𝔥𝔦𝔢 𝔖𝔱𝔯𝔢𝔢𝔱 were used for the programme's opening and closing credits, and some small amount of outdoor filming was done here until 1968 when the street was demolished.

▸ Granada TV, p. 47.

Trafford Road

The main entrance to Manchester Docks was on Trafford Road, which was also home (at the eastern end of No. 8 Dock) to the Dock Office, built during the construction of the Ship Canal as a church for the benefit of the navvies who worked on the waterway. It was here during the docks' heyday that dockers would meet to see which ships had entered the Ship Canal and therefore what work would soon be available, information that was written in slate on one of the windows.

Around the turn of the nineteenth century Trafford Road was the setting for public debates, with some of the greatest speakers and figures of the day, which took place outside the Social Democratic Federation Club at 𝔑𝔬. 43. William Morris spoke about the state of the nation, giving a speech entitled 'What Shall We Do Now', on 11 March 1894 in front of around 2,000 hardy souls battling against a bitter wind that blew along the Irwell. On 6 July 1901 James Connolly, the leading Irish nationalist, spoke on socialism and war, in particular the Boer War, which was then raging, bravely condemning the British military campaign. The popularity of these street meetings worried Salford Corporation which eventually fenced off the land to stop it being used.

Trafford

A hybrid borough, created in 1974 from Altrincham, Sale, Stretford and Urmston, Trafford is the Norman form of the Anglo-Saxon Stretford, and takes its name from the major traditional local landowners, the De Trafford family, who enjoyed an uninterrupted line of male heirs from the twelfth century until the twentieth. Before the Second World War the name Trafford was synonymous with the huge Trafford Park industrial estate. Nowadays it is indelibly linked with Old Trafford, test cricket venue and more famously Manchester United's stadium.

FIRSWOOD

An anonymous suburb to the north of Chorlton filled with streets of near identical 1930s semis set around the junction of King's Road and Great Stone Road.

King's Road
Morrissey's address (1969–84), No. 384
In a drab suburban semi, situated in an equally drab west Manchester suburb, one of the most fateful meetings in music history occurred. It took place in 1982 when Johnny Marr, a hopeful young guitarist, knocked at the King's Road home of the Morrisseys, a family of Irish background who had moved to Trafford in 1969 when their Hulme terrace was condemned. Marr, thrilled by stories of early rock 'n' roll US songwriting duo Leiber and Stoller, was looking for a competent lyricist, and was directed to Steven Morrissey, would-be intellectual and recluse, who had impressed a number of Manchester musicians with his burgeoning songwriting skills and was infamous in city circles for sending the *New Musical Express* a series of provocative letters in the 1970s.

Morrissey handed Marr some lyrics he had written. These included 'Suffer Little Children', a paean to the victims of the Moors Murders based around their cries for help and conversations between the perpetrators, Ian Brady and Myra Hindley. As soon as Marr read the words to the song

'Suffer Little Children': The Smiths and the Moors Murders

The Smiths owe much to the Moors Murders, Manchester's darkest episode – including their name. In his adolescence Morrissey read Emlyn Williams's powerful tale of Myra Hindley's and Ian Brady's murders, *Beyond Belief*, which constantly mentions 'the Smiths' – Maureen and David Smith (Hindley's sister and her husband) – who shopped the child-killing pair to the police.

The book provided Morrissey with ideas, titles and lyrics. Williams describes how women at Holloway prison spat the words 'Suffer Little Children' at Myra Hindley when she was first jailed, words taken from the Bible's Mark 10:14 ('Suffer the little children to come unto me . . .'), which Morrissey used for the title of the closing track on the group's debut album.

When Hindley was moved to Durham jail in 1977 she was mortified and announced: 'Society owes me a living,' a line Morrissey used on 'Still Ill' from that album. Even the seemingly innocent 'I Don't Owe You Anything' from the same album is little more than a well-concealed account of the murderers' early romance. In subsequent albums Morrissey has inserted a number of oblique references to the crimes.

As Morrissey once explained to journalists puzzled at his obsession with the murders, when he was at school in the 1960s he genuinely feared that he might become a victim – as doubtless did countless of his contemporaries. He spoke of how mothers at the school gates would talk in hushed tones about the story. 'It was like living in a soap opera.'

he realized that their meeting could have a greater bearing on the future of music than even Leiber's visit to Chez Stoller. 'I was taken aback completely because the content was so serious but at the same time very poignant and poetic,' the guitarist later recalled. The two went on to form the Smiths, Manchester's greatest rock band.

▶ Manchester music scene, p. 67.

OLD TRAFFORD

A sprawling inner suburb which takes in urban wastelands of empty weed-strewn plots and boarded-up shops near Hulme, bland industrial zones of crinkly tin warehouses near the canals, and old-fashioned working-class brick terraced houses near Brooks's Bar, is by a historical accident part of the contrived borough of Trafford rather than the more appropriate City of Manchester.

Chester Road

1857 Art Treasures Exhibition Hall, site of White City retail park

Old Trafford was still a semi-rural suburb when it was used as the setting for the 1857 Art Treasures Exhibition, the most ambitious civic venture ever staged in the North and the largest exhibition ever held in Europe.

The exhibition, held in a hall between the Botanical Gardens and the railway (now Metrolink), was organized to show that Manchester was about more than smoking chimneys, cotton spinning and making money – that it could be the home of culture as well. The hall was a vast iron and glass building designed by the local architect Edward Salomons, laid out like a cathedral, with a transept and a massive organ, and Alexander Pope's lines: 'To wake the soul by tender strokes of art' displayed at one end.

To acquire exhibits a committee sent out requests to Britain's wealthiest families, but not all complied. William Cavendish, seventh Duke of Devonshire, remarked:

'What in the world do you want with art in Manchester? Why can't you stick to your cotton spinning?' It was vital to obtain royal assent for the venture, and it duly came from Prince Albert, who enthused about plans to 'illustrate the history of Art in a chronological and systematic arrangement [which would] speak powerfully to the public mind'.

Some 16,000 works were displayed at Old Trafford. There was sculpture, metalwork, ceramics, jewellery and paintings by Michelangelo and Rembrandt. There were some works by British painters which critics were keen to praise – lest art be thought the preserve of continentals – but much of the British collection consisted of pale watercolours and hackneyed animal paintings. Exceptions were the section devoted to the newly emerged Pre-Raphaelites and Henry Wallis's *Chatterton*, which two policemen protected from the crowd.

The exhibition was a great success, and was attended by more than one million visitors, including Benjamin Disraeli, Florence Nightingale and Charles Dickens. The travel agent Thomas Cook even ran special trains that left Newcastle at midnight, arrived in Manchester for breakfast and returned in the evening. The exhibition's legacy was not just an improvement to Manchester's art galleries but, indirectly, the creation of the Hallé Orchestra, for Charles Hallé organized a group of musicians to play in the hall, then stayed in the city after the exhibition closed to found the orchestra that bears his name.

The Botanical Gardens closed in 1907 and later became White City amusement park. It was a greyhound racing stadium from 1926 until 1981 after which it was developed as a retail park.

▶ Manchester Art Gallery, p. 17.

Chorlton Road
Amalgamated Union of Foundry Workers, No. 164

The kind of excitement rarely seen at a trade union headquarters greeted Soviet cosmonaut Yuri Gagarin, the first man to walk in space, when he visited the foundry workers' union building by Brooks's Bar on 12 July 1961. Gagarin, who was dressed in a bright green uniform that contrasted with the workers' dark overalls, was given a gold medal. When he told the assembled workers, 'I was a foundry worker too for a long time and although I am doing a different job now I am still a foundry worker at heart,' they cheered heartily and gave him a chorus of 'For he's a jolly good fellow'. Earlier in the day Gagarin had visited Manchester Town Hall, where the Red Flag fluttered beside the Union Jack, while across Manchester schoolboys dressed up in home-made space suits in honour of the visit.

King's Road
Working Class Library (1953–87), No. 111

Ruth and Eddie Frow created Britain's most remarkable private library in their modest King's Road semi after the Second World War, accumulating a collection of some 30,000 books, pamphlets, leaflets and political tracts that attracted visitors from far and wide.

Eddie Frow was a trade union official and a long-standing local political agitator. He was a member of the Liverpool Communist Party delegation that visited Moscow in 1930, and soon after he carried out a survey of poverty in Salford, finding furniture that had been pawned and replaced with orange boxes, and people living on bread, margarine and tea. A year later Frow took part in Salford's infamous Battle of Bexley Square demonstration against unemployment (p. 181). He knew his political sympathies did little for his employment prospects, and claimed that he lost twenty out of twenty-one jobs because of his beliefs and trade union activity.

In 1953 Frow met Ruth Haines, a teacher who had joined the Communist Party in 1945. Gradually they amassed a book collection which by the 1980s was too large for their modest home. Salford council bought

the library and moved it to the Crescent in 1987 (p. 183). Eddie Frow died in May 1997.
► Political demonstrations in Stevenson Square, p. 72.

Sir Matt Busby Way
Manchester United (1910–)
The world's most famous football team, England's best supported club and its most successful side other than Liverpool has done more to give Manchester an international standing than any other local institution.

Founded in east Manchester and known as Newton Heath until 1902, the club moved to Old Trafford in 1910. Early years at the new stadium were a bizarre mixture of triumph and disaster. United won the championship in 1911 but four years later needed to beat Liverpool at home on Good Friday to avoid relegation. Although they achieved the desired result, the referee and the paltry 15,000 crowd realized that some of the Liverpool players were acting strangely during the match. It later transpired that four players from each side had decided to fix the result, and that some United players had placed bets with local bookmakers on the 2–0 victory. Eight players were banned for life, though the bans were subsequently lifted in view of the culprits' good war record.

Between the wars United endured their least successful era, and came close to relegation to the Third division. Salvation arrived courtesy of a Scot, Matt Busby, who had played for Manchester City. Busby took over as manager in February 1945 when the club had a £15,000 overdraft, a ground that had almost been destroyed by wartime bombs (where the dressing rooms stand today was a hut), and played their home matches at City's Maine Road stadium. Busby revolutionized United through his eye for a quality player and his man-management skills. Reinvigorated, United finished second in the League for three consecutive years after the war and won the Cup in 1948. The championship came four years later at the start of an era dominated by the rise and tragic fall of the 'Busby Babes', a group of home-grown young stars who took the club to two more championships but most of whom perished in a plane crash at Munich airport in February 1958. Lost in the disaster was the club's brightest talent, Duncan Edwards. A surprise survivor was Busby himself, over whose injured body the last rites had been read.

Busby painstakingly rebuilt the team around another Munich survivor, the indomitable Bobby Charlton, and although it was some time before United approached their pre-Munich levels, the task was completed in May 1968 when the club, with George Best starring alongside Charlton, became the first English side to win the European Cup. The European achievement became a millstone to United once Busby retired. Decline set in, the playing stock deteriorated in quality and relegation followed in 1974. United swiftly returned, and under Tommy Docherty, Dave Sexton and Ron Atkinson regularly finished high in the League as well as savouring occasional FA Cup success. However, as far as the club was concerned this wasn't enough: United needed to be League champions.

It took twenty-five years from Busby's last title to United's next. The guiding hand was again that of a Scot, Alex Ferguson, but the contrast with the suave and sober Busby couldn't have been greater. Where Busby had charmed and inspired all who met him, Ferguson was at best annoying, at worst embarrassing. Where Busby was calm, Ferguson was manic. Where Busby was represented on the pitch by Bobby Charlton, the most impressive English footballer the game has ever seen, Ferguson's ruthless spirit was embodied by a captain (Roy Keane) who once boasted of deliberately injuring an opponent and a forward (Eric Cantona) best remembered for vaulting into the crowd and attacking a supporter. Nevertheless during Ferguson's twenty-year-plus reign United won the championship more times than almost every other club has *ever* won it, thanks to outstanding long-term

Manchester United miscellany

• The last official football match held in England before the professional game was put under wraps during the Great War was the 1915 FA Cup Final at Old Trafford. It did not involve United but Sheffield United and Chelsea, who contested what became known as the Khaki Cup Final which the Yorkshire team won 3–0. When Lord Derby presented the trophy to Sheffield United, he told them: 'You have played with one another and against one another for the Cup; play with each other for England now.'

• News of Matt Busby's arrival as manager on Monday 19 February 1945 was greeted in a matter-of-fact manner by the *Manchester Evening News*: 'Company Sergeant-Major Instructor Matt Busby, Liverpool right-back and Scotland captain, today signed an agreement to become manager of Manchester United when he is demobilized.'

• United fans were amazed to discover during the summer of 1950 that winger Charlie Mitten had left the club for Santa Fe of Colombia. The incentive to go abroad at a time when few players left their country of origin was the size of the wages the South Americans were offering him. At United Mitten was earning £12 a week; the Colombians would be paying him a signing-on bonus of £2,500 and an annual salary also of £2,500. Life in Bogotá was not so grand, however, and Mitten soon returned to England.

• After the 1958 Munich air disaster only Harry Gregg and Bill Foulkes of the team that played the previous match were fit enough to play Sheffield Wednesday in the next game. In the programme for the Wednesday match the United chairman, Harold Hardman, wrote:

Although we mourn our dead and grieve for our wounded, we believe that great days are not done for us. The sympathy and encouragement of the football world and particularly of our supporters will justify and inspire us. The road back may be long and hard but with the memory of those who died at Munich, of their stirring achievements and wonderful sportsmanship ever with us, Manchester United will rise again.

• Film director John Schlesinger used Manchester United's ground in a scene from the kitchen-sink classic *Billy Liar* in 1961. Fifty students from UMIST were paid 30 shillings each as extras to run towards a turnstile as Billy Liar himself (played by Tom Courtenay) imagines a roar from a Nuremberg rally-style crowd saluting him.

players such as Paul Scholes and Ryan Giggs, and in 1999 achieved the unprecedented treble of League, FA Cup and European Cup.

▶ Manchester United in East Manchester, p. 153.

Warwick Road
Lancashire County Cricket Club
An occasional Test Cricket venue, enshrined in popular myth as the ground most likely to suffer a rainstorm, has also been home to Lancashire County Cricket Club since 1857. The first Test Match took place here in 1884 when England drew with Australia, and one of the most famous Tests was in 1956 when Jim Laker took a record haul of wickets. In

the Alfred Hitchcock mystery *The Lady Vanishes* (1838) the comic duo Charters and Caldicott spend the entire film desperately trying to get to Old Trafford for the Test. Eventually they arrive at the last minute after an extraordinary journey, only to find it has been rained off.

TRAFFORD PARK

The world's first industrial estate, still buzzing with activity, if no longer quite so remarkable an economic powerhouse, occupies three square miles at the western edge of Manchester. Trafford Park is a relatively

Major matches at Old Trafford
● **24–26 July 1902, England v Australia, closest result in English test history** Australia beat England by only 3 runs after Victor Trumper scores a century before lunch on the first day.
● **17–19 July 1952, England v India, visitors humbled by one-sided win** England beat India by an innings and 207 runs as the tourists are bowled out for 58 and 82. Freddie Trueman takes eight wickets in the first innings.
● **26–31 July 1956, England v Australia, Jim Laker's record haul** For the only time a bowler – England's Jim Laker – takes all ten wickets in a Test, in the second innings, as the home team beat the tourists by an innings and 170 runs. Laker had taken nine out of ten wickets in the first innings.
● **27–30 July 1995, England v West Indies, Dominic Cork's hat-trick** In the first over of the Sunday morning session the fast bowler took the consecutive wickets of Richie Richardson, Junior Murray and Carl Hooper – the first England hat-trick for nearly forty years – and England beat the visitors.

modern phenomenon as far as the region's industrial history is concerned. The land on which it stands was a deer park owned by the de Trafford family until 1897. As its southern boundary was the Bridgewater Canal and its northern one the Manchester Ship Canal, it was getting increasingly hard for the owners to resist development, especially given the incongruous sight of deer roaming near huge steaming vessels bringing the world's goods to Manchester.

In 1896 the de Trafford family put the land up for sale. The buyer was not the Manchester Corporation, as many expected, but what the local papers described as a 'London syndicate'. This turned out to be Ernest Terah Hooley, a financier from Derby, who paid £360,000 for the site and formed Trafford Park Estates Ltd in August 1896.

Hooley planned to develop the area as a luxury village in the style of London's Regent's Park, with golf courses, shooting ranges and 500 villas for the wealthy, set in landscaped grounds screened from the Ship Canal. However, Marshall Stevens, general manager of the canal company, persuaded him to reconsider and develop Trafford Park for what the *Manchester Guardian* described as the 'incense of industry'. But this was to be no ordinary industrial estate. Here there would be no cotton mills or textile factories. Instead Trafford Park would pioneer new industry for a new century:

commerce with an international (i.e. American) outlook, capital intensive, embracing the latest technology – a centre of skilled, rather than mass, labour.

At first Trafford Park attracted carriers, warehousing firms, timber merchants and flour millers. In 1901 there were twenty-four firms; by 1914 there were ninety-seven, including oil companies, engineering works and even car manufacturers, for Trafford Park was Ford's UK base from 1911–31. Indeed Trafford Park was Britain's centre for advances in transportation. Its firms made aircraft, jet engines and equipment for trams and trolley buses.

Throughout the estate was a myriad of railway lines and sidings which allowed companies to move their goods to and from the Ship Canal efficiently. The locomotives shunting across the area were originally named after cities connected with Trafford Park, such as Hanover and Hamburg, but this system was abandoned during the Great War when vehicles bearing these names were stoned by impassioned locals, who threatened to throw their drivers into the canal.

Trafford Park suffered its first slump in the 1930s, but revival came during the Second World War when the area became the country's biggest arsenal, making Lancaster bombers and even the trailer caravans used by Field Marshal Montgomery, despite heavy bombing which destroyed Trafford

Hall. After the war Trafford Park became best known for major companies such as ICI, Procter & Gamble, Hovis, Brooke Bond, Guinness, who sunk artesian wells for a brewery, and Kellogg's, who adopted an American system for numbering buildings, No. 1 being the workmen's toilet, Number 2 the canteen, and so on.

The 1960s saw decline due to lack of new investment, outmoded factories, strikes and overseas competition. But regeneration has recently occurred through the Trafford Park Development Corporation, which has concentrated on attracting major institutions such as the Trafford Centre and the Imperial War Museum North.

First Avenue

Trafford Park has never been merely an industrial estate. A village was built from 1899 with money supplied by the American-owned Westinghouse company that employed half the local workforce of 12,000. This village had an American-style grid pattern of roads. Those that ran north–south were given the title 'avenue' – First Avenue, Second Avenue and so on – those that ran east – west were 'streets'. Although the company's blue-collar workers could walk to their factories the village was never a success socially. There were too few amenities, it was too remote from central Manchester (even Trafford Park railway station was a long walk away), and its residents lived too close to the pollution and noise of the industrial estate.

The 1970s saw the demolition of much of the original village. A strange-looking survivor is the monstrous 1902-built Trafford Park Hotel, one of the largest and emptiest pubs in Britain.

Westinghouse Road
north side
Ford (1910–31), west of Mosley Road
The Ford motor car company arrived in Trafford Park in 1911 – a move its employees celebrated by driving a Model T up Ben Nevis – and was soon the country's leading car manufacturer. The company produced

vehicles using the most up-to-date methods such as conveyor belts. They were serviced by workers standing in a pit assembling the cars as they moved along at a required average rate of one every 2 minutes 48 seconds, a system which was far from popular. One unnamed employee recalled in a biography of local industrial activist Eddie Frow that 'the Ford worker was not a worker but a robot – part of the ever flowing mechanism. The work was exceedingly monotonous; everything organized to suppress the individual personality'.

Ford employees were obliged to wear a one-piece uniform and badge, and those who turned up at the gate without them would be sent home, their pay docked for the time taken before they returned. Nor was trade union membership allowed. However, wages were high and jobs were at a premium. Even the floor sweepers were paid as much as £5 a week, which around the time of the Great War put them in the working-class aristocracy as far as Manchester was concerned.

Despite producing some 230 cars a day, Ford didn't last long in the North. Competition from southern-based car makers such as Morris and Austin resulted in the company's move to Dagenham, east London, in 1931. Over one weekend that September 2,000 employees were taken south to the new plant on chartered trains. The company briefly returned to Trafford Park during the Second World War to make Merlin aeroplane engines.

south side
British Westinghouse/Metropolitan Vickers, between Mosley Road and Bridgewater Canal
Trafford Park's major employer was British Westinghouse (later known by a variety of names such as Metrovic's) which arrived in 1899 as the British subsidiary of the American firm George Westinghouse. The company built big factories with heavy turbines, traction engines and power plant equipment, and a distinctive water tower in what was the largest engineering works in

Britain. It was modelled on American lines, and the best managers, known as the Holy Forty, were trained in Pittsburgh. Yet the owner, George Westinghouse, was so enamoured of Trafford that he borrowed the name when he built Trafford City in Pennsylvania in 1902. Westinghouse himself relinquished control in 1909, and ten years later the firm was renamed 𝔐etropolitan-𝔙ickers, popularly known as 𝔐etrovit's. (In Walter Greenwood's *Love on the Dole* it is called Marlowes.)

Manchester's first radio station began broadcasting from the premises on 15 November 1922 with the words '2zy calling, 2zy calling. Our transmission tonight will consist of late news followed by musical items . . .' Later that decade, as economic conditions deteriorated, political meetings began to be held outside the factory gates. At one of these, in March 1930, Eddie Frow (who later ran the Working Class Library in Firswood) exhorted the crowd: 'Come to my assistance, comrades. Shoot for it, comrades, as they have done in Russia. Three cheers for machine guns. Down with the Labour government,' for which he was imprisoned for a month.

Also arrested, in March 1933 in Moscow, were six 𝔐etrovit electricians invited by the Soviet Union to improve the Communist state's electricity network. They were interned on Stalin's orders for supposedly spying, which led to a diplomatic crisis and earnest statements from 𝔐etrovit's denying any wrongdoing. Research conducted by Gordon Morrell in the 1990s showed that the men were in fact spying – on the British government's orders.

During the Second World War the company aided the war effort by making Lancaster bombers. The 𝔐etropolitan-𝔙ickers

name was dropped in 1960 when the works became AEI (Manchester) Ltd, a company taken over by GEC in 1967. The firm left the area in 1992, to much dismay.

Across the Atlantic

In 1919 two pioneering local airmen, John Alcock and Arthur Whitten Brown, convinced 𝔐atrovit's to finance an air trip across the Atlantic Ocean. On 14 June that year the two men left Newfoundland, Canada, in a Vickers-Vimy aircraft that had been shipped across the Atlantic in crates for assembly there. Despite sleet and ice that 'chewed bits out of our faces', they made it to Ireland after 16 hours 12 minutes and landed their plane in a bog at Clifden. Alcock and Whitten Brown had become the first men to fly across the Atlantic.

Trafford Wharf Road
Imperial War Museum North

Manchester's twenty-first-century direction is embodied in grandiose projects such as the Imperial War Museum North. The museum is based in a building designed by the fêted international architect Daniel Libeskind in the form of a shattered globe, offset by three shards representing air, earth and water – the three theatres of war. One of the museum's shortcomings is the lack of artefacts; the building itself, rather than its contents, is the main attraction.

Nearly opposite on the other side of the Ship Canal in Salford stands the equally challenging Lowry Centre (p. 109).

Bibliography

Archer, John (ed.), *Art & Architecture in Victorian Manchester*, Manchester: Manchester University Press, 1985

Atkins, Philip, *Guide Across Manchester*, Salford: North West Civic Trust, 1976

Ayerst, David, *Guardian: Biography of a Newspaper*, London: Collins, 1971

Bracegirdle, Cyril, *The Dark River*, Altrincham: John Sherratt & Son, 1973

Brooks, Ann and Haworth, Bryan, *Boomtown Manchester 1800–50: The Portico Connection*, Manchester: The Portico Library, 1993

Burgess, Anthony, *Little Wilson and Big God*, London: Heinemann, 1987

Burn, Gordon, *Best and Edwards: Football, Fame and Oblivion*, London: Faber & Faber, 2006

Cardus, Neville, *Autobiography*, London: Collins, 1947

—, *Second Innings: More Autobiography*, London: Collins, 1950

Curtis, Deborah, *Touching from a Distance: Ian Curtis and Joy Division*, London: Faber & Faber, 1995

Deakin, Derek, *Wythenshawe: The Story of a Garden City*, Chichester: Phillimore, 1989

Dobkin, Monty, *Rothschild in Manchester*, Manchester: Neil Richardson, 1998

Dunphy, Eamon, *A Strange Kind of Glory*, London: Heinemann, 1991

Farnie, D. A., *The Manchester Ship Canal and the Rise of the Port of Manchester 1894–1975*, Manchester: Manchester University Press, 1980

Foot, Paul, *Red Shelley*, London: Sidgwick and Jackson, 1980

Frangopulo, Nicholas J., *Rich Inheritance: A Guide to the History of Manchester*, Wakefield: S.R. Publishing, 1969

—, *Tradition in Action: The Historical Evolution of the Greater Manchester County*, Wakefield: EP Publishing, 1977

Frow, Ruth, *Edmund Frow: The Making of an Activist*, Salford: Working Class Movement Library, 1999

Grant, Roderick, *The Great Canal*, London and New York: Gordon & Cremonesi, 1978

Gray, Ted, *A Hundred Years of the Manchester Ship Canal*, Trafford: Memories, 1993

Haslam, Dave, *Manchester England: The Story of the Pop Cult City*, London: Fourth Estate, 1999

Herbert, Michael, *The Wearing of the Green: A Political History of the Irish in Manchester*, London: Irish in Britain Representation Group, 2001

Hunt, Tristram, *Building Jerusalem*, London: Weidenfeld & Nicolson, 2004

Inglis, Simon, *Played in Manchester*, London: English Heritage, 2004

Jones, Steve, *Manchester: The Sinister Side*, Nottingham: Wicked Publications, 1997

Joyce, J., *Roads & Rails of Manchester 1900–1950*, London: Ian Allan, 1982

Kargon, Robert H., *Science in Victorian Manchester: Enterprise and Expertise*, Manchester: Manchester University Press, 1977

Kennedy, Michael, *Portrait of Manchester*, London: Robert Hale, 1970

Kidd, Alan, *Manchester*, Keele: Keele University Press, 1993

Knowlson, Joyce, *Red Plush and Gilt*, Manchester: J. Knowlson, 1984

Lee, C. P., *Shake, Rattle and Rain: Popular Music Making in Manchester 1955–95*, Ottery St Mary: Hardinge Simpole, 2002

Melly, George, *Owning Up*, London: Weidenfeld & Nicholson, 1965

Messinger, Gary S., *Manchester in the Victorian Age: The Half-Known City*, Manchester: Manchester University Press, 1985

Middles, Mick, *From Joy Division to New Order: The Factory Story*, London: Virgin, 1996

Nicholls, Robert, *Trafford Park: The First Hundred Years*, Sussex: Phillimore, 1996

Parkinson-Bailey, John J., *Manchester: An Architectural History*, Manchester: Manchester University Press, 2000

Reid, Robert, *The Peterloo Massacre*, London: Heinemann, 1989

Robinson, Brian R., *Aviation in Manchester: A Short History*, London: Royal Aeronautical Society, 1977

Rogan, Johnny, *Morrissey and Marr: The Severed Alliance*, London: Omnibus, 1992

Rohde, Shelley, *Lowry: A Life*, Salford: Lowry Press, 1999

Walker, Martin, *With Extreme Prejudice*, London: Canary Press, 1986

Walmsley, Robert, *Peterloo: The Case Reopened*, Manchester: Manchester University Press, 1969

Waterhouse, Robert, *The Other Fleet Street: How Manchester Made Newspapers National*, Altrincham: First Edition Ltd, 2004

Williams, Bill, *The Making of Manchester Jewry 1740–1875*, Manchester: Manchester University Press, 1976

Williams, Emlyn, *Beyond Belief*, London: World Books, 1968

Williams, Philip Martin and Williams, David L., *Hooray for Jollywood: The Life of John E. Blakeley and the Mancunian Film Corporation*, Ashton-under-Lyne: History On Your Doorstep, 2001

Wyke, Terry, *A Hall for All Seasons: A History of the Free Trade Hall*, Manchester: Charles Hallé Foundation, 1976

Wyke, Terry and Rudyard, Nigel, *Manchester Theatres*, Manchester: Manchester Central Library, 1994

Index

For areas, streets, etc., use the main Contents List and the lists at the beginning of each section.

(B) indicates a reference to text within a box.

Adamson, Daniel 106, 168
Addy, Mark 114, 115
Afro-Caribbean community 127, 132–4, 135–7, 136–7(B)
Agate, James 25
Agricola (Roman general and governor) 2, 48–9
Ainsworth, Harrison 85, 184
Albert, Prince 2, 39
Alcock, John 167, 193(B)
Alexander, Samuel 32(B)
Allen, Peter 56
Allen, Peter Anthony 163
Allen, William 183
Allies and Morrison (architects) 35, 36
Allison, Malcolm 138
Anderson, Lindsay 46(B)
Anderton, James 90, 137(B)
Ando, Tadeo 35
Anti-Corn Law League 14, 21, 25, 47, 58, 72, 92, 172
    see also Corn Laws
Arkwright, Richard 83(B), 84
art, art galleries 2, 17–18, 36(B), 40, 53, 71, 77, 109, 120, 125, 145, 183, 187–8
Asian community 170
Assheton Bennett family 18
Atkinson, Clive 135
Atkinson, Ron 189
Aytoun, Roger 98

Baker, Stanley 20
Balfour, Arthur 38, 161
Ball, Alan 138–9
Ball & Elce (architects) 92
Bamford, Samuel 23(B), 24(B), 82, 113, 183
Banda, Hastings 125
Banks, Isabella Linnaeus 24(B), 85, 112, 149
Bannister, Jimmy 38
Barbirolli, John 32–3(B), 64, 66, 74
Barker & Ellis (architects) 15
Barlow family 165
Barr, Billy 182
Barry, Charles 17, 40

Barton, Edward 86, 130–31
Baseley, Godfrey 36
Beaumont, J. W. 9
Beaverbrook, William Maxwell Aitken, Lord 147
Beecham, Thomas 32(B), 35, 46
Behan, Brendan 75
Behrens, Gustav 177
Bell, Erinma 135
Benedict-Smith, Caroline 98
Bennett, Keith 154–5(B)
Bennett, Richard Rodney 88
Bentley, J. J. 16
Bernstein, Sidney 18, 47–8
Best, George 57, 75, 108, 134, 166–7, 182, 189
Beyer, Karl 142(B), 156, 169
Birkett, I. R. E. 19
Birley, Hugh Hornby 124, 169
Birley, Joseph 169
Björk 88
Blair, Cherie 124
Blair, Tony 124
Blakeley, John E. 9, 171
Bland, Lady Ann 79, 81
Blatchford, Robert 13–14
Blondin, Charles 30
Bohr, Neils 121
Bonaparte, Napoleon 71
Book, Tony 138
Booth, Eva Gore 144(B)
Booth, Henry 51, 182
Booth, Josiah 10
Booth, Tony 124
Bradshaw, George 4
Brady, Ian 19, 65–6, 133, 154, 154–5(B), 164, 186, 187(B)
Bramah, Martin 79
Brideshead Revisited 27, 92
Bridgewater, Francis Edgerton, 3rd Duke of 102, 105
Brighouse, Harold 25, 26(B)
Bright, John 5, 29(B)
Brindley, James 53, 102–3, 105, 108, 116, 118
Brittan, Leon 75

PENGUIN HISTORY

THE LONDON COMPENDIUM

ED GLINERT

The streets of London resonate with secret stories, from East End lore to Cold War espionage, from tales of riots, rakes, brothels, anarchy and grisly murders, to Rolling Stones gigs, gangland drinking-dens, Orwell's Fitzrovia and Lenin's haunts.

Londoner Ed Glinert has walked the city from Limehouse to Lambeth, Whitehall to Whitechapel, unravelling its mysteries along the way. Here he uncovers the tales of the hidden metropolis – street by street, area by area and building by building. Now updated and with a new subject index to help you discover the secret city, this book reveals London as you've never seen it before.

'One of those books, destined to be read until they fall apart, that map the unmappable and make it live' Iain Sinclair

'Splendid ... brings the underground to the surface, be it in the form of psychedelic rock clubs, suffragettes and political radicals, or the secret tunnels that link buildings across the capital in case of war' *Daily Telegraph*

He just wanted a decent book to read ...

Not too much to ask, is it? It was in 1935 when Allen Lane, Managing Director of Bodley Head Publishers, stood on a platform at Exeter railway station looking for something good to read on his journey back to London. His choice was limited to popular magazines and poor-quality paperbacks – the same choice faced every day by the vast majority of readers, few of whom could afford hardbacks. Lane's disappointment and subsequent anger at the range of books generally available led him to found a company – and change the world.

'We believed in the existence in this country of a vast reading public for intelligent books at a low price, and staked everything on it'
Sir Allen Lane, 1902–1970, founder of Penguin Books

The quality paperback had arrived – and not just in bookshops. Lane was adamant that his Penguins should appear in chain stores and tobacconists, and should cost no more than a packet of cigarettes.

Reading habits (and cigarette prices) have changed since 1935, but Penguin still believes in publishing the best books for everybody to enjoy. We still believe that good design costs no more than bad design, and we still believe that quality books published passionately and responsibly make the world a better place.

So wherever you see the little bird – whether it's on a piece of prize-winning literary fiction or a celebrity autobiography, political tour de force or historical masterpiece, a serial-killer thriller, reference book, world classic or a piece of pure escapism – you can bet that it represents the very best that the genre has to offer.

Whatever you like to read – trust Penguin.